New Ways of Doing Business

IBM Endowment for
The Business of Government

The IBM Endowment Series on The Business of Government

Series Editors: Mark A. Abramson and Paul R. Lawrence

The IBM Endowment Series on The Business of Government explores new approaches to improving the effectiveness of government at the federal, state, and local levels. The Series is aimed at providing cutting-edge knowledge to government leaders, academics, and students about the management of government in the 21st century.

Publications in the series include:

E-Government 2003, *edited by Mark A. Abramson and Therese L. Morin*
E-Government 2001, *edited by Mark A. Abramson and Grady E. Means*
Human Capital 2002, *edited by Mark A. Abramson and Nicole Willenz Gardner*
Innovation, *edited by Mark A. Abramson and Ian D. Littman*
Leaders, *edited by Mark A. Abramson and Kevin M. Bacon*
Managing for Results 2002, *edited by Mark A. Abramson and John M. Kamensky*
Memos to the President: Management Advice from the Nation's Top Public Administrators, *edited by Mark A. Abramson*
The Procurement Revolution, *edited by Mark A. Abramson and Roland S. Harris III*
Transforming Organizations, *edited by Mark A. Abramson and Paul R. Lawrence*

New Ways of Doing Business

EDITED BY

MARK A. ABRAMSON
IBM ENDOWMENT FOR
THE BUSINESS OF GOVERNMENT
and
ANN M. KIEFFABER
IBM BUSINESS CONSULTING SERVICES

ROWMAN & LITTLEFIELD PUBLISHERS, INC.
Lanham • Boulder • New York • Oxford

ROWMAN & LITTLEFIELD PUBLISHERS, INC.

Published in the United States of America
by Rowman & Littlefield Publishers, Inc.
A wholly owned subsidiary of The Rowman & Littlefield Publishing Group, Inc.
4501 Forbes Boulevard, Suite 200, Lanham, Maryland 20706
www.rowmanlittlefield.com

PO Box 317
Oxford
OX2 9RU, UK

British Library Cataloguing in Publication Information Available

Library of Congress Cataloging-in-Publication Data Available

ISBN 0-7425-3359-X (alk. paper)
ISBN 0-7425-3360-3 (pbk. : alk. paper)

Printed in the United States of America

™ The paper used in this publication meets the minimum requirements of American National Standard for Information Sciences—Permanence of Paper for Printed Library Materials, ANSI/NISO Z39.48-1992.

TABLE OF CONTENTS

CHAPTER ONE

Toward Government of the Future: New Ways of Doing Business

Mark A. Abramson
Executive Director
IBM Endowment for The Business of Government

Ann M. Kieffaber
Vice President, Public Sector, Global Strategy and Solutions
IBM Business Consulting Services

Introduction

The title of this book—*New Ways of Doing Business*—was intentionally chosen. An alternative title was *New Ways of Managing,* but that was rejected because the term *managing* does not adequately describe the changes now either under way or being contemplated by government at all levels in the United States and, indeed, across the world. In the 1990s, the emphasis in government, as well as in the private sector, was on better management of internal operations of an organization. Good managers focused on improving the efficiency and effectiveness of internal operations and motivating employees to do their best. While these activities are still important within any organization, 21st century government can already be characterized by a different management emphasis: how and by whom can the tasks of government best be performed?

In the old days of 20th century government, the "default" for government was to perform its tasks in-house with public employees. While government has always used a variety of different "tools"—such as grants, loans, and contracts—the presumption was that the first choice of government was to perform all activities by itself.[1] While it might dip into its tool kit from time to time, the range of decisions on which tools to use was limited. Running a government activity was relatively straightforward: You first tried to do it yourself and if for some reason you decided *not* to do it yourself, you would then select an appropriate tool, such as a contract, to carry out the activity.

The world of 21st century government is more diverse. The presumption for government to do everything itself is no longer in place. There are now many more ways to do business. The process for government to decide how to do its business has grown more complicated. The number of potential tools that government can use has increased. This book describes new approaches that government is now deploying to carry out its business.

Changing the Internal Operations of Government

New ways of doing business does not mean that public employees no longer have important and interesting roles to play in undertaking the activities of government. In many ways, the job of the public servant is becoming more interesting and more challenging. Chapters two and three present examples of public servants who have dramatically redefined their jobs and the way they go about delivering services.

In 20th century government, a monopoly situation characterized the internal operations of government. Internal services were delivered "in-house"; managers had no choice of whether or not to buy those services. Decision making was easy. Each individual government department delivered services to its own employees, who had no choice but to purchase those services. This began to change in the 1990s. A major tenet of former Vice President Gore's National Performance Review (NPR) was that line managers should have a choice as to whether to "buy" services from within their own department or to go elsewhere—either to another department or outside of government. Civil servants would no longer be mandated to buy services from within their own department. The premise of NPR was that competition for services would inevitably lead to lower costs and higher quality services.

In chapter two, Anne Laurent describes how civil servants in many agencies across government have begun to make the shift to become entrepreneurs and to act like businesspeople in response to this drive for internal competition. She describes how "old-line" federal departments, such as the Department of Agriculture, have turned their employees into real-life entrepreneurs who sell services both within and outside of the federal government. But the road has not been easy for these government pioneers. Some of the enterprises described initially by Ms. Laurent in 2000 have fared better than others. All have had their ups and downs in responding to a changing world. Her chapter includes lessons learned about what factors might drive government to continue this trend toward increased public sector entrepreneurship.

In chapter three, John Callahan provides additional examples of public servants who have become businesspeople. Callahan focuses specifically on the six franchise funds that were authorized by the Government Management Reform Act of 1994. From the six franchise funds, Callahan selected two for in-depth analysis: Federal Occupational Health in the Department of Health and Human Services and the Department of Treasury Franchise Fund. While there were clearly areas for improvement in each of the two franchise funds examined, Callahan concluded that the funds were meeting their original expectations and held promise for continue to deliver high-quality services to government organizations. The two continue to exist as of this writing, May 2003, and are excellent examples of government "charging" for its own services and the creation of a competitive environment within government.

Changing the External Delivery of Services to Citizens

Breaking up internal government monopolies is one major change in the way government is doing business. Part II of this book presents three dramatic changes in the way in which services to the public can now be delivered:

- Online via the Internet
- Via contracts performed by private or nonprofit organizations
- Via non-traditional organizations, such as faith-based organizations and business improvement districts

Delivering Services Online

The 1990s witnessed a dramatic revolution with the advent of the Internet as a vehicle for both the public and private sectors to deliver services online.[2] The nation moved from "in line" to "online." In chapter 4, Professors Steven Cohen and William Eimicke present an overview of how the Internet made it possible for government to rapidly change the way it did business. The early days of government's presence on the World Wide Web, according to Cohen and Eimicke, could be characterized as making information available to citizens online. As the decade of the 1990s ended, government increasingly began the move to performing more and more transactions online. Cohen and Eimicke point to examples such as obtaining passport applications and tax forms online, contesting or paying traffic fines, ordering government publications, filing requests for zoning variances, and reserving space for athletic events or tee times on public golf courses. They provide six in-depth case studies of success stories in government's move to the use of the Internet to deliver services.

Just as public servants are learning entrepreneurship, they are also undergoing a learning process about how to use the Internet as a vehicle for delivering services. Cohen and Eimicke provide a valuable checklist for government managers to use in deciding how and when to use the Internet for service delivery. Based on the six case studies and their assessment of the future of online services, they conclude that government organizations must assess in detail the cost and benefit of online services and use that information to shape the form, services offered, fee structure, and the timing of the launch of a website. Cohen and Eimicke write, "The Internet is a tool.... It is a complex undertaking. When used with care it can help government improve its ability to serve the public."

Delivering Services via Contracts Performed by Private or Nonprofit Organizations

One of the most controversial new ways of government doing business is the trend toward the use of contracted agents to deliver government services. Various terms are used to describe this trend: outsourcing, privatization, contracting out, and public-private partnerships.[3] As with government's experience with entrepreneurship and the use of the Internet to provide internal and external services, the public sector is undergoing a significant, often difficult, learning process of how to best deploy and manage these contracts.

In chapter five, Professors Jocelyn M. Johnston and Barbara S. Romzek describe the experience of Kansas in moving to contracts for social services. While contracting for social services has its own special issues and concerns, similar challenges face all government organizations when they decide to "outsource." In a recommendation similar to the one proposed by Cohen and Eimicke regarding the delivery of services online, Johnston and Romzek urge government officials to take time to carefully consider the design of a contract, the proposed staff and any specific cost factors associated with implementation of contracts. Equally important is making clear performance expectations for both the government and the contractor.[4] These expectations, recommend Johnston and Romzek, should be negotiated in advance of awarding the contract.

Based on the Johnston-Romzek analysis of the Kansas experience with contracting for social services, it is clear that we are again in the early stages of a significant change in the way government does business. The trend toward contracting out will clearly continue. It is interesting to note that the Kansas contracting initiative was launched by a Republican governor but was continued and supported by the newly elected Democratic governor, who took office in 2003. While clearly political and often ideological, there appears to be growing support for and interest in contracting out among Democrats and Republicans.

Delivering Services to Citizens by Non-Traditional Organizations

A third interesting, and also highly controversial, change in the way government does business is the delivery of governmental services by non-traditional organizations. Two examples of non-traditional organizations are presented in this volume. In chapter six, John P. Bartkowski and Helen A. Regis describe Mississippi's experience with the charitable choice initiative contained in the Personal Responsibility and Work Opportunity Reconciliation

Act of 1996 (PRWORA). Bartkowski and Regis interviewed 29 Mississippi pastors to probe their attitudes toward the implementation of charitable choice initiatives. Based on the interviews, the authors developed a series of recommendations on how charitable choice type initiatives might best be implemented.

Since 1999, when the Bartkowski-Regis report was originally published, interest in charitable choice, now called faith-based programs, has continued and is actively supported by President George W. Bush. While the administration's faith-based legislative proposals proved to be highly controversial and have not been fully accepted by Congress, the President has been able to implement many of his faith-based proposals by Executive Order.[5] The door has thus been opened to the delivery of services by faith-based organizations. As with many of the new ways of doing business described in this book, there is a steep learning curve facing all involved in faith-based programs: the government and the faith-based providers. It is clearly going to be a difficult learning experience as both sides gain the necessary experience needed to make the delivery of such services less controversial and ideological. Mistakes (or mini-scandals) may occur. The key question will be whether governments can become learning organizations and modify these programs based on real-life experience and learning.

Less controversial has been the creation of Business Improvement Districts (BIDs) across the United States. In chapter seven, Professor Jerry Mitchell examines this non-traditional approach to the delivery of traditional government services in downtown business areas, such as street cleaning, street signage, and safety patrol. While legal status and funding sources differ dramatically among BIDs, they are largely outside of government and frequently receive funding directly from the beneficiaries (downtown store owners) being served by the BID. They often are organized as a nonprofit organization, a government corporation, or a public-private partnership.

The growth of Business Improvement Districts represents a growing trend in American governance: the practice of charging a specific group of beneficiaries for additional services they receive above and beyond those provided by government to the general public. There are clearly other examples of special user fees throughout the nation, such as homeowner associations and gated communities. One can speculate whether fiscal constraints at all levels of government will drive the creation of more BID type enterprises.

Changing the Delivery of Environmental Programs

If there is one policy arena in government that has been highly experimental and innovative in the use of tools to deliver government programs and implement policies, it has been the environment. Chapters eight, nine, and ten provide three perspectives on new ways to achieve national environmental quality goals through innovative approaches to government regulatory policies.

In chapter 8, Professor Richard C. Hula describes Michigan's experience in developing an innovative approach to brownfield redevelopment policies. An interesting aspect of the Michigan brownfield experience was the change in the role of the state government agency responsible for overseeing brownfield policies. Hula describes the shift in the Michigan Department of Environmental Quality from focusing mainly on the environmental cleanup aspects of brownfields to also being concerned about the redevelopment and economic aspects of brownfields. This changing focus is likely to be seen in other governmental organizations across the nation as the public sector adopts new ways of doing business.

The Michigan brownfield case study also points out another trend in the changing ways in which government will do business in the decades ahead. Hula recommends that local officials be given sufficient flexibility to respond to market-driven redevelopment opportunities. It is likely that government at all levels will become more market driven in the future.

In chapter nine, Dennis A. Rondinelli describes an alternative to the traditional command-and-control orientation of environmental policy. A major goal of environmental policy is pollution prevention. Rondinelli argues that pollution prevention can also be accomplished by voluntary environmental management systems now being used by an increasing number of private sector companies. The specific approach advocated by Rondinelli is eco-efficiency, which seeks not only to reduce waste in manufacturing, but also to reduce environmental impacts and conserve resources throughout a business's entire operations, from the acquisition of input and raw materials to the final disposal of products by consumers.

A major driving force for seeking alternatives to the traditional command-and-control approaches to the environment of the 1970s is the changing nature of the private sector. Rondinelli argues that there are now four sets of forces that are driving companies to more aggressively pursue pollution prevention: increasing regulatory demands, stronger stakeholder pressures, increasing costs and savings potential, and stronger competitive requirements. Based on these forces, Rondinelli recommends a new way to accomplish pollution prevention by placing greater emphasis on eco-efficiency to achieve environmental performance improvements while "maintaining a sound regulatory system as the foundation for ensuring current levels of achievement." Thus, Rondinelli is, in effect, arguing for multiple approaches to pollution prevention beyond traditional command-and-control techniques. He writes, "New environmental management policies should focus on performance improvements rather than regulatory compliance, use economic incentives to encourage clean manufacturing and the adoption of pollution prevention technologies and processes, and forge public-private partnerships for improving environmental quality."

In chapter ten, Gary C. Bryner examines emissions trading and other market-based regulatory tools for achieving improved environmental quality. In this area, the public sector has been highly creative in developing market-based tools for environmental regulation. Examples of market-based tools include deposit/refund systems, fees, reporting requirements, subsidies, tax incentives, and pollution charges. As with faith-based initiatives, some of these tools are very controversial and the debate over them has often become highly politicized.

Bryner examines both the strengths and weaknesses of emissions trading as a tool for pollution prevention. His conclusions set forth circumstances in which emissions trading can be used effectively as a regulatory tool. An important point made by Bryner is that emissions trading can be viewed as an interim tool as additional tools are developed. Bryner argues that emissions trading should lead to other, more powerful regulatory innovations that will effectively encourage ecologically sustainable activities. The concept of interim tools can be applied to many of the new ways to do business described in this chapter. Bryner writes, "Emissions trading programs should be designed as a transition to a system of emissions fees or taxes and other efforts to reflect true costs in prices and to create more powerful incentives to reduce and prevent pollution. The ultimate test of an emissions trading program is its contribution to a more fundamental shift in practices aimed at reducing pollution, improving efficiency, and conserving resources."

Looking to the Future

In the future when we look back upon government in the early years of the 21st century, it will be readily apparent that government was undergoing its most significant transformation since the decade of the 1930s when direct government-delivered services grew significantly as part of the New Deal. Because we are in the early days of this major transformation, government will continue to undergo change and experiment with additional new ways of doing business. It should also be expected that governments will make some mistakes along the way as they undergo this transformation. The challenge for government in the years ahead is to learn to manage its risk and not pursue the traditional approach of avoiding risks until shifts in ways of doing business are adopted. Public managers will have to become more comfortable with a trial-and-error approach to doing business. They will not have all the answers as they undertake new approaches and will not be able to foresee all the unanticipated consequences of their actions. Government by managing risks will be required.

Endnotes

1. For an extensive discussion of tools, see Lester Salamon (ed.), *The Tools of Government: A Guide to the New Governance,* (New York: Oxford University Press, 2002).

2. For in-depth discussions of the public sector's move to the use of the Internet to deliver services, see *E-Government 2001* (Abramson and Means) and *E-Government 2003* (Abramson and Morin), two volumes in the IBM Endowment Series on The Business of Government (Lanham, Md.: Rowman and Littlefield).

3. For an in-depth discussion of each of these terms and the differences between them, see Jacques Gansler, *Moving Toward Market-Based Government: The Changing Role of Government as Provider* (Arlington, Va.: IBM Endowment for The Business of Government, 2003.)

4. Larry Martin provides an excellent discussion of performance-based contracts in Chapter 4 ("Making Performance-Based Contracting Perform: What the Federal Government Can Learn from State and Local Governments) in Abramson and Harris, *The Procurement Revolution* (Lanham, Md.: Rowman and Littlefield, 2003).

5. For an in-depth discussion of the politics of the administration's faith-based initiative, see Dana Milbank, "Bush Legislative Approach Failed in the Faith Bill Battle," *The Washington Post*, April 23, 2003.

PART I

Changing the Internal Operations of Government

CHAPTER TWO

Entrepreneurial Government: Bureaucrats as Businesspeople

Anne Laurent
Deputy Editor
Government Executive
Washington, D.C.

This report was originally published in May 2000, revised May 2003.

Preface

Much has changed since I wrote this report at the end of 1999. I've updated it to some degree, but I've probably missed some changes, and others will occur even as this book is published. What hasn't changed is the zeal and smarts of federal workers infected with the entrepreneurial spirit.

Most of the entrepreneurial outposts I wrote about three and a half years ago still are going strong. Sales under the General Services Administration's Federal Supply Schedules, for example, tripled between 1997 and 2001, from $4.3 billion to $14.4 billion. Use of government-wide acquisition contracts, such as the Transportation Department's Information Technology Omnibus Procurement (ITOP), increased as well.

Forest Service enterprises have been so successful that the agency planned to expand the program to two new regions in 2003 and to more regions in later years. The enterprise initiative also was a semifinalist in the 2000 Innovations in American Government Awards program.

The Agriculture Department's National Finance Center is one of four agencies selected to consolidate the federal government's 22 payroll systems and providers. NFC will partner with another entrepreneurial organization, the Interior Department's National Business Center.

Building businesses inside federal agencies isn't such a new concept anymore. It has become common enough that the Office of Personnel Management's management development centers are offering classes in how to do it—for a fee, of course!

Anne Laurent
May 2003

Acknowledgments

This chapter relies heavily on research and reporting done originally for *Government Executive* magazine. The author thanks *Government Executive* President and Editor Timothy Clark for his support and encouragement. My deepest appreciation to Lauren R. Taylor and Susan Fourney, who provided invaluable editing and moral support. Special thanks to Michael Serlin for his insights and for his story, "The Company Goes Commercial," (*Government Executive,* August 1999), which is the basis of the CIA anecdotes in this chapter. Thanks also to Katy Saldarini for her groundbreaking reporting for *GovExec.com* on the controversy surrounding the General Services Administration's decision to close its warehouses and to Brian Friel for his discovery of the Gov.Works.gov trademark battle.

Introduction

Unbeknownst to most American taxpayers and to many federal employees, the government is growing its own businesses. Entrepreneurial outposts are taking root inside federal agencies in the fertile soil of management reform, new purchasing rules, downsizing, and performance pressure. Government's business people are shaking off the shackles of limited congressional appropriations and staving off job threats using money they earn selling services within their own and other agencies.

As in the early days of American capitalism, success in this new bureaucratic business world often goes to the entrepreneur who gets there first. Some craft new contracts to provide computer equipment and services that every agency wants. Others benchmark against the best private-sector administrative service providers. A few are selling their personal expertise. But no matter how they operate, government's business people are ahead of the pack in taking advantage of fast-paced changes in regulations, laws, and government culture.

These pioneers are hacking their way out of the stodgy, stovepiped, red-tape-entangled bureaucracy to create new businesses good enough to win work that might otherwise have gone to private-sector firms. They are bureaucrats turned canny entrepreneurs, walking a tightrope between the Industrial Age federal monolith and the lean, fast, and flexible Information Age government of the new millennium.

Government entrepreneurs are bridging the gap between the past and future roles and structures of government. The continual birth and evolution of entrepreneurial federal entities is attended by great consternation about whether government can become businesslike and about whether it should. Opponents argue that anything entrepreneurial belongs in the private sector and that pecuniary interests will distract government from its true goal: carrying out the directives of Congress and thereby the will of the American people.

Despite these concerns, businesslike enterprises are springing up each year. The phenomenon has received little attention and the conditions creating it even less. This chapter describes those conditions and some entrepreneurs' creative responses to them. This first comprehensive look at entrepreneurial activities within the federal government also provides guidance and cautions for would-be entrepreneurs.

Background

Plenty of business opportunities exist inside government today. For example:

- Some organizations are following the cross-servicing model created by the 1932 Economy Act, which permits agencies whose services are operating at less than full capacity to perform reimbursable work for other agencies.
- Six agencies are operating franchises—fee-for-service administrative service centers—under the 1994 Government Management Reform Act (GMRA). A handful of others have won permission to operate franchises through special legislation. (See chapter three for profiles of two of these franchise funds.)
- Procurement offices that suffered deep staff cuts under former Vice President Al Gore's National Performance Review (NPR) are staying alive by crafting broad contracts for popular products and then making other agencies pay to use those purchasing agreements.
- A growing number of Forest Service employees are starting businesses, selling their expertise within their home region and beyond.

Starting in the early 1990s, reinvention spotlighted fee-for-service operations and improved conditions for them to proliferate. The National Performance Review—later known as the National Partnership for Reinventing Government—gave businesslike government a kick-start in 1993 with its first report, *From Red Tape to Results: Creating a Government that Works Better & Costs Less.* In addition to recommending elimination of 252,000 federal jobs, the report suggested that organizations providing administrative support services compete with one another for clients across government. "Most federal managers must use [agency] monopolies to handle their printing, real estate, and support services," the NPR study found. "A monopoly's managers don't even know when they are providing poor service or failing to take advantage of new, cost-cutting technologies because they don't get signals from their customers. In contrast, competitive firms get instant feedback when their customers go elsewhere."

Citing a number of private firms' successes in competitively providing administrative services, the NPR advocated a similar approach in government. "Competition for services will inevitably lead to lower costs and higher quality," the NPR found. "No manager should be confined to an agency monopoly. Nor should agencies provide services in house unless the services can compete with those of other agencies and companies." The report called for every agency to have a revolving fund to collect fees for competitive services.

The report offered as a model the Treasury Department's Center for Applied Financial Management, a consulting business created in 1991 to help agencies meet Treasury's reporting standards. The center provided systems support, financial advice, education, and accounting operations assistance for a fee. The center's experience showed the limits on truly businesslike federal operations in the early 1990s. As an entity created under the Economy

Act, the center couldn't reinvest the fees its customers paid—it had to break even and start over again every year—because the 1932 law precludes federal organizations from retaining fees beyond the end of the fiscal year in which they are collected. The center's first director, Michael Serlin, was frustrated by his inability to carry over funds and reinvest and told his staffers "to break even vigorously."

Because of his work on the center, Serlin was tapped as one of the earliest NPR participants focusing on financial management. His and others' frustration with reimbursable organizations' inability to carry over funds and engagements from year to year led them to help push through the Government Management Reform Act in 1994. Until the NPR focused on competitive services as a reinvention tool and GMRA set standards for it, "cross-servicing was very haphazard and not self-sustaining," Serlin says. The law provided pilot testing for a new breed of fee-for-service enterprises called "franchises."

GMRA permitted agencies to create working capital funds under which franchises not only could use income from customers to finance current operations, but also could accumulate up to 4 percent of earnings annually for major capital investments and management improvements. Franchises also could carry over funds from year to year. They were to be competitive and to support themselves entirely from fees, unlike cross-servicing operations, which were set up under other authorities and sometimes rely on subsidies from appropriated funds to shore them up when costs exceed income. Six agencies now are running GMRA franchises: the Environmental Protection Agency and the Departments of Health and Human Services, Commerce, Veterans Affairs, Treasury, and Interior. Congress separately granted the Central Intelligence Agency (CIA) and the Department of Transportation permission to establish franchise-like operations.

As the NPR was exhorting administrative service organizations to compete and GMRA was establishing the new franchise business model, other reimbursable services were spreading and improving their operations. PricewaterhouseCoopers conducted a survey for the Treasury Department Chief Financial Officers Council and found in April 1999 more than 300 cross-servicing agreements throughout government operating under the Economy Act and non-franchise working capital funds. Pressure to downsize administrative functions and make them competitive has produced a number of entrepreneurial responses, particularly among acquisition organizations, which have used acquisition reforms to build fee-for-service buying businesses that help their agency customers purchase needed technology quickly and effectively while enabling acquisition offices to remain open.

Entrepreneurs: Case Studies

Company Business: The Central Intelligence Agency

Richard Calder
Central Intelligence Agency

The CIA won its franchise authority through the 1998 Intelligence Authorization Act, though its Directorate of Administration had been charging internal customers since 1994. As is common among federal agencies, the directorate had little idea of its costs, and its customers were accustomed to receiving its services without charge. Before the directorate began billing, demand was high for shipping, financial management, armoring vehicles, and other services the directorate provided. But downsizing had whittled away staff even as demand grew, and the directorate was increasingly unable to provide timely, efficient service. In 1996, newly appointed directorate chief Richard Calder hired a consulting firm to develop an accurate cost accounting system. He also forced administrative operations to benchmark against their private-sector counterparts, come up with business plans, and gain the approval of the newly created Business Transformation Office on the road to becoming franchise members.

Four enterprises made up the CIA franchise: the Central Warehouse transportation and storage facility; the telephone service; the Transportation Service Center motor pool and package delivery services; and a software development center. The Central Warehouse began franchising as part of its struggle to win back disgruntled agency customers. Increasingly, CIA directorates were turning to Federal Express and United Parcel Service instead of the warehouse for priority deliveries. As part of its marketing and sales strategy, the warehouse ran an in-house public relations campaign with the slogan "Doing Business Like Business." Success allowed the warehouse to give back to its customers funds that were appropriated to it by Congress. When customers became responsible for paying warehouse fees out of their own budgets, they prioritized and reduced their demands for warehouse services. That, in turn, allowed the warehouse to consolidate expensive overseas shipments and save $6 million in the first year of operations.

The CIA's franchise businesses also won non-CIA customers, such as the National Imagery and Mapping Service for the warehouse and the Agency for International Development for the Transportation Service Center. Adding external customers allowed the franchises to spread their costs among more customers, decreasing per-unit costs for all.

Cross-Servicing Creativity: The National Finance Center

The Agriculture Department's National Finance Center (NFC) is a classic example of pre-franchise cross-servicing. Since 1983, it has been providing payroll processing for other agencies on a reimbursable basis. The NFC currently handles payroll for more than 450,000 federal employees at 125 agencies. It also keeps the records for the Thrift Savings Plan—the federal government's 401(k).

The NFC's history is a roller coaster of successful expansion followed by retrenchment ordered by an anxious parent agency and then a cautious return to growth. In addition, its payroll operations have been buffeted by the ripple effects of downsizing in human resources (HR) offices since 1993. Through all of the changes, the center has exhibited the resilience and resourcefulness that are hallmarks of small businesses, but uncommon among bureaucratic organizations.

For example, the center faced up to rapid change in government human resources operations not by hunkering down, but by cooking up a new idea for contracting with software manufacturers. Short-staffed HR offices across government installed enterprise software systems to move large portions of personnel processing online. NFC was being forced to alter its own software in order to exchange data with the fast, new online systems.

Between 1993 and April 1999, reinvention cost the executive branch more than 340,000 jobs, many of them in administrative fields—human resources, procurement, finance and the like. Human resources offices were targeted for a 50 percent staff cut by the end of fiscal 1999. The number of personnel specialists dropped 21 percent between 1993 and 1997. Some offices lost as much as 40 percent of their workforce since 1992. These cutbacks forced HR officials to find ways to let managers and employees obtain and manage more HR information directly, without HR staffers' help. To accomplish this, agencies purchased enterprise software systems that allow managers to process personnel actions from their desktop computers and that permit employees to enter address and insurance plan changes, and charitable contributions by phone or computer. Enterprise software also allows agency managers to keep closer track of training and staff costs agencywide and to make better strategic decisions about when to add staff, eliminate jobs, or consider outsourcing.

The move to these strategic systems forced business adjustments at the NFC. The large center's mainframe-based payroll systems couldn't keep up with the seamless, online, real-time world of enterprise software. As a result, customers became restless for better service. In response, former NFC Director John Ortego embarked on a risky quest to convince an enterprise software firm to front the money for a new, commercial, state-of-the-art system.

Photo: Mike Posey

John Ortego
National Finance Center, Department of Agriculture

In return, the firm would get a fee for each person successfully paid using the new system.

Ortego's "share-in-success" venture was a classically entrepreneurial response to reinvention-induced business pressure. "If they share in the risk, they should make a handsome profit," said Ortego of his prospective software partner. "If it doesn't work, they get nothing." What's more, even if it flopped, the approach wouldn't saddle NFC, its agency customers, or taxpayers with the cost of a large, failed computer system. "I [will have] suffered a major defeat, but I [will not have] asked my client to pay for that defeat," said Ortego.

Procurement Pioneers: The Technology Buyers

That Ortego should have chosen an innovative purchasing technique to help his business catch up and keep up with rapid HR technology changes should come as no surprise. The explosive evolution of information technology (IT) in the 1990s blew open the formerly closed-in, tightly controlled, rule-bound world of federal acquisition. Information technology advances set off a statutory and regulatory big bang that spun off a new, fast-paced, performance-focused government IT marketplace and a constellation of daring, flexible buying businesses.

In the late 1980s, the federal government awoke from decades of dominating the IT market to discover it was no longer the biggest buyer in the store. Private industry was replacing costly employees with computers. Agencies under downsizing and streamlining pressure from NPR also were turning to technology for relief. With more flexible, faster buying processes, corporations were able to keep up with accelerating IT upgrades and innovation. Snared in cumbersome, time-consuming purchasing rules left over from another era, government fell behind. Frustrated by contract after contract that took years to complete and left users with outdated machines, agencies prevailed on lawmakers to loosen procurement laws. At the same time, the NPR was targeting procurement offices for staffing cuts.

The 1994 Federal Acquisition Streamlining Act (FASA) was the first break in the logjam. The law was intended primarily to speed up small purchases in order to reduce workload in procurement shops destined for downsizing. But a few lines in the new law encouraged agencies with an ongoing need for certain goods or services to negotiate long-running task- and delivery-order contracts instead of holding lengthy and complicated full and open competitions for every purchase. Further, in order to ensure competition, the law directed agencies to award these contracts to more than one company and have them bid against each other for every order. For IT buyers, FASA was a godsend, enabling them to speed the purchasing cycle once an indefinite-delivery, indefinite-quantity (IDIQ) contract was in place.

FASA's innovations, while welcome, couldn't keep up with the IT demand. Government still was squandering vast sums on huge, complicated systems that quickly exceeded their budgets and schedules and then failed to deliver. To check the hemorrhaging funds and forestall failures, Congress and President Clinton put in place the 1996 Information Technology Management Reform Act (ITMRA), later renamed the Clinger-Cohen Act in honor of co-sponsors former Rep. William Clinger of Pennsylvania and former Sen. William Cohen of Maine. Clinger-Cohen created a new IT acquisition model that included careful strategic decision-making before purchases are made and judicious modular procurement to guarantee that each element of a big system that is installed delivers value even if the entire package doesn't ultimately get built. Clinger-Cohen also replaced the 1965 Brooks Act, which had made the General Services Administration (GSA) the gatekeeper for agencies that wanted to open their IDIQ contracts for use governmentwide. The freedom brought by Clinger-Cohen fired the imaginations of a handful of IT procurement entrepreneurs.

These acquisition trailblazers saw that the combination of FASA's multiple-award IDIQ authority and the end of the Brooks Act meant they could put together long-term governmentwide acquisition contracts (GWACs) with top vendors of sought-after IT products. Once the multiple-award contracts were in place, the agencies that had created them could let other agencies pay to use them rather than negotiate their own. "FASA said we encourage multiple awards and streamlining, and it opened things up," said Emmanuel "Manny" DeVera, who pioneered some of the most envelope-pushing GWACs for the National Institutes of Health's Information Technology Acquisition and Assessment Center (NITAAC). "[Clinger-Cohen] ended the Brooks Act. It was the combination [of it and FASA] that made the opportunity to get into business," DeVera added.

Manny DeVera
Federal Technology Service, General Services Administration

Pushing the System

And DeVera needed business. By the mid-1990s, NIH's central acquisition office had nearly lost the loyalty of the agency's 25 institutes. "I saw it was time to push the system a little bit to get it moving faster so the scientists could get what they wanted," DeVera recalled. He hoped the fee-for-service NITAAC could create governmentwide IT contracts that were so economical, fast and easy to use that they would lure other agencies and then bring NIH's own institutes back to NITAAC. By buying through an existing contract, even after paying the sponsoring agency a fee, agencies save considerable amounts of time and money they otherwise would invest in conducting full and open competition among contractors for every IT purchase.

"The money is in charging the agencies for using GWACs," said DeVera. "The agencies save money by buying off your contract for a fee. We showed we could get better prices and easier and faster purchases with an IDIQ called the Electronic Computer Store [a computer equipment contract negotiated in 1995]," DeVera said. "Once it became popular, the institutes started using it. The NIH business has come back to NITAAC now," added DeVera, who left NIH in September 1998 to become director of GSA's new IT Solutions Regional Center.

Richard Lieber
Transportation Administrative Services Center, Department of Transportation

DeVera wasn't alone in recognizing the opening created by technology's rapid evolution, acquisition reform, and downsizing. In 1996, the Transportation Department bundled 10 lines of administrative services into a franchise—the Transportation Administrative Services Center (TASC). Richard Lieber headed the center's acquisition business line. "When we became fee-for-service, it was a huge paradigm shift," Lieber said. "Now we're all focused on customer service and a fair price." Lieber's challenge was to maintain customer service as he was losing staff to downsizing. He decided to promote Transportation's new IT contract in order to reduce his dwindling staff's workload while catering to agencies hungry for technology.

The contract, known as ITOP (Information Technology Omnibus Procurement), had been let in May 1996, as TASC was being formed. "We can issue task orders within six to eight weeks where ordinarily it took a year to let a contract," Lieber said. Through February 1999, agencies, including the Transportation, Defense, Justice, and Energy Departments, and others, made 250 orders worth $851 million using ITOP. Fees vary depending on the level of involvement by the ITOP special projects office.

Free Enterprise: The Forest Service

Al Gore's NPR logically chose administrative services—such as those offered by the CIA's Administration Directorate, NFC, and acquisition shops—as the most likely candidates for entrepreneurship and competition inside the federal government. In the early 1990s, they were monopolistic, not customer-focused, and could be benchmarked against similar services in the private sector, which also offered competing services. But in the late 1990s, a group of imaginative Forest Service employees began pushing the NPR's vision to its limits. Instead of transforming administrative organizations into competitive fee-for-service operations, the Forest Service is allowing individual employees to become itinerant small-business people selling core Forest Service functions, as well as administrative services, throughout California's 18 national forests in the Pacific Southwest Region (Region 5)—and sometimes beyond.

Staff cuts and flat budgets through the 1990s left the Forest Service increasingly short of the skills needed for safeguarding and harvesting trees, granting grazing rights, and providing recreation facilities for visitors. But instead of trying to make ends meet by putting longtime, highly skilled employees out of their jobs, hiring private firms to fill in, or simply by doing less, the Forest Service in California is turning employees loose to open their own businesses to accomplish needed tasks.

As federal agencies follow industry's lead by shedding all but their inherently governmental functions, the Forest Service enterprises offer a new model for accomplishing that core work. The enterprise experiment is bringing to fruition the predictions of management theorists that "full-time, forever" employment will fade and be replaced by armies of floating, flexible freelancers hopping from one enticing project to the next. "In the years ahead, organizations will no longer have a permanent workforce or even a temporary workforce; instead they will have what I call a 'situational workforce,'" said former Office of Personnel Management Director Janice Lachance in an October 1999 speech. "Work will be done by a blend of core employees in cross-functional teams and by temporary employees, consultants, and contractors, when necessary," she told the International Personnel Management Association's federal section conference in Washington. "Full-time, lifelong jobs and job descriptions are already disappearing and instead, employees are increasingly being called upon to be generalists—omnivores in the new world order, with the tools to survive and flourish at many tasks and in many different environments."

"Infusing Innovation"

The idea of itinerant internal enterprises washed into the Forest Service on a wave of reinvention. It arose independently but simultaneously in the agency's Washington, D.C., headquarters and in Region 5. The term "enterprise" first appears in "Excellence in Administration," a report published by Region 5 in October 1994. The report envisions administrative work in the region being "provided in an entrepreneurial and choice-based manner" by five operations teams. "These teams will compete with each other for sufficient work to justify their salaries. If a customer (forest business unit) is unsatisfied with service, that unit may have its administrative processing performed by another team," according to the report.

Two months later, in December 1994, Forest Service headquarters staffers published "Reinvention of the Forest Service: The Changes Begin," which also included a vision of competitive, self-supporting businesses within the agency. "We are moving away from large staff organizations toward a model in which units that use their budgets to care for land and serve people can purchase the services they need from internal enterprises," the reinventors wrote. "The result will be an evolving and self-correcting system governed by market forces rather than hierarchical decision-making."

David Radloff
Forest Service, Department of Agriculture

The growing consensus on some form of enterprising gave a solid focus to Forest Service reinvention chief David Radloff, who was new to his job in 1995. He created a team to further develop the notion. "The real idea was that reinvention in general, and enterprises in particular, were a way of infusing innovation and excitement and spirit into an organization that had gotten kind of stodgy and had driven the entrepreneurial spirit out of people," Radloff said. In California, Mike Duffy, then Region 5 financial management director, was looking for a way to streamline administrative services. He brought together the group that came up with the idea of competing administrative teams and named them "enterprises." Cross-fertilization was provided by Pacific Southwest Regional Forester Lynn Sprague and John Phipps, then forest supervisor of Region 5's El Dorado National Forest, whom Radloff calls "one of the most fearless innovative thinkers in the agency." The two men sat on Radloff's team and were key players in Duffy's search for excellence in administrative organizations. Duffy and Radloff also were acquainted.

Photo: Debra Lex Photography

Mike Duffy
Forest Service, Department of Agriculture

Said Radloff, "My team was still talking mostly in the abstract about enterprising, and I was coming to think that we just needed to find a place to try it. Region 5 came up just at the right time. We needed a place as large as a region because we needed to have a big enough market to find enough people to try the approach and enough managers willing to buy their services."

In 1996, Duffy spoke with Radloff's team about Region 5's enterprising idea. "Two months later, I was in Washington briefing Radloff and Doug Farbrother of Vice President Gore's National Performance Review staff, and a month later we became a reinvention laboratory," Duffy recalled. Reinvention laboratories were innovative organizations or activities established under NPR guidance to test or prototype new ways of doing business and share their lessons across government.

Breaking into Business

By 2003, there were 22 enterprises operating in Region 5. Most began with one employee and grew to hire others. Their services range from trail planning and assessing trees for their timber yield, to billing the state for federal firefighting assistance and handling workers' compensation claims. Enterprises are fully self-supporting, using the fees they charge forest managers. They must cover all the overhead costs they incur wherever their offices are housed as well as their salaries and benefits. To prevent forest supervisors from altering enterprisers' work priorities and to guard the businesses from downsizing, Duffy arranged for them all to report to the reinvention lab.

The lab also runs a bank for the enterprises, doing all their bookkeeping, providing advice and counsel, and even creating a form of workers' compensation insurance for enterprisers, who could lose their businesses if they were injured or ill and unable to work. To pay for the banking, advisory, and other services, the lab charges each enterprise a $5,000 licensing fee plus 1 percent of revenues. Enterprise backers convinced the Forest Service general counsel to allow the reinvention lab to use the agency's working capital fund for enterprise banking. The lab keeps careful track of its money in the fund and how much belongs to each enterprise. "As a result, the enterprises have very good accounting information—they know what funds are available, what have come in, what's still out, and where their money is going," Radloff said. "They are learning a level of financial management most Forest Service managers don't have."

The enterprises set off a cascade of cost-consciousness throughout Region 5, a real boon to the Forest Service, which is under perpetual fire from Congress for poor financial management. Enterprisers are deeply aware of costs since they must bring in enough money to cover them. They often negotiate hard with other Forest Service organizations for price cuts or service improvements. That bargaining, in turn, prods those operations to get a better handle on their own costs. Forest managers blanch at enterprisers' fees—often their first encounter with the true hourly cost of labor in government. But once the shock wears off, they become conscious of the high cost of full-time employees and begin considering better ways to use them. The majority of the enterprises started business in August 1998. Most more than covered their first-year costs.

The enterprisers and their supporters acknowledge that getting into business has been an uphill climb. "It has taken a lot of leadership and care [to create enterprises] because the agency's immune system is so strong," Radloff said. "People have learned to work to the position description, and enterprises don't fit that. Their goal is to bring in innovation and enthusiasm and flexibility. They do threaten people and that's how the immune system gets triggered. Some employees fear losing their jobs through this, but it's more likely to create jobs because enterprises can be profit centers. They also fear loss of control and power, so we're going slow, keeping them small and unthreatening, and building a support system."

The Challenge of Running Entrepreneurial Organizations

Getting Started

Growing carefully, flying under the radar, and spending lots of time allaying fears are hallmarks of savvy government businesses. Entrepreneurial operations are threatening to the governmental status quo for many reasons. Among them:

- They use funds not directly controlled by Congress.
- They do work for entities other than their parent organizations and agencies.
- They bring managers face-to-face with the true costs of accomplishing projects, forcing them to acknowledge inefficiencies and reorder priorities.
- They raise questions about the best mix of full-time, regular employees; government businesses; and private sector contractors.
- By demanding better service and by following rules inventively, they push the agencies and organizations in which they live to become more innovative and responsive to customers.
- By marketing their services and competing, they compel other organizations—inside and outside government—to improve their offerings and prices, or lose customers.

- Because they are beholden primarily to customers for survival, they threaten the control of the managers of functional silos, such as human resources, acquisition, and financial management.

Because they threaten power centers ranging from department headquarters and Congress to federal unions and contractors, government businesses need strong, savvy leaders and well-placed champions to nurture and protect them. For example, without a firm endorsement from Region 5's top official—then Regional Forester Lynn Sprague—the enterprise experiment never would have been launched. "The regional leadership met quite a few times to discuss it, with a lukewarm to cool response," Radloff said. "At one point, Lynn Sprague said, 'I've decided we're going to give this a try. We're going to go slow and put systems in place to support it. Managers don't have to support it, but you can't sabotage it.' That was the leadership support needed."

David Sutfin
Gov.Works, Department of the Interior

The staff of Gov.Works, a fee-for-service acquisition business within the Minerals Management Service (MMS), credits MMS' leaders for creating an environment in which entrepreneurs could flourish and take risks. "We're very lucky to have senior managers open to change and experimentation and making the workplace better," said David Sutfin, chief of the MMS procurement operations branch that became Gov.Works.

MMS was created about 15 years ago to manage the resources of the Outer Continental Shelf and to collect royalties from oil and gas exploration. The agency considers itself a profit center for the government, returning to the treasury $5 billion to $6 billion a year over its operating budget. MMS is an ideal business incubator: It's a relatively new organization, has close relations with private sector companies, and is strongly focused on customer service. "We're nimble because we're small and young and customer-oriented," said Bob Brown, MMS associate director for administration and budget. "We don't have a massive history with involved procedures. Because of that, we are able to staff up with people who are unencumbered by hidebound rules."

Photo: Liz Lynch

Bob Brown
Minerals Management Service, Department of the Interior

Leaders of government businesses not only must be open to change and nontraditional approaches, they must be evangelists for them. The CIA franchise's Calder, like many entrepreneurial leaders, regularly proselytized among the managers of his enterprises as well as potential customers, preaching the need for change in administrative practices, the power of competition, and the lessons of progress. He didn't shy from sharing bad news. Calder sponsored at least one "town meeting" among his entrepreneurial flock during which a leader of one of the franchise businesses outlined the mistakes she made starting out.

Champions and Coaches

The birth of the Forest Service's enterprises was attended by a number of champions. Agency reinvention chief Radloff enlisted NPR support through Farbrother. NPR support eased creation of a reinvention lab to shield the fledgling enterprises. "Radloff and Farbrother said the lab [would] give us license to do stuff and get us through the bureaucratic maze," Duffy said. "Being a lab has given us status within the organization. We're viewed as something that's not going to go away very quickly. What we wanted and got was encouragement, advice, leads on people to talk to and assistance when needed—a support system."

Duffy became the Region 5 reinvention lab's chief scientist, supporting the enterprise experiment by catalyzing useful connections throughout the agency and brewing up the business approach. He put together a laboratory staff and an enterprise steering committee, figured out financing, won the union's cooperation, sold the idea to regional managers, and campaigned for their cooperation.

Operators of buying businesses also credit others with protecting and assisting their operations. ITOP's Lieber said much of the support that allowed him to experiment in creating his fee-for-service contracting model came from George Fields, then director of the Transportation Administrative Service Center, which included ITOP. TASC sold data management, acquisition, HR, learning and development, facilities and space management, security, and a variety of other services. Of Lieber's acquisition business, Fields said, "I'm merely the coach. There are times when the business case has to be played out before the leadership of the department and of the administration. That's my job. If [Lieber] is on the line executing, someone has to make sure they understand what the benefits are."

ITOP was one of the last GWACs to be authorized by GSA under its Brooks Act authority. When it became clear that ITOP would meet in two and a half years the $1.13 billion sales limit GSA had intended to last for seven years, Fields had to convince officials at Transportation and the Office of Management and Budget that a second contract was needed. "There was a legitimate argument [against it]. There is such a proliferation of GWACs, [was] there a need to continue this one? I had to make the case for the relevance of ITOP—in other words, why we needed [OMB's blessing] to provide the service across government and what harm would come to agencies if we were not able to." Fields was successful. ITOP II, a $10 billion multiagency pact, was awarded in January 1999.

Getting the Numbers Right

Private sector businesses are made or broken on how well they can match the prices of their goods and services with customers' desire for them. It's no different in government. What is different is that government organizations rarely have experience determining the cost of what they do, let alone the demand for it or an appropriate price. The decision to charge for services and live on fees inevitably sets off a cultural revolution in an entrepreneurial government enterprise and its parent organization and often among its customers. Indeed, cost-consciousness is the key to creating a lean, flexible, customer-focused and performance-based government.

Only when agencies must account for the results their operations achieve and the costs of accomplishing them will they truly be forced to respond to their customers, internal or external. "A lot of what drives the [traditional bureaucratic government] system is the appropriations process...that's why it is so difficult to bring change, because the behavior drivers don't change," said Joseph Coffee, who is known as an expert in federal agency culture for his 1993 dissertation, "Organization Culture Change in Federal Agencies." Coffee and others agree that entrepreneurial enterprises, with their focus on a true financial bottom line, can fundamentally reshape government's culture. After all, cost accounting is the first and most basic skill entrepreneurial organizations must learn. To stop relying on appropriations and become self-sufficient, they must have full and detailed information about all their costs. To become competitive, they must figure out how to cover those costs while at the same time not pricing themselves out of the market. This kind of common business sense often is unfamiliar to would-be entrepreneurs working in the federal system.

Shocked into Success

Staffers at the General Services Administration's Federal Supply Service (FSS) were shocked into business success when they were forced to benchmark against private-sector firms and become a fee-for-service operation. FSS negotiates and oversees governmentwide contracts covering 4 million items—ranging from test tubes to inner tubes—offered by more than 6,300 companies to every agency in government. Using the size of the government as leverage, FSS's employees negotiate below-market prices on most items and services. The GSA schedules, as the contracts are called, are booming. Sales are up nearly 100 percent, from $4 billion in 1997 to $14 billion in 2001. Behind the boom in sales is a revolution in business brought on by near catastrophe in 1995.

Photo: Liz Lynch

Sue McIver
Federal Supply Service, General Services Administration

That year, the Clinton administration targeted GSA as an example of bureaucracy gone bad. To save itself from elimination, GSA underwent a top-to-bottom business review that subjected every business line, including FSS, to rigorous comparison with private-sector counterparts. Lines that couldn't compare were closed. FSS was forced to shape up from being a slow, rigid operation offering limited quantities of low-quality goods at mediocre prices to a lean, fast, hungry, customer-oriented, hard-bargaining buying shop. FSS has transformed itself into a fee-based enterprise and that, said Sue McIver, former director of FSS's services acquisition center, has made all the difference. "The 60 people [on my staff] have a very different perspective of their role than they did five to 10 years ago," McIver said of her staff. "I have a financial manager who pulls together data and presents it in town hall meetings so people can see the revenue and costs their products are creating. It's been fascinating to watch people taking ownership."

For example, when one of McIver's teams had to give up a successful management-consulting contract to a faltering sister center, McIver's team suffered some heartburn about how they would cover their costs before they ramped up a set of new contracts. "We try not to have them be nervous about not bringing in revenue," McIver said. "We're not going to put a schedule in place and cover $100 million in costs in [the first] year." Nevertheless, that anxiety about making ends meet has helped to power the transformation of FSS.

Billable Hours

When Forest Service enterprisers open their businesses, they go through a learning process similar to that of McIver's staff. Enterprisers learn quickly how few hours are billable in an average federal employee's working year and how hard it is to convince managers to pay the true cost of those billable hours. The fees enterprises must charge to cover their costs "take the breath away from a manager," Radloff said. "Enterprisers are calculating prices based on true costs, salary, and fringes (retirement, future use of annual leave, insurance). You have [to account for] annual leave, sick leave, training, and meetings, so you quickly find that the number of billable hours is smaller than

2,080 [the average annual hours of a full-time federal employee], and enterprisers have to recover all their costs during those shortened hours."

"When I do marketing, I ask them what total percentage of time they think the typical employee puts in in effective project hours. Some say 80 percent," said Kelly Fike, owner of Streamline, an environmental analysis and training enterprise. "Billable hours are more like 45 percent. I'm dealing with career government bureaucrats, and nothing ever brings them face to face with full costs."

Once they're won over to using enterprisers, forest managers more carefully weigh the cost of full-time employees. "We look at the cost differences between maintaining a full-time employee and paying an enterprise," said Margaret Boland, former deputy supervisor of the Los Padres National Forest. "We're in a high-cost area, so adding people is [expensive] for us. Enterprises are much more cost-effective for a one-time kind of thing."

As they come to appreciate the true value of a dollar, enterprisers also become more careful and canny spenders. Several have moved to new offices when offered lower rent. They also are demanding better, faster service from support organizations within the agency. For example, to challenge human resources staffers to become more responsive and creative in working with the enterprises, the reinvention lab held a competition for its business among HR offices in the region. Enterprisers already are pushing the winning office to become more businesslike. Jeni Bradley, owner of Recreation Solutions, a trail planning and consulting enterprise, asked for a price schedule for special services. "If they say it's going to cost an extra $500 to get a job classification within 30 days, we'll say fine," she said. "If I can hire quickly to win a $100,000 project, $500 is not going to mean anything to me."

The Price Is Right

Like Bradley, other federal entrepreneurs constantly are looking for ways to shave their costs to keep their prices at or below what the market will bear. For example, competition drove Lieber's ITOP price-setting policy from the start. "I looked at what the competition was charging and I said, 'I can't charge more than that,'" he said. Lieber kept costs, and therefore prices, low in creative ways. For example, he hired contract employees, rather than full-time federal workers, to administer task and delivery orders under the GWAC. "I couldn't hire federal employees because the whole idea is that since I'm now a business, I need the flexibility to expand and contract based on the level of business," Lieber explained.

Problems in handling fluctuating workload have dogged franchises, according to an April 1998 report to Congress from OMB, the six GMRA franchises, and the Chief Financial Officers Council Entrepreneurial Government Committee. "Organizations that operate without direct appropriated funds take risks beyond those required in an appropriated environment," the council observed. "Artificial [staffing] controls unnecessarily exacerbate the risk inherent in a non-appropriated environment." In many cases, downsizing in parent agencies has reduced franchise staffing, as well. According to the report, some franchises rely on technological productivity enhancements and cross-training to help their staffs handle workload ebb and flow. "In addition, a majority of the franchises turned to contracting ... as an efficient short-term solution to resource limitations," the report says.

In addition to keeping a stable of contract employees, Lieber employed other strategies to keep ITOP prices competitive. He set a range of fees based on how much work customers were willing and able to do themselves. "I'm offering a couple levels of service," said Lieber. "The first would be that I would delegate contracting authority to the customer. That's a 1 percent fee [based on the amount of the order]. Then, if they come to my special project office, we'll help them do a statement of work and be the source selection office. For that joint effort it's 2 percent. If I write the statement of work and do more, it's 2.75 percent. The majority [pay] 2 percent."

Money Matters

Fee-for-service operations also invariably need a place to bank their fees. In addition, they need some method of building up reserves so they can pay bills that exceed available cash. Federal agencies are prohibited from incurring cash deficiencies. All the franchises and a number of other entrepreneurial organizations do their banking with working capital funds, which are allowed to maintain operating reserves. Franchises have the added advantage under GMRA of a retained earnings incentive. They can keep up to 4 percent of total revenues in order to buy capital equipment, put in place financial management and other support systems, and make management improvements. This ability to "make money" is an incentive to improve efficiency.

Gov.Works, the MMS acquisition-shop-for-hire, owes its success in large part to becoming part of the Interior Department's franchise and working capital fund. When the procurement shop decided to go fee-for-service in 1996, staffers didn't yet know that MMS's parent department had a franchise fund. Instead, the MMS procurement staff was considering offering their services under the much more restrictive Economy Act. That would have meant the funds they collected could not be retained beyond the end of a fiscal year and that potential Gov.Works customers would have to make burdensome Economy Act determinations that supplies or services could not be obtained as conveniently or economically from the private sector.

Brown, the MMS associate director for administration and budget, helped Gov.Works find its way into the franchise fund. "If Interior hadn't had a franchise fund, we would have had to look for a working capital fund to become part of or [we would have had to] get one through Congress," Brown said. "We could have done some work through the Economy Act, but generally the funds are transferred under an agreement that runs out at the end of the fiscal year. That's no good if you are providing a service that you can't cut off because you will lose your investment, or because it's impractical." Discovering the Interior Franchise Fund proved a lifesaver to MMS, allowing it to take on work over more than a single fiscal year, build reserves, and, someday soon, begin setting aside funds for future capital acquisitions. "So far, our revenues have more than covered our expenses," said Gov.Works Director Sutfin in 1999.

The Forest Service's Region 5 reinvention lab placed such a high value on getting under the agency's working capital fund umbrella that lab director Duffy brought in the fund's creator to help. "The Washington, D.C., director of financial management had retired and moved to California, so we picked him up as a re-employed annuitant," Duffy said. "He had set up the agency's working capital fund and helped us get our system up and running. Absent him, I'm not sure we could have done it."

The lab's enterprise bank set up an overlay accounting system to translate the data coming from the fund into separate accounts for each enterprise. "We do accrual accounting to match [each enterprise's] revenues with the expenses of a fiscal year," said Kathleen Wolcott, then head of the enterprise bank. "It matches expenses to the period in which the revenue is earned whether or not the money has come in or the check has been written." In this way, enterprises and the bank can keep track of what's been billed, what money has come in, and what's on hand to cover costs. If an enterprise temporarily runs short of cash, the enterprise bank provides loans at 10 percent interest.

New Ways of Operating

Partners in Success

Innovative partnerships are characteristic of successful Information Age companies. In *The Complexity Advantage: How the Science of Complexity Can Help Your Business Achieve Peak Performance* (Business Week Books, McGraw Hill, New York, 1999), Susanne Kelly and Mary Ann Allison tout collaboration as one of their 14 steps for business success. "In our current environment of rapid change, networks of vendors, academics, and even competitors are out there learning new things far more rapidly than we will on our own," they write. "We have to recognize the strength that exists in partnerships and to leverage it intelligently so that we can work effectively with each other."

Federal entrepreneurs are bringing people together on all levels. Both the NIH and Transportation Department GWACs, for example, were run by specialized contracting offices that joined purchasing professionals with IT experts. "I've always said that if you get the technology and the procurement sides together, anything can be achieved," said ITOP's Lieber. "In reality, ITOP is an information resources management program housed in procurement."

The Forest Service enterprises found ways to partner to increase their marketability. "One of the things happening now is alliances, partnerships, two enterprises getting together to take on a job," said Region 5 reinvention lab director Duffy. "For example, Kelly Fike of Streamline [which does environmental analysis and team-building] teamed with ACT 2 [a writing and editing enterprise]. I think the enterprise [partnerships] are going to grow and probably do bigger and more complicated things."

A Knack for Niches

Be they in government or in the private sector, fledgling businesses find the safety they need to grow strong by anchoring themselves in market niches. Finding the unmet need, the underserved clients, or the unexploited specialty has launched more than one successful first entrepreneurial foray. NIH's DeVera, for example, struck gold by building a contract that offered the perfect combination of popular vendors and must-have computer technology. ITOP's Lieber went DeVera one better by offering technology services on his contract. "There was a significant yearning in government to have a good, efficiently run IT services vehicle. We found a niche," Lieber said. "We knew there was a market for IT services out there. What we didn't really know was the extent."

Not to be outdone, DeVera, too, saw the market in IT services. Not long after ITOP was awarded, he raced into existence the Chief Information Officer Solutions and Partners (CIO-SP) contract based on IT management reforms. "I knew [the 1996 Clinger-Cohen Act] was coming and that it was based on IT solutions, not hardware and software," DeVera recalled. "Our target market was CIOs and program managers. The real issue was to get something going that people would identify with the Clinger-Cohen Act."

Specialization Sells

Gov.Works, the MMS acquisition business, has specialized in helping agencies with IT purchases. Gov.Works bet that specialization would draw business to it and away from agency procurement shops that get bogged down buying everything from office products to IT services. "What Gov.Works sells is nothing that anybody else couldn't sell," says MMS budget chief Brown. "It's the same contracts and the same systems as anybody can sell. [But Gov.Works also sells] responsiveness, sensitivity, and the ability to deliver. We get people willing to pay a fee to get that—program people who feel lost, displaced, and not supported." Gov.Works leader Sutfin frankly acknowledged that Gov.Works trades on the failures of other acquisition offices. "Program managers come to us because they are looking for an alternative," he says. "If you have to spend months getting through the acquisition process, you're losing money. We're able to do it faster than most."

Forest Service enterprisers are making a living out of specialization, parlaying their unique skills into small businesses. Tree measurement expert Merl Sturgeon was about to lose his job because his forest could no longer support an expensive employee with top-notch timber skills at a time when tree harvesting was declining. But among all 18 forests in Region 5, there was more than enough demand for Sturgeon's special skills. The answer was to free him from old-fashioned employment, set him loose as a small businessman, and let him work forest to forest capitalizing on his finely honed abilities.

The women who started Region 5's Compensation Resolution Brokers enterprise turned their expertise in handling workers' compensation claims into a thriving business. The large size of Region 5 and the fact that its heavy fire seasons produce lots of injuries each year mean demand for compensation claims processing talent is high. Region 5 spends more per year on workers' compensation and medical benefits than any other region in the Forest Service. In addition, before the enterprise began, each forest handled disability cases on its own, often catch-as-catch-can, allowing cases to languish for years before checking to see whether employees receiving compensation were fit to work again.

"We found that with the numbers of cases they had to handle, a lot of casework was falling through the cracks," said Geralyn Bolong, a resolution broker with the enterprise. "The five of us just handle [compensation cases] as opposed to other duties. We have a lot more energy and time so we're getting resolutions a lot faster." In their first year, the brokers resolved eight cases, saving the Forest Service $244,000 in the short term and potentially more than $4 million over the full course of the eight employees' working lives.

Forest Service reinvention czar Radloff said specialized services give enterprises an edge that helps them overcome the perception that regular full-time employees are less expensive. "Enterprises are overcoming the barrier of built-in subsidized competition by being in specialty niches and by being available and willing to go where the work is and having a real customer service attitude," he added.

Advertising Anxiety

Entrepreneurial federal operations quickly learn that all the specialization in the world won't help if no one knows you're in business. Selling means advertising, but promotion and PR aren't the normal province of federal managers, and entrepreneurs have made notable marketing missteps. For example, NIH acquisition innovator DeVera gained notoriety for radio advertisements he placed at the end of fiscal 1996 to woo federal buyers and to take advantage of the newly enacted Clinger-Cohen IT reform law. The ads ended up running during the morning rush hour on "shock jock" Howard Stern's program. "I hired an advertising firm to [find] me the three most listened-to stations during a.m. drive time," DeVera recalled. "They didn't tell me what the [names of the] shows were. They did the ad, I listened to it, and they put it on the three shows. One happened to be Stern's."

Needless to say, running an ad amid Stern's antics brought DeVera a raft of criticism. The furor grew when *Federal Computer Week* newspaper ran a story about the ad placement a week later. Some say the firestorm stirred by the Stern show ad contributed to DeVera's ouster from the NITAAC directorship in November 1996. Despite the brickbats, DeVera says the ad worked. "A whole lot of government people listen to Stern," he says. In addition, "there was money made off [the ad] because of phone calls that came off the *Federal Computer Week* article about it," DeVera says. "It was outrage marketing. The whole notion of a government agency putting the ad on radio was a good idea."

Perhaps, but others have taken a different lesson from DeVera's experience. Three years after the Stern affair, Gov.Works decided it had reached the limits of word-of-mouth advertising and decided to engage a firm to craft a "customer awareness campaign." Gov.Works staffers were careful to seek endorsement from the leadership of their parent agency, MMS. "We sold the idea at several levels of the agency and had no negative reaction," said Sutfin. "We discussed the types [of media]. Radio and TV got a thumbs-down. We all know Manny [DeVera]."

Branding a New Business

"Advertising" and "marketing" are words still spoken in whispers among many entrepreneurial federal organizations. In the early days after GMRA was enacted, congressional staffers often warned franchise founders not to risk legislators' fragile support of businesslike government by appearing too aggressive in generating sales. "A staff director of a congressional committee told me unequivocally to be careful how we market," said Ernest Hardaway, then vice president for national marketing and reinvention of government at the Department of Health and Human Services' Federal Occupational Health franchise fund. "He indicated that something euphemistic like 'customer awareness' or 'education campaign' would be far more appropriate."

Fully aware of such concerns, Gov.Works took a careful approach to rev up sales. "We were concerned somebody might have a negative political take on it—should government be doing this type of thing?" says MMS budget chief Brown. But despite its trepidation, the acquisition enterprise gambled on advertising. "We knew [the name] MMS wasn't working. We had to create an identity," said Sutfin. Gov.Works hired Osborn & Barr, a $60 million St. Louis advertising firm known for its brand campaign for agricultural equipment manufacturer John Deere—"Nothing runs like a Deere." "It was amazing to me how well they understood the frustrations we were trying to piggyback on—[that] if you're a project manager, the last thing you want is to have somebody in the acquisition shop tell you why you can't do something," said Sutfin. "They already had the Gov.Works logo ready. We went out to buy an awareness program, but subsequently I realized we were buying a brand," Sutfin adds.

Osborn & Barr studied publications about government to learn federal program managers' problems and how a fee-for-service acquisition organization such as MMS's Gov. Works could help them. The firm also understood the sensitivities of working with an entrepreneurial governmental entity. "We knew there were some politics involved, that MMS could be seen as coming in and superseding the procurement offices of other agencies," said Mark Vogel, Osborn & Barr executive vice president for brand management. The firm placed ads in *Government Executive* magazine and *Federal Computer Week*. "We only put ads in publications aimed exclusively at the population we're trying to serve," says Brown. "Clearly it's aggressive, but we think it's honest."

Branding is bringing Gov.Works new business. "We've gotten a lot of calls and they've been productive calls," Sutfin said. In July, the value of contracts Gov.Works handled in fiscal 1999 had almost reached $74 million, the total for fiscal 1998, and Gov.Works finished 1999 at $98 million, with $20 million booked for fiscal 2000. Gov.Works charges fees ranging from 2 percent to 4 percent, and projected income for fiscal 1999 was about $2 million, up from $1.7 million in 1998 and $700,000 in 1997.

By early 2000, Gov.Works' brand had become so important to the new business that it was contemplating a lawsuit to protect it. Though Gov.Works has purchased the Internet address "govworks.gov," as a government entity it couldn't buy "govworks.com." Sure enough, about six months into the new branding campaign, Gov.Works found out that a New York-based Internet firm calling itself "gov.Works.com" was planning to offer assistance to federal, state and local governments that want to offer citizens service via the World Wide Web. Gov.Works began negotiating with the dot.com, and had to decide whether to sue to prevent the start-up from violating its trademark or to sell the rights to the trademark it has built. The dispute marks the first time a government business has confronted a private business over the right to use a government-owned brand name. It won't be the last if entrepreneurial government continues making headway.

The Costs of Success

Other officials at cross-servicing units still flinch when asked how they market. "We prefer to approach the marketplace as an [accounting] or law firm approaches it," said NFC's Ortego. "We depend on our presence in the community." Ortego is candid about his understated approach. "I don't want to get under the skin of some congressman that I'm out marketing business away from the private sector."

Ortego has reason to worry. NFC's success in attracting customers almost put it out of business. In 1983, at the request of the Office of Management and Budget, NFC expanded its data processing services to begin cross-servicing for other agencies. In the early 1990s, payroll-processing income from other agencies first exceeded that generated from the Department of Agriculture (USDA). Soon thereafter, Agriculture put a moratorium on NFC cross-servicing and the center took in no new customers until 1998.

The public explanation was that USDA wanted NFC to focus on redesigning its software to support Agriculture systems. Most observers agree that the real reason for the moratorium was that USDA headquarters wanted to rein in the exuberant business mentality of the New Orleans center. Under former Director Clyde McShan, NFC had prospered, adding 600 new employees and hauling in nearly $100 million a year largely by processing pay for 500,000 employees at USDA and other agencies. NFC won praise for expanding, and McShan wrote and spoke about possibly taking it out from under USDA control.

Soon after the moratorium was in place, McShan was demoted; he subsequently left Agriculture to become deputy chief financial officer at the Commerce Department. He has since left government. "It was a disagreement about expansion," McShan said of his demotion. It also was an opening for other federal payroll providers. "Since I left, NFC sat dormant for about five years or better," McShan said. "When I was there people knew we were open for business and were flocking to us." NFC rebuilt its reputation as a cross-servicing powerhouse under the leadership of Ortego, who had the full support of former USDA Chief Financial Officer Sally Thompson. "One of the things the center does outstandingly well is payroll and payment processing," Thompson said. "I expect they would continue to expand the line."

Public-Private Competition

NFC's ups and downs, DeVera's ouster, and the self-censorship Gov.Works exercised vis-a-vis TV and radio advertising illustrate the limits of bureaucratic entrepreneurship. Prospering can be perilous if it arouses jealousy among those higher up in the hierarchy. Tooting your own horn can bring unwelcome attention from congressional and private sector opponents. Indeed, there is a strong current of criticism of entrepreneurial government among businesses and, consequently, on Capitol Hill.

Among the leading opponents has been the Professional Services Council (PSC), a national trade group representing professional and technical services contractors. "The public sector should not be trying to emulate the entrepreneurial behavior of the private sector by seeking to grow and expand into new products, services, or markets at its constituents' expense," according to "Rationalizing Public and Private Sector Roles," a 1998 PSC position paper. "Government's entrepreneurial energies should be directed toward achieving excellence and greater efficiencies in performing inherently governmental functions, and developing and managing outsourcing programs that make the best use of private sector capabilities."

PSC denounces franchising, cross-servicing, federally funded research centers, and a variety of other practices as forms of improper "public-private competition." "Public-private competition fosters competition for resources rather than cooperation among government agencies, places the private sector in competition with its government clients, and raises questions about conflicts of interest for the government when governmental entities are potential future competitors on work the private sector currently performs," the council asserted. Agencies' entrepreneurial activities "shift [their] energies away from fulfilling their own missions...solely to legitimize the existence of excess capacity," according to a council report, "A New Model for Public-Private Competition," published in 1999.

The Clinton administration responded to such criticism by suggesting that barring federal organizations from competing for government work is unfair. G. Edward Deseve, then acting OMB deputy director for Management, detailed the administration's position in March 1998 testimony before a Senate Governmental Affairs subcommittee. "As agencies seek lower costs and best value support service offerors, they will test and improve their in-house, contract and franchise (cross-servicing) support mix," Deseve said. "Federal employees are some of our nation's most highly trained and dedicated employees. They operate within a complex system of rules, regulations, and laws. They respond to a vast array of missions, public concerns, and operational requirements. They deserve, as does the private sector, the opportunity to compete for their jobs on a fair and level playing field." Deseve also pointed out that March 1996 revisions to federal service contracting rules made certain interagency servicing arrangements available for bid by both federal and private operations.

What's more, the experience of franchises and cross-servicing operations demonstrates that the private sector hardly is shut out of business won by federal enterprises. "Franchising is by no means a 'government vs. private sector' contest," wrote former Office of Federal Procurement Policy

Administrator Alan Burman in the September 1999 issue of *Government Executive* magazine. "Governmentwide, nearly 80 percent of the revenues generated by franchises go to private companies who support their activities. In this way, franchising is doing what years of outsourcing proposals have failed to accomplish—making much greater use of the private sector to provide government administrative services."

Business vs. Governance

Critics of entrepreneurial government believe the notion that government can share characteristics with business is faulty. In "The Importance of Public Law: New and Old Paradigms of Government Management," in the *Handbook of Public Law and Administration* (Jossey-Bass, 1997), Ronald Moe called this "sector blurring" and denounced it. "This philosophy of replacing a public service ethic with a private sector, pecuniary-based ethic for managers is not without its risks," Moe wrote. It "replaces political accountability with economic accountability. In effect, the executive branch gets to define and reward its own success without direct accountability to Congress," he contended.

What was lost amid the NPR's calls for internal government competition, customer service, and focus on the budgetary bottom line, wrote Moe, was "that the primary purpose of government management is not to make manifest economic axioms but to implement laws passed by the people's representatives in Congress." Moe said that hewing to that traditional legal framework does not prevent agencies from innovation, as Vice President Gore argued. In fact, Moe wrote, "given a straightforward, definable mission, an appropriate organizational structure, and funding in a manner that encourages economically efficient behavior, governmental institutions are remarkably creative instruments for achieving public purposes."

Moe has a point. In fact, when their entrepreneurial efforts clash with "public purposes," businesslike agencies do get into trouble. GSA, which remade itself by benchmarking against private industry in the mid-1990s, ran smack up against such a conflict. In 1999, GSA announced it was closing its eight FSS warehouses in order to make ordering, shipping, and delivery of supplies to agencies vendor-direct, virtual, and more cost-effective.

Between 1988 and 1998, warehouse sales had fallen 15 percent, from $908 million to $772 million. Meanwhile, the FSS schedules, through which agencies order and receive goods directly from private vendors, saw sales increase nearly 100 percent, from $4 billion in 1995 to $7.7 billion in 1998, and best $10 billion in fiscal 1999. "Because [running the warehouses] involves high fixed costs, we have found ourselves in a catch-22 position of constantly having to raise our prices to break even," said then

FSS chief Frank Pugliese. "We will create new partnerships with the private sector and continue transitioning stock items to other sources, such as schedules."

As a business decision, closing the warehouses was a no-brainer, but the warehouses were more than just a business operation; they served societal, and thereby political, purposes as well. For more than 50 years, GSA has been the primary distributor of the products made by agencies associated with National Industries for the Blind (NIB). NIB President James Gibbons said the closings would affect as many as 1,400 blind and disabled workers who produce warehouse products or work in customer service positions for contractors. The organization said products made by those workers make up one third of GSA's stock program, and 60 percent of NIB's distribution was through GSA. "The domino effect could jeopardize the whole program," Gibbons said, including large and small community agencies that provide rehabilitation, job training, and job placement for the blind. Both NIB and the organization that provides jobs for severely disabled people operate under the Javits Wagner O'Day (JWOD) program, created by Congress to ensure federal agencies buy goods from workers with disabilities.

At the same time GSA was awakening to the social consequences of closing its warehouses, the American Federation of Government Employees, which represented warehouse workers, was filing a grievance against the action. The union charged that GSA failed in its obligation to bargain before making the decision that could put as many as 2,000 employees out of work. An arbitrator agreed. After promising increased marketing help for JWOD agencies, GSA reversed its decision. But in the end, GSA consolidated warehouse operations at two depots, closing six. In this case, a federal acquisition law with a social purpose interrupted an entrepreneurial agency's attempt to further streamline government buying and improve its own bottom line. GSA is only one example of the almost inevitable clash between entrepreneurial and law-enacting government. The conflict undoubtedly will play out in many forms as government evolves to its new size and shape for the Information Age.

Business-Permeable Government

It may be true that, in the long run, government will be pared back to an inherently governmental nub that is significantly smaller than it is today. But in the short term, the future is likely to hold continual evolution of federal-private conglomerations and partnerships and new forms of entrepreneurship within government. Glimpses of a new, more business-permeable government can be seen in the proposed "share-in-success" payroll software contract contemplated by NFC's John Ortego and in the vendor advisory councils supporting governmentwide IT contracts. They're also visible in Richard Lieber's use of contractors to help run ITOP.

Attempts to lobby, legislate, shame, or frighten these developments out of existence will founder, as do all efforts to hold back change. The better course may be to climb aboard and find ways to benefit from and guide them. The ride is sure to be wild, rapid, and unpredictable, but the likely long-term outcome is new business in government, more business for industry, and better business for taxpayers.

Those who doubt the inevitability of further entrepreneurial morphing by federal agencies should consider that holders of the nation's deepest secrets at the CIA became venture capitalists in 1999. In-Q-Tel is a nonprofit firm underwritten by the CIA with offices in Washington and Silicon Valley. It's partnering with developers of cutting-edge IT projects useful to the CIA that also have commercial applications. The CIA hopes to find more effective methods, including using the Internet, to mine the piles of data it collects worldwide.

The CIA's foray into cyberbusiness was denounced in an op-ed in the *New York Times* as an unsound use of federal dollars that would be better spent contracting with Internet innovators. Nevertheless, if secretive agencies such as the CIA can throw off their cloaks and enter the scramble for stock in private companies, then entrepreneurial government no longer is a fad, it's a *fait accompli.*

Lessons Learned

Forms of federal entrepreneurship vary widely, but successful entrepreneurial organizations share a number of traits that developed as they first fought to create their businesses and then to run them. Organizations hoping to nurture entrepreneurship or create their own businesses would do well to take note of the lessons and characteristics of the pioneers.

1. An event or circumstance that demonstrates the futility of status quo operations and the need to change.

Every single one of the entrepreneurial ventures described here came into being after its founders got a kick in the pants—an event or circumstance, such as downsizing, a threat of closure, a loss of confidence, or plummeting funding—that demonstrated the futility of the status quo and the need to change or die. Acquisition organizations were under severe pressure to speed up technology purchases while downsizing. The California forests were running out of funds to support some of their most experienced, but also most specialized, employees. The CIA administration directorate had too little staff to keep up adequate service standards and was losing customers to the private sector. Without such do-or-die conditions, entrepreneurial leaders would have had a much harder time making the case for change and nudging staffers into taking risks they otherwise might have been able to avoid.

2. A knack for finding unmet needs, underserved customers, or unexploited specialties, and for occupying those business niches.

For example, Forest Service enterpriser Merl Sturgeon found he could support himself by plying his specialized timber skills across Region 5's forests even though a single forest couldn't afford him year-round. The women of Region 5's Compensation Resolution Brokers parlayed skills and connections honed for years into a business resolving workers' compensation cases that the Forest Service had allowed to languish. Government's buying businesses are clustered in one area of purchasing—information technology—because it is the fastest growing and changing segment of government acquisition. This cottage industry of internal acquisition businesses survives by feeding off of agencies' seemingly unquenchable appetite for IT equipment and services.

3. Strong, savvy, well-placed leaders and champions.

Entrepreneurial organizations have little chance of establishing themselves unless they have strong, wise, well-placed leaders and champions to enact the business vision; run interference and keep opponents off guard; provide protection, advocate, and agitate throughout the parent agency; license experimentation and mistakes; and build useful connections and support structures. Forest Service enterprises owe their creation and survival to a cast of protectors including David Radloff at Forest Service headquarters and Douglas Farbrother at the then-National Performance Review, along with Mike Duffy, Lynn Sprague, and John Phipps in Region 5. Each played a role in smoothing the way for the small businesses to come into being. Duffy and his reinvention lab cleared obstacles and built a support structure to allow the enterprises to flourish. Without George Fields, then chief of the Transportation Department's administrative services franchise, Richard Lieber's ITOP contract might never have been renewed. In every case, visionary leaders have created the space in which government businesses could grow. The confluence of reformed regulations and new business needs alone wasn't enough to sustain entrepreneurs in the skeptical, if not downright hostile, bureaucratic environment.

4. Cost consciousness and a bottom-line orientation.

Government businesses must quickly develop a keen sense of cost-consciousness and a bottom-line orientation if they are to survive. Those that have done it almost immediately become hard bargainers with the organizations that provide them services, setting off a search for efficiencies throughout the parent operation. Many entrepreneurial organizations have found they can't afford full-time federal staff, turning instead to contract labor they can augment or diminish with surges and declines in workload. The customers of entrepreneurial organizations also are forced to grapple with costs as they try to find money to pay for services they once thought of as free and try to determine whether the prices they're paying are fair. Where competition is lively, as among government's buying businesses, agencies quickly become canny purchasers, moving from one contract to another or from contracts to the GSA schedules and back again in search of the best deals. Forest managers in California are becoming wiser users of their full-time regular employees now that they have discovered the true cost of federal labor by paying enterprisers' fees.

5. The ability to build and maintain financial reserves and to rely upon effective, reliable accounting systems.

All the cost-consciousness in the world can't help entrepreneurial organizations if they have no way to bank their earnings. Just as the banking industry grew alongside capitalism, so working capital funds are proliferating as government becomes more businesslike. Government businesses simply cannot survive without the ability to build and maintain financial reserves and to rely upon effective, reliable accounting systems. In order to ensure the survival of its enterprises, the Region 5 reinvention lab not only won them use of the Forest Service working capital fund, it also is built them a bank to keep their books and offer them loans. Of course, just as in the private sector, these financial services come at a price, one that enterprisers must absorb through greater efficiency or pass along to their customers in higher prices. The need for accounting and banking services is growing as more and more cross-servicing organizations are becoming self-supporting, losing the margin of safety provided by occasional support from their parent agencies' appropriations.

6. Unswerving customer focus.

Self-supporting organizations must charge prices that can be difficult for their customers to swallow. That's why these operations must have an unswerving focus on making whatever changes are necessary—as well as legal and appropriate—to win and keep customers. Both the CIA's administration directorate and NIH's contracting shop, for example, were forced to become entrepreneurial because they were hemorrhaging customers. And when the directorate began charging for its services, its CIA customers balked at first. Likewise, Forest Service enterprisers were forced to justify their fees by educating first-time customers about the relatively small portion of billable hours in an average Forest Service employee's day. The education usually was coupled with a sales pitch. Enterprisers explained that when managers hire enterprisers, they get 100 percent of their time as opposed to regular employees, who often are pulled off a project to attend meetings, answer calls, handle crises, or respond to e-mail, among other activities. What's more, each of the entrepreneurial organizations described here has tailored its offerings in response to customers' desires. From ITOP's sliding fee scale based on customers' desired levels of participation in their task orders to NFC's efforts to obtain better software to interface with customers' ERPs, government businesses are attempting to meet, exceed, and even anticipate customers' needs.

7. The ability to apply information technology to improve productivity and keep staffing levels low.

Many entrepreneurs are relying on technology both as a lure to attract business and a way to reduce their costs of doing business. As NFC's Ortego shopped for a new software partner, he was both attempting to acquire cutting-edge ability to catch up with his customers' new systems and to reduce costs by replacing a legacy system with heavy maintenance requirements with one that required little human intervention. Wherever they can, entrepreneurs use technology to reduce their need for costly staff. In addition, a number of government entrepreneurs have fashioned businesses to feed agencies' insatiable IT appetites. The technology-buying businesses occupy the most active and innovative market within the larger world of government acquisition. The rapid evolution of innovative ways to purchase information technology matches the speed of change in technology. To survive, IT-buying businesses must remain nimble, flexible, and innovative. The fact that the complexity of technology makes it challenging to purchase works in buying businesses' favor so long as they remain focused on selling the technology smarts that many agencies lack but desperately need.

8. Openness to partners.

Successful entrepreneurs both in the private and public sectors rarely are loners. Instead they are skilled practitioners of the art of partnership. Gov.Works might never have gotten off the ground but for an early partnership with the Federal Systems Integration and Management Center (FEDSIM), a fee-for-service IT support operation within GSA's Federal Technology Service. FEDSIM used Gov.Works to handle overflow contracting work and at one time accounted for 75 percent of Gov.Works' business. The percentage went down to a healthier 50 percent after FEDSIM, seeking to bolster its in-house contracting shop, issued a short-term policy requiring all FEDSIM staff to check first with the home office before using an outside contract shop. But early on, the FEDSIM partnership was crucial to Gov.Works' success.

9. Creativity in dealing with fluctuating workloads.

From its FEDSIM slowdown, Gov.Works quickly learned that part of the secret of business success is creativity in dealing with fluctuating workloads. The work of national forests ebbs and flows with the seasons, so a number of the Forest Services enterprisers have had to diversify their services in order to maintain their incomes year-round. Fee-for-service operations have little choice but to accommodate to the cycles of business and work. Ironically, since many government businesses came into being in part to preserve their founders' jobs, they almost always end up hiring contractors for some jobs or using contract labor as a portion of their workforce. It's just too hard and too costly to use entirely federal staffs when work isn't steady, they've found. It's far more efficient to bring on contractors when they're needed and let them go when they aren't or to outsource whole projects or lines of work. Federal franchises have learned to creatively leverage the workload of other agencies. A good portion of the value added by franchises comes not in performing administrative work themselves, but in aggregating the demand of numerous small agencies unable on their own to provoke price-reducing competition for their business. Wielding the needs of a number of agencies, franchises are able to attract bidders and contract out work for lower prices than individual agencies could achieve. Nearly 80 percent of the revenues of federal franchises go to private firms.

10. Marketing ability.

Many federal entrepreneurs have or develop a flair for promotion. They need it, of course, if they are to attract business and bring in fees. Few are as brazen as Manny DeVera with his ads on radio shock jock Howard Stern's drive-time show, but some are getting braver. The trick, as demonstrated by Gov.Works' branding campaign, is to develop a feel for how far to go in advertising before the political sensibilities of legislators, sponsors, and customers are violated, and the ability to push the PR campaign right up to those limits. NFC's former chief Clyde McShan may have pushed too far by talking too soon about taking the center out from under the Agriculture Department's umbrella. Subsequent Director John Ortego preferred a quieter approach to sales, which he likens it to the high-brow collegial networking of an accounting firm.

11. Willingness to take risks and to make mistakes.

From DeVera's bravado to Merl Sturgeon's dogged stick-to-itiveness to the Gov.Works' staff's drive to control their own destiny, government's business people all have shown themselves ready to dare greatly. Sometimes, like NFC under Clyde McShan, or DeVera at NIH, they lose and get punished. But, like all good entrepreneurs, government's business pioneers just lick their wounds and try again, each time a bit smarter, cagier, and more creative than before.

For Additional Information

Anne Laurent, *Government Executive,* "Tree Enterprise," November 1999 (electronic version: http://www.govexec.com/features/1199/1199s1.htm)

Anne Laurent, *Government Executive,* "Brand New Business," October 1999 (electronic version: http://www.govexec.com/features/1099/1099s3.htm)

Anne Laurent, *Government Executive,* "Shifting the Risk, Top 200 Contractors," August 1999 (electronic version: http://www.govexec.com/features/99top/08a99s1.htm)

Anne Laurent, *Government Executive,* "Sales Force," July 1999 (electronic version: http://www.govexec.com/features/0799/0799s3.htm)

Anne Laurent, *Government Executive,* "Pay Dirt," June 1999 (electronic version: http://www.govexec.com/features/0699/0699s2.htm)

Anne Laurent, *Government Executive,* "The Buying Business," April 1999 (electronic version: http://www.govexec.com/features/0499/0499s2.htm)

CHAPTER THREE

Franchise Funds in the Federal Government: Ending the Monopoly in Service Provision

John J. Callahan
Adjunct Professor
School of Public Affairs
University of Baltimore

This report was originally published in February 2002, revised May 2003.

Introduction

The franchise concept has a long legal and economic history. In England, franchises were royal grants by the king to his subjects. In our own legal tradition, *Black's Law Dictionary* notes that a franchise "... is a privilege or immunity of a public nature which cannot be legally exercised without legislative grant."[1]

In economic parlance, franchising is defined as "a contractual arrangement under which an independent franchise produces or sells a product under the brand name of the franchisee and to his specifications and with marketing and other support."[2]

The six governmental franchise funds authorized by the Government Management Reform Act (GMRA) of 1994 are grounded in the legal and economic traditions of the franchise concept. They are specifically authorized to operate by federal law; they are granted certain powers and rights not accorded to other fee-for-service instrumentalities; and their day-to-day operations are similar to private sector franchise operations. They offer services according to the dictates of their sponsoring agents—their governmental service customers. They provide services on a voluntary basis, and are expected to operate within the federal financial management landscape designed to maintain the fiscal integrity of their operations. Their overall legal and operating construct is not dissimilar to that of private franchise operations.

While this analogy to the private sector is not perfect, these governmental franchise funds operate as entrepreneurs in the public service arena. They "sail on their own bottoms," as it were and succeed or fail, in great part, on the price, quality, and responsiveness of their service offerings.

Thus, we should determine whether franchise funds in the federal government are achieving the objectives envisioned by the National Performance Review (NPR), whether they should be expanded, or whether they should be regarded as just an isolated bureaucratic experiment designed to provide a limited set of services on a highly selective basis.

This chapter analyzes the origin and legislative background of the GMRA franchise fund pilots authorized in 1994. It provides a summary description of these franchise funds and examines in detail two such funds now operating at the Department of Health and Human Services (HHS) and the Department of the Treasury. The latter part of the chapter sets forth several criteria for evaluating the success or failure of these two franchise funds and ends with a set of recommendations that should be borne in mind as the Congress and the White House consider whether these funds should be permanently authorized or expanded.

The lessons learned from this chapter should inform executive and legislative branch decision makers as they consider ways to increase government efficiency and effectiveness in the provision of services without diminishing the public mission behind the provision of governmental services by these franchise funds. Indeed, the question may not always be an either/or proposition of whether a service will be provided entirely by a public bureaucracy, partly by private contractors, or be totally privatized. Rather, the question may be more appropriately whether the service to be provided can have a transparent cost and pricing structure and whether the service can be provided with high quality levels that will meet the needs of the paying customer.

The franchise fund initiative analyzed in this chapter should answer a number of questions about the viability of these instrumentalities and whether they should be continued, terminated, or expanded as a means of promoting greater efficiency and cost-effectiveness in the delivery of a number of public services.

Franchise Funds: Legislative Origins

Franchise funds trace their legislative origin to the Government Management Reform Act of 1994, but derived their basic impetus from the early efforts of the National Performance Review. Among its many initiatives, NPR also sought to promote a more entrepreneurial approach to the provision of selected governmental services.

As part of an overall program to reinvent government, the NPR wisely sought to devote more attention to eliminating service monopolies in common administrative services and to providing such services on a competitive basis similar to that in the private sector. As a 1994 NPR report on the subject of franchises noted: "Like the concept in private industry, franchise organizations must meet customer needs in order to be financially self-sustaining. If the franchise organization cannot compete in the environment in which it operates, it will eventually cease to exist."[3]

The rationale could not be clearer. Government service monopolies were to be a thing of the past. New cross-servicing organizations were to be created that would provide for a more competitive playing field for the provision of administrative services. Duplicative services would be eliminated, economies of scale would be realized, the unit cost of administrative services would be reduced over time, and services would be provided on a voluntary basis.

A further impetus for this concept came from the realization that entrepreneurial organizations already existed at the federal level. The 1994 NPR report noted that as of that time there were over 100 entrepreneurial organizations operating throughout the government, the most significant being the 49 Cooperative Administrative Support Units (CASUs) that were prevalent in federal regions.[4]

Again, another positive message came from the NPR. Franchise funds were not only desirable from a "better business" point of view, but also the federal government had enough practical experiences with the entrepreneurial dimensions of the concept due to the long-standing nature of CASUs and other financial instrumentalities like working capital funds. Franchise funds were not being invented from scratch. Rather, they were to be a more expansive and refined application of existing mechanisms that emphasized more fully the concept of entrepreneurial government.

Having promoted the concept, NPR staff at the working and senior levels sought a legislative foundation for these mechanisms, ultimately resulting in the passage of the Government Management Reform Act of 1994 (P.L. 103-356).

The House action on a broad government reform measure, H.R. 3400, was nearly unanimous; it passed by a vote of 429-1 on November 22, 1993. The Senate was unable to pass the omnibus bill, containing more than 50 NPR-inspired reforms including franchise funds, that passed the House. One of the obstacles to passage was that opposition developed around the number of franchise funds to be authorized by the bill and the fact that such franchise funds would face far less regular fiscal scrutiny of their operations by congressional appropriations and the Office of Management and Budget (OMB) staff.

The Senate Governmental Affairs Committee subsequently reported a bill that comprised selected provisions of the House measure as S.2170 almost a year later and then passed it on September 28, 1994. The House then passed this measure, and it was signed into law on October 13, 1994 as the Government Management Reform Act of 1994.[5]

The genesis of franchise funds then derived from two basic sources. First, they were the more entrepreneurial successors of service and financing mechanisms that already existed in various agencies, most of which had no explicit legislative construct. Second, they were the brainchild of NPR staff, who felt that they should have a legislative construct, be put in place throughout government, and be more cross-servicing and voluntary in nature than their predecessors so that a full-scale competitive process could be injected into the provision of selected governmental services. OMB and the Chief Financial Officers Council (CFOC) developed a series of business principles to serve as operational guidelines for franchise funds.

OMB prepared two reports on the performance of franchise funds with the active participation of the CFOC in the first several years of the pilots' existence.[6]

These two reports provided generally favorable assessments of the franchising concept, but acknowledged that individual pilot franchise operations warranted improvements in various areas.

The first report was prepared pursuant to a requirement in GMRA to report to the Congress on the performance of the franchise pilots. The report recommended extension of the franchise fund pilots with continued emphasis on the 12 business operating principles for effective franchise fund management.

The second report, communicated to Congress in late 2000, provided the legislative justification that the franchise concept be made permanent and that the franchise fund concept be extended to other departments as well, with OMB involved in a more formal approval and monitoring role as more franchise funds were created.

The proposed legislation that was sent to the 106th Congress would have codified many of the franchise fund operating principles endorsed by OMB and the CFO Council. It also advocated a greater administrative role for OMB in the creation and oversight of franchise funds. Each franchise fund would be expected to have its own separate budget account, provide services on a full-cost basis, be subject to an annual financial audit, as well as being held to annual financial management performance goals and indicators. Furthermore, as many of the pilots were already doing, franchise funds would be able to retain up to 4 percent of annual receipts for capital, information technology, and financial management improvements. A significant new provision would have permitted new franchise funds to obtain at least partial funding through federal debt financing. As in the private sector, such debt would eventually have to be retired as the franchise fund became successful.

The Bush administration in its FY2002 budget proposed a one-year extension of the pilot franchise funds. However, at the same time, it has advocated more outsourcing of services through competitive sourcing and called for a more thorough scrutiny of the terms and conditions of interagency service projects.[7]

As of this writing, the Senate Governmental Affairs Committee has reported out legislation providing for a one-year extension of franchise funds—S.1198—and the full Senate approved it by a voice vote. The House of Representatives has yet to act on this legislation. However, a one-year extension for existing franchise funds was enacted as part of the FY2002 Treasury-Postal Appropriations bill.

In sum, the idea of franchise funds was driven largely through an executive branch process aided and abetted by interested agencies that wished to put these instrumentalities on a sounder legislative footing and thereby give them greater incentive for more aggressive agency and interagency cross-servicing. Bureaucratic entrepreneurs who headed these operations stood ready to market their services on a competitive basis and were given free rein to do so during the first several years that franchise funds existed. By 2000, these franchise funds had strong supporters in OMB and the CFOC, both of which recommended legislative permanence for the concept.

Franchise Fund Pilots: An Overview

Six franchise fund pilots were created pursuant to the Government Management Reform Act of 1994. They operate in five departments and one independent agency and vary in size, scope of service offerings, governance structure, and the degree to which they provide service beyond the department's jurisdiction.

Five of the six franchise funds have been in operation since May of 1996 and one since January 1997. Thus, at the end of FY2001, they had been in operation for five years. The Bush administration requested a one-year extension of franchise funds in the FY2002 budget[8] while at the same time seeking a more thorough examination of interagency cross-servicing procedures.[9]

Once established, franchise funds were expected to operate according to 12 business operating principles (see Table 3.1).[10] These principles were enumerated to insure that these funds were to be truly entrepreneurial in nature and provide various administrative services on a fully voluntary, market-based basis to all interested government agencies.

The funds were expected to succeed on their own, having no subsidy from appropriated funds but financing their operations solely from the revenues received from their business operations. Most funds had authority to retain up to 4 percent of their earnings to finance either periodic upgrades of their infrastructure or cope with surges and contractions of business. However, accumulation of these funds was predicated on the assumption that their business operations were self-sustaining and that such business lines would succeed or fail depending on their ability to attract and retain satisfied government customers. Or as Curtis Coy, former director of the Program Support Center (PSC) at the Department of Health and Human Services, said, "Franchise funds are established to drive business processes and behavior towards efficiency—the better, faster, cheaper model."

The customers of franchise funds were to be government agencies within and outside of the departments or agencies in which the funds were located. Internal customers were valued because they could help produce rapid economies of scale in administrative agencies. In addition, internal customers were also seen as beneficial as departments or agencies sought to meet their downsizing FTE mandates from the Office of Management and Budget and Congress and contend with the fiscal pressures caused by declining program management budgets.

At the same time, other federal agency customers of franchise funds were an equally if not more important gauge of franchise fund success. Such external customers would also benefit from service economies of scale, but an increasing number of external customers would also indicate that the franchise fund was providing a high-quality, high-value service with a quality and cost mix that was superior to other providers. This competi-

Table 3.1: The Franchise Fund Pilot Program, 12 Business Operating Principles

1.	**Competition**	The provision of services should be on a fully competitive basis. The organization's operations should not be "sheltered" or be a monopoly.
2.	**Voluntary Exit**	Customers should be able to "exit" and go elsewhere for services after appropriate notification to the service provider and be permitted to choose other providers to obtain needed services.
3.	**Self-Sustaining/ Full Cost Recovery**	The operation should be self-sustaining. Fees will be established to recover the "full costs," as defined by standards issued in accordance with FASAB [the Federal Accounting Standards Advisory Board].
4.	**Surge Capacity**	Resources to provide for "surge" capacity and peak business periods, capital investments, and new starts should be available.
5.	**FTE Accountability**	Full-Time Equivalents (FTEs) would be accounted for in a manner consistent with the Federal Workforce Restructuring Act and OMB requirements, such as Circular A-11.
6.	**Initial Capitalization**	Capitalization of franchises, administrative service, or other cross-servicing operations should include the appropriate FTE commensurate with the level of effort the operation has committed to perform.
7.	**Adjustments to Business Dynamics**	The ability to adjust capacity and resources up or down as business rises or falls, or as other conditions dictate, is necessary.
8.	**Cessation of Activity**	The organization should specify that prior to curtailing or eliminating a service, the provider will give notice within a reasonable and mutually agreed time frame so the customer may obtain services elsewhere. Notice will also be given within a reasonable and mutually agreeable time frame to the provider when the customer elects to obtain services elsewhere.
9.	**Organization**	The organization would have a clearly defined organizational structure including readily identifiable delineation of responsibilities and functions and separately identifiable units for the purpose of accumulating and reporting revenues and costs. The funds of the organization must be separate and identifiable and not commingled with another organization.
10.	**Services**	The enterprise should provide only common administrative support services.
11.	**Performance Measures**	The organization must have a comprehensive set of performance measures to assess each service that is being offered.
12.	**Benchmarks**	Cost and performance benchmarks against other "competitors" are maintained and evaluated.

Source: OMB. 1997 Report on Franchise Funds

tive environment would put pressure on other franchise funds and/or other government service providers to enhance service quality and/or reduce the cost of their services to gain a competitive advantage, or else run the risk of losing customers or going out of business altogether.

While franchise funds were expected to be competitive service providers within and outside of their departments, they were also expected to observe uniform rules of prudent and transparent financial management. They were expected to undergo independent, annual financial audits. They were to have full cost accounting and full cost recovery for their business operations. Furthermore, they were encouraged to monitor customer satisfaction, set performance objectives and measures, and engage in benchmarking. Benchmarking could enable franchise fund managers to better manage their costs, while incorporating lessons learned from the best practices of other organizations to measure the efficiency and effectiveness of their own operations and better manage their costs. Finally, they were expected to abide by all current laws and regulations dealing with competition with other public and private sector service providers to government agencies.

Essentially these franchise funds were expected to be entrepreneurial in the truest sense of the word. They were to offer competitive, high-quality services. They could not "low ball" their service offerings since they could not run a fiscal deficit. They could not "pad" their bills since their services were required to be offered on a full cost recovery basis. Moreover, they had to have fully transparent pricing for their services and maintain continuous customer feedback as to the quality and cost of their service offerings.

What has been the general record of franchise funds during their existence? By a number of measures, franchise funds appear to have succeeded well in their service mission (see Tables 3.2, 3.3, and 3.4).

Their overall record is perhaps best summarized by a 1999 report of the Entrepreneurial Government Committee of the Chief Financial Officers Council. The report stated, "Overall the franchising concept appears to be adding value to government operations, as foreseen by the NPR. During their first two years of operation, franchise funds have generated more than $600 million in gross revenues through the delivery of common administrative services. Furthermore, nearly three-fourths of the revenue generated by these pilots is attributable to cross-servicing arrangements with external customers. Accompanying this impressive level of production across the pilot, many franchise funds have been able to support more effective or efficient operations of their customers by either reducing the costs and/or improving the quality of products and/or services provided—achieved, in part, through both competition and collaboration with other public and private sector providers."[11] Put another way by Curtis Coy of the HHS Program Support Center, which now supervises the Federal Occupational Health

Table 3.2: Initial Features of Franchise Fund Pilots

Franchise Fund	CEO	Start Date	FY97 Rev. ($millions)	FY97 FTE	Services Offered By Fund
Commerce Department	CFO	October 1996	$12M	39	Acquisition management, financial services, engineering, environmental compliance, and IT services
HHS Department	Deputy Sec.	January 1997	$81M	103	Clinical occupational health, environmental health, and employee assistance program services
Interior Department	Deputy CFO	October 1996	$3M	12	Administrative, IT, facilities management, and training and development services
Treasury Department	Deputy CFO	July 1996	$37M	84	Financial consulting, administrative management, accounting, financial systems, and financial education services
Veterans Affairs Department	Asst. Sec. Mgt.	October 1996	$59M	433	IT and telecommunication, records management, law enforcement and investigations, and financial services
Environmental Protection Agency	CFO	October 1996	$104M	65	IT, telecommunications, and postal services

Source: OMB, The Franchise Fund Pilot Program: An Interim Report, 1997.

(FOH): "The key element in a franchise fund is responsiveness. Government customers really want responsiveness and control over the services that they receive. The key here when competing for business is to shut up and listen to the customer."

Table 3.3: Selected Characteristics of Franchise Fund Pilots, FY97-FY98

	Treasury	Interior	VA	EPA	HHS
Sales Growth 1997-1998 (in $millions)	$37–$80M	$3.4–$19.3M	$59.2–$88M	$104–$111M	$81–$82M
Full Time Equivalent (FTE) Employment Growth/Decline 1997-1998	84–120 FTE	12–58 FTE	433–546 FTE	65–59 FTE	103–90 FTE
Service Efficiencies Recorded 1997-1998	7% Mail 27% Admin/ Support Cost Reductions	N.A.	83% Unit Rates Decreased	9.6–20% Cost savings for Business units	Reduced Clinical Training costs
Full Cost Recovery Policies in Place	Yes	No; not complete	Yes	No; not until 2000	Yes
Unqualified Opinion on Financial Audit	Yes Unqualified Opinion, FY97, 98	Yes	Yes FY98 only	Yes Material Weakness	No Separate FOH Audit Performed

Source: OMB 1999 Report of Franchise Funds

Franchise fund pilots discussed here have voluntary service offering policies, a successful service competition record, and deliver a large if not predominant part of their service through private sector subcontractors.

Sales growth occurred during the early years, though some of the franchise funds actually dropped some service lines because of declining customer demand and/or loss of business to other government service providers. FOH has revised some of its standard packages of services to better meet the service needs and price demands of its customers. More progress appears to be needed on some critical aspects of financial management, such as the conduct of annual financial audits, development and

Table 3.4: Additional Characteristics of Franchise Fund Pilots, FY97–FY98

	Treasury	Interior	VA	EPA	HHS
% of Customers from External Agencies	91% External	84% External	36% External	All Internal	93% External
Service Provision on Voluntary Basis	Yes	Yes	Yes	No	Yes
# of Competitive Service Bids Entered and Won	50%/ 10 Bids No challenges	50%/ 4 Bids	100%/ 25 Bids	None	43%/ 21 Bids No challenges
% of Business Handled by Private Sub-contractors, FY98	84%	85%	50%	95%	87%

Source: OMB 1999 Report on Franchise Funds

use of performance measures, and implementation of full cost recovery policies and practices—a critical element in franchise fund financial self-sufficiency.

The most recent assessment of franchise funds came at the end of 2000 during the closing days of the Clinton administration. This report, prepared by the CFO Council and presented to OMB, commented favorably on the success of the franchise fund concept since it encouraged agencies to consolidate administrative service provision and have such services provided on a competitive basis. It further noted the fiscal benefits of cross-servicing, the competitive spirit engendered by franchise funds, and the continuous ability of franchise fund customers to enter into and exit from service agreements with the funds. The report concluded by noting that proposed legislation making the franchise concept permanent and extending the concept to all government departments and agencies would "… help make franchise funds a better model for accountable, non-subsidized offerings of administrative services.… As the franchise fund concept is expanded, future policy makers could consider whether the other non-appropriated funds should be subject to the same safeguards that franchise funds are."[12]

In summary, through the end of 2000, the franchise concept appears, for the most part, to have proven its worth and lived up to the initial expectations of its founders. Franchise funds:

- Increased sales volume, especially on cross-servicing agencies;
- Operated on a voluntary fee-for-service basis; and
- Provided the bulk of their service through small-business subcontractors and did so with a high degree of customer satisfaction.

To that end, they received the endorsement of OMB and the CFOC to propose permanence for the franchise fund concept and to extend it to other departments with OMB approval.

While this summary assessment of franchise funds is helpful, a more detailed look at two franchise funds in the Department of Health and Human Services and the Treasury Department is now in order.

Franchise Funds: Two Case Studies

This part of the report examines in more detail the operations of two specific franchise funds: the HHS franchise fund—the Federal Occupational Health (FOH)—and the Department of the Treasury Franchise Fund (TFF).

Public records of the funds were examined and a series of in-depth interviews were held with senior governmental officials responsible for or familiar with the operations of these funds.

Federal Occupational Health (FOH)

The FOH was the last franchise pilot to be established under the Government Management Reform Act. Yet, the FOH had a long history in the provision of basic occupational health services, formerly being a part of the hospitals and clinics division of the Health Resources and Services Administration (HRSA). By 1984-85 as part of a cost-cutting initiative of the Reagan administration, FOH was directed to be funded on a wholly reimbursable basis from the government customers that it served. Senior HHS officials at the time took FOH into the fee-for-service arena and operated it on a fully reimbursable basis, with annual sales totaling $50 million by 1993.

The FOH was recommended to be a franchise fund by John Hisle, director of FOH, and Dr. Ernest Hardaway, deputy director of FOH, who had been an agency representative to the National Performance Review and was active in developing the franchise concept. Other officials at HHS, including the secretary, deputy secretary, CFO, and deputy CFO, strongly endorsed this recommendation and requested that OMB designate the FOH as a franchise fund. While some internal consideration was given to designating the newly created Program Support Center at HHS as a franchise fund, the complex operations and financing of the PSC suggested that a smaller, more focused franchise fund be created, hence the choice of FOH as the department's designated franchise fund.

As John Hisle said, "The franchise fund designation gave us the 'Good Housekeeping Seal of Approval.' It also helped us retain up to 4 percent of our revenues, which aided with our business development efforts and further helped us deal with the surge and flow of FOH business."

John Hisle was named to head FOH in 1993, and he changed in a fairly dramatic way the operation of the FOH. Previously it had operated on a decentralized basis with business being generated from 10 regional FOH offices. Hisle moved away from this decentralized, regional approach toward a more centralized one that could compete for national contracts with a uniform rate structure.

In February 2002, the FOH had 84 "core" FTE and over 1,600 persons who are hired through a variety of contractual agreements (both on a part-time and full-time basis). Of particular interest is the teaming effort that FOH has with the Magellen Corporation. Magellen contracts with FOH to provide Employee Assistance Program services and at the same time it has a non-compete clause with the FOH. This arrangement benefits contractors since they obtain a guaranteed line of business and basically supply services as set forth in a service agreement developed by the FOH. Thus, the FOH, in effect, becomes a financial intermediary for Magellen and other subcontractors and insures that a private contractor delivers effectively the services for the government customer.

At the same time, there is competition between the FOH and other federal fee-for-service instrumentalities (i.e., CASUs) and with private providers like Ceridian that provide Employer Assistance Program services on the GSA schedule, something that the FOH is prohibited from doing. But the FOH ascribes its success to its responsiveness to the customer. It seeks to provide a high-quality service at a reasonable price. This indicates that the FOH is selective in what work it competes for. FOH does not compete with low-end public or private sector providers who offer lower value occupational programs at substantially lower costs. Again, as FOH Director Hisle states, "The FOH prides itself on the quality of its services. We pride ourselves on this point. We will not offer low-quality services even if they can be delivered at a cut-rate price."

Past business plans for the FOH projected $87 million in revenue in FY2000 rising to $96 million in FY2002. The FOH projects an annual growth rate of 5 percent or more in sales in 2002 and beyond due to developing a more skilled marketing workforce, greater outreach to a wider range of federal agencies, and a continued high-quality "branding" of their services (see Tables 3.5 and 3.6 and Figure 3.1).

The FOH is a geographically dispersed service provider. It has 210 permanent clinical service locations, 290 counseling service centers in 50 states, and 52 wellness/fitness centers operating throughout the country.[13]

The FOH services 1.2 million federal employees with its Employee Assistance Program (EAP) services; 200,000 employees with basic clinical services; and another 500,000 employees with specialized clinical or EAP services. All in all, 493 separate organizations have concluded service agreements with the FOH.

The history of the FOH suggests that it has become attuned to changing customer service needs and, therefore, has been able to expand and diversify its service offerings over time. It has noted a gradual shift from basic occupational health services (BOCHS) to other specialized clinical, environmental, and employee assistance programs. The movement here suggests that agency customers were expanding service agreements pursuant to various labor agreements and also due to their desire to customize

Table 3.5: Federal Occupational Health Top 12 Customers (FY99 Billings)

Rank	Customers	FY99 Billings
1.	U.S. Postal Service	$24,771,637
2.	Treasury	10,005,082
3.	Justice	6,228,388
4.	Environmental Protection Agency	5,033,584
5.	Health and Human Services	4,903,432
6.	Army	4,439,459
7.	Interior	2,959,088
8.	Social Security Administration	2,621,042
9.	General Services Administration	2,510,755
10.	Defense	2,411,164
11.	Agriculture	2,180,258
12.	U.S. Courts	2,067,344

Source: Federal Occupational Health

Table 3.6: Services Offered by Divisions of the Federal Occupational Health

Occupational Health Services Division		Federal Law Enforcement Medical Program Division	
Basic Occupational Health Services	**Specialized Clinical Services**	**Environmental Health Services**	**Employee Assistance Program**
• Walk-in care and first emergency response • Personal physician services • Health education programs • Annual workplace visits • Ongoing health screenings • Individualized health counseling • Occupational health records • Routine immunizations	• Medicare surveillance services • Specialized physical examinations • Medical clearance examinations • Occupational health consultation • Medical opinions on ADA [Americans with Disabilities Act] and Family Leave Act matters • Education and training on disease control and management • Illegal drug-use detection programs • Individual/corporate health-risk appraisals • Defibrillator training and quality assurance • Smoking cessation programs	• Industrial hygiene surveys • Environmental surveys • Workplace safety surveys • Training in hazardous exposure protection • Hazard surveillance and risk assessment • Occupational health and safety program assessment • Environmental sampling and laboratory services	• Supervisor consultation and training • Short-term problem resolution • Community resource referral • Crisis counseling • Health promotion • Family support services (Department of Defense primarily) • Dependent care and referral services • Workplace violence prevention

Source: FOH FY2000-2002 Business Plan

Figure 3.1: Total FOH Revenue by Year, FY96–FY01

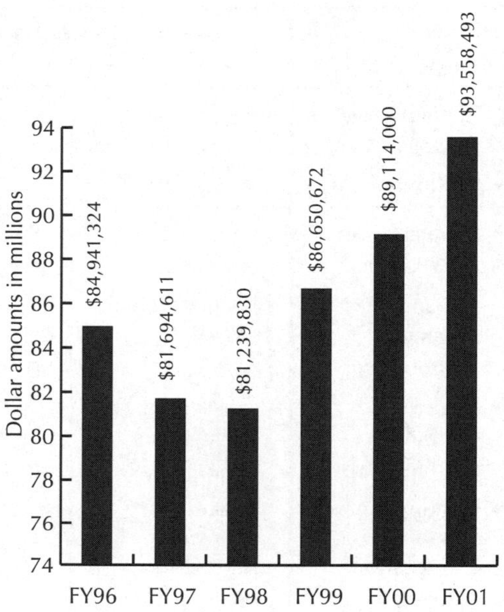

Source: Federal Occupational Health

their specialized clinical service offerings from among those that were being offered by the FOH. As a result, specialized clinical service agreements produced 60 percent of all clinical product line revenues by FY2000.

One example of the ability of the FOH to offer new services on a fast-paced basis was the agreement between the FOH and the U.S. Army to provide anthrax inoculation and other specialized medical services to the Army on an as-needed basis. After approval by the HHS Service and Supply Fund Board and the department, the FOH offered the service so that the Army could better utilize in-house personnel and reduce the maintenance of fixed locations for such services. Thus, the FOH provided the service on an as-needed and just-in-time basis.

Yet, in another case, the FOH sought approval to supply environmental remediation services to the U.S. Navy at selected environmentally contaminated "surplus" Navy base sites. This proposal was turned down by the HHS Service and Supply Fund Board when it was determined that HHS might have to assume legal liability for the sites once FOH services were offered at the locations. So even though the FOH was aggressive in seeking new business opportunities, other overiding considerations prevented this new FOH business venture.

A number of factors appear to have contributed to the FOH's service success in its first several years of operation. On the fiscal front, it had a healthy level of retained earnings and was able to offer lower rates for some of its offerings, especially EAP services. It could also document substantial dollar savings for some of its customers after they received service from the FOH.

Perhaps the most important feature of the FOH was its intense attention to customer service. "Core" staff continuously monitored customer service and was insistent that FOH subcontractors maintain high-quality service levels. In this regard, they appear to have been aided by their subcontractors, many of which were small businesses eager to maintain their business with the government. These small businesses found that the FOH could act as a general contractor for their services. The FOH could design and negotiate a service agreement with an agency, and the subcontractor would simply execute the contract. This arrangement assured a revenue stream for the subcontractor but continued to enhance the ability of the FOH to negotiate and monitor service-level agreements.

In sum, the FOH has developed as a successful franchise fund and fulfilled its promise as a vehicle for public-sector entrepreneurship. It has offered services consistent with its mission. It has done so through carefully crafted service agreements and backed this up with continuous monitoring of customer satisfaction with service offerings. Its "customer first" spirit, its efforts to hold down unit costs of service where possible, and its ability to offer new and custom-tailored services to its customers have insured its success as a franchise fund (see Figure 3.2). In sum, as a senior HHS official, Deputy CFO George Strader, put it, "The Federal Occupational Health franchise fund is well connected to its original mission and has excellent entrance and exit rules for its customers."

Treasury Franchise Fund (TFF)

The Treasury Franchise Fund (TFF) was designated as a pilot in 1996, and its first year of full operation was FY97. The TFF originally had five units—the Center for Applied Financial Management and four CASUs that were administered by the Internal Revenue Service and that operated in Baltimore, Los Angeles, Cincinnati, and Seattle. Since there were a variety of separate fee-for-service instrumentalities operating within Treasury, it was felt that the TFF would be a "holding company" for these units and thereby promote more systematic franchising.

The TFF was created according to a highly systematic process, guided in some measure by the NPR operating principles for franchise funds. Detailed risk-assessment studies were conducted, and the TFF charter was designed with input from a wide variety of Treasury officials including the

Figure 3.2: Summary of FY2000 FOH Customer Satisfaction Survey—% of Customers Who Rated FOH "Excellent" or "Good" on Selected Measures

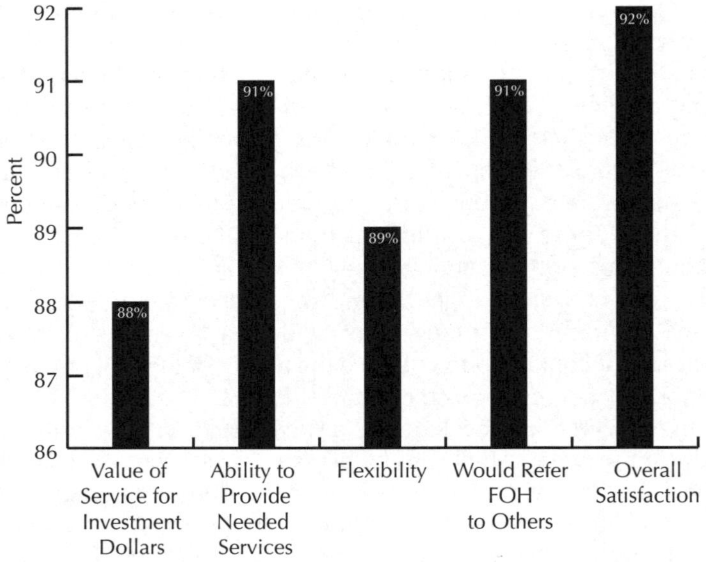

Source: Federal Occupational Health FY2000 Business Plan

inspector general. They also helped draft a rigorous set of rules for any Treasury entity that wished to come under the umbrella of the TFF. The main rules were: 1) no subsidy for operating costs, 2) total cost accounting for all services rendered, 3) quarterly financial statements, 4) annual financial audits, and 5) benchmarks for service.

Additional units have been brought into the TFF over time, with the major addition being the Administrative Reserve Center (ARC), located in Parkersburg, West Virginia. This has become the most successful business unit in TFF and has been adding customers both inside and outside of the Treasury Department.

Business offerings have increased substantially during the history of the TFF (see Tables 3.7 and 3.8). The most successful business unit, the ARC, first sought business from small government agencies and then expanded to the D.C. Pensions Board and the Financial Management Service in Treasury. Senior Treasury officials describe the success of this burgeoning service unit as coming from an entrepreneurial spirit that just "drips customer service." Or as Barry Hudson, director of the Office of Financial Management, put it, "The Treasury Franchise Fund is distinguished by the fact that we under-

Table 3.7: Services Offered by Treasury Franchise Fund

- Accounting Services
- Alternative Dispute Resolution
- Auditor Training
- Background Investigations
- Collaborative Consulting with Leaders
- Computer Repair Maintenance
- Conference Room Management
- Copier Management
- Court Reporter Services
- Employee Assistance Programs
- Equipment Rental
- Federal Benefits Information Systems
- Financial Education and Training
- Financial Management Consulting
- Financial Systems Consulting
- Laser Cartridge Services
- Leasing
- Mail Room and Management Services
- Messenger Service
- Moving Services
- Personnel Services
- Procurement Services
- Records Management Destruction
- Resource Management Program
- Space Planning and Design
- Telecommuting Services
- Temporary Help
- Training Services

Source: Department of the Treasury Franchise Fund 2000 Accountability/Annual Report

Table 3.8: Treasury Franchise Fund Business Organization & Units

Consolidated/Integrated Administrative Management	Financial Systems Consulting and Training	Financial Management Administrative Support
FBA Central FBA East	Center for Applied Financial Management	Administrative Resource Center
FBA Midwest FBA St. Louis	Financial Consulting Group	
FBA San Antonio FBA West FBA Seattle	Inspectors General Auditor/ Training Institute	

Source: U.S. Department of Treasury, 2000 Accountability/Annual Report stand our customers better than anyone else. This is even better than, say, going through a GSA schedule for service where there is not an intimate, continuous relationship between the provider and the customer."

At the same time TFF CASU units have dropped some product offerings, such as conference services, and all Treasury Franchise Fund business units are under constant scrutiny to insure that their business offerings do not operate at a loss.

The TFF is governed by the deputy chief financial officer and the director of the Office of Financial Management. These chief officers hold quarterly meetings at which the Treasury inspector general and all directors of the business units of the TFF must attend. Quarterly financial statements are prepared for all TFF units and examined at these meetings, again to insure that all services being offered will be done on a self-sustaining basis (see Table 3.9).

The TFF currently has 11 business units, offering 30 distinct products or services to nearly 1,500 customers. They have a "core" staff of 490 employees, yet 83 percent of their revenues go to private subcontractors. Their revenue has grown from $38 million in FY1997 to $165 million in FY2000, and they have doubled their number of external customers in four years of operation (see Figures 3.3, 3.4, 3.5, and 3.6).

The TFF also notes that customers using their services have reduced administrative costs as part of their overall budget from 7.3 to 5.5 percent. This has helped these customers move toward greater consolidation of such administrative support services as accounting, procurement, travel, and personnel services.

The TFF has many elements of success similar to that of the FOH. It has a large and growing number of customers; its sales volume has increased dramatically. The strength of its core mission has meant a considerable plus in marketing its services within and outside of Treasury.

More so than FOH, the TFF has prided itself on its full cost accounting and its unqualified financial opinions over the years. It is scrupulous in following the various federal financial mandates, ranging from OMB Circular A-76 to various Statements of Federal Financial Accounting Standards (SFFAS), and it has maintained a positive net position in its fiscal statements since its inception.

Other principal reasons for success appear to be the TFF's determination to have all its business units operate on a self-sustaining basis and not to impose rigid hierarchical rules and regulations on them. Also, they have greatly expanded their private subcontractor base as noted in their annual financial statements. Yet, at the same time they have successfully insisted on a strong customer-service ethos on the part of their service managers and vigorously demonstrated how agency use of their services can reduce customer administrative costs.

Table 3.9: Treasury Franchise Fund—Progress in Meeting Performance Goals

	Benchmark	FY2000	FY1999
Goal: Ensure Business Activities Are Self-Sufficient			
1. Annual financial results are equal to or greater than break-even (total expenses equal total revenues)	Positive Net Position	Met	Met
2. Current Ratio	1.2	1.2	1.4
Goal: Customer Satisfaction			
1. Satisfaction Approval Rating	80% approval	Exceeded	Exceeded
2. Sales Volume Growth	10% increase	20%	72%
3. Growth or Decline of Customer Base	10% increase	57%	1%
Goal: Ensure Compliance with Legal & Regulatory Requirements			
1. Results of Management Controls Reviews	No Deficiencies	Met	Met
2. Results of Annual Audit	Unqualified "Clean" Opinion	Met	Met
Goal: Ensure Competitiveness			
1. Program Voluntary	All agreements have customer escape clause	Met	Met
2. Growth in Customer Base	10% increase	14%	1%

Source: Department of the Treasury Franchise Fund 2000 Accountability/Annual Report

At the same time, Treasury officials are concerned about a series of future issues. First, they see the need for permanent reauthorization of the franchise fund legislation if the TFF is to remain in business. As Steve App, former deputy CFO at Treasury, put it, "If the franchise fund legislation is not made permanent, we will suffer. We are still viewed as pilots. Without permanency, we eventually will not succeed." Second, they see the need for strong succession planning for "core" TFF managers, and they fear the loss of institutional knowledge due to impending retirements of TFF staff. Finally, although it is a muted concern, they are anxious to insure that there is a level playing field among franchise funds and like instrumentalities in the

Figure 3.3: Treasury Franchise Fund 1997-2000

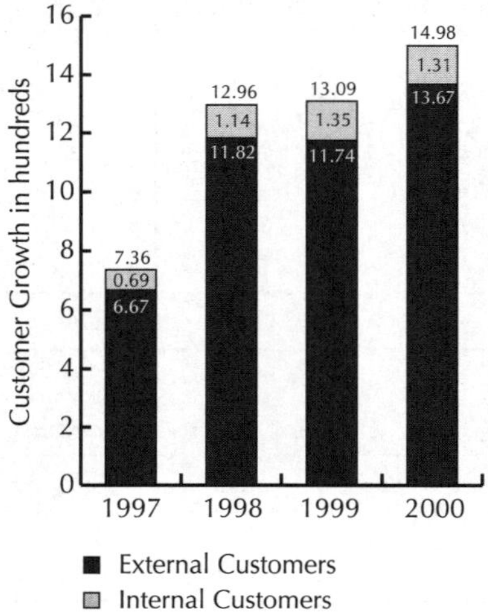

Source: Treasury Franchise Fund
Note: Customers = number of separate service agreements with entities inside and outside of the Treasury Department

Figure 3.4: Treasury Franchise Fund Revenue Growth 1997-2000

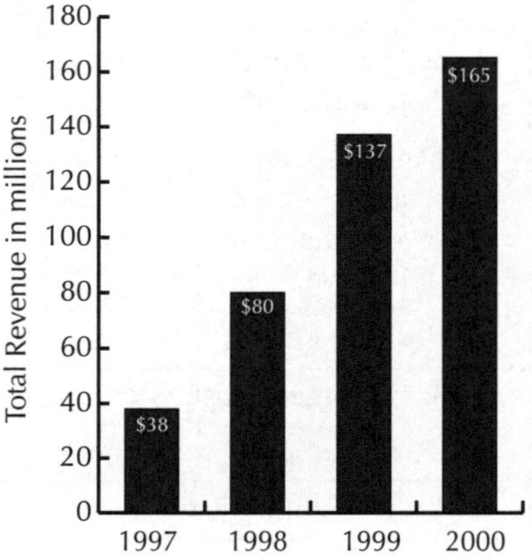

Source: Treasury Franchise Fund

Figure 3.5: Treasury Franchise Fund Private Sector Participation

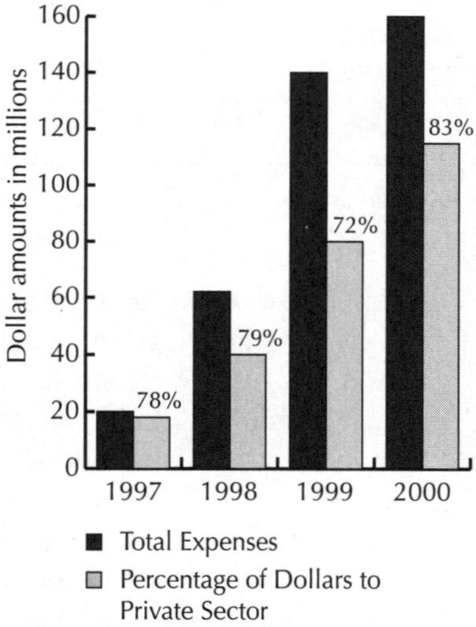

Source: Treasury Franchise Fund

Figure 3.6: Accounts Receivable Collection Trends FY1997-2000

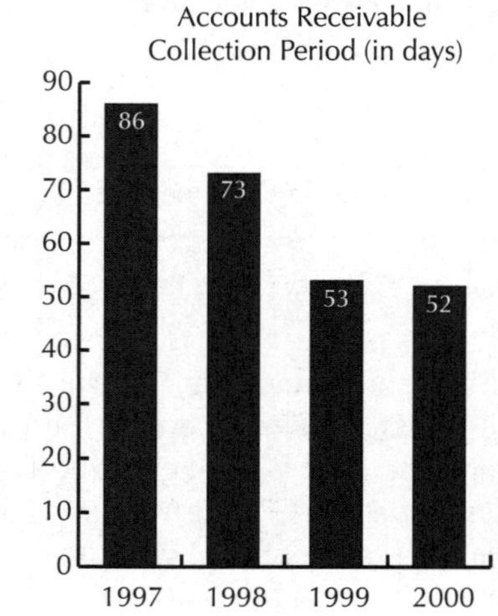

Source: Treasury Franchise Fund

competition for service offerings, a problem that sometimes extends to the component service units of the TFF.

Unlike the FOH, the TFF is really a holding company for a variety of component fee-for-service units that once operated independently within Treasury. Its governing board does not include political appointees like that of the HHS Service and Supply Fund Board, to which the FOH ultimately reports. Moreover, TFF's dramatic sales growth, excellent record in meeting financial management mandates, and generally superior fiscal position do distinguish it from the FOH.

Both franchise funds have specific strengths and weaknesses and concerns, but they both demonstrate that franchise funds can be successful service entrepreneurs. They can be truly customer centered and be so without relying on internal subsidies, all the while providing high-quality services on a fully competitive basis.

Franchise Funds: Criteria for Evaluation

The franchise fund pilots have been in operation for several years. So by what measure have they been successful or not? While this chapter does not examine in full detail the operations of all franchise funds, it is important to provide some criteria by which one can judge their successes and shortcomings.

One key way of evaluating the success of the franchise fund pilots would be to determine whether they have adhered to the 12 business operating principles jointly developed by the National Performance Review, Chief Financial Officers Council, and the Office of Management and Budget (see Table 3.1). A second broad criterion would be to assess whether the operations of these mechanisms were better than traditional methods of providing service—either keeping the service in house or contracting it out by traditional methods.

Three of the operating principles—competition, voluntary exit, and full cost recovery—appear to have been well met by the franchise funds studied in this chapter. Customers are free to seek or terminate service offerings from the FOH and the TFF. Both franchise fund pilots have engaged in processes whereby they compete for customers; they have both won and lost these competitions according to prescribed A-76 rules, and when they have won these competitions, their successful bids have not been challenged. Both franchise funds have lost customers during the time they have been in existence, and they have dropped or modified business offerings that have been found not to be self-sustaining. Also, both funds have maintained their services on a full cost recovery basis, with the Treasury Franchise Fund reviewing the fiscal status of all their business units on a quarterly basis. With regard to these principles, these two franchise funds are truly voluntary in nature; they have provided their customers with alternative means to providing service either in house or through total outsourcing. To that end, they have ended the inefficient internal government service monopolies that the National Performance Review found to be so wasteful.

The next broad set of business operating principles—capacity to accommodate business growth, FTE accountability, initial capitalization, adjustments to business dynamics, and cessation of activity—are principles that the two studied franchise funds have largely, but not completely, adhered to.

Both franchise fund pilots have been adequately capitalized and thus have had a sound fiscal footing by which to undertake their operations. It appears that the TFF had a greater level of initial capitalization and, with an expanding customer base, has not had to fully use that capitalization over time. The FOH, on the other hand, did lose some business when a major customer—the U.S. Postal Service—modified their business with the FOH. Overall revenues for a brief period actually declined somewhat, and the FOH did have to dip into their capital reserve to adjust for the business loss, all the while continuing to assess ways of revising their pricing structure to encourage more business over the long term.

The record of these two franchise funds with regard to surge capacity to accommodate business growth, adjustments to business dynamics, and cessation of activity also appears to be positive. The record of both franchise funds in attracting new customers, especially that of the TFF, is notable. Two major customer service initiatives undertaken by the FOH, one with the U.S. Army and the other with the U.S. Navy, one successful and the other unsuccessful, also highlight FOH's aggressiveness in seeking new business opportunities. And while both franchise funds have dropped or revised services on occasion, this elimination or revision of services was done without any damage to exiting customers or their customer base.

With regard to FTE accountability, the author can find no record of dissatisfaction with franchise fund staffing on the OMB front. While franchise funds were specifically exempted by OMB and the President's Management Council from the government-wide FTE ceilings imposed by the Workforce Restructuring Act, it is fair to say that both franchise funds see their FTE policies as a means to an end—that of providing superior service to their customers. Both franchise funds emphasize that their "core" employees should be customer-centric in their approach to franchise fund operations. They both provide resources to help their core employees become better service marketers and service managers, and both are concerned that impending retirements and lack of suitable pay and benefits may eventually erode the ability of these core employees to sustain the business successes over the long run.

The last set of operating principles—organizational structure, the provision of common administrative services, performance measures, and benchmarks —is an area where these franchise funds do not fully follow the business operating principles, and to some degree with good reason.

Both franchise funds have well-defined organizational structures. The TFF is in reality a holding company for 11 distinct business units. These units all report quarterly on their business operations and finances to the Treasury deputy CFO and the director of financial operations, and all their business units have to be self-sustaining, or face the possibility of going out of business. The FOH is headed by a director who supervises a relatively small core staff, who in turn are in charge of several business lines throughout the country. These core employees are responsible for managing service contracts with government agencies and the subcontractors that provide the actual service. The director now reports to the director of the HHS Program Support Center and the HHS Service and Supply Fund, headed by the HHS deputy secretary. The funding of both organizations is, of course, entirely separate from any other organizations, and the business units in the franchise funds have operated on a self-sustaining basis.

Both franchise funds provide common administrative support services, though the definition of such services has certainly changed over time. Thus, the FOH service offerings have changed from providing basic occupational health services to also providing new services such as the work/life component of its employee assistance programs, an example of benefits that often accrue to federal employees as a result of labor management contracts put in place in recent years. In the same vein, TFF services provided by that franchise fund's business units sometimes extend to such services as the safe disposal of medical waste.

With regard to performance measures and benchmarks to measure services against competitors, the two franchise funds do not follow fully the business operating principles to the letter and with some reason. First, their core staffs are relatively lean and almost fully devoted to managing customer accounts and service needs. While they do customer satisfaction surveys and respond almost on the spot to customer concerns, they do not have the time or the luxury to develop overly elaborate performance measures or perform extensive benchmarking. This, in some ways, is an overhead function that does not command the attention of franchise fund personnel. They are first and foremost interested in obtaining and retaining service customers, who are the best judge of whether franchise funds meet the needs of their government agencies.

Thus, the two franchise funds appear to meet the bulk of the business operating principles. They are competitive, voluntary, self-sustaining, customer centered, and prudently managed. In that sense they do adhere, in the main, to the business operating principles that were set forth to guide the operation of franchise funds.

Another broad-gauged criterion to judge the success or shortcomings of franchise funds is to ask the question of whether these mechanisms add value to the federal financial landscape. Are they superior to providing these services in a traditional manner, either by maintaining them in house or by fully contracting them out to the private sector?

Here again, franchise funds should be given favorable marks. So by what grounds can they be viewed as successful? First, their record of customer satisfaction and customer growth is a strong indicator of their success. Government managers chose in large numbers to do business with these entities. They did so because they were treated like true customers—they could define the terms and conditions of their service requirements, and they could obtain these services at a reasonable price. Moreover, with respect to both the TFF and the FOH, they respected the depth of traditional expertise brought to bear by these instrumentalities on the services that they offered.

Second, the private sector benefited from the use of franchise funds. Private contractors conducted the bulk of the day-to-day operations of these franchise funds, the bulk of whom were small business concerns, many of whom might otherwise not have provided services to the government. With the franchise fund as a financial and management intermediary, businesses were able to offer their services without going through a time-consuming and otherwise expensive process of bidding for a government service. In short, the franchise fund negotiated the prime contract with the department or agency, set up the terms and conditions for providing the service, and then expeditiously moved to select a subcontractor. So while business expertise and efficiency was directed toward the delivery of the service, overall management of the service rested with the franchise fund. This was a division of labor that greatly benefited the private sector.

Benefits also accrued to the government as well. First, franchise fund managers—the core personnel of the franchise fund—became skilled service marketers and service managers in the process. They continually engaged with government customers to understand and define their service needs. They negotiated service contracts that provided services at a reasonable price, and they expertly managed the private subcontractors that provided the service. In effect, they became general contractors for the provision of selected administrative services, insuring that the services offered to the department or agency were characterized by high quality, reasonable cost, and timely responsiveness. So the government achieved the benefit of developing a cadre of "government-business" professionals who could structure and manage service contracts in a fully entrepreneurial manner.

Finally, the government benefited by the ability to retain some of the "inherently governmental" nature of the government service-contracting process. Too often, federal agencies, in fully offloading services to the private sector, may lose the ability to effectively manage and/or monitor their private sector service providers. When the government customer loses the knowledge base and the skill sets needed to manage a service contract, the door can be left wide open to service inefficiencies and cost overruns. With franchise funds this does not appear to be the case. These funds maintain a critical mass of "core" employees that can expertly structure and manage service contracts. They know the business lines that their funds are offering; they maintain continuous customer contact about their service offerings; and they come to know the expertise and efficiency of their private subcontractors. And since they are governmental employees, they recognize the fact that the provision of their administrative support services helps the support of the overall mission of the government customer they are there to serve.

So do franchise funds make a difference? Are they useful means of providing a government service? Are they a constructive alternative to continuing to provide a service entirely by the government or entirely by a private sector concern? The answer to all three questions is a resounding "yes"!

While every individual franchise fund must be evaluated on its own record, the concept is sound, and the two franchise fund pilots studied in this chapter suggest that federal decision makers would do well to embrace strongly this service mechanism as a way of doing business in government in the years ahead.

Recommendations

Franchise funds have operated on a pilot basis for over five years. It now remains for the executive branch and the Congress to determine their future. Based on this chapter, the following recommendations are in order. These recommendations are directed to the Congress, the executive branch, the General Accounting Office, and the Office of Management and Budget.

Recommendations for the Congress

First, the Congress should pass legislation that permanently authorizes the franchise concept.

Second, in passing this authorizing legislation, the Congress should also extend the franchise fund concept to other agencies. The "pilot" franchise funds are proof-of-concept that service franchising can work. Therefore, the Congress should permit all departments and independent agencies to set up franchise funds that operate according to the same principles that now govern the operation of existing franchise funds.

Such new authorizing legislation should require each department and independent agency to survey all fee-for-service instrumentalities within their jurisdiction to determine whether they are operating according to the same financial management and service delivery principles as existing franchise funds. The goal here would be to determine whether these fee-for-service instrumentalities should be recast as separate franchise funds or subsumed by other existing franchise funds. As Michael Serlin, former senior NPR official who helped bring the franchise fund concept into operation, said, "Franchise funds should be established with permanent legislation. More agencies should be given authorization for such a fund, or series of funds, to help reduce the overhead cost of government. Moreover, every intra-government fee-for-service organization should be put on a plan, a glide path, to meet the same standards and become a true franchise fund."

Finally, congressional legislation should require GAO to undertake a comprehensive review of franchise funds every three to five years to determine their continuing viability and also to assess the ways in which the "best practices" of various franchise funds can be transmitted to all franchise funds.

Recommendations for Executive Departments

First, the heads of all departments and independent agencies should survey all franchise funds and similar fee-for-service operations within their jurisdiction. This survey would assess whether the franchises are achieving the objectives of GMRA and are properly applying relevant business operating principles. The survey would also assess the price and quality of their service offerings, their cost-recovery policies, and whether their services are offered on a fully voluntary basis. Additionally, analysis should be conducted as to whether franchise funds and fee-for-service instrumentalities have engaged in A-76 competitions and undergone thorough FAIR Act analyses. This would help departments determine whether various fee-for-service instrumentalities should be set up as independent franchise funds or consolidated into other franchise funds.

Second, departments and independent agencies should determine whether their component organizations are effectively utilizing existing franchise funds or fee-for-service instrumentalities that would be potential franchise funds, instead of continuing to provide common administrative services on an in-house basis. Here studies should be made of the true costs of providing services according to the quality and responsiveness of the service required by the customer. Costs, service quality, and responsiveness could be combined in a service-level agreement that could provide the basis of whether the service in question should be provided wholly by the government, by a suitable franchise fund, or be totally outsourced to the private sector.

Third, department and agency heads should insure that all franchise funds and fee-for-service instrumentalities that administer services most commonly provided by franchise funds are developing and implementing performance measures. This service analysis should, of course, became an integral part of a department's or agency's annual budget process.

Finally, departments and agencies should also insure that "core" franchise fund federal employees be trained as high-quality service marketers and managers, adept at improving service quality and reducing service costs through improved business practices. To that end, such employees should be accorded suitable innovative pay and benefits. This would be essential to help franchise funds continue their basic role as service intermediaries that would seek out service customers and manage high-quality service providers from both the public and private sectors.

Recommendations for the General Accounting Office

The General Accounting Office should maintain constructive financial management oversight of franchise funds and insure that all franchise funds practice full cost recovery and undergo annual financial audits. Independent GAO review of these financial management concerns will provide constructive guidance to the Congress, OMB, and executive departments about the financial integrity and service efficiency of these service providers.

Recommendations for the Office of Management and Budget

First, the Office of Management and Budget should maintain a full inventory of all franchise funds as well as other fee-for-service instrumentalities that might become franchise funds. Continuing analysis of this inventory will enable the OMB to develop plans for the expansion, consolidation, or termination of franchise funds.

Second, the deputy director for management at OMB should produce, as part of the annual federal budget, a comprehensive analysis of the business operations of franchise funds in the federal government along with recommendations for improved service delivery and service management by these funds. These recommendations might also take the form of annual legislative submissions to the Congress as well.

Third, OMB should have a role in the creation of new franchise funds. It should set up and maintain service and financial management criteria that should be met by new franchise funds, but it should not have blanket authority to prevent the creation of new franchise funds if they meet the preset criteria set forth by the OMB. OMB also should not recommend preset levels or quality of services to be offered by franchise funds. Franchise funds have proven their value to their customers without meeting such predetermined service requirements. Customers, through their individual service-level agreements with franchise funds, should negotiate these service offerings. They can punish franchise funds that do not meet these service levels by seeking alternative service providers. This is the best means of insuring satisfactory customer service.

Finally, OMB has an important oversight role in monitoring appropriate competition among franchise funds. A balance might have to be struck to insure that overly large franchise funds do not dominate the service field whether within or among departments or agencies while at the same time encouraging the highest-quality franchise funds to be the "best practices model" for other franchise funds. This could lead to a future where a few specialized franchise funds could offer their services on a competitive basis to all governmental agencies, with the resulting competition providing the best means of raising service quality and maintaining suitable costs for franchise fund service offerings.

Conclusion

The franchise fund experiment has been a success. Franchise fund pilots have provided quality services and registered considerable customer satisfaction in doing so. They have conducted their operations in a fiscally sound and prudent manner, and they have advanced the goal of entrepreneurial service competition in the federal sector. Accordingly, franchise funds should become a permanent and expanding part of the service-provider network in the federal government.

Postscript

As of the current date, all six franchise funds created pursuant to the Government Management Reform Act of 1994 are still in operation. Budgetary information on these franchise funds is contained in the FY 2004 President's Budget, released in February 2003.

The Federal Occupational Health program at HHS is now part of the HHS Program Support Center, and legislation has been proposed to give it authority to enter into individual service contracts with professional, administrative, and occupational health professionals. All franchise funds may be required to recompete service contracts, costing more than $1 million annually, pending final A-76 revised regulations to be issued by the Office of Federal Procurement Policy.

Business volume at the various franchise funds continues to expand with both Federal Occupational Health and Treasury franchise fund outlays growing by 25 and 21 percent respectively between 2002 and 2004.

The Bush administration has proposed reauthorizing franchise funds through October 1, 2004. (Section 625 of the General Provisions of the Fiscal Year 2004 Budget; The Appendix, page 11.) It has not proposed making franchise funds permanent or extending them throughout the government. So the franchise fund concept is still a limited experiment, despite the strong entrepreneurial character of these instrumentalities.

John J. Callahan
May 2003

Endnotes

1. *Black's Law Dictionary* (West Publishing Co., revised fourth edition), p. 786.
2. Graham Reynolds, R.E. Baxter, and Evan Davis, *Penguin Dictionary of Economics* (London: Penguin Books, 1998), p. 162.
3. National Performance Review (NPR), "'Franchise' Internal Services," *Improving Financial Management* (Accompanying Report of the National Performance Review) (Washington, D.C., NPR, 1993), p. 41.
4. Ibid., p. 3.
5. Congressional Quarterly, Inc. (CQ), *1994 Congressional Quarterly Almanac* (Washington, D.C.: CQ, 1995), p. 143.
6. Office of Management and Budget (OMB), *Report to the Congress: The Franchise Fund Pilot Program—An Interim Progress Report* (Washington, D.C.: OMB, 1997), and Chief Financial Officers Council (CFOC), *The Franchise Fund Pilot Program: Assessment of Operations* (Washington, D.C.: Chief Financial Officers Council, 1999).
7. Colleen O'Hara, "OMB to Broaden Competition," *Federal Computer Week,* July 2, 2001.
8. Office of Management and Budget (OMB), *The Budget of the United States Government, 2002, The Appendix* (Washington, D.C.: OMB, 2001), p. 875.
9. Colleen O'Hara, op.cit.
10. Chief Financial Officers Council (CFOC), op. cit., p. 1.
11. Ibid.
12. Chief Financial Officers Council, op. cit., p. 13.
13. Division of Federal Occupational Health (FOH), *2000-02 Business Plan* (Washington, D.C.: February 2000).

Bibliography

Chief Financial Officers Council (CFOC). *The Franchise Fund Pilot Program: An Assessment of Operation.* (Washington, D.C., September 1999).

Daniel, Lisa. "Cashing In." *Government Executive* (August 1999): 39-44.

Department of Treasury. *2002 Franchise Fund Accountability and Annual Report.* (Washington, D.C., 2000).

Dorobek, Christopher J. "Focus on Competition Widens." FCW.COM (July 9, 2001).

Dorobek, Christopher J. "ITOP Contract Draws Scrutiny." FCW.COM (July 16, 2001).

Federal Occupational Health Service. *2000-2002 Business Plan for Federal Occupational Health.* (Washington, D.C., February 2000).

Landauer, Bill. "Agencies' Foray Into Services Draws Ire." *Federal Times* (February 7, 2000): 1ff.

National Performance Review. *Creating A Government That Works Better and Costs Less.* (1993).

Office of Management and Budget (OMB). *The Franchise Fund Pilot Program: An Interim Report.* (Washington, D.C., 1997).

O'Hara, Colleen. "OMB to Broaden Competition." FCW.COM (July 2, 2001).

Peckenpaugh, Jason. "White House wants more federal workers to face competition." GovExec.Com. (July 23, 2001).

Posner, Michael. "Franchise fund programs get another year in Senate bill." GovExec.Com (August 6, 2001).

Serlin, Michael D. "Buyer's Market." *Government Executive* (September 1998): 31-38.

Serlin, Michael D. "The Competitors." *Government Executive* (June 1996): 29-33.

PART II

Changing the Delivery of Services

CHAPTER FOUR

The Use of the Internet in Government Service Delivery

Steven Cohen
Director, Graduate Program in Earth Systems Science, Policy, and Management, School of International and Public Affairs
Columbia University

William Eimicke
Director, Picker Center for Executive Education
School of International and Public Affairs
Columbia University

This report was originally published in February 2001.

Introduction[1]

Background

A wide variety of governments have begun to use the World Wide Web to assist in service delivery. This includes, but goes far beyond, the dissemination of information to the general public and involves a variety of other governmental functions. Examples include:

- Obtaining passport applications and other federal tax forms
- Contesting or paying traffic fines
- Ordering government publications
- Filing requests for zoning variances
- Reserving space for athletic events or tee times for public golf courses

In reviewing some federal, state, and local government websites it is clear that the use of the web for service delivery is still in its infancy. Nearly any function that now requires a person to stand in line and submit a paper form could be delivered through the web. The issue of verification of identity is undoubtedly subject to technological innovation. Personal Identification Numbers, scanned fingerprints, and other techniques will soon make it possible for licensing and minor police and adjudication processes to be delivered through the web.

The types of services that can be delivered via the web are still in the process of being imagined and organized by both governments and the private sector. Over the next decade we can expect to see a great deal of experimentation and organizational learning in this area. The purpose of this chapter is to accelerate this learning process by studying several noteworthy current government efforts to use the web for interactive functions.

The Study

The methodology of this study is to select a number of illustrative case studies on the use of e-commerce and the Internet in government service delivery and communications. The study includes a content analysis of selected state, local, and federal government websites and, where available, an analysis of the costs and benefits of switching to web-based service delivery.

The analysis describes and compares the ways in which different governments plan to use the web in improving the level of customer satisfaction as well as the effectiveness and efficiency of the services they deliver. The specific research questions we address include:

1. What content does government in the United States now provide on the web?

2. What transactions with government can customers use the web to complete?
3. What government services are provided through the web?
4. How are these services funded? What are the costs and benefits of service delivery through the web?
5. What new information and services do they plan to deliver through the web over the next one to two years? Over the next three to five years?
6. Do governments plan to increase the use of e-mail to communicate and interact with citizens? If so, in what ways?

We have selected cases in Alaska, the U.S. Internal Revenue Service, the city of Boston, Florida, Indiana, and Texas. We discuss the lessons learned from the cases and their broader implications for government service delivery. Then we present a checklist of the steps that governments should take when utilizing the web to deliver services. Finally, we provide background on the websites we reviewed, discuss the development and implementation of each site, and analyze its costs and benefits.

Lessons Learned from the Cases: Implications for Government Service Delivery

In researching these cases we discovered that most governments in the United States are beginning to utilize the web for both service delivery and information dissemination. We did not have the resources in this study to conduct a systematic survey of government websites and believe that a systematic sample survey should be conducted. Nevertheless, to produce the six case studies reported in this study we contacted well over 50 government organizations that had websites we considered well developed and that provided citizens with a direct service. We found that less than 15 percent of the government organizations we contacted had collected data on the costs and benefits of using the web as a means of delivering services. Very few of these organizations had analyzed the costs and benefits of using the web before launching their sites.

Most of these organizations had obtained funding for their sites by convincing senior management that the web was the "wave of the future"; website development was a defensive reaction to the need to appear to be on the cutting edge of this new trend. Funding was more a function of fashion than a result of an analysis of cost savings of expected benefits. Most officials assumed that the use of the web would increase customer satisfaction and was self-justifying.

When costs were assessed in the cases presented in this chapter, we found that typically services delivered over the Internet were less expensive to deliver than those delivered in-person. In one instance we found that it cost less to process mail-in forms than either web-based or in-person form processing. The unit costs of electronic service provision benefited from economies of scale, due to the large cost of setting up infrastructure and the relatively low cost of operation and maintenance. We found that as an agency's customers got more comfortable with web-based service delivery and used it more frequently, unit costs dropped dramatically.

We also found that electronic service delivery could change human resource deployment patterns and improve organizational performance. It freed up staff to provide better service to in-person customers, and allowed workers to focus less on routine tasks that could be easily handled by computers.

The business potential of electronic service provision was highlighted by the Indiana case. Since service recipients would pay for the ease of use, and lower costs of obtaining service through the web, a revenue source was found to fund the capital, operation, and maintenance costs of a website. Many government licenses, permits, and services require user fees. An additional fee can be charged for the convenience and potential time/labor savings of online processing.

A second source of revenue for electronic service provision is savings generated from reduced costs. There are several problems with this source of "revenue." First, it may take several years to materialize. E-services require an investment in computers, communication infrastructure, software, and web design and expert staff. Once the service is up and running, it will take time before customers are aware of the service and feel capable and comfortable enough to use it. The benefits of reduced service costs will tend to occur in a different fiscal year from the year that costs are incurred.

If our impressions are correct, most advocates of web-based service delivery do not collect or use data on unit costs when planning these service enhancements. Moreover, it is not clear that data is collected or projections are made on benefits either. The absence of business planning will almost certainly lead to mistakes in developing these services. When sites do not produce immediate benefits, or other operational problems develop, sites that may have great potential may be abandoned prematurely.

The six cases we analyzed demonstrate the potential for lower costs and improved services through the use of the web. In several of the cases we see government moving into new areas with care and thoughtful planning. Among the cases we reviewed but did not write up were numerous examples of web-based services developed without a business plan and without a projection of costs and benefits. We conclude, therefore, that government must obtain additional management assistance before launching these new enterprises. Consulting firms, academics, and other experts with experience in launching these new ventures should be hired by agencies that are planning to deliver service using the web. An effort should be made to assess costs and benefits and use that analysis to shape the form of the site, the services offered, the fee structure, and the phasing.

Some analysts of government operations have considered the web as a potentially revolutionary force in service delivery. The impression we gain from this study is that the impact of the web on government service delivery will be slow and incremental. It will likely result in gradual, small-scale service enhancements. Customers will be provided with alternative modes of access to government and will notice some improvement in service delivery. In some instances the cost of service delivery will be reduced. When mistakes are made, or when redundant points of access are provided to please customers, the costs of service delivery will rise.

A Checklist for Using the Internet to Deliver Services

1. Create a web strategy

There is evidence to suggest that development of a strategy is one of the most important factors in developing successful technology applications (Christensen and Hughes, 2000; p. 564). A structure for developing such a plan should be as simple but comprehensive as possible (see for example, Cohen and Eimicke, 1998; pp. 15-29). Some of the key steps include a problem and opportunity analysis, establishment of clear priorities, identification of key players, and an organizational and situational analysis. To ensure that the process achieves widespread organizational buy-in under a cross-functional task force.

2. Identify, describe, and analyze the operational steps of the web-based delivery service

When government is considering the use of the web to deliver a service that is now performed in-person, by phone, or by mail, the first step is to develop a complete description and then analysis of the method(s) in which the service is currently performed. Follow these steps:

a. Interview or hold a group meeting with individuals who implement the service. Ask them to make a flowchart of the steps involved in service delivery. The flowchart should include details on steps, time to complete tasks, and delays. It should note who does what and when.

Based on the research in this chapter, we have identified a set of steps that governments should undertake in order to implement web-based services:

1. Create a web strategy.
2. Identify, describe, and analyze the operational steps of the web-based delivery service.
3. Benchmark against similar services in other jurisdictions or organizations.
4. Develop a pilot project to test web use in one district or in one element of the service.
5. Analyze the results of the pilot project.
6. Develop options for instituting wide-scale web-based delivery of the service.
7. Conduct a costs and benefits analysis of piloted alternatives.
8. Select an option.
9. Develop a data collection system for operational performance of the service, its costs, and benefits.
10. Analyze performance data, costs, and benefits.
11. Perform periodic reviews of service delivery, then modify the web format and operations.

b. Circulate the flowchart for comments from individuals with knowledge of the process.
c. Revise the flowchart to reflect comments.
d. Analyze the flowchart for disconnects and waste, and the critical path.
e. Identify targets for web-based delivery.
f. Project potential savings in cost and time and potential benefits to customers in cost and level of satisfaction. A key factor to consider is whether customers will be comfortable using a higher level of technology to complete these activities and how long it might take to achieve that level of comfort. In a public sector environment, such technological innovations must follow the annual budget cycles and fit within two- or four-year election political cycles if partial funding and failed implementations are to be avoided.
g. Identify potential risks in adopting a web-based service structure and develop appropriate risk-management strategies.

3. Benchmark against similar services in other jurisdictions or organizations

Most government functions are not unique to a particular jurisdiction. We often can learn important lessons about policy, management, or service operations by visiting with colleagues in other towns, counties, states, or nations. Even in our own location we may find an organization performing a similar or related function from which we can learn. While not everyone is open to allowing their operations to be observed, imitation is the most sincere form of flattery, and most organizations permit benchmarking visits. In order to benchmark a function for web-based service delivery follow these steps:

a. Conduct a web search to identify similar programs with web presence.
b. Review existing websites (or a sample of sites) from those identified.
c. Conduct an informal survey of key contacts in other jurisdictions and organizations to identify those with a reputation for excellence on the web.
d. Identify the top five to 10 websites and seek appointments with the managers and technical staff responsible for developing and maintaining the site.
e. Develop an interview guide for key questions and subjects to be covered during benchmarking interviews.
f. Conduct field research.
g. Project team members should use the site themselves and create a list of advantages and weaknesses.
h. Analyze research and develop a list of key factors to emulate and avoid in your own web-based service.
i. If your web-based application does go forward, revisit the current benchmark sites in the future to periodically update and upgrade your services.
j. Among the categories to include in a benchmarking survey, Christensen and Hughes (2000, pp. 566-567) provide a very useful list, including customers, contact information, graphics, page design and presentation, content, speed, hardware, software, development, personnel, maintenance training and user support, and web hosting (if outsourcing is considered).
k. The agency's legal affairs group should ensure that the materials and pictures posted as well as the links made do not violate any intellectual property laws and do not even imply (through its links) that the agency is exceeding its legal authority or jurisdiction.
l. The agency's technology staff must assess the security risks inherent in web access to certain databases and develop a fail safe plan to protect confidential and sensitive information from unauthorized use.

m. Human resources staff must assess the initial and ongoing training that will be needed to launch the contemplated web-based applications, maintain them, and use them.

4. Develop a pilot project to test web use in one district or in one element of the service

A pilot test is a small-scale experiment, limited in duration, with performance data collection and analysis built in. Before moving to delivery of a service on the web, government agencies should experiment with elements of a service or with an entire service in a particular geographic area, or a "trial site" labeled explicitly as an experiment. It is important that the web-based service be fully integrated into the organization's standard operating procedures. Information provided online must be accurate, and actions promised through the web must be carried out. Records cannot be lost and servers cannot be unreliable. A pilot test allows the organization to experiment and innovate, but is small enough in scale that mistakes can lead to institutional learning instead of organizational scapegoating or destruction. The downside of pilot testing is that it takes a great deal of work to launch even a relatively modest web-based pilot. Therefore, care should be taken to choose a test service or area that is particularly important to the organization and its mission. If the pilot is successful, the potential benefits of system-wide change will be more clear.

5. Analyze the results of the pilot project

A web pilot test should address the following questions:

- Does the web-based version of the service provide adequate and appropriate service?
- What is the level of customer satisfaction with the service? How does it compare with other modes of delivery?
- What are the unit costs for the web-based service? How does it compare with the costs of service delivery in other media?
- Does the organization know how to operate the web-based service? If not, how will they learn?
- What improvements should be made before wide-scale implementation of the service is begun?

The answers to these questions will facilitate the development of a high-quality, customer-oriented and cost-effective web-based service. The analytic strategy should be designed to address the operational issues involved in developing a web-based service. Overall, proponents of web-based technology stress better, faster, and cheaper service. In practice, the benefits seldom live up to the initial promises and frequently do not achieve results in each of the three categories. Managers need to consider whether the innovation can be justified even if it is not cheaper but faster and better, or some other combination of those three key elements of success.

6. Develop options for instituting wide-scale web-based delivery of the service

The analysis of the pilot project should generate three to five web-based service options. There might be different levels of graphic complexity, site design might vary, the intervals for content updates might be different, access to various databases, e-mail, downloading and print options, forms and printed materials might vary, there are server options, different internet connections, and a wide variety of server and site management software choices. Personnel choices include network administration, user application support, technical support, programmers, hardware maintenance, and telephone help personnel. There is also the possibility of outsourcing some or all of these activities. Finally, there's the issue of what kind of training to offer and whether it will be ongoing. These options can form additional pilot tests or can be exposed to focus groups. The options should be developed sufficiently that they can be seen as discrete choices.

7. Conduct a costs and benefits analysis of piloted alternatives

Before deciding on an option, it should be analyzed for costs and benefits. It should also be compared with non-web-based services. The unit costs of web-based services will come down as more people learn about the service and as more people become web proficient. The cost-side analysis should include more than dollars and cents. It is sometimes difficult to price the effect on morale of relief from tedious clerical tasks through automation. It is also difficult to price opportunity costs as freed-up labor is devoted to other more creative and possibly more important tasks.

Moreover, technological change may threaten some employees, disrupt work patterns and communications flows, and raise user expectations well beyond the capacity of the organization to respond. Confidentiality and privacy issues may also arise as internal and external users have more access to the organization's databases.

On the benefit side of the equation, the analysis should factor in increased speed and accuracy of service delivery, and increased customer satisfaction. Web-based access to public agencies has the potential to make government much more open and transparent to all interested public audiences. Sites also have the potential to be interactive, giving citizens the opportunity to comment, make requests, and/or receive additional and customized information. Employee morale may rise as organization members get positive feedback from customers, feel more empowered and effective, and take pride in working for a more "cutting edge" organization. Managers must also recognize that the impact of technology on organizations is evolutionary. What begins as a benefit in terms of relief from routine requests for information may turn into a new cost, as consumers realize what kinds of information the organization may be capable of providing.

8. Select an option

Once the analysis is completed, an option should be selected and wide-scale web-based service can begin. You should expect that the initial option you select will evolve along with the service itself and changes in computer technology, capacity, software, and graphic design. It is important that the service be permitted to change and not get locked in to a particular design. You should program resources, including management time, for periodic review and redesign of the site and service. To do this effectively and manage a web service, you must measure the performance of the service delivery system.

9. Develop a data collection system for operational performance of the service, its costs, and benefits

When the web-based service is being developed, it is important to design performance measures and mechanisms for collecting, reporting, and analyzing these data. The first step is to decide on the appropriate performance measures. How can we measure the service's costs and benefits? What are our goals? How can we track accomplishments? What type of data on customer satisfaction do we need to collect? Developing a performance measurement system includes standard operating procedures for collecting and reporting data and a periodic analysis by management of the meaning of the data. Some of the data should be collected as a routine part of accessing and delivering the services. Counts of web hits on particular pages can be counted automatically. Counts of specific services provided and response times can also be counted automatically. Measures of customer satisfaction can be placed on the web site or automatically e-mailed to customers on a random basis or to an entire population.

Performance measures should be designed up-front to avoid expensive retrofits and to ensure that longitudinal data can be collected. Performance will hopefully improve over time and early measures can help develop an accurate baseline. This is not to say that measures should not be changed and added as the service delivery system evolves. However, to the extent possible, you should attempt to anticipate the evolution of the service system and develop measures that can be used for a long period of time.

10. Analyze performance data, costs, and benefits

As noted above, the analysis of service system performance should be a regular organizational function. In commercial retail operations, data on store sales is transmitted directly from cash registers to analysts and from analysts to management. In some cases the reporting is automatic and simply sent electronically directly to management. The reporting of performance data on the government web-based service should emulate the private sector. Key measures should be sent to management on a frequent, predictable basis.

In addition to simple reporting of data, analysts should prepare periodic trend analyses and identify problems, opportunities, and successes that are worthy of management attention. Problem analysis should be presented with potential solutions as well as work plans for pilot testing and implementing improvements. The analyses should be designed to be as straightforward as possible, in an attractive, easily understood format, to facilitate the use of the information by management.

To properly assess the impact of web-based solutions on organizational performance, public managers need to assess the impact of the innovation in terms of the organizational goals, existing performance measurement indicators, public approval rating, media image, legislative profile, and reputation with the chief executive. Measures need to be taken at regular intervals and performance assessed over time, among divisions and services, and across relevant geographical boundaries.

11. Perform periodic reviews of service delivery, then modify the web format and operations

The purpose of the performance measurement system is to allow management to improve performance and to ensure that improvement targets are derived from data rather than "common wisdom." The most effective organizations hold high-priority periodic service reviews with key personnel and senior management in attendance. These reviews provide deadlines for analysis and a regular cycle of reporting, analysis, and decision making, leading to continuous improvement. A specific portion of the review process should focus on web-based service delivery. During reviews of web-based service delivery, it would be useful to include technical personnel who can discuss potential system modifications as well as limits to modifications. While we are in the early stages of web-based public services, research indicates that quality is critical to the favorable impact of such technological innovations (Specht, 2000; p. 148).

The above checklist provides a road map to organizations considering using the web to deliver services now delivered in other ways. We hasten to note that we are still learning how to develop and manage this new technology, and we expect that over the next several years we will need to expand and modify these steps. There is a great deal we need to learn about this topic. A decade ago there were fewer than 100 sites on the World Wide Web; we do not want to even guess how many sites will be in existence a decade from today.

The Case Studies

This section reviews the case data that informed the analysis and discussion presented earlier in this chapter. These cases represent success stories and are among the very few examples of governments that conducted cost analyses before launching online services.

CASE 1: Alaska's Department of Motor Vehicles

Background

Motivated by negative newspaper articles, long lines, and dissatisfied customers, former Governor Tony Knowles of Alaska issued an executive order in January 1997 to reengineer the Department of Motor Vehicles (DMV). The first stage of creating a more efficient and effective DMV was to move it from under the Department of Public Safety, whose first concern was police functions, to the Department of Administration, where it would receive more attention. Once under the Department of Administration, DMV underwent a critical analysis of its core functions in order to develop a new approach to service delivery. Two transactions were identified as targets for Internet delivery: 1) renewing of motor vehicle registrations and, 2) ordering personalized license plates. These were simple services that were performed daily and were selected for pilot project experiments.

Previously, DMV had conducted these two transactions through the mail or through in-person counter transactions in the DMV offices. Regis-

Alaska's DMV

website: www.state.ak.us/local/akpages/ADMIN/dmv

Description: Alaska provides two Department of Motor Vehicle (DMV) transactions on the web: renewing motor vehicle registrations and ordering personalized license plates.

Assessment: Worthwhile project due to increased customer satisfaction. As core services are streamlined through web-based service delivery, employees benefit from increased opportunity to meet more challenging responsibilities.

tration renewals through the mail could take anywhere from several days to three weeks. Similarly, ordering personalized license plates through the mail took from four to six weeks to check name availability and order the plates. While counter transactions were significantly quicker for both services, they still could take anywhere from 15 minutes to 1 1/2 hours for registration renewals and several weeks to check name availability and order personalized plates.

Currently, DMV e-services have decreased the time spent per transaction. Registration renewals take approximately 100 seconds over the Internet and personalized license plate transactions take about 30 seconds. Not only did the introduction of e-services for these two transactions decrease the amount of time per transaction, but they also enabled counter employees to deal with more complex transactions, such as the issuance of driver's licenses.

The Emission Inspection (I/M) station registration process also uses the Internet to facilitate transactions, is a public-private partnership between DMV and private I/M stations in Anchorage and Juneau, and enables private partners to renew vehicle registrations while the vehicle receives a mandatory emissions test. The private stations access the DMV database through the Internet at the end of each day to update the registration system and to transfer the funds they collect throughout the day. This brief, daily interaction enables the stations to conduct the transactions without DMV assistance or interference. The stations use their own credit card machines, contracts, and labor. Some I/M stations charge for the registration service, while others view the increased number of customers who use the service and may buy other products as adequate compensation.

Finally, the DMV website also includes video footage of the office sites and the customer lines. The video frames change every five minutes between 8:30 a.m. and 4:30 p.m. They enable the consumer to identify ideal times to go to the DMV office for counter transactions.

Development

Before conducting registration renewals or ordering personalized plates online, DMV had to create the infrastructure to support these transactions. DMV hired SAGA Software, a consulting firm based in Reston, Virginia, to create the systems program. For this initial stage, the consultants were paid a one-time fee of $50,000. In-house employees from both DMV and the Information Technology Group (ITG), another governmental agency also housed under the Department of Administration, wrote the web scripting. It was estimated that an additional $250,000 was spent on employees and equipment, making the total setup costs $300,000.

ITG employees are responsible for maintaining the site, which costs approximately $440 per month (three hours per week of analyst programmer time at $100 and $40 per month of regular employee time) and DMV employees are responsible for transactions and responding to customers.

Implementation

Registration renewals and search and order of personalized plates were available as online transactions by the end of 1997. In 1998, 4,828 customers used the Internet to reregister their vehicles, a number that rose to 10,115 in 1999. While this was only 4.7 percent of the DMV registration renewals for that year, the alleviation of those 10,000 transactions influenced the entire registration process. By diverting a portion of the overall transactions, in-person and mail-in services were provided more quickly.

More significantly, in 1999 private I/M stations renewed 24.2 percent of the vehicle registrations for that year. During the first half of 2000, I/M stations completed 25.7 percent of the total registration renewals. This partnership has diverted and consolidated a significant proportion of DMV transactions into single daily transfers from each partner.

Prior to the new registration options, DMV received negative press about its inefficiency and long lines. While the DMV did not formally measure

Table 4.1: Automobile Registration Renewals in Alaska[a]

Year	Number of Online Registration Renewals	% of Total DMV Registration Renewals
1998	4,828	2.06%
1999	10,115	4.73%
2000 (Jan. to April)	4,691	7.195%

Notes:

[a] *Data appeared in an unpublished memorandum sent from Mary Marshburn, director of the Department of Motor Vehicles in Alaska, on 6/14/2000.*

Table 4.2: Cost of Automobile Registration Renewals in Alaska[a]

Type of Transaction	Direct Labor[b]	Direct Materials[c]	Overhead[d]	Development Cost	Credit Card Cost	Total Unit Cost
Counter	$4.15	$0.11	$3.48	—	—	$7.74
Mail-in	$1.56	$0.48	$1.31	—	—	$3.35
E-service	$0.52	$0.53	$0.40	$0.85	$1.32	$3.62

Notes:

[a] *Figures on e-service transactions appear in an unpublished memorandum written by Mary Marshburn, director of the Department of Motor Vehicles in Alaska, on 6/14/2000. Figures on counter and mail-in transactions appeared in a memorandum written by Tom Cherian, finance officer for the Department of Administration in Alaska, on 10/13/97.*

[b] *Direct labor costs are assumed to consist of 80 percent of total personal service expenditures for the DMV Field Service component. Direct labor costs are allocated to each major class of transaction based on the amount of time required to process the transaction type and the total number of transactions processed during the year.*

[c] *Direct materials include the cost of postage, license plates, license tabs, photo costs, and forms. The direct materials cost data were obtained from DMV Deputy Director Chuck Hosack.*

[d] *Overhead is determined using the same methodology that was used to allocate direct labor. That is, overhead is allocated to transaction classes based on processing time and number of transactions. The components consist of building lease costs, equipment amortization costs, and three support staff from the Driver Services component.*

customer satisfaction with the Internet transactions, it has noticed significant improvement, indicated by increased utilization of e-services and an increased number of unsolicited customer compliments. Mary Marshburn, director of the Department of Motor Vehicles, has found that each year more customers are using the Internet to renew their vehicle registrations.

In addition, most customer e-mails are no longer negative, but tend to thank DMV "for the most pleasant vehicle registration process of my life" and for "an outstanding, informative, and useful website." Since Internet transactions were begun, the DMV is a very different place; lines are shorter, customers are happier, and staff are more accessible because they do not have to spend as much time responding to complaints.

In addition to these improvements, the Internet services also cost less than the in-person transactions. An Internet registration renewal costs $3.62 to process per transaction, while a counter registration renewal costs $7.74 per transaction. Mail-in registration is still the most cost effective at $3.35; however, this method has the longest turnaround time. Furthermore, as more individuals use e-services, they will become more cost effective because the primary incremental expense is the credit card cost, which decreases when a higher volume of transactions is completed.

Analysis

This project was worth doing because customers are more satisfied with the speed and convenience of the new e-services. The Internet allows customers to perform transactions in a variety of different venues, which increases access to DMV. Similarly, employees are more satisfied because they are no longer spending as much time dealing with dissatisfied customers and service complaints. As core services are streamlined, the employee's role is slowly shifting away from direct customer service toward more challenging roles as trainers and auditors for the I/M station registration renewal program. As a result of this redistribution of tasks, DMV reclassified positions and all employees received a two-grade increase.

In addition to customer and employee satisfaction, this initial program puts in place the infrastructure to expand services. The Alaska DMV plans to increase services to include renewal of driver's licenses and address changes online. By increasing services provided over the Internet, the entire program becomes more cost effective. Furthermore, as services are new, there is still room for improvement. Currently, about 95 percent of a transaction is completed through the Internet, with only five percent of the process completed manually. The manual labor is needed when an error occurs in the system and someone must investigate and correct the inaccurate data. In addition, someone must manually change disks and enter forms. While DMV has automated most of the process, its goal is to have transactions that are 100 percent automated. This would result in even more efficient transactions.

Alaska's long-term goal is to develop a portal system that can accommodate all state government Internet transactions at a single point of contact. Currently, each department is responsible for the development and maintenance of its specific transactions, which has resulted in a significant amount of duplication and competition among varying state agencies. This case raises the issue of coordination of the technical infrastructure needed to support Internet-delivered services. It also indicates that electronic service delivery affects both customers and administrative operations. In this case, the Internet reduced demands on administrative staff and allowed them to provide better service to customers who did not use the Internet.

CASE 2: The City of Boston

Background

Boston's overall city website has a clear mission of delivering good content to citizens, and it is an excellent example of how e-government can work if well funded and designed. Beyond the typical features of obtaining forms and reviewing restaurant inspection reports, users of Boston's website

The City of Boston
website: www.ci.boston.ma.us
Description: Boston's site offers good content, serves as an engaging information resource, and provides an impressive list of online services like paying parking ticket fines, registering to vote, obtaining a dog license, and more. **Assessment:** Successful project of interest to casual information seekers and those seeking access to Boston city government services. Conveniently and efficiently facilitates a variety of services for citizens. Excellent example of well-funded and well-designed e-government.

can access a great deal of serious information as well as interesting background on the city, and also take care of many onerous city-related tasks.

Set up clearly and logically, the first area of the site directs different categories of users to different parts of the site based on whether they are residents, business people, or visitors. Each type of user can then access a wide range of information pertinent to his or her needs. Visitors, for example, can find out historical information on the city, the locations and hours of popular tourist sites, and even find great locations for film shoots if they are visiting from Hollywood.

Residents have several areas in the site. Most popular is the "Mayor's Food Court," containing the recent inspection reports for all restaurants in Boston, with explanations of violations and total scores. There are also pages where residents can manage obligations to the city; the section for excise tax payment, for example, has been successful. On this page, you can pay your motor vehicle excise tax with a credit card, a tax that previously had to be paid in person or by mail. Similarly, citizens can pay their parking tickets online using a credit card and file for dismissal as well. Even more information can be accessed. Missing a dog license? Looking to register to vote? There are few city services now available online here.

Businesses also have a thorough selection of available services. As in the residential section, users can both access forms and conduct transactions. For the former, over 20 different forms are available, the vast majority of the paperwork needed to conduct business in the city. Transactions online are similarly comprehensive, allowing businesses to search for available real estate or bid on city contracts via an online RFP process.

Development

One of the most interesting aspects of the Boston site is that its development occurred completely in house. Boston recognized the need for a website as vital, and created a partnership with Hitachi, who has become its single private provider, providing all hardware (e.g., Web servers) in exchange for prominent mention on the Boston site. The equipment is cutting edge, able to facilitate over one million hits a day; the value of the donation exceeded $200,000.

The development costs also included two full-time in-house staff, which today has grown to a full-time staff of six. Additionally, they purchase some software upgrades. Boston uses the latest web technology, using ASP programming language, for example.

However, city staff, is determined that the website not be driven by costs, and to keep tight control over content, development, and maintenance. According to the manager of the site, this is how the site has become so successful, winning many awards.

Implementation

By all accounts, Boston's site is a success. According to the site's manager, many features have shown significant increases in use since the site was launched. Motor vehicle excise tax payment, for example, increased by 300 percent from mid-1999 to mid-2000. In the year 2000, an average of 3,000 tickets were paid over the Internet each month. Although no specific data were provided to us, people managing the site believe that it saves the government money. With the motor vehicle excise tax, for example, the city formerly saw many payments at city hall and, as a result, had a huge backlog of paperwork. It is estimated that about 6,000 payments were made online during the first year of service, collecting about $500,000. The time that administrative staff has had to spend on filings related to the tax has decreased substantially since the payment option has gone online. Such a decrease certainly creates an opportunity for more efficient staff allocations.

Analysis

The success of Boston's site is evident even to the first-time user. Compared to sites such as New York's, for example, Boston's is aesthetically more pleasing, easier to navigate, and provides more options. The site can even have an effect on the public's perception of government, as citizens come to see that the government has become easier to work with.

CASE 3: The Florida Online High School

Background

To equalize access to education for all Florida residents, the Florida Department of Education initiated a transition from the traditional learning

The Florida Online High School

website: www.fhs.net

Description: The Florida High School site seeks to build on and expand the traditional idea of the online school and can serve any student in the state.

Assessment: Ambitious attempt to use Internet technology for high school education that achieves outstanding success in its graduation rates and other measures. Pushes the envelope on e-government.

environment to the Florida High School (FHS) online environment. The Florida High School's goal is to build a quality education system that eliminates the shortcomings of the traditional educational delivery system. This site can in fact serve any student in the state, from rural students who need more course selection to working students who need hours that are more flexible. The FHS has had a major impact on Florida education, with teachers from all over the state providing curricula for the virtual school. Student participation has grown, perhaps drawn by the freedom implicit in the motto, "any time, any place, any path, any pace."

The program seeks to build on and expand greatly the traditional idea of the online school. One example of such a school was the Orange County Public School's 1996 experimental online program, the "WebSchool." This school offered SAT preparation and computer programming to Orange County, Florida students. These specialized programs have been available for some time; before online, they were available in disk form, but did not have broad enough offerings to replace actual high school course work.

While Orange County piloted its "WebSchool," Alachua County proposed a statewide online high school. This was a more ambitious idea, with the goal of delivering actual high school course material to students online. The U.S. Department of Education identified the two sites as having similar goals and suggested collaboration, offering a seed grant as a catalyst. The counties met and decided to collaborate, and created the Florida High School, originally offering five online courses. According to the website, the project's mission is "to place a complete high school online by the year 2001 and include those student services that will enable students to successfully transition to postsecondary educational institutions and to the workplace." To ensure high quality of course content, the program will aim to meet the Florida Sunshine State Standards and other more stringent criteria supported by the education and business communities. It will also use the Internet to deliver facilitated instruction to students, an innovative use of the web.

The program has both a brick-and-mortar location and website. The site is organized around the coursework and curriculum, the integral part of the program. Each course has its own section on the site, accessed from the main course area. The online syllabus shows the assignments and required reading for the course. The high school has aimed to have as much of the required activity available on the site as possible; links take students to other sites for articles, and textbooks are offered on CD-ROM. There are also additional links for students with a particular interest in topics covered, making it easy for them to explore in as much depth as they like. The school appeals to and creates self-motivated students with a drive to learn. It also helps develop solid technical skills and facility with the Internet.

Class discussion is clearly not possible in this environment, a potential drawback. The Florida High School tries to replace classroom discussion with e-mail and a virtual "CourseRoom." The CourseRoom is a chatroom where students are expected to join in discussion of topics, asynchronously. This concept has the limitation of not effecting actual discussion, which is clearly hard to approximate, but fits within the overall motto of the school of 24/7 access, not limited by any schedule.

In addition to the web-based services available to students, teachers are also accessible by telephone. Furthermore, some classes work with traditional brick-and-mortar classes to support their activities, such as the drama class that eventually meets together with a traditional class to watch a production.

The Florida High School claims that the overall approach is more student centered than that offered in a traditional high school, since students are free to move at their own pace, without being required to stay with the group in-class discussions. In turn, it claims more success in developing higher learning skills as well as more practical, employment-related skills due to the technical literacy required to succeed.

Development

The FHS developed its web capability through a partnership of public and private sources. As mentioned earlier, funding came originally from the federal Department of Education with a $200,000 starter grant via the "Break the Mold" program. This was followed by a $1.3 million appropriation from the Florida Legislature. The first $1.5 million, however, primarily went to staff and curriculum development. Costs for the actual website development were approximately $350,000, provided from in-kind donations from private sources, Lotus Development, and IBM. A service provider, Interalia, maintains and hosts the site on its servers in an ASP solution.

Technical problems often develop with the site, as noted on several of the pages. To overcome them, the school maintains a technical support staff (via Interalia).

Implementation

The Florida High School grew significantly in its first three years, from 150 students in 1997 to 2,300 in 2000. Additionally, the number of school districts affiliated with FHS has grown to include all but two of the state's districts, as well as three charter and 25 private schools.

The "customers" of the site appear to be doing well in school, based on their high grades and test scores coming out of the program. In 1999-2000, 59 percent of all students earned A's and 24 percent B's, a figure the School attributes in part to the extensive personal attention given each student (although it must be pointed out that the FHS student body is probably not similar to a typical high school's). Advance placement scores are also impressive, with 72 percent passing these tests at FHS.

Costs are another matter, with Florida mentioning in its literature that "cost-effectiveness studies that focus only on dollars probably will not capture [all the] ... data." However, even if the school is not producing savings now, it is clear that costs are decreasing as the school grows, reflecting the economies of scale for this sort of endeavor. It is also difficult to quantify the benefit side of the equation that will come over the long run due to improved grades and test results.

Analysis

The Florida High School project has been one of the most ambitious attempts to wed Internet technology and high school education. The school uses several progressive education methods, self-paced learning, personalized attention, and technology, and has achieved outstanding success in its graduation rates, average grades, and success on placement exams. Similarly, educators have flocked to the program—the faculty has tripled over the course of the site's development—and report high satisfaction with the flexibility of the schedule and the motivation of the students.

Beyond the good marks from students and faculty, the school has built an infrastructure that will allow expansion over the years. Specialized courses hold particular promise for expansion and seem to be a goal of the school, since traditional high schools that may not have enough student interest for Latin or economics can direct their students to FHS. In addition, the school has moved to offer a full range of courses with the goal of providing the complete high school experience for full-time students.

Florida's venture into cyberspace to create an entire high school is noteworthy because it pushes the envelope of e-government to offer an expensive and complex service over the web. The danger is that the state may not have the patience to see out the expansion of the school to an efficient and money-saving scale. Educators should hope that this does not happen and that FHS can continue to innovate.

CASE 4: Access Indiana

Background

Recognizing the need to increase citizens' access to the government, but wishing to reduce the capital expenditures to government, Indiana formed a creative public-private partnership to deliver services over the Internet. Indiana contracted with a private partner who provided start-up capital and covered costs of developing, marketing, and managing the site in return for the right to charge service fees to its customers. This enabled citizens to have one point of contact for all government transactions, while deploying advanced technological resources without major capital investments to the state. In 1995, Indiana engaged in a public-private partnership with Indian@Interactive, Inc. to form Access Indiana, the Internet portal for the state. Through Access Indiana, residents can utilize 130,000 web pages and engage in over 175 interactive services.[2]

Internet services provided through Access Indiana range from filing income taxes to renewals of professional and recreational licenses. One simple transaction that has resulted in significant savings is the online physician license search. Hospitals, clinics, and physician's offices are required by law to verify the licenses of all health-care providers: physicians, nurses, LPNS, and physical therapists. Prior to online verification, medical facilities had to contact the Health Professions Bureau and request verification of an employee's license. Then the office had to access the license, print a verification form, and mail it to the requesting agency. Since accreditation requirements mandate that medical facilities update their licenses every two years, this resulted in at least 100,000 requests per year.

Three years ago, online verification of medical licenses simplified this process. Now, Access Indiana enables subscribers to access the state database of medical licenses and download the needed verifications immediately. Not only does this save the government money in printing costs, but it also saves time for both state and medical personnel.

Development

In order to conduct this exchange, the Health Professions Bureau needed access to the technology that would support this process. The state of Indiana was able to obtain this infrastructure through the public-private partnership, Access Indiana. Instead of creating the infrastructure for Internet transactions in-house, they utilized the technology and knowledge of the private industry. As Indian@Interactive, Inc., the private partner, is responsible for all capital and developmental costs, the state government incurs no capital expenses from this project. However, while the government has no financial investment in the project, the partnership ensures that the state owns the site and has oversight powers with regard to content and transaction

Access Indiana

website: www.state.in.us

Description: Site provides residents with access to thousands of web pages and over 175 interactive services, including income tax filings and renewals of professional or recreational licenses.

Assessment: Indiana has one of the most comprehensive state sites: it serves customers well and can be used by all of its departments and agencies. Because a creative public-private partnership produced the site, the government did not incur development and capital costs.

fees. The state established a governing board that reviews the transaction and subscription fees to ensure that they are reasonable and that the private partner complies with state policies and procedures.

The private partner is responsible for all costs, which they recoup through "market-driven convenience fees" on some of the services. Approximately 95 percent of the information on the 130,000 Internet pages is free, while approximately 5 percent of the services charge a fee. Most of these transactions carried a fee when the service or information was provided through more traditional methods. The program uses a self-funded model that leverages the revenues of the portal to assist in the development of applications and content for agencies without using government funds.

Implementation

The online license verification process has completely eclipsed the traditional verification process due to its ease and convenience. As a result, the Health Professions Bureau no longer verifies individual licenses through the traditional process. Instead, all transactions are accomplished through verbal verification over the phone or through Internet verification. In its first year, the program resulted in savings of $86,000 in copier and paper expenses alone, not including savings in labor and postage. Furthermore, as there were no investment costs to implement this program, the savings to government were immediate.

Not only easier and more convenient, this new transaction can also result in overall savings to medical facilities. With the traditional method, requesting parties could access one to 50 licenses at a time for $30, or they could purchase the entire list of licenses following a renewal period. Before undergoing the online license verification project, Access Indiana Information Network conducted a survey that found, on average, it cost the requesting agency $3 to process a verification. This is because most agencies do not need to update 50 licenses at a time and with the traditional system you could not pay per verification. With online verification, hospitals or other large medical facilities can subscribe to Access Indiana for $50 per year, enabling the facility to download verifications immediately for $1 each. As a result agencies can save money by paying only for the verifications needed. If individuals do not wish to pay the subscription fee, they can access a verification for $2.20 with a credit card.[3]

Analysis

The Indiana state government has created a system that can be used by all of its departments and agencies. This alleviates any duplication that might otherwise occur if each department developed its own individual website, which happens in many states. This model results in governmental savings, as agencies and constituents have access to cutting-edge technology without any capital expenses.

In addition, customers are more satisfied because they are able to access needed information more quickly and conveniently. Agencies are able to quickly access important information that previously took two to three weeks to obtain. Furthermore, hospitals now receive individual verification sheets for each licensee that can be placed in the individual's personnel folder, which is an improvement over the older system with a single sheet containing anywhere from one to 50 verifications.

In the future, the Health Professions Bureau plans to expand the transactions available on the Internet. It is in the process of increasing the downloadable information on the website to include statutes and board rules. Furthermore, it plans to make applications and other forms available via the Internet. This will reduce the amount of time lost between sending and receiving information and will result in additional savings in postage and staff time.

The public-private partnership between the government of Indiana and Indian@Interactive, Inc. has provided the government with the technological infrastructure to provide Internet services to the public, with no developmental or capital costs. As a result, Indiana has one of the most comprehensive state websites without the expenditure of government funds. The only people charged for this service are those who use the service. This is an important model that other states and larger jurisdictions would be well advised to at least consider.

CASE 5: The U.S. Internal Revenue Service Electronic Tax Administration (ETA)

Background

The Electronic Tax Administration (ETA) is part of the Internal Revenue Service (IRS) and is critical to their mission of providing quality service to

The Internal Revenue Service ETA

website: www.irs.ustreas.gov

Description: Site enables individuals to file their taxes online and provides downloadable forms and instruction booklets.

Assessment: The Internal Revenue Service's electronic filing initiative is faster, more convenient for customers and saves government money. Additionally, less paper use complies with the Paperwork Reduction Act.

U.S. taxpayers. Every year the IRS receives over 200 million tax returns and over one billion information returns, issues 88 million individual returns, answers more than 110 million assistance calls, and collects $1.7 trillion dollars. In light of the tremendous amount of customer transactions, the IRS's reliance on resource-intensive processes for interacting with taxpayers is costly. Paperbound and error-prone processes divert critical resources from areas such as customer service and compliance.

The ETA was created in 1986 to help revolutionize how individuals, businesses, and tax practitioners transact and communicate with the IRS. This includes how Americans file tax returns, pay what is owed, and receive assistance and information to comply with tax laws. In the late 1980s the IRS conducted its first pilot test of electronic filing. In 1986, approximately 25,000 individual tax returns were filed by a handful of professional tax practitioners. By 1999, 13 years later, one out of every four individual tax returns is filed electronically.

Prior to 1986, all federal tax forms were filed through the mail. Individuals either prepared their own paper tax forms or they paid an accountant or tax practitioner to prepare the forms for them. Individuals who prepared their own tax forms usually went to the library, the post office, or other government agencies where they could get copies of the forms needed, along with lengthy instruction booklets for each form. While this method is still the most prevalent, increasing numbers of taxpayers are utilizing one of the three electronic methods to file their federal tax forms. Individuals can choose to file via the telephone utilizing the TeleFile system, over the Internet via a personal computer, or electronically through an IRS-authorized Electronic Return Originator (ERO).

While these new methods are more convenient for taxpayers, there are still many supplemental forms that cannot be filed over the Internet, and most transactions are not completely paperless. In 1999, one million taxpayers participated in two pilot projects, which enabled them to have a totally paperless filing experience. However, most taxpayers must still mail in W-2 forms, along with certain paper-only forms and schedules. As a result, many taxpayers continue to use the traditional mail-in method.

In addition to enabling individuals to file their taxes over the Internet, the IRS website also provides downloadable forms and instruction booklets. Similarly, taxpayers can e-mail questions to an IRS representative and a "What's Hot" page alerts taxpayers to current problems and issues affecting them. All of these new tools enable the IRS to reduce the amount of paperwork that they produce to assist taxpayers. This is in accordance with the Paperwork Reduction Act that attempts to minimize the burden of federal-paperwork demands through use of technology.

Development

Before taxpayers could file their taxes over the Internet, the IRS had to create the infrastructure to support these transactions. Much of the initial work was done in-house; however, as the demand for e-filing increased and the options available became more complicated, the IRS recognized the need to rebuild the computing infrastructure of the ETA. At the end of 1998, the IRS awarded a contract to Computer Service Corporation and a team of leading technology and consulting firms to be major partners in managing the modernization of IRS's core business and technology systems.

In developing an e-filing system, there were many problems. For instance, the need for authentic W-2 forms and the taxpayer's signature have deterred many filers from using the online options, because they would be forced into a two-step process: sending in the necessary paper after completing the online transaction. The ETA is dealing with this problem by conducting pilot projects that enable small numbers of taxpayers to work around these issues. By piloting different options, the ETA is able to determine the best ways to make the system more user friendly for everyone.

An additional barrier to e-filing is the public's perception that they are more likely to be audited if they file electronically. To combat this obstacle, the ETA developed a marketing campaign that dispels this false perception. The campaign explains that audit selection criteria does not take into account how a return was filed. Furthermore, the campaign points out that those who file using traditional mail-in methods are actually 40 times more likely to receive subsequent contact with the IRS than those who file electronically. Another obstacle that ETA faces concerns the privacy and security of taxpayer's personal information. The ETA is working on safeguarding taxpayer's information. Simultaneously, it is streamlining forms to minimize the amount of personal information needed to file electronically. Finally, it is implementing pilot projects to develop a safe and secure method for using personal identification numbers (PINs) to enable individuals to file electronically.

Implementation

In 1999, online filing increased 161 percent over 1998 filings with 2.5 million taxpayers utilizing this option. The IRS is projecting continued increases in the utilization of e-filing services, as the services improve and as customers become more familiar with and more confident in electronic filing methods. In addition to the transactional increases, in 1999 the IRS homepage received over one billion hits for information or downloadable tax forms. The increased utilization of the Internet to provide instructions and information has reduced the amount of paperwork the IRS produces and processes.

In addition to decreasing the amount of paperwork, these new filing options have extremely high accuracy rates and customer satisfaction reports. The IRS has consistently achieved a 99 percent accuracy rate on all electronically filed tax returns, with a 99.2 percent rate in 1999. As a result, customer satisfaction is also very high. In 1999 the Russell Marketing Research, Inc. conducted a satisfaction survey on the three methods of e-filing. Of those who used the practitioner file and online file, 75 percent reported they were "very satisfied," compared with 85 percent of those who used TeleFile. Furthermore, when you included those who claimed that they were "somewhat satisfied," the scores increased to 95 percent for practitioner file, 97 percent for online, and 99 percent for TeleFile. These figures were confirmed by the President's Management Council (PMC) Customer Service Results.

Table 4.3: Individual IRS Tax Filings[a] (in thousands)

<table>
<tr><th>Year</th><th>TeleFile</th><th>Practitioner File (ERO)</th><th>Online File</th><th>Total IRS e-file</th><th>Total Tax Forms Filed</th></tr>
<tr><td>1998</td><td>5,955</td><td>17,669</td><td>942</td><td>24,580</td><td>1,225,000</td></tr>
<tr><td>1999</td><td>5,664</td><td>21,223</td><td>2,458</td><td>29,346</td><td>1,251,000</td></tr>
<tr><td>2000 (projected)</td><td>7,000–7,800</td><td colspan="2">25,000–31,000 (projections combined)</td><td>33,600</td><td>1,269,000</td></tr>
<tr><td>2003 (projected)</td><td>8,000–9,600</td><td colspan="2">31,800–43,000 (projections combined)</td><td>44,100–45,600</td><td>1,321,100</td></tr>
<tr><td>2007 (projected)</td><td>9,400–12,700</td><td colspan="2">40,000–57,000 (projections combined)</td><td>55,500–64,300</td><td>1,386,000</td></tr>
</table>

Notes:

[a] *All IRS Data drawn from: IRS Electronic Tax Administration's "A Strategy for Growth," Washington D.C., December 1999.*

The IRS recognized that customer satisfaction was only one way to measure success, and therefore also conducted surveys to rate the satisfaction of tax practitioners and ETA employees with e-filing. The ERO survey found that tax practitioners believed that the e-file program was fast, accurate, and improved customer satisfaction. Of those surveyed, 75 percent were "very satisfied" with the practitioner file and approximately 95 percent were at least "somewhat satisfied" with this service. Similarly, employees were surveyed to determine their level of satisfaction on 12 different indices, ranging from training to empowerment to performance measurement. The overall scores on the 12 indicators ranged from a low of 55 percent to a high of 74 percent. The IRS is using the employee survey and the information it uncovered to create new initiatives for employees, such as training programs and communication efforts. Furthermore, managers have incorporated the 12 indicators into their work groups and were held accountable for acting on the indicators in FY2000.

In addition to the high levels of satisfaction with the e-file methods, they also cost less than traditional mail-in services. In 1999, a unit mail-in transaction cost $4.28 per 30 million transactions. Similarly, a unit e-file transaction cost $4.14 per 30 million transactions. While these savings are relatively small, the projected savings over the next several years are much more significant (see Table 4.4). These savings are based on the assumption that as the volume of e-transactions increases, the IRS should be able to amortize its fixed costs, which will allow the per-transaction cost to decrease. Furthermore, the IRS also has a number of techniques to increase customer usage, which will in turn decrease unit costs. These include deploying an authentication approach, enabling debit and credit card payments, automating the ERO application and suitability process, and consolidating and modernizing service center assets.

Analysis

The Internal Revenue Service's electronic filing initiative must be judged a success. First, it is faster and more convenient for customers, thereby increasing their customer satisfaction. Similarly, it saves money per transaction. Furthermore, this project is in compliance with the Paperwork Reduction Act that attempts to replace paper transactions with paperless technological transactions. While most users are currently satisfied with their e-filing experiences, future enhancements should make the experience even better. Finally, this project is consistent with the goal of the federal government to increase the use of the Internet to provide government services.

Over the next several years, the ETA plans to make electronic filing, payment, and communication so simple, inexpensive, and trusted that taxpayers will prefer these methods to phone and mail options. They are cur-

Table 4.4: IRS Transaction Costs[a] (Unit cost per 30 million transactions)

Year	Traditional Mail-In Transaction	Electronically Filed Transaction
1999	$4.28	$4.14
2003(projected)	—	$3.50
2007 (projected)	—	$2.00

Notes:
[a] *Source: "A Strategy for Growth": op. cit.*

rently developing a comprehensive plan to remove barriers, increase benefits, and broaden the appeal of electronic transactions to all segments of the population. IRS plans to expand the pilot projects that enable taxpayers to have a completely paperless filing process and to acclimate more individuals to this new option. Similarly, they plan to increase the number of forms and schedules that individuals can file online. This should increase the number of taxpayers opting to use one of the e-filing methods. The overall goal is to have 80 percent of individuals filing their taxes online by the year 2007. This increase in use should result in large reductions in cost per transaction, because the fixed development and implementation costs will be spread across more transactions.

Over the last 14 years the IRS, and specifically the ETA, has greatly improved electronic filing. It has expanded and enhanced the services provided. Both experience and new technology have contributed to better, more comprehensive options for taxpayers. With electronic filing, customers and practitioners are more satisfied and costs per transaction are decreased. While the ETA improved e-filing significantly, there are many improvements to come. The ETA's strategic plan outlines a comprehensive plan that should result in 80 percent IRS transactions occurring electronically by the year 2007. In order to accomplish this, it plans to continue to invest time and resources into the infrastructure and marketing of the project.

CASE 6: Texas Electronic Compliance and Approval Process (ECAP)

Background

In 1998, the oil and gas industry in Texas was facing historically low oil prices and declining production. In an attempt to reduce the cost of regulatory processes and encourage the drilling of new wells, the Texas Railroad Commission, in conjunction with the oil and gas industry that it regulates, proposed a pilot project to streamline oil and gas permits, the Electronic

Texas ECAP

website: www.rrc.state.tx.us/ecap

Description: Site streamlines the oil and gas permit process by improving communication and saving both time and money for government and private industry.

Assessment: While this pilot program incorporates a long-term strategy to reduce administrative complexities and costs of drilling in Texas, initial results include a more flexible, accurate approval process that requires less time and money to complete.

Compliance and Approval Process (ECAP). This technological solution is comprised of an integrated database linked to an Internet-based interactive permitting system. The overall goal is to use Internet technology to improve communication, save money and time for both the Commission and industry operators, and streamline regulatory compliance processes through electronic workflow systems.

The Commission chose the drilling permit application process as the first to transform into a completely electronic transaction. It was the ideal transaction to use in the pilot project because it is complicated, involving signatures, electronic fund transfers, and record archiving and storage. In addition, it is the first step in any regulatory process. Prior to the ECAP process, drilling permits were either processed through the mail or through an expedited walk-through process at the commissioner's office in Austin. It takes approximately four days to process mail-in applications, and an expedited mail-in application takes about eight hours. A walk-through application takes about two hours depending on the number being processed on a particular day. The drilling permit process is linear in nature, thus delays are experienced if one step in the process is not working or hits a bottleneck. Furthermore, once an application is approved, industry operators either wait several days while the approval is returned through the mail or they can pay the $50 expedite fee. Finally, once applications are approved, they are either stored in paper format, which makes it difficult to access valuable information in the future, or the information is keyed into a computer database, which is time consuming and can result in clerical errors.

In May 2000, the ECAP project provided an alternative method for industry operators to submit the drilling permit application. Now, the Commission utilizes the Internet to accept, file, review, and approve a portion of the approximately 15,000 drilling permit applications received per year. This new process not only reduces the amount of time and money spent processing an application, it also reduces errors and mistakes. The online application form asks for key data that enables the program to fill in other fields on the form. This streamlined application reduces the time spent filling out forms and increases the data accuracy. Similarly, it reduces the time spent processing incorrect forms and resubmitting corrections. The electronic application allows the various steps in the process to occur simultaneously, further expediting the process. Critical correspondence previously performed through the mail or in-person now takes minutes through the Internet, and permits are usually approved within 24 hours. Finally, the Commission receives data in the same format that it will be stored, eliminating the need to store paper documents or computerize paper data.

Development

The development process for this project is broken down into three separate phases. The estimated cost for developing and implementing the entire ECAP pilot program is $1.4 million. In February 1999, the Texas Railroad Commission received a $700,000 grant from the U.S. Department of Energy to use toward this project, and in May 1999 the Texas Legislature appropriated $1.4 million. This funding enabled ECAP to begin the developmental process, and in April 2000 it completed the first phase. Phase 1 cost approximately $333,000, which included contracting out the initial development costs, such as programming services to four independent contractors. The labor costs for this phase were based on 15 person-months of programming time at $100 for analysis and work design and $75 for pure programming services. Capital expenditures, such as increased server storage capacity, were estimated at $37,000. The completion of this stage took approximately eight months and now enables the Railroad Commission to accept, process, and approve drilling permit applications. This phase focused on building the primary infrastructure, such as secure system access, credit-card payments, mainframe database updates via the Internet, and limited online data validation and editing capacities.

In late 2000, ECAP was working on the second phase of the pilot project, which is projected to take approximately five months to complete and cost an estimated $516,000. This phase expands the core systems to include full editing capabilities and a comprehensive workflow system. It will require approximately 11 person-months of programming, or $254,000, to enable the system to process more complex work permits. In addition, the procurement of commercially available workflow software would enable multiple processes to occur simultaneously. Software expenses and additional contracted programming services to adapt the software to the Commission's process were estimated at $262,000.

The third and final phase of this project should take approximately seven months to complete and is estimated at $555,000. During this phase, contractors will complete the development process and will fully integrate the new system with the existing mainframe databases. This will enable ECAP to provide comprehensive online permit approvals. It will require approximately five person-months to complete and will cost approximately $107,000. The main expense incurred during this phase is the procurement of a commercial bridging software, which will enable the new Internet based system to replace the manual process while still maintaining the accuracy of the Commission's files. The estimated capital expenditure, including hours required to implement and test the software, is $448,000.

During the three-phase development and implementation plan, contractors will participate in the maintenance of the site; however, they will be under the direction of Commission personnel. Once development process is complete, the Commission staff will be responsible for maintaining the site. The ongoing maintenance costs will be approximately $322,000 per year.

The Commission encountered several obstacles through the initial phase of development. These included delays in the government procurement process and compatibility issues with changing technology. As a result, it established a project management team that reviewed the impact of the varying problems and developed solutions. For instance, when dealing with technical compatibility issues, it defined change management processes and escalation procedures. In addition, it ensured that future steps in the project had contingency plans and time frames for sufficient testing of application issues.

Implementation

Since Phase 1 was completed in May 2000, one consulting firm and 34 organizations have filed the necessary agreements and security forms required for utilizing the ECAP system. However, there are over 8,000 operators in the state, so the Commission expects more registrations to occur in the following months. Since the ECAP project was actually initiated by industry operators and not the Commission, high enrollment is expected to follow, as operators become more familiar with the new system. Similarly, once industry operators realize the savings that will result from this new approval process, more will register.

During the development phase of this project, the Commission worked with industry representatives to determine the administrative savings that operators will realize when applying for permits electronically. Together they determined that the reduction of processing and approval time would result in a $200 to $400 savings per permit. If there is a 25 percent utilization of electronic filing, then total annual industry savings is expected to reach $17 million. These savings help meet the Commission's goals of decreasing industry costs in an effort to ensure continued drilling in Texas.

Table 4.5: Estimated Costs of ECAP's Pilot Program[a]

ECAP	Labor	Capital	Total
Phase 1	$296,000	$37,000	$333,000
Phase 2	$254,000	$262,000	$516,000
Phase 3	$107,000	$448,000	$555,000
Total Project	$657,000	$747,000	$1,404,000

Notes:

[a] *Source: The Railroad Commission of Texas, "ECAP (Electronic Compliance and Approval Project) Report," December 15, 1998.*

While saving money for industry operators is the primary goal of the ECAP project, the Commission projects that savings for the government will be realized in later years. Initially, the Commission will have to maintain two application processes until the electronic process is completely operational. However, once the system is finalized, the streamlined approach will save the government time and money, especially as capital costs are dispersed among more transactions.

Analysis

This project will immediately begin to meet the Commission's overall goal to reduce the administrative costs for industry operators. The electronic process not only saves time and money for the government and private industry, it also provides a more flexible and accurate approval process. In addition, permit information is more consistent and accessible due to the database system.

The Commission expects to complete the second phase of the ECAP project by the end of 2000, which will allow the processing of more complex drilling permits and attachments. This addition should increase the utilization of electronic filing. Similarly, utilization and savings should increase further as the third phase is completed. Phase 3 is scheduled for completion by September 2001, ending the development process and resulting in a fully integrated database system. Once the system is complete, the Commission plans to expand ECAP to include compliance permits and performance reports. The goal is to have a 50 percent paperless regulatory environment by the year 2005.

Over the last two years, the Texas Railroad Commission has worked closely with industry operators to develop a streamlined permit application process. The project was primarily driven by the private industry and should result in savings for operators and eventually for the government. Utilizing the expertise of private operators enabled the Commission to create a comprehensive, long-term strategy to reduce administrative costs of drilling in Texas.

Conclusions and Recommendations

The six cases we analyzed indicate that the web can serve as a mechanism for improving government service delivery.

While some of the government sector's development of web-based services has followed thoughtful planning, more often web-based services have been developed without a business plan and without cost and benefit analysis. The principal conclusion of this study is that governments must obtain management assistance when they begin to develop these web-based services. Experts with experience in launching these new ventures should be hired by any government organization that is planning to deliver service using the web. An assessment of costs and benefits should be conducted that then should be used to shape the form of the site, the services offered, the fee structure, and timing.

The potential of the World Wide Web for government is great, but should not be overestimated. Just as Barnes and Noble bookstores benefit from having both virtual and physical stores, governments should assume that different types of customer needs should be addressed through different modes of interaction. Face-to-face contact and physical presence is sometimes required for effective transactions. Web-based service delivery can relieve pressure from the physical "store" by removing some general traffic and people who'd rather "shop at home." It can also save money when properly managed.

Even if web-based government services were a bad idea, many governments would still need to explore them due to citizen demand. Fortunately, there is ample evidence that the Internet can be a valuable aid to government. It is important to ensure that services are carefully planned, and that costs and benefits are constantly evaluated. Poorly planned web-based services can increase an agency's costs without significantly improving citizen satisfaction. The Internet is a tool and not a cure-all. It is a complex undertaking. When used with care it can help government improve its ability to serve the public.

Endnotes

1. The authors are grateful for the research assistance of our students in Columbia University's Graduate Program in Public Policy and Administration: Candace Winkler (lead researcher), Kelly Christensen, and Lisa Dimas.

2. Personal e-mail communication with Robert Knapp, director of marketing for Access Indiana, July 18, 2000.

3. Source of data in this section: personal e-mails from Herb Price, systems analyst for the Health Professions Bureau, September 13 and October 2, 2000.

Bibliography

Christensen, E. W. and Hughes, J. E. "Putting Your Agency on the Web" in David Garsen (ed.) *Handbook of Public Information* (New York: Marcel Dekker Inc., 2000).

Cohen, S. and Eimicke, W. *Tools for Innovators: Creative Strategies for Managing Public Sector Organizations* (San Francisco: Jossey-Bass Publishers, 1998).

Specht, P. H. " The Impact of IT on Organizational Performance in the Public Sector" in David Garsen (ed.) *Handbook of Public Information* (New York: Marcel Dekker Inc., 2000).

CHAPTER FIVE

Implementing State Contracts for Social Services: An Assessment of the Kansas Experience

Jocelyn M. Johnston
Assistant Professor
Department of Public Administration
University of Kansas

Barbara S. Romzek
Professor
Department of Public Administration
University of Kansas

This report was originally published in May 2000, revised May 2003.

Introduction[1]

In the mid-1990s, support coalesced among elected officials in Kansas for increased privatization and contracting out of government services.[2] Both the state legislature and former Governor Bill Graves, whose professional background is in business, were supporters of the principle of privatization for state services. The Department of Social and Rehabilitation Services (SRS), which was viewed by elected officials as uncontrollable and unwieldy—a "monster agency"—provided a target of opportunity for pursuing this agenda (Myers, 1997). The then-secretary of SRS, Rochelle Chronister, was a supporter of the concept. As Governor Graves's appointee, Chronister brought her 17 years of experience as a state legislator to the job of reforming the state's social service programs. Her legislative experience, including her tenure as chair of the House Appropriations Committee, gave her the insights and networks to deal effectively with legislators and to garner their support for her efforts to privatize SRS activities.

The Department of Social and Rehabilitation Services had a history of repeatedly requesting mid-year supplemental appropriations to fund social service programs. These requests were driven by rising Medicaid costs from the mid-1980s on, by a traditional Kansas pattern of stringent budgets for all state agencies, and by the general difficulty of projecting the fiscal needs of entitlement programs. Partly as a result of this pattern, SRS developed an image of being too big and cumbersome to be well managed and accountable. For example, both the SRS budget and full-time equivalent (FTE) staff expanded by 21 percent between fiscal years 1993 and 1996 (Governor's Budget Reports, 1993-1998). Clearly the state could not afford to sustain these staff and budget increases for the long term. And demographic projections, especially for the Medicaid-eligible elderly, suggested even greater need for services in the future.[3]

The 1996 federal welfare reform, the Personal Responsibility and Work Opportunity Reconciliation Act (PRWORA), required a new intensity of employment services for recipients of Temporary Assistance for Needy Families (TANF), the cash assistance program that replaced Aid to Families with Dependent Children (AFDC). PRWORA came on the heels of new state discretion for the Medicaid program. That discretion led many states, including Kansas, to contract with health maintenance organizations (HMOs) for health care services and to reconfigure services for the elderly to prevent unnecessary nursing home care. These program developments, combined with the privatization emphasis shared by the state's political leaders, led to a number of state contracts in a variety of social service program areas. Contracting occurs in all of SRS' individual units or "commissions."[4]

In order to better understand the dynamics of state contracting for social services, we conducted in-depth case analyses of five contracts associated with PRWORA and Medicaid (see Table 5.1 on research method). The contracts examined are:

- Medicaid case management services for the frail elderly
- Medicaid managed-care HMO services
- Contracts for administration and oversight of Medicaid managed care
- Provider agreements for employment preparation services
- Comprehensive employment preparation services contract

The objective of the research was to focus on the contracting decision processes associated with these contracts and on the adaptations of the state and the contracting agencies to the new contractual arrangements. By drawing on previous research in the area, and by analyzing data from extensive interviews with state and contracting agency officials, we identified

List of Acronyms

AAA Area Agencies on Aging: nonprofit agencies with which the state of Kansas contracts for case management services for elderly Medicaid clients.

AFDC Aid to Families with Dependent Children: the federal cash assistance program for welfare eligible households prior to 1997.

DOA Kansas Department on Aging: the agency with administrative responsibility for case management services for elderly Medicaid clients.

HCFA The federal Health Care Financing Administration: the agency within the Department of Health and Human Services that administers Medicaid, Medicare, and other federally financed health care programs.

HMO Health Maintenance Organization: a medical care entity that provides services in the private market, and to Medicaid recipients under contracts with states.

PRWORA The Personal Responsibility and Work Opportunity Reconciliation Act: the 1996 federal welfare reform bill that eliminated the federal entitlement to welfare benefits under AFDC, and which took effect in October 1997.

RFP Request for proposal: the strategy used to solicit nongovernmental agency proposals for state contracts.

SRS The Kansas Department of Social and Rehabilitation Services: the state agency with administrative responsibility for most of the state's social welfare programs, including TANF and Medicaid.

TANF Temporary Assistance to Needy Families: the program that replaced AFDC, as stipulated by PRWORA, the 1996 federal welfare reform.

Table 5.1: Five Contracting Cases

	Number of Contracts	Contracted Services	Dates of Contracts	Reimbursement Method	Performance Measurement Focus	Related Subcontracts or Other State Contracts
Medicaid Case Management Services for the Elderly	11	AAAs provide case management services for elderly Medicaid home and community-based services	January 1997, ongoing	Reimbursement based on client contact hours	Performance measurement focuses on client plans of care	Blue Cross and Blue Shield of Kansas, in-home care providers
Medicaid Managed-Care HMO Services	1*	HMO provides capitated (pre-paid) comprehensive health care services for eligible Medicaid clients	State began annual contracts with HMOs in 1997; current HMO contract began May 1999.	Reimbursement based on pre-existing fee-for-service rates for individual health services	Performance measurement based on health indicators, utilization patterns, and client satisfaction	BCBS, Kansas Foundation for Medical Care, others
Contracts for Administration and Oversight of Medicaid Managed Care	2**	Various administrative and oversight tasks. Kansas Foundation for Medical Care assesses HMO performance through data analyses. BCBS collects HMO data and manages client and provider enrollment, consumer hotline, and other program components	BCBS: 11/96 (for three years); KFMC: three-year contract through 6/99; currently under extension	Reimbursement varies; ranges from per enrollee fee (for BCBS) to per HMO fee (for KFMC)	Performance measured through contract deliverables, data and analytic reports, focus studies, etc.	HMOs, other contractors for administration and oversight

Table 5.1: Five Contracting Cases (continued)

	Number of Contracts	Contracted Services	Dates of Contracts	Reimbursement Method	Performance Measurement Focus	Related Subcontracts or Other State Contracts
Provider Agreements for Employment Preparation Services	not known***	Wide variety of organizations provide components of welfare-related employment preparation services	Ongoing for several years; often open ended	Reimbursement typically based on services rendered to welfare clients	Performance focuses on client contact—hours of program attendance, etc.	
Comprehensive Employment Preparation Service Contract	1	One contractor provides all components of employment preparation services for welfare clients in 11-county area	Services began June 1998	Reimbursement based on outcomes such as client employment with performance bonuses	Performance based on outcomes such as employment, process for client contact, etc.	

* *Kansas had contracted, at various times since the 1997 inception of Medicaid managed care, with five different HMOs. For a brief period, ending in December 1998, the state contracted simultaneously with three HMOs. Since that time, only one HMO has contracted for Kansas Medicaid services.*

** *Although not discussed in this chapter, Kansas contracts with other organizations for Medicaid managed-care related services, including external evaluations, consulting for various program issues, actuarial analyses, etc.*

*** *The SRS central office Grants and Contracts Unit is presently devising a strategy to consolidate information on SRS local office provider agreements. The Grants and Contracts Unit estimates that between 5,000 and 8,000 provider agreements currently exist statewide. The Unit is unable to identify the number of employment service provider agreements. SRS is attempting to rectify this problem.*

common themes and variations in decision making as well as adaptations across the five contracts. The research shed light on the motivations underlying the decisions and on the major administrative challenges and adjustments required by contracts for these types of services. What follows is a general discussion of the contracting process.

The Contracting Process

Contracting for state social services presents a broad array of administrative challenges. The contract decision process typically involves both political and fiscal considerations, but the important issues of design and implementation often are not addressed until after the contracting decision has been made.

Implementation of these contracts requires substantial adaptation on the part of the agencies involved. Kansas' experience confirms that good contracts for social services are hard to write and equally challenging to manage. One of the major problems is that sound contracts often require more information about pre-contract program cost than public sector agencies have.

Good contracting requires a clear understanding of costs, understandable and clear statements of the scope of work, clear specifications of performance expectations, and defined obligations on the part of the contracting agency and contractor. Contracts need clarity regarding the contract deliverables, including contractor reports to facilitate state monitoring of cost and performance. While all players involved in state contracting know these conditions are central to success, they are not always able to meet these terms for social service contracts.

Effective contracting is also facilitated by appropriate institutional supports. For SRS, those supports are formally provided both externally by the state's Department of Administration and the recently formed Kansas Performance Review Board, and internally by the SRS Grants and Contracts Unit. The nature of support derived from these organizations varies from program to program, but in any case, SRS has access to external and internal advice as it considers contracts for social services.

Contract Monitoring Issues

As governments contract out social service programs, they take on increasing responsibilities for managing and monitoring the contracts. They face a number of issues related to contract monitoring. They must identify those who will monitor contract performance, as well as the components of performance to be monitored. Governments must stipulate how and from whom they will obtain reliable data on contractor performance. Once these data are available, the state must evaluate contractor performance and decide what, if any, response to make to its findings.

Who monitors?

The answer to this question is not always as straightforward as it appears at first glance. Sometimes the state agency will have its own staff serve as monitors. In other instances it will it rely on self-reporting by the contractor or ask a third party to monitor the contract performance.

The transition to contract monitoring is complicated by the fact that the contracting decision often is driven by cost-saving rationales that do not allow for hiring experienced contract management staff. The typical response is to have former program staff within the state agency assume contract management responsibilities. Yet individuals who make this transition need substantial specialized training in the complexities and unique challenges associated with monitoring contracts. Such circumstances raise important questions about contract managers' skills, credentials, and degree of independence from the contractor.

If the strategy chosen is to shift state agency personnel from service provision to contract management, staff face new job tasks that often require a dramatic shift in emphasis from service provision and responsiveness to client needs to contract management and monitoring of contractor performance and client well-being. Often this shift is a wrenching one for program staff asked to make the transition.

What aspects of performance will be measured?

The issue of performance measures is a complex one. Good contracts specify performance measures in advance. But the reality of social service contracts is such that performance measures are difficult to identify and reliably measure. Performance measures originally specified in contracts frequently undergo extensive revision, and others are sometimes developed after the fact, based on experience with the contract.

Historically, contract management has focused on measuring inputs (such as costs and caseloads) and processes that typically emphasize paperwork and timeliness issues. Recent management reforms seek to shift the emphasis toward outputs (such as head counts, contact data, and client-satisfaction survey data) and outcomes (such as sustained independence for frail elderly, employment for former welfare clients, and improved health for HMO clients). The difficulty in outcome measurement lies in the fact that contractors' performance is often only one factor in a complex social context that affects the desired outcomes.

Access and reliability of performance data

Once the contracting agency and contractor agree on what performance measures to use, questions of data access and reliability must be addressed. Are the selected measures good indicators of success? Are the contract monitors able to access those data? Does the contract require the contractor to collect performance data and provide them to monitors? Or will these activities and their associated costs be borne by the state agency?

Contractor performance

All contract monitoring is ultimately targeted toward ensuring that the contracted services are appropriately and successfully delivered to the relevant clientele. Depending upon contractor performance, the state agency will face decisions regarding what to do about those findings. Should it continue the contract at its present levels? Should the contracting agency adjust subsequent performance measures to more accurately reflect the outcomes sought by the state? The state agency faces questions regarding its options when contractor performance is inadequate. Should it offer technical assistance? Revoke the contract? Let the contract run its course and seek a new provider for the next round of contracting? If the state terminates the contract due to poor performance, can it find another contractor? Or must the state be prepared to resume direct service delivery?

The Kansas Experience

The Kansas experience confirms that contracting for state social services poses substantial challenges to administrators of state and contracting agencies, in both the decision and implementation phases of the contract. In this section, we present research findings related to our examination of the contracting decision process. We also provide detailed case studies of five social service contract areas. We analyzed the decision process and contract management experiences associated with each contract to identify administrative strategies and their strengths and weaknesses. Our analysis revealed patterns and common themes in the decision processes and in the implementation phases of these contracts.[5]

The Kansas Contract Decision Process

In Kansas, state social service contracting decisions are made in a political environment that, until very recently, has strongly encouraged the use of contracting whenever and wherever possible in state government. In

1996 the legislature, led by proponents of alternatives to government service provision, created the Kansas Performance Review Board (KPRB). The purpose of the KPRB is to conduct

> a continuing process to review functions of state government to determine whether current programs, functions, or agencies are being executed in the most efficient and effective manner possible, and to recommend the privatization, elimination, retention, or modification [PERM] of them accordingly (Kansas Performance Review Board, 1998, p. 1).

All state agencies are supposed to follow the "PERM" contracting decision process as recommended by KPRB.

In some instances, the decision to contract out social service programs has moved very quickly, in part to minimize the opportunity for opponents—political or administrative—to block the decision.

The SRS contracting process tends to begin informally; formality increases with the incorporation of discussions with potential contractors, administrative staff, and other state agencies. After the contract is signed, a combination of formal and informal interactions occur between the state and its contractors. Frequently, these interactions develop into a "partnership" type of approach to the service, with mutual support systems serving to facilitate implementation of the contract and to ease the adjustments required by both parties to the contract. The genesis of the contracting idea for any given social service contract typically comes from within SRS. If the idea is seen as viable by those with the power to carry it forward, a work team is formed. The SRS Grants and Contracts Unit can contribute by helping to formulate a statement of work (i.e., to specify and articulate the service SRS wants to purchase).[6] Although they may not be represented formally on the SRS team, the interests of the SRS secretary, the governor, and the legislature are also considered by the team.

Under standard conditions, the state's Department of Administration, which is responsible for overseeing state purchasing and contract negotiations, is formally involved in the contracting decision, but only relatively late in the process. The Department of Administration is charged with assisting state agencies with contract preparation, the bidding/negotiation process, and the finalization of the contract. Once the contract is signed, Department of Administration staff are no longer formally involved in the contract, although they may be asked for help if contract problems arise. However, unless they are approached by the relevant state agency, they have no further role and may only hear about contract problems "through the grapevine." Contracts for Medicaid managed-care HMOs are exempt from Department of Administration oversight, and Administration has virtually no role in local provider agreements for employment preparation services.[7]

SRS (along with most Kansas agencies) uses an "any willing provider" approach to solicit proposals for most of its contracts. Reimbursement rates are not negotiated, but are published in the requests for proposal (RFPs). SRS requests proposals from all providers willing to accept the rates in return for specified services.

Ultimately, unsatisfactory contract proposals are eliminated after review. The work team then meets with all remaining organizations that have submitted proposals to the state. At that point, a final negotiation process ensues, and "bidders" are asked to submit their best and final offer. If agreement is reached with an organization, a final contract is signed.

Interviews suggest that the genesis of and processes used for each contracting decision are contingent on a variety of contextual factors. However, one common theme emerges: If agency administrators see a need for more personnel for service delivery, they are well aware that in the current political environment, contracts with outside organizations provide the only likely method to staff such needs. Medicaid managed-care administrators solicited contracts for several elements of managed-care oversight because they knew that the legislature would not support additional staff expansion for contract management or performance measurement of Medicaid managed-care providers. One Medicaid official noted that "we can get all the money we need for contracts. We just can't get money for staff." In the area of employment preparation services, the comprehensive state contract resulted in part because the SRS area office felt it would not be possible to hire new staff to devote to the services. This condition applies also to the multiple provider agreements for employment preparation service components in SRS area offices throughout the state.

This theme is echoed by other agencies in state government. The state's Legislative Division of Post Audit notes, for example, that most state contracting decisions result from budget problems as opposed to idealized agency evaluations of organizational strengths, weaknesses, needs, etc. (Legislative Post Audit, 1996, p.29).[8] Yet, in the view of Post Audit, the agencies clearly recognize that contracts are not likely to generate cost savings.

The preponderance of the evidence indicates that many of SRS' contracting decisions result from agency responsiveness to political pressures to contract, as opposed to analyses of the economic and provider supply conditions necessary for a good contracting environment. The state's Department of Administration and other observers recognize that for many SRS services, there may be only one potential contractor available to provide the service. This environment tends to complicate the contract management process because the provider efficiency theoretically associated with competition may not materialize.

Five Contracting Cases

1. Medicaid Case Management Services for the Elderly

In 1996 Kansas received one of the earliest waivers from the federal Health Care Financing Administration (HCFA) to construct a new Medicaid service delivery system for the state's "frail elderly." A major objective of the reform was the consolidation of all services for the elderly and the creation of a "single point of entry" to state health and social services. The logic of the reform was to increase home and community-based services to minimize the use of more expensive skilled nursing facilities for the elderly. To accomplish this objective, the state adopted a two-pronged reform.

First, the state decided to contract out case management services for clients who needed assistance with daily living chores such as laundry, meals, bathing, and paying bills, and who might be forced into nursing homes without such services. In January 1997, the state contracted with 11 Area Agencies on Aging (AAA) located throughout the state for all Medicaid case management services for the elderly.[9]

Cash Flow
Medicaid Case Management Services for the Elderly

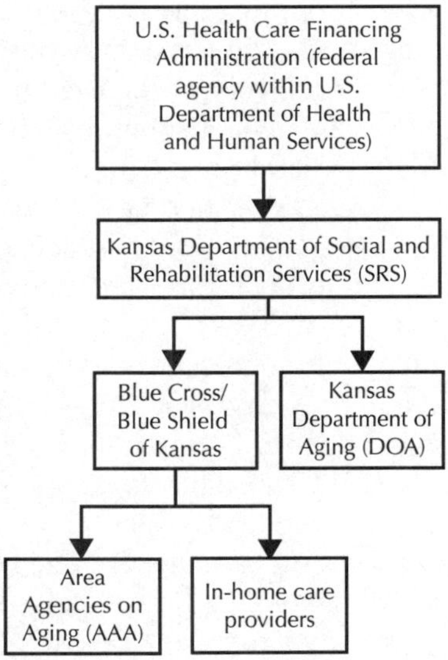

Second, in July 1997 the state transferred administrative responsibility for Medicaid case management services for the elderly from SRS to the Kansas Department on Aging (DOA). SRS remains the designated Medicaid contact agency directly accountable to HCFA and is responsible for paying service providers for Medicaid-funded in-home services; it does so through a contract with Blue Cross and Blue Shield of Kansas, the state's Medicaid fiscal agent.

The experience of the state of Kansas with this reform has illuminated some of the opportunities and constraints associated with administrative reform and contracting arrangements. The policy reform moved quickly, in part because it enjoyed broad ideological support, including that of the former governor and key department heads. The state legislature also was eager to reduce the size and cost of SRS, the largest state agency. The AAAs as a group had lobbied vigorously for the reform.

The reform required the DOA to grow quickly and substantially as it assumed responsibility for administering the Medicaid case management program. When DOA took on the elderly Medicaid program its budget increased from $18 million in FY97 to $302 million in FY98 and its staff nearly tripled in that same period, from 57 to 160 FTE. (Legislative Post Audit Report, 1999). And the AAAs around the state found that they, too, had to grow quickly and develop the capacity to provide services to a much larger and needier population than they had previously served.

Implementation of the policy reform was an iterative process, reflecting the fact that this reform was new territory for both the state and the contractors. Many aspects of the reform were worked out through negotiations among key agents as issues arose during the early months of implementation. Some aspects of the reform involved changes in state agency operations, such as the transfer of state agency authority from SRS to DOA, and the accompanying shift of some staff from SRS to DOA. Other issues related to contract management between the state and AAAs, such as contractor reimbursement rates, timeliness, quality and frequency of oversight and monitoring of case management decisions, and standards to be used for nursing home resident status reviews.

During the lead-up to the reform, SRS offered training sessions for AAA directors, case managers, and data-entry staff to help prepare them for their new roles. Of course, in a program representing such a massive shift of responsibilities, training is not a substitute for experience; the inevitable transition problems surfaced during the transfer.

The elderly Medicaid reform was designed to head off budget problems within SRS (related to escalating nursing home costs), but the reform itself created budget problems for contractors because early estimates of the cost of delivering the case management services were too low. Consequently, the contractor reimbursement rates were inadequate and were subsequently increased.[10]

Basic performance monitoring presented challenges as well. While extensive training was offered to the AAAs, there was minimal training for contract monitors within SRS and DOA. When SRS made the transition from direct service provision to contract management in January 1997, program staff were shifted to contract monitoring/quality review duties, but these staff had not received adequate training in their new responsibilities. Although they had extensive program and service expertise, staff were far less familiar with the skills required to monitor the performance of outside agencies. Interviews with SRS staff indicated that there was no formal internal agency training for contract management staff. One SRS manager observed that former program staff often take a "soft, people-oriented" approach to their jobs; as a result, as contract managers they are sometimes "softer on people than they ought to be." As individuals not personally inclined to ask tough questions about whether contractors have been successful, they typically need training to make a successful transition to monitoring duties.

By July 1997, when administrative responsibility for the elderly Medicaid program had shifted to DOA, performance monitoring of case management was handled by 30 DOA Medicaid quality reviewers, most of whom had previously worked as SRS case managers for the Medicaid elderly. Relations between SRS quality reviewers and AAA case managers were strained from the beginning due to lack of clarity regarding monitoring standards and status discrepancies between reviewers case managers.[11] Medicaid quality reviewers are required by legislation to review 10 percent of case plans of care on a monthly basis. As a result, 100 percent of all cases are typically reviewed during the year. (The AAAs view this intensity as excessive and inefficient.) These reviews include on-site file reviews, in-home visits, and interviews with clients. Although the long-term outcome sought is continued independence of the frail elderly, contract monitoring measures in the Medicaid program tend to emphasize process and paperwork issues. Plans of care are submitted for approval to DOA area offices through its electronic database, the Kansas Medicaid Information System (KAMIS). While there were the usual problems during the transition and start-up of the KAMIS, the system enables DOA to generate AAA performance reports without requiring periodic reporting from individual AAAs. However, performance outcome measures, such as extended independence or reduced nursing facility use by the frail elderly, have been difficult to develop.

AAA case managers are well positioned to assess the performance of in-home direct care service providers for elderly Medicaid clients.[12] But they have no authority over these providers.[13] Consequently, AAA case managers are limited to reporting observed problems with in-home care providers and must rely on other agencies to terminate or enforce contracts with these providers in the event of performance shortcomings. They also encourage clients to report inadequate service to the state. This arrangement illustrates the complications that can arise from the use of multiple contractors and sub-contractors in one program area. Case management services can be compromised or limited by poor performance on the part of in-home service providers that also contract with the state, but that have no accountability to the case managers. Under the current system, client satisfaction is assessed separately for in-home services.

After several years, some program stability is emerging. An audit of the performance of DOA and the Medicaid elderly program, conducted by the Legislative Division of Post Audit, found that DOA is doing a good job monitoring the case management program. It found a few potential weaknesses in the monitoring that related to lack of follow-up regarding subsequent resolution of minor problems, validity of decisions to deny services, and spot-checks when clients received fewer services than were approved in their plans of care (Legislative Post Audit, 1999).

While the state and AAAs are still wrestling with definitions of quality, the reimbursement rate problems are resolved. KAMIS is now up and running. The state can generate its own reports about comparative performance of the AAAs. There is greater consistency and consensus on quality review standards for case management. And most of those involved in quality reviews (reviewer and reviewed) have come to terms with interpersonal and status discrepancies.

AAAs are coming out of their crisis mode. Case managers now know their jobs, and performance expectations are well established. Agencies have confidence that they are doing something important by helping the frail elderly maintain independence. And they can see the outcomes of their cases. Previously, they might not know what happened to a client after the referral was made. Their role as advocates for the elderly regarding health has grown.

A major problem for the program relates only tangentially to contracting. It concerns more traditional issues of funding scarcity. Facing a projected revenue shortfall due to a series of ambitious tax cuts, the 1999 Kansas legislature shifted its funding principle for the elderly Medicaid program away from an entitlement program. Instead it authorized a budget ceiling for the program, leaving DOA and the AAAs with more eligible clients than they had funds to serve. This situation has been exacerbated by the success of the AAAs in outreach efforts to identify and serve eligible Medicaid clients. This development illustrates the potential results of shifting service responsibility from a state agency to an advocacy organization. In this case, the AAAs, the advocacy organizations, have been successful in reaching out to eligible Medicaid clients. The state agency, on the other hand, played a more passive role in identifying clients and also adopted a "gatekeeper" function in its service provision. These different approaches reflect the tradeoff between serving all eligible clients and adding to budgetary strain, and serving fewer clients while holding spending growth. One could speculate that the AAAs have been "too successful" in their mission, and that the state's decision to contract with the AAAs is unlikely to reduce Medicaid cost growth despite the potential for reduced nursing home admissions.

In July 1999 the DOA announced the creation of waiting lists for elderly clients seeking Medicaid assistance with home and community-based care. Those individuals who were currently receiving in-home care services would be able to continue. But any new applicants to the program would be evaluated and placed on a waiting list depending upon need. In October 1999 the former governor announced that he would ask for (and that key state legislators would support) a supplemental appropriation for the DOA to allow services to clients currently on waiting lists. The irony is that the history of SRS requests for supplemental appropriations was part of the basis for supporting this reform. Now DOA looks a lot like SRS to state legislative leaders.

2. Medicaid Managed-Care HMO Services

In the spring of 1994, Kansas mandated that by July 1, 1997, most of its non-elderly and non-disabled Medicaid population would receive health care services through a managed-care program. This decision applied to all clients who qualified for Medicaid as a result of receipt of welfare benefits. In effect, the state had just 18 months to move from a system in which virtually all of its welfare Medicaid population was served through fee-for-service reimbursement to a statewide managed-care system. Like other states, Kansas had been plagued by high rates of growth in Medicaid expenditures during the late 1980s and early 1990s. Medicaid annual cost growth in Kansas had exceeded the national average between 1988 and 1993 (Winter-bottom et. al, 1995). The legislature had grown exasperated with SRS requests for supplemental budget appropriations to cover unanticipated program cost growth during this period.

In November 1995, SRS was granted permission through an HCFA waiver to extend its limited pilot Medicaid managed-care program to all counties, and to contract for HMO capitated managed-care as warranted. The broad objectives of this waiver were to assure adequate access to quality care, prevent unnecessary utilization, reduce inappropriate utilization, and reduce costs for Medicaid beneficiaries. By August 1997, managed care was available throughout the state through a non-capitated managed-care program called *HealthConnect*.[14] *HealthConnect* technically met the objectives of the state legislative mandate, but the legislature was very interested in using the capitation strategy wherever possible to maximize cost savings.

Cash Flow
Medicaid Managed-Care HMO Services

Kansas Medicaid HMO contract managers were caught between the political mandate for expansion of capitated managed care and an environment that does not support that expansion. Provider supply is a big problem, with HMOs expressing virtually no interest in Medicaid contracts.[15] Choice among capitated plans has been minimal for the state's Medicaid enrollees; only seven of the state's 105 counties were ever covered by more than one Medicaid HMO, and only for a year. By December 1998, only one financially shaky HMO, known as *Horizon*, continued to contract with the state.[16] Nonetheless, SRS has succeeded in enrolling 90 percent of the state's welfare-related Medicaid enrollees in either *HealthConnect* or the *Horizon* HMO.

Medicaid managed-care contracts with HMOs are exempt from the usual Kansas Department of Administration oversight of state contracts. While this exemption maximizes the flexibility of the Medicaid agency in soliciting and finalizing contracts, contracting for Medicaid is less accountable to normal contractual oversight by the state's top administrative agency. Potential Medicaid HMO contractors must meet the commercial health plan financial viability and licensure standards required by the

Kansas Department of Insurance. Some SRS officials indicate that these standards may be too low for HMOs serving Medicaid clients, given the financial challenges faced initially by providers serving this population. Accordingly, after the Department of Insurance has approved the HMO, SRS conducts an additional review of the HMO's financial and corporate structure.

Because of the lack of provider competition for capitated Medicaid managed care in Kansas, SRS is in a fairly weak position with regard to holding Medicaid HMO contractors accountable. It appears that fairly drastic performance failures would have to be evident before SRS would terminate a contract with an HMO. SRS has occasionally invoked mild corrective action when quality or access problems surpass a threshold of acceptability, but in the case of *Horizon*, SRS has gone to extraordinary lengths to keep the HMO afloat. And SRS engaged in a variety of efforts to maximize the retention of other Medicaid HMO contractors prior to December 1998, when two of the three HMOs decided not to renew their Medicaid contracts.[17]

In addition, in 1998 the legislature authorized $10 million to augment selected Medicaid reimbursement rates. However, SRS Medicaid officials viewed this augmentation as a mere "drop in the bucket," estimating that an additional $100 million would be required to allow reimbursement rates to approximate private rates. Another rate increase was authorized in the spring of 1999 when the *Horizon* Medicaid contract was purchased by an HMO known as *FirstGuard.* SRS also conducted a study of administrative oversight requirements (reporting, etc.) imposed on all managed-care providers in order to minimize compliance burdens. However, SRS officials found that most of their oversight requirements are required by HCFA and must be continued.

Throughout the program's history, Medicaid officials have had to administer contracts with some HMOs that they feel are unable to maintain financial viability and/or services to enrollees. On the other hand, Medicaid officials have urged some commercial HMOs to respond to the state's "any willing provider" requests for proposals, despite the fact that the HMOs are quite skeptical that they can meet Medicaid performance requirements. The implication is that Medicaid officials make judgments about the viability of potential contractors, and sometimes engage in efforts to solicit proposals from HMOs that are not interested in Medicaid contracts but which are seen by the agency as capable of providing high-quality services to enrollees.

Most of the SRS staff assigned to Medicaid managed care were program staff promoted from within SRS, with little or no experience with contract management. For the most part, the staff had to take the "learn as you go" approach. Training has been minimal.[18]

3. Contracts for Administration and Oversight of Medicaid Managed Care

The combination of the privatization and cost-control emphases by state political leaders has led SRS to contract out many of the administrative and oversight tasks associated with Medicaid managed care. The state has a major contract with Blue Cross and Blue Shield of Kansas, the organization that serves as the state's Medicaid fiscal agent, and a smaller contract with the Kansas Foundation for Medical Care (KFMC). Blue Cross and Blue Shield is responsible for a variety of services, including claims and encounter data administration, management of client and provider enrollment, information systems administration, and customer services such as grievance procedures and toll-free hotlines.[19] KFMC helps the state to monitor HMO contracts by providing regular analyses of Medicaid HMO performance in the areas of health care quality and access and patient satisfaction. SRS officials estimate that the combined annual cost for the administrative contracts totals nearly $5 million.[20]

The state's ability to oversee the activities of the administrative contracts is clearly related to its ability to enforce contracts with the HMOs. Most reporting from the HMOs goes directly to the oversight contractors, where the information is compiled into reports for SRS. Yet HMOs have been chronically late in submitting data,[21] which limits the capacity of the oversight contractors to meet their contracts with the state. All contractors have experienced problems related to information management, in part because most of their systems are not compatible. This has further complicated the ability of the administrative contractors to produce performance reports. SRS has limited capacity to penalize the administrative contractors because of a classic problem with some government contracts: an inability for the state to quickly re-assume responsibility for tasks that have been contracted out. SRS would be very hard-pressed to handle even a small fraction of the administrative contractors' tasks.

These complications are exacerbated by the relationships between the SRS, the HMO contractors, and the administrative contractors. Capitated Medicaid managed-care HMOs consistently complain that SRS's reporting requirements are excessively burdensome, relative to what is encountered in the private sector. HMO officials indicate that they had "no clue" what they were getting into. Commercial HMO staff, like the staff of many government contracting agencies, are often unprepared for the level of regulation and scrutiny involved. The HMOs have also been exasperated by requirements to report to three organizations—SRS and its two administrative contractors.

Similar issues are cited by Blue Cross and Blue Shield (BCBS) and KFMC. Much of their reporting to SRS is contingent on getting timely and reliable data from either the HMO or another administrative contractor. For example, the bulk of KFMC reporting to SRS relies on data from Blue Cross

Cash Flow

Contracts for Administration and Oversight of Medicaid Managed Care

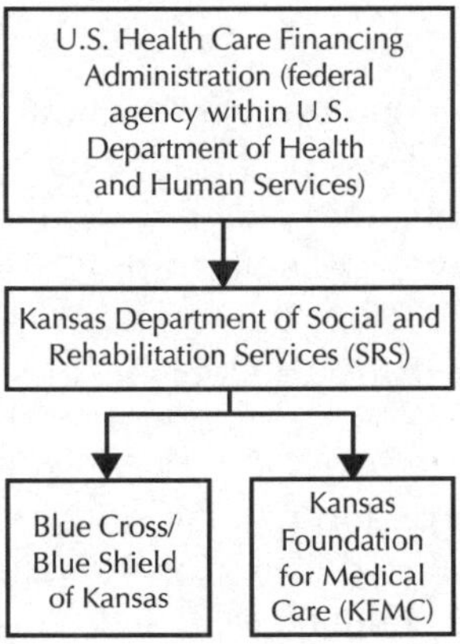

and Blue Shield (which in turn relies on data from the HMO) or from the HMO. The dearth of HMO data hampers the efforts of BCBS and KFMC to comply with their contractual requirements. Interviews with KFMC staff indicate minimal SRS specification of contractor performance expectations in their contract. This lack of specification caused severe problems for KFMC because they encountered numerous situations in which SRS expected reports and services that were not really required under the contract; in essence, SRS dealt with KFMC as if the contractor were on a state retainer.

Most—if not all—of these complications in relationships with contractors are linked to resources. If HMO reimbursement rates were higher, and if the Medicaid agency had access to more resources for staffing and training, it is likely that the state would be more successful in inducing capitated managed-care providers to supply required information. This, in turn, would ease the plight of the administrative contractors.[22] As a contractor, KFMC faced tension between its desire to be responsive to SRS and its own efficient use of organizational resources. Likewise, if more resources were directed to reimbursement rates, HMOs would feel less pinched by administrative burdens and the required adjustments involved in government contracts. To paraphrase one contract agency official, "we can't continue to subsidize the state's underfunding of Medicaid."

Despite these difficulties, from a technical perspective, SRS capacity to oversee HMOs has generally improved over the years. Moving from a small managed-care pilot program to statewide mandatory coverage in a short time frame was a major accomplishment. Simply by virtue of time and experience, SRS officials have become more adept at contract management. Yet, like Medicaid administrators in other states, they are plagued by continued information challenges and difficulties associated with evaluating the work they have done (Fox et. al, 1998).

4. Provider Agreements for Employment Preparation Services

Compared to the other areas of this investigation, the provider agreement approach to contracting for welfare-related employment preparation services follows a relatively decentralized model that has been used successfully for quite some time. But the federal Personal Responsibility and Work Opportunity Reconciliation Act, with its focus on fostering independence among the unemployed, brought a resurgence of activity in this area. The Kansas response to PRWORA has been to emphasize work first, focusing more on short-term, job-specific skills training programs and to reduce spending on long-term education and training for welfare recipients. Most employment services contracts take the form of provider agreements between SRS local area offices and local social service organizations, including government organizations (such as local vocational schools) and nonprofits. The SRS central office Grants and Contracts Unit estimates that there are between 5,000 and 8,000 provider agreements covering a wide range of program areas throughout the state. In contrast to the Medicaid arena, dollar amounts are very small, and the entire process is far less burdensome for providers.

This decentralized provider agreement approach allows area offices to contract for services that are tailored to local capacity, clientele, and workforce needs. Typically the area office decides to enter into a provider agreement based on a number of criteria; key among them are whether the area office can do the program in-house and, if so, whether they can do it "better" than alternative providers. Provider agreements are often the result of long-standing relationships between community social service providers and local area offices, where the area offices know which services the local agencies are able to provide well and are able to obtain services suited to local population needs. Area offices tend to contract for small, discrete components of employment preparation services (e.g., job club, job search, etc). Likewise, available providers know the area office staff and what they need; they sometimes approach an area office with a proposal to provide services.

For example, the Wichita Area Office has long-standing collaborative relationships with employers in the area to provide targeted employment training. Sometimes these provider agreements reflect formalized training and job-placement programs for welfare recipients, such as the celebrated

Cash Flow
Provider Agreements for Employment Preparation Services

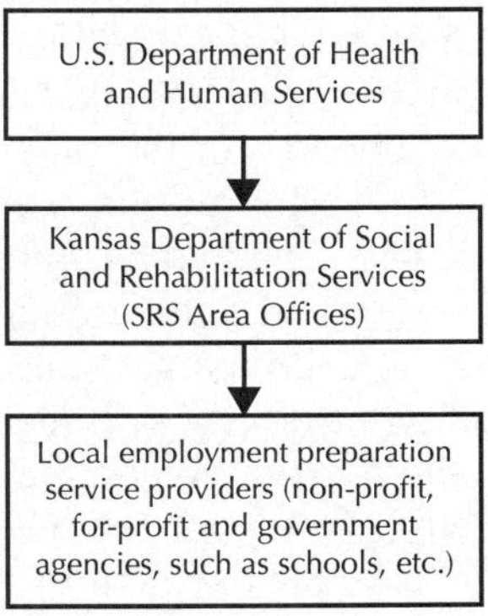

21st Street Project sponsored by the area office and Cessna.[23] At other times the working relationships are much more informal.[24]

Provider agreements are subject to relatively little SRS central office oversight; performance monitoring of the providers is the responsibility of local area offices. Monitoring under these provider agreements tends to be relatively informal; performance is monitored primarily through process measures such as head counts of client program participation or through provider contributions to job placements. There appear to be relatively low conflict levels between providers and area offices, and agreements are easily terminated.

Compared to the Medicaid contracts, these provider agreements seem to offer more provider choice, more flexibility, more goodwill, and a closer connection between program staff in area offices and contract agency staff. Many of the agreements for employment preparation services are well established, yet it is relatively easy for the area office to re-assume services in-house if necessary. The agreements are smaller in scale and relatively easy to manage. Significantly, there is no state dictated "one size fits all" approach as we see in Medicaid contracts. To the extent that contract complications exist for employment preparation services, they are associated with the large, formal, outcome-oriented contract used by one area office (described next), as opposed to the dozens of small, process-oriented, tailor-made local provider agreements.

5. Comprehensive Employment Preparation Service Contract

An exception to this pattern is the contract between one area office and Curtis & Associates for a comprehensive employment preparation service program. In contrast to most provider agreements, this contract was negotiated in conjunction with SRS headquarters staff. The decision to pursue such a contract was driven by the PRWORA mandate to get welfare recipients into the workforce and the recognition that the local area office (which is responsible for an 11-county area of the state) would not get the funds necessary to hire staff to handle the increased employment service workload. While there are arguments for retaining employment preparation services in-house, such as reduced span of control, reduced coordination/time costs, and better accountability, these arguments were insufficient to overcome the lack of area office flexibility in hiring staff with the necessary skills. For this area office, the decision to contract was more about political responsiveness to pressure from the governor and state legislature to privatize rather than about effective management or cost control. Recognizing the need to contract for the services, the area office made the decision to go with Curtis & Associates based on their familiarity with and respect for the quality of materials that Curtis & Associates had developed previously for components of employment service programs in other areas of the state.

Management of the Curtis & Associates contract tends to involve many of the dynamics associated with contracting for Medicaid case management and managed care. The area office and Curtis & Associates both found the contract tasks to be more challenging than they had anticipated. Curtis had a hard time coming up to speed, specifically with regard to hiring sufficient staff and opening offices to provide services to all clients in the 11-county area covered under the contract. Unlike most SRS contracts, this contract reimbursement is contingent on success as measured through outputs and employment outcomes. Reports from participants in the negotiations indicate that central SRS administrators were somewhat resistant to the performance-based contract because it was so different from the employment preparation services process measures—or client "nose counting"—with which they were more familiar.

From the perspective of SRS' central office and area office welfare caseworkers, the contract is perceived as more expensive than necessary.[25] Several SRS staff noted that, with the funds available to the contractor, the SRS staff could have done an equally good job.[26]

Area office staff have acknowledged that they have a vested interest in seeing the Curtis & Associates contract succeed. But they also have concerns about contractor performance. Contract monitoring started out at a very intense level.[27] Initially the area office contract manager developed a checklist, met weekly with the contractor, and maintained her own duplicate database to monitor client services and placements under the contract.

Cash Flow
Comprehensive Employment Preparation Service Contract

While this was very costly in terms of communication and time, it was deemed necessary to establishing a level of trust between the area office and the contractor. After six months, the area office had gained sufficient experience managing the contract and had enough confidence in the contractor's performance to relax the intensity of its monitoring. The contract manager now relies on the contractor's reports and contacts with clients for performance monitoring.

As noted in the discussion of the Medicaid contracts, issues of coordination also challenged staff associated with this contract. Area office staff emphasize that it would be far easier and less cumbersome to have employment service staff in-house. Discussions about clients would be less time consuming and more straightforward. Everyone would have ready access to relevant client information and could engage easily in group approaches if necessary. Area office staff now have to "depend on others for information," and they feel like they're not "always in tune with what's happening with the client."

In sum, the contracting problems that we observed in the three Medicaid contract areas have emerged here as well. Program people were "converted" to contract management; they were often left to learn contract management skills on the job, with little if any training or professional development on the subjects of quality control and contract monitoring. There are extensive coordination and management costs associated with the contracts, and the coordination and management of information systems posed significant problems.

Study Findings

Finding 1: Despite their participation in the contract decision process, it is often the case that neither the state agency nor the contracting organization is prepared for the changes required under the contract arrangement.

All parties seem to fully understand the elements of a good contract, but executing a contract proves to be surprisingly difficult for all parties involved. Participants often underestimate the time required to design, implement, and work out the contract. Contractors reported, in hindsight, that they had "no clue" what they were getting into regarding the scope of programs, costs, and accountability obligations.

Implementation of the contract is likely to entail an iterative policy decision process. The implementation of the contract results in consecutive rounds of negotiation and "give and take" that continue as the contract is implemented. This iterative process allows both parties to the contract to address new policy issues that inevitably emerge during the startup phase; however, issues continue to change as the contract matures.

Parties underestimate the "mechanics" of the implementation process. Contract management capacity is usually sorely tested, partly as the result of complications for which parties to the contract are not prepared. The "devilish details" challenge all contractual parties. For example, DOA has all the responsibility and none of the authority to administer Medicaid case management services. The statutory requirement that SRS remain the single Medicaid contact agency has placed a barrier to the free flow of communication between DOA, the agency managing the program, and HCFA, the federal funding agency.

There are dramatic impacts on all parties to the contracts—impacts that require major institutional adjustments. Common themes emerge across programs, including contractor surprise at government regulatory requirements, information systems problems, resistance to change among some state agency staff, and coordination burdens (such as weekly meetings and phone tag) for both parties to the contract.[28] Many contractors reported difficulty finding qualified staff.

It is difficult to guard against bureaucratic drift and the "governmentalization" of some contracting organizations, particularly nonprofits. Although the state may initially contract with a nonprofit advocacy and service organization, over time that organization is likely to evolve into a new and different agency partly in response to the new contract and to related revenue concerns.[29] These nonprofits have become more "government" like in their operations. On the other hand, state contract managers must also be prepared for the development of more "businesslike" behaviors and attitudes on the part of the contractors. Contracting agency staff may shift to strategies designed to enhance "billable hours." For example, one contract agency director instructed staff to "think like attorneys" when billing hours under the contract. These contracting agency adjustments require corresponding adjustments on the part of state contract management staff. As contracting organizations respond to incentives, they may develop in ways that undermine the very traits that made them attractive as contractors.

Finding 2: Genuine goodwill often exists between the state and most contracting organizations.

Most state and contractor staff exhibit goodwill to one another. There is a sense of shared mission among policy professionals. Most parties to the contracts use words like "team" and "partnership." All parties to these contracts favor a collaborative approach to contracting. Parties to the contract note that "we're all friends here." Contractors dealing with more than one state reported positive feelings about dealing with Kansas social services staff, and felt that Kansas staff try hard to work with contractor concerns. Staffs at both the state agencies responsible for managing the contracts and the contracting agencies share common commitments to serving the targeted populations.

A shared professional service mission does not make up for insufficient resources or inadequate planning, nor does it overcome the disjoint between the government agencies accustomed to dealing with regulations and the contractor staff who are used to more flexibility. This is especially challenging for Medicaid and other intergovernmental programs, which are highly regulated.

Finding 3: Neither the state agency nor the contracting organization is able to accurately project program costs.

State policy reformers found it difficult to accurately project costs for the contracted services. These officials frequently did not have good initial figures on the real cost of providing the programs, partly due to the cross-subsidies often built into state program administration and to pressures to live within budgets. Initial figures generated are often "guesstimates" and result in unrealistic contract cost projections.

The cost-saving motive that drives much of state contracting also contributes to state cost estimates erring on the low side. Both state agencies and contractors tend to underestimate necessary resource investments. State pressures on contract reimbursement rates, especially if they result in unrealistically low rates, are likely to constrain contractor performance. For example, some contractors have had to cover short-term deficits with reserves. This is a real hardship for many of the service-oriented organizations that seek to contract with the state. At the same time, investment in state staff preparation for contract management is likely to be minimized in order to reduce costs. This combination is one that is likely to generate serious complications for all parties to the contract.

The monetary costs associated with administrative adaptation and coordination under contracting tend to be underestimated by the state and by contracting organizations. Examples include staff training, contract management activity, and consultation time in which state and contracting organization staff interact during and after the implementation phase.

Costs tend to become more visible under contracting because nonprofits and other nongovernmental organizations typically have more experience in costing out their services and have a greater incentive to do so.

Several of these contracts use a "one size fits all" cost approach. For example, the AAAs all receive the same case management reimbursement rate, despite substantial variations in staff and other program costs in different areas of the state.[30]

Tensions between the state and contracting organizations are higher for those contracts that used a "fixed" reimbursement approach, which entails a shift of financial risk to the provider. In such cases, unanticipated costs are problematic and may generate ill will among parties to the contract. This has been especially evident in the contracts with HMOs for Medicaid managed-care services. HMO reimbursement rates are based on legislatively driven, pre-existing fee-for-service rates for individual health care services, such as newborn delivery, and are regularly adjusted through actuarial analyses. SRS and the HMO staff agree that the HMO reimbursement rates are woefully inadequate. On the other hand, contracts involving reimbursement on a for-service basis, such as the provider agreements for employment preparation services, generate fewer conflicts, but may be less likely to produce reliable cost savings.

Without realistic cost/benefit assessments that factor in the full (or more realistic) costs, it is extremely difficult to assess whether contracting generates cost savings.

Finding 4: The need for training in contract management/contract monitoring is often underestimated.

Because contracting is often undertaken in response to budgetary pressures, the state is typically not in an investment mode and is loath to invest the resources necessary to train contract management staff to monitor performance.

Most state contract management and monitoring staff are former program personnel; their familiarity with clients and services facilitates their assessment of contractor performance. But as former program staff they can sometimes have difficulty shifting from a service mentality to a monitoring mindset. Ironically, their familiarity with the program may interfere with their oversight of the contract.

Contract management training is particularly important in an environment devoid of provider competition. In such cases, contract managers are in an especially weak position with regard to contract enforcement.

Development of performance measures is slow. There is a temptation to rely on easier process and paperwork reviews rather than outcomes. This, in essence, substitutes a public bureaucracy with an increasingly bureaucratized nongovernmental organization.

The dynamics of performance evaluation and contract enforcement may conflict with a partnership arrangement between state agencies and contractors.

Finding 5: Contracting decisions and implementation processes are infused with political considerations.

Most contracting decisions are driven by political imperatives to contract out as many state social services as possible. These imperatives flowed from both the former governor's administration and from the legislature. Despite the absence of provider competition for many of the contracted services, the state has forged ahead with many contracting initiatives.

A substantial portion of contracting activity results from legislative antipathy toward SRS, which has been perceived as too large, unwieldy, and insufficiently accountable to the legislature. Several SRS officials commented that they could get the legislature to fund service contracts, but could not get adequate funding for the programs if they continued to be provided in-house. This observation holds across all programs reviewed for this chapter, as well as for other contracted services, such as foster care and adoption.[31]

Several contracting decisions have moved very quickly, in part to head off potential political resistance from interest groups, opposing legislators, and others. This speed has given rise to several complications in contract implementation and management for both the state and contracting agencies.[32]

Finding 6: Contracting problems arise when there are only a few available service providers.

For most of these contracted services, only one or two potential providers exist. As a result, many of the benefits associated with competition among providers are absent, such as comparisons regarding acceptable contractor costs and performance. Without competition, contract management becomes much more difficult for government overseers. Typically, state contract managers do not have complete information about the possibilities and constraints within the contracting agency environment; as a result, state monitors are not well situated to urge greater operational efficiencies on contractors.[33]

The pressure to contract out means that the state is sometimes desperate to seek and retain contractors. This can lead to contracts with providers who have not had to withstand close scrutiny by state administrators regarding their capacity to provide services and meet performance expectations. In some cases, in the interest of obtaining multiple proposals, the state has asked providers to consider contracting with the state despite doubt on both sides that the provider is capable of meeting performance expectations.

The provider agreements for welfare employment preparation services, which are far less formal, more closely resemble the idealized market environment in which there are multiple providers available to provide the service. In such instances, if one provider proves to be inadequate, other contractors are available for the state to recruit. These provider agreements, which are highly decentralized and which build on relationships between local service providers and regional staff offices, rely on process measures and are limited to discrete components of the total employment program. There is no "one size fits all" approach to these agreements, and state retention of services in-house is a viable option frequently used, especially in rural western Kansas, where few nongovernmental providers exist.

Finding 7: Contract relationships can create problems of accountability.

All contract parties appear to have strong commitments to ensuring accountability for contract performance. The iterative policy implementation process gives contractor organizations the opportunity to influence state policy and the contract accountability mechanisms used to assess their performance.

Contractor organizations face high costs related to complying with the regulations inherent in most intergovernmental social service programs. Reporting requirements are mentioned by all contracting organizations as costly, both in terms of staff time and related administrative burdens such as information systems compliance. These issues are particularly salient for the two Medicaid program reforms.

All parties need better understanding and implementation of accountability measures. Contractors are "shocked by the [state's] scrutiny and need for accountability," and some contractors in programs that we did not include in our study indicate that SRS officials "were impossible to work with in a businesslike manner" (Shields, 1999). Contractors sometimes expect total privatization of the service and cannot understand why the state retains regulatory and monitoring authority.

Subcontracting arrangements complicate contractor performance and state contract management. For example, contractors providing administrative oversight for the state's Medicaid managed-care program interact directly with HMO contractors in order to obtain data required for performance studies and to facilitate other contractual oversight activities. As a result, HMO contractors feel that their compliance burdens are duplicated by the need to communicate with both the state agency and the administrative oversight contractors. On the other hand, administrative contractor performance is dependent on HMO performance and cooperation in order to provide required performance reports to the state. If any of the parties are not performing, the system breaks down. Similarly, AAA case management for the Medicaid elderly is affected by the quality of care offered by in-home service providers, yet these providers contract with a different state agency and are not accountable to the case managers. Consequently, when case managers observe poor-quality in-home care, they have limited ability to rectify the situation.

Reliance on advanced information systems to reduce costs and increase accountability is an unreliable strategy. Nearly all parties report serious difficulties with information systems. And it always takes longer to get new information systems up and running than projected. These difficulties include adjustments to new systems, requirements to create new reporting systems, staff training on the new systems, and coordination between existing systems in contracting organizations and state systems.

From the perspective of contracting agencies, there has been too much emphasis on process and paperwork compliance and not enough on output or outcomes measures.

Finding 8: Contracting with advocacy organizations may be "too" successful.

State agencies tend to simultaneously provide services and act as gatekeepers that ration services. Advocacy organizations, on the other hand, are likely to adopt highly successful outreach mechanisms in order to maximize service provision to needy clients. This approach may threaten cost savings associated with the contract. As a result, the Kansas legislature "capped" the Medicaid frail elderly program and, because of budget constraints, instituted waiting lists for eligible elderly in need of in-home services. The legislative response was driven in part by the unanticipated growth in eligible elderly Medicaid clients. However, the legislature was challenged by a wide range of advocates for the elderly and has been forced to reconsider its decision. This experience underscores the point that the political consequences of budget cutting are very different when the budgets affect advocacy organizations as opposed to government agencies.

Recommendations

The findings reported give rise to several recommendations for governments considering the contracting option for the provision of social services.

Recommendation 1: Take enough time in contracting decisions to adequately consider program design, staff, and cost factors, and to identify state and contractor responsibilities.

Speedy decisions can yield reasons for regret on both sides of the contract. In considering decisions to contract out, it would be helpful to make sure the "rationale" for the reform has some basis in the reality of the contracting plan. For example, if the proposed contracting rationale is to save money, have firm cost estimates in hand before making the decision to contract. Likewise, if the proposal is to downsize an agency, have plans for reductions-in-force in place, including some understanding of who will do the work that remains to be done after the downsizing is complete. If the proposal anticipates the need for contractors to hire new staff, have analyses of workforce availability and detailed staffing plans in hand before shifting responsibilities to contractors.

If accurate cost projections are not available, the contracting decision needs to be subjected to extraordinary scrutiny and extended planning. If accurate cost and caseload projections are not possible, then the government needs to rethink the decision to pursue contracting. Realistic cost/benefit assessments are important to both the state and the contracting organizations.

Once the decision is made to contract out for a service, contracting agencies need to undertake substantial planning regarding the necessary funding and program changes that the reform will entail. This is especially important in the area of identifying responsibilities.

Recommendation 2: Avoid the one-size-fit-all approach to contract design.

While it is tempting to try to build upon the experience of other states that have engaged in similar contracting programs or use uniform statewide reimbursement rates, be sure to tailor the contract specifications to accommodate any important regional and/or unique policy circumstances.

Recommendation 3: Performance expectations for both state agencies and contractors should be negotiated in advance of awarding the contract.

States must be reconciled to some loss of control over program performance.

Contractors need to recognize that they will have more regulations and different accountability relationships even if the program is promoted under the rubric of privatization.

Both state agencies and contractors must carefully consider the disruptions likely when high-tech information systems are planned as a way to monitor performance with reduced staff. Problems in the development and implementation of complex information systems are common.

Recommendation 4: Examine all costs.

When estimating contracting costs, factor in increased costs due to contract management, training, and accountability requirements for the contractor.

Expect high administrative costs for administrative adaptation and coordination. Recognize the importance of investing in training for state contract management staff and budget for it.

Former program staff will need training to develop new attitudes, language, and skills to effectively perform their new contract management duties.

Recommendation 5: Identify the presence of multiple providers with both the fiscal and administrative capacity to provide the service.

States seeking contracting partners need to identify an adequate number of providers to insure a competitive provider environment. Otherwise, contracting could merely shift from a governmental monopoly of service provision to a private provider monopoly.

Organizations that face viable competition for the government contract will face greater pressure to be responsive and to perform efficiently and effectively.

Recommendation 6: State agencies and contractors need to examine and project financial consequences of contract proposals that shift risks from the government to the contractor.

All parties to such contracts should have contingency plans regarding funds and staff. In addition, the state needs to develop contingency plans in the event of contractor failure.

Postscript

Since this report was originally published in 2000, the political landscape for contracting in the state of Kansas has changed. A Democratic governor who previously served as state insurance commissioner replaced the former Republican governor, who served the maximum two terms and was a strong supporter of privatization. Kansas politics continues to be split three ways among conservative Republicans, moderate Republicans, and Democrats. The state fiscal situation is under severe strain. State agencies faced modest recisions in FY 2003, and the state faces a revenue shortfall for FY03 and

FY04, with little political will to raise taxes. Since a significant portion of the state's discretionary spending is in the area of social services, these programs have faced cuts, resulting in reduced services for many individuals and waiting lists for others. Due to budget cuts, the state Department of Social and Rehabilitation Services is contemplating consolidating its area offices.

Since the research published in this chapter was written, we have extended our research into another area of social services contracting: foster care and adoption. These contracts put the state of Kansas in the national forefront in social services contracting and were very controversial in their design and implementation. There have been significant consequences for contractors in this policy area, with several well-respected, faith-based nonprofit institutions encountering substantial financial difficulties providing foster care and adoption services under the state contracts. Two of the five contractors declared bankruptcy after absorbing multi-million-dollar costs associated with providing services under the state contracts. When it became apparent that the reimbursements were inadequate, the state allocated major balloon payments to help contractors with their financial difficulties. As a result, the state's cost for these contracts has risen by a significant factor.

The state of Kansas has continued most of its social service contracts. Some of the enthusiasm for contracting has been tempered by the experiences of the state and the contractors with implementation difficulties and the recognition that contracting typically does not reduce costs. The state has discovered that contract management poses challenges that are different from administering the programs directly. And the contractors continue to deal with the reality that although state contracts allow nonprofits to expand the reach of their services, the contracts present serious complications.

The contracts between the state's Department of Aging and the 11 Area Agencies on Aging for home and community-based services for the frail elderly described in this chapter are now firmly established. The state and AAAs continue to negotiate about federal and state regulations that are not adequately stipulated in the contracts. Static state funding levels for these contracts, combined with a growing client base, have resulted in waiting lists for clients needing services.

SRS continues to rely on provider agreements for welfare-related employment preparation services that are negotiated and administered by local offices. These offices find that, while paperwork associated with provider agreements has been reduced, the administrative burdens associated with the provider agreements have intensified. The state did not continue its pilot contract for comprehensive employment preparation services with a for-profit corporation. While the contract with the for-profit corporation was deemed to be working well and meeting the needs of the clients, it was considered too costly per individual. Instead the state now relies on provider agreements to purchase services from local nonprofits. Compared to the comprehensive pilot contract, the state spends an equal or greater amount for services, and outcomes are less positive.

Contracts for Medicaid managed care services have expanded to incorporate a model that combines Medicaid and the State Child Health Insurance Program (SCHIP). There is still only one HMO contractor, and although contract terms and administration are stable, the HMO continues to face challenges in terms of recruiting and retaining health care providers. The administrative contractor for enrollment and other services has changed. Blue Cross Blue Shield of Kansas opted not to bid to continue its contract with the state, and EDS is the current contractor. The quality assurance and management contract remains with the Kansas Foundation for Medical Care.

In sum, many of the lessons learned in our initial research are still relevant, and the contracting culture has become firmly established in the state's social services community. However, both the state and the nonprofit sector have come to the realization that, contrary to expectations, contracting raises many challenges and does not solve some of the fundamental problems in providing social services. There have not been any new initiatives to do contracting of any kind since the child welfare contracting of the mid-1990s. Adequate funding remains a key issue, and competitive contracting is difficult to achieve and sustain. Kansas administrators, together with nonprofit administrators, continue to work together to deal with this new environment.

Jocelyn M. Johnston
Barbara S. Romzek
May 2003

Appendix: Research Method

For each of the five contract program areas covered in this chapter, we interviewed numerous state agency officials and managers, and contracting agency employees. The state officials included key state administrators within the Kansas Department of Social and Rehabilitation Services and the Kansas Department on Aging, the Kansas Performance Review Board, the Kansas Department of Administration, the Kansas Legislative Division of Post Audit, the regional federal Health Care Financing Administration office, and key members of the legislature, including members on committees charged with overseeing these contracting initiatives. Other state officials included administrative and case management staff in SRS area offices around the state. Among the contracting agencies' staffs, we interviewed Area Agencies on Aging directors and case managers, representatives of a Medicaid HMO and the Medicaid administrative contractors. We also interviewed staff from agencies that provide employment preparation services through provider agreements, as well as staff from the organization with the state contract for a comprehensive employment preparation service program.

Our analysis is based on 75 interviews conducted over a two-year period. (The interviews were conducted in four waves: spring 1997, fall 1997, fall 1998, and spring-summer 1999). The IBM Endowment partially funded 33 of these interviews, all of which were conducted in the spring and summer of 1999. These latest interviews included follow-up work on earlier contract program areas and the addition of two new contract program areas to broaden our analysis.

Using semi-structured personal interviews, we asked members of each group of administrators and staff (state, contracting agency, etc.) to respond to a standard list of questions designed to identify key issues in the contract. We also sought assessments of their understanding of the contracts, including the contracting decision process, performance oversight features, and state and agency capacity for managing the contracts. To supplement the interview data, we obtained and reviewed a number of relevant administrative and legislative documents concerning the contracts. The use of both types of data enabled us to better understand the impetus for the actual contracting decision, as well as its execution.

Endnotes

1. Funding from the IBM Endowment for The Business of Government enabled the authors to expand previous research in this area, which was partially funded by the Rockefeller Institute of Government's State Capacity Study through the W. K. Kellogg Foundation and the University of Kansas (General Research Fund #2301148).

2 Although the terms "contracting" and "privatization" are used throughout this chapter, we note that state officials frequently refer to contracting for social services as "privatization." True privatization would entail a complete shift of responsibility and financing for a program to a nongovernmental agency. In the Kansas cases, the state retained ultimate responsibility for the contracted services.

3. For example, in the mid 1980s, Kansas had a greater percentage of its population over the age of 65 living in nursing homes than all but two other states, and the average functioning level of those residents was relatively high, suggesting that expensive institutional care was probably inappropriate for many of the residents. The state doubled its expenditures on nursing homes between 1985 and 1989, despite the fact that its per diem nursing home costs were below average. In addition, Kansas had one of the oldest populations: it ranked fifth in terms of percent of the population age 85 and older (Johnston, Davis and Fox, 1998).

4. These include Adult and Medical Services (which administers Medicaid and other health programs); Employment and Economic Support (which administers most components of TANF, including employment preparation services); Children and Family Services (which administers foster care and adoption services, which have been extensively "privatized"); Alcohol and Drug Abuse Services; Mental Health/Developmental Disabilities Services; Rehabilitation Services; and Administrative Services.

5. Our research covers the period ending in the fall of 1999. It is important to note that developments in late 1999 and early 2000 indicate that state decision-makers are looking more critically at contracting. A number of highly visible problems, particularly in the areas of state contracts for foster care and adoption services, have led to executive and legislative review of contracting. In addition, a controversial state contract for consultant services to the Kansas Department on Aging raised the profile of contracting in general. This contract was rescinded, and the political fallout from the contract led to the resignation of the Secretary of Aging. The combination of this incident and the foster care and adoption problems has slowed the inclination for state contracting.

6. The SRS Grants and Contracts Unit was created recently, partially in response to a study by the Legislative Division of Post Audit that criticized SRS' grants and contracting activity. The study noted that SRS had no central registry of agency grants and contracts, that it sometimes paid grantees and contractors without verifying that services had been delivered, and that grant and contract monitoring activities were inadequate (Legislative Post Audit, 1995).

7. Our interviews indicate that the Department of Administration has historically viewed itself as a service—not a regulatory—agency. The culture of the agency would preclude interference in other agency decisions. Department of Administration staff would not be inclined to tell other agency secretaries that they could not or should not engage in a particular contract.

8. The Division of Legislative Post Audit staff have been substantially influenced by a "privatization" guide used by the Colorado State Auditor's Office. Post Audit's assessment of Kansas contracting decisions relies heavily on the Colorado model (see State of Colorado Office of State Auditor, 1989).

9. AAAs were created under the federal Older Americans Act of 1965. The traditional role of the AAAs has been to serve as local facilitators and coordinators for state and federally funded elderly assistance programs. Eight of the Kansas AAAs are certified nonprofit agencies; three are county agencies that receive stipulated portions of property tax revenues in addition to the state and federal funds received by all AAAs.

10. The state initially reimbursed for case management services at a rate of $30 an hour. After several AAAs reported severe difficulties providing case management at those rates, and one came close to financial failure, the reimbursement rate was increased by 33 percent, to $40 an hour.

11. Shifting the case management services from SRS to DOA and the AAAs required the layoff of SRS caseworkers. Several former SRS caseworkers remained in state employment in the newly created DOA Medicaid quality reviewer positions. As a result, many of the reviewers were monitoring AAA case managers who had, in effect, assumed their former jobs and served their former elderly Medicaid clients. Early in the contract, this dynamic created some resentment on both sides of the contract: some former SRS caseworkers were dissatisfied with the AAA case management services, and some of the AAA case managers resented the oversight of former SRS caseworkers. This was especially problematic in the few AAAs that insisted on higher education and experience standards for their case managers, relative to those that had been required for SRS case managers.

12. The HCFA authorized direct care services for the Medicaid elderly include 1. adult day care; 2. wellness monitoring; 3. respite care; 4. sleep cycle support; 5. medical and non-medical attendant care; 6. residential personal care; and 7. medical alert devices.

13. The in-home care providers do not contract directly with the AAAs or with DOA. Their contracts are negotiated directly with SRS, and are administered by Blue Cross and Blue Shield of Kansas in its role as Medicaid fiscal agent contractor for the state. Furthermore, in-home care providers are licensed by the Kansas Department of Health and Environment.

14. *HealthConnect* is a primary care case management (PCCM) program in which physicians are paid a monthly case management fee for each Medicaid patient, but are reimbursed on a fee-for-service basis for all health services provided to that patient. Capitated HMOs, on the other hand, provide managed care through a pre-paid monthly arrangement; the HMO receives a monthly payment from the state for each enrolled Medicaid client, and the HMO must use that payment to cover all costs of care for that client.

15. Low reimbursement rates and high administrative burdens preclude provider participation and competition for the state's business, as demonstrated by the withdrawal of all but one commercial HMO from the state's Medicaid program.

16. Many HMOs have terminated state Medicaid contracts recently (Abelson, 1998; Steinhauer, 1998). In Kansas, this trend is complicated by the fact that the state never had many HMOs to begin with.

17. These efforts included mandated HMO enrollment for all Medicaid recipients in the seven counties covered by more than one HMO. In these counties, the non-capitated managed-care option was eliminated for welfare-related Medicaid enrollees. This measure was designed to maximize HMO market share of Medicaid clients in these counties.

18. Most training for the managed-care staff has been obtained informally, often from the contractors themselves. Some staff attend professional conferences, where they are able to obtain management information from the staffs of other states. Periodic HCFA regional training conferences share "best practices" among the states in the region. In

addition, funds have been authorized to subscribe to some professional publications and journals that serve managed-care professionals.

19. In most state Medicaid programs, HMOs submit encounter data to document treatment of Medicaid clients. Encounter data is used to simulate claims submitted by fee-for-service Medicaid health care providers.

20. Blue Cross and Blue Shield of Kansas is reimbursed on a per enrollee basis for its Medicaid HMO oversight and administrative services contract. Reimbursement rates were re-negotiated in the second year of the contract because of the drop in Medicaid enrollments (most likely attributable to declining welfare caseloads experienced in Kansas and many other states after the enactment of PRWORA). KFMC is reimbursed on a flat rate based on the number of active Kansas Medicaid HMO contracts. With only one current HMO contract, compared to the three contracts that existed in 1998, KFMC Medicaid contract revenues have declined.

21. Most states have faced substantial difficulties in collecting data from capitated Medicaid HMOs. According to Landon et al (1998), twenty-two states reported collecting encounter data in 1996, but many "lacked the ability to analyze meaningfully encounter data from multiple health plans, " indicating that the capacity to engage in access, quality, and utilization comparison among plans continues to elude most state Medicaid contract managers.

22. KFMC submitted a low bid for its contract with SRS and consequently had a lean staff. KFMC officials were comfortable relying on informal negotiations to work out performance expectations. But turnover within SRS meant that it was difficult for KFMC to maintain long-term interpersonal relationships, and SRS developed little institutional memory regarding informally negotiated agreements about performance expectations. As a result, KFMC often had to resort to reviewing minutes of meetings to document agreements regarding expectations.

23. President Clinton visited Wichita in November 1997, and hailed the 21st Street program as a "model for the nation" (McLean 1997).

24. Collaborators in the Wichita employment services network pride themselves on avoiding written rules and using common sense. But, as one Wichita area office official put it, both the providers and area office staff are always careful to "act as if [ABC's investigative news show] 20/20 were going to investigate."

25. Curtis receives $1,000 for each client placed in a 30 hour-per-week job, and generous bonuses are included at the end of 180 days of sustained employment, and also for jobs with starting wages that exceed $6 per hour or that include medical benefits.

26. This sentiment has been echoed for other service contracts as well. A highly visible example is provided by SRS contracts for foster care services. Contractors have recently engaged in widely noted lobbying in the legislature for contract reimbursement increases from the state. In the 1999 session, the legislature agreed to increase rates by 47 percent from the previous year, from $68 million to $100 million (McLean, 1999). Many former and current SRS employees, and several interest group observers note that had those resources been allocated to SRS, the agency probably could have provided the services more effectively without the painful disruptions that have plagued the contract.

27. No one trained the area office staff member dedicated to managing the contract; she just used "common sense." However, she was guided by a supervisor who had come from the private sector and was familiar with performance measurement, and who was determined to use a performance contract model.

28. For example, once the AAAs took on the Medicaid case management program, AAA caseloads ballooned in size, resulting in significant jolts to the organizational culture, both positive and negative. AAA missions have been distorted by size, clientele

needs, and the regulatory demands of Medicaid. Increased caseloads required accelerated new hires and those new hires brought higher levels of professionalism to the AAA staff.

29. The AAAs, for example, now find that their former service orientation has been altered by their assumption of the Medicaid case management program, which accounts for up to 50 percent of their budgets and a large portion of their staffs.

30. The state's initial reimbursement rate did not allow for AAA case manager travel time, yet in some rural parts of the state, case managers had to travel great distances to see their elderly clients. Over time, this cost issue has been addressed by allowing the AAAs to count travel time as client contact time eligible for reimbursement.

31. The SRS secretary's decision to "privatize" foster care and adoption services was motivated in part by recognition that legislative funding for foster care caseload reductions would not materialize, and that the only way to obtain the resources from the legislature necessary to increase program effectiveness was to "privatize."

32. The state's decision to "privatize" foster care and adoption services has followed this pattern. The SRS secretary purposely accelerated the contracting decision in order to head off potential opposition.

33. For example, in the area of Medicaid managed care, the limited number of HMOs willing to participate in the program reduces the enforcement position of state contract management staff.

Bibliography

Abelson, Reed (1998). "Oxford health posts big loss for 2nd quarter," *New York Times*, August 12.

DeHoog, Ruth H. (1984). *Contracting for Human Services: Economic, Political and Organizational Perspectives*. (Albany: State University of New York Press).

Fox, Michael H., Jocelyn Johnston, Raymond Davis, Robert Lee, Mary Zimmerman, Janice Moore and Kara Lindaman (1998). "An Evaluation of the Medicaid Managed Care Program in Kansas." Research report submitted to the Kansas Department of Social and Rehabilitation Services, June.

Governor's Budget Report, State of Kansas, Fiscal Years 1993-1998.

Johnston, Jocelyn M. (2000). "Implementing Medicaid Managed Care in Kansas: Politics, Economics and Contracting," *Case Studies in Medicaid Managed Care*, The Rockefeller Institute of Government, Albany, N.Y.

Johnston, Jocelyn M. and Barbara S. Romzek (1999). "Contracting and accountability in state Medicaid reform: Rhetoric, theories, and reality," *Public Administration Review*, September/October, 59, 5: 383-399.

Johnston, Jocelyn M. and Kara Lindaman (1998). "Implementing Welfare Reform in Kansas: Moving, But Not Racing," *Publius*, Summer, 28, 3: 123-142.

Johnston, Jocelyn M., Raymond Davis and Michael Fox (1998). "Medicaid Reform in Kansas: A Cautious Approach," in Mark R. Daniels, ed., *Medicaid Reform and the American States*. (Westport, Conn.: Auburn House).

Kansas Performance Review Board, 1998. *Performance Review Methodology*. September 22.

Kettl, Donald F. (1993). *Sharing Power: Public Governance and Private Markets* (Washington, D.C.: The Brookings Institution).

Landon, Bruce, Carol Tobias and Arnold Epstein (1998). "Quality management by state Medicaid agencies converting to managed care," JAMA, 279, 3, 1/21/98: 211-16.

Legislative Division of Post Audit, 1999. *Performance Audit Report: Reviewing In-Home Services to Elderly Kansas: A K-GOAL Audit of the Department of Aging*, 99-04, A Report to the Legislative Post Audit Committee, State of Kansas, February.

Legislative Division of Post Audit, 1996. *Performance Audit Report: Reviewing State Contracting for Consultants and other Professional and Technical Services*, 96-38, A Report to the Legislative Post Audit Committee, State of Kansas, March.

Legislative Division of Post Audit, 1995. *Examining Contract Oversight by the Department of Social and Rehabilitation Services*, 95-52, A Report to the Legislative Post Audit Committee, State of Kansas, July.

McLean, Jim. 1997. "Graves agreeable to bailout of foster care and adoption," *Topeka Capital-Journal*, March 14.

McLean, Jim. 1997. "Clinton Hails Cessna Program," *Topeka Capital-Journal*, November 18.

Myers, Roger. 1997. "SRS is Losing its 'Monster' Image," *Topeka Capital-Journal*, July 23.

Nathan, Richard P. et al (1996). "The 'nonprofitization movement' as a form of devolution," in *Capacity for Change? The Nonprofit World in the Age of Devolution*. Indiana University Center on Philanthropy.

Rehfuss, John (1990). "Contracting out and accountability in state and local governments: The importance of contract monitoring," *State and Local Government Review*, Winter: 44-48.

Romzek, Barbara S. and Jocelyn M. Johnston (2000). "Reforming State Social Services through Contracting: Linking Implementation and Organizational Culture" in *Public Management: New Developments in Theory, Methods, and Practice*, Jeffrey Brudney, Laurence O'Toole, Jr., and Hal B. Rainey, eds. (Washington, D.C.: Georgetown University Press).

Romzek, Barbara S. and Jocelyn M. Johnston (1999). "Reforming Medicaid through contracting: The nexus of implementation and organizational culture," *Journal of Public Administration Theory and Research*, 9, 1, January: 107-140.

Roper, Richard W. (1998). "A shifting landscape: Contracting for welfare services in New Jersey," *Rockefeller Reports*, December 23, The Nelson Rockefeller Institute of Government, Albany, N.Y.

Savas, E.S. (2000). *Privatization and public-private partnerships*. (New York : Chatham House).

Savas, E.S. (1987). *Privatization: The Key to Better Government*. (Chatham, N.J.: Chatham House Publishers.)

Savas, E.S. (1982). *Privatizing the Public Sector: How to Shrink Government*. (Chatham, N.J.: Chatham House Publishers).

Shields, Mike (1999), "Contractor: Working with SRS 'Impossible'," *Lawrence Journal-World*, May 30.

Smart, Tim (1998). "Humana to scale back HMO plans; Move will affect some Medicare and Medicaid patients," The *Washington Post*, September 16.

Smith, Steven Rathgeb and Judith Smyth (1996). "Contracting for services in a decentralized system," *Journal of Public Administration Research and Theory*, April, 6: 277-296.

Smith, Steven Rathgeb and Michael Lipsky (1993). *Nonprofits for Hire: The Welfare State in the Age of Contracting*. (Cambridge, Mass.: Harvard University Press).

State of Colorado Office of State Auditor, 1989. *Privatization Assessment Workbook*. Denver.

Wallin, Bruce (1997). "The need for a privatization process: Lessons from development and implementation," *Public Administration Review*, 57, 1, January/February: 11-20.

Weisbrod, Burton A. (1997). "The future of the nonprofit sector: Its entwining with private enterprise and government," *Journal of Policy Analysis and Management*, Fall, 16, 4: 541-55.

Winterbottom, Colin, David Liska and Karen Obermaier (1995). *State-Level Databook on Health Care Access and Financing*, Second Edition and Supplement. (Washington, D.C.: The Urban Institute).

CHAPTER SIX

Religious Organizations, Anti-Poverty Relief, and Charitable Choice: A Feasibility Study of Faith-Based Welfare Reform in Mississippi

John P. Bartkowski
Associate Professor of Sociology
Department of Sociology, Anthropology, & Social Work
Mississippi State University

Helen A. Regis
Assistant Professor of Anthropology
Department of Geography & Anthropology
Louisiana State University

This report was originally published in November 1999, revised May 2003.

Introduction

Background: Welfare Reform and the Emergence of Charitable Choice

Although policy experts hardly agree on the merits of recent welfare reform legislation, many would concur that the Personal Responsibility and Work Opportunity Reconciliation Act (PRWORA) has dramatically changed the face of public assistance programs in at least two ways. First, PRWORA replaced Aid to Families with Dependent Children (AFDC) with Temporary Assistance to Needy Families (TANF). In contrast to the virtually unlimited assistance provided by entitlement-based AFDC, TANF provides strict time limits on the disbursement of federal funds to needy families. Among its other provisions, TANF requires adults to work for pay within 24 months after they begin receiving assistance. Second, PRWORA has altered the avenues available for the disbursement of temporary assistance funds.

Consistent with the philosophy of political devolution, welfare reform provides states and, ostensibly, local communities with greater autonomy in the distribution of public assistance monies. PRWORA provides states with a federal allocation of block grants—i.e., a fixed annual sum of federal monies which are dispersed to state governments and then matched by state funds. Champions of political devolution charge that creative and effective relief programs are more likely to be conceived and implemented by local officials who understand the unique dynamics of their communities more intimately than distant officials in Washington.

Because of the discretionary latitude associated with block grants, a provision in PRWORA called "charitable choice" (Title I, Section 104) requires that states who contract with local nonprofit organizations for social service delivery to include religious communities as potential contractees in the competitive awarding of block grant funds (see *A Guide to Charitable Choice* 1997; Chaves 1999; Sherwood 1998). The rudiments of charitable choice legislation are discussed in the accompanying sidebar, "What is Charitable Choice?"

Although charitable choice was introduced into the 1996 welfare reform law by former Missouri Senator John Ashcroft (now Attorney General of the United States), it was Marvin Olasky's *The Tragedy of American Compassion* (1992) that initially catapulted the prospect of faith-based welfare reform into the public consciousness. Supporters of charitable choice such as Olasky contend that religious organizations will be more effective providers of social services than government agencies because of both the grassroots character of congregations and the unambiguous moral values they embrace.

In 2000, Presidential hopefuls from both parties—Al Gore and George W. Bush—supported charitable choice. This initiative has attracted forceful

What is Charitable Choice?

Charitable choice became law as part of the 1996 welfare reform legislation, the Personal Responsibility and Work Opportunity Reconciliation Act (PRWORA) (see *A Guide to Charitable Choice* 1997). As outlined in Section 104 of PRWORA, state governments that opt to contract with independent-sector social service providers cannot legally exclude faith-based organizations from consideration simply because these organizations are religious in nature. Consequently, the language of "choice" in this legislation is designed to underscore the importance to giving religious congregations the same opportunities that secular nonprofit agencies enjoy in competing for purchase-of-service contracts with state governments. Furthermore, charitable choice aims to ensure that state governments cannot censor religious expression— i.e., religious symbols or practices—among faith-based organizations that are selected to provide state-funded social services.

Even as it protects the religious expression of faith-based organizations, charitable choice provisions in PRWORA are intended to preserve the civil and religious liberties of welfare recipients. Charitable choice provisions mandate that states which utilize religious congregations as social service providers offer welfare recipients the choice of receiving assistance from faith-based or secular organizations. Moreover, religious congregations that provide state-funded social services to the needy cannot legally force beneficiaries of such services to participate in religious practices. In the end, the charitable choice provisions found in Section 104 of PRWORA strive to manage the tension between several potentially competing aims: (1) the state's obligation to provide poverty relief without fostering welfare dependency; and (2) the protection of civil liberties for both religious communities and welfare recipients, such that religious organizations may be awarded government monies to provide public sector anti-poverty services along with guaranteed protections for the particular sensibilities (religious or secular) of welfare recipients.

criticism from civil libertarians, who worry about government-sponsored religious favoritism and faith-based proselytization with the use of public monies (e.g., Boston 1998; Pinkerton 1999; Fritz 1999). Other commentators question the practicality of this initiative in the late 20th century (e.g., Wolfe 1993), and some religious communities are leery of perceived government "intrusion" into faith-based relief work (e.g., Burger 1996; Jewish News 1999; Raasch 1999).

Interestingly, Mississippi was among the first states to implement a collaborative church-state anti-poverty program. Before the passage of charitable choice legislation in PRWORA, the governor's office in Mississippi implemented a statewide program called "Faith & Families of Mississippi" with the assistance of Mississippi's Department of Human Services. Attracting national attention (e.g., Harrison 1995a, 1995b; Yardley 1996), Faith & Families of Mississippi sought to have local religious congregations adopt needy families receiving welfare (*Faith & Families of Mississippi* nd-a, nd-b).

Ideally, a welfare family sponsored by its adoptive local church could use a combination of public administrative and faith-based resources to move from government assistance into stable, long-term employment. Mississippi's Department of Human Services currently utilizes former Governor Fordice's Faith & Families program as its primary means of implementing faith-based welfare reform within the state. Given growing federal momentum for charitable choice implementation, there is a chance that such efforts may be expanded. However, an official at Mississippi's Department of Human Services suggested that some theologically conservative congregations in Mississippi might remain leery of an anti-poverty alliance between churches and the government.

Study Objectives, Context, and Research Methodology

In light of welfare reform legislation and ongoing debates about charitable choice, this study aims to address one basic question: What are the potential advantages and disadvantages associated with utilizing rural religious communities as collaborative providers of social services previously disbursed by the state? Many studies suggest that religious communities can—and often do—provide their members and local needy populations with safety nets that buttress the effects of poverty and personal misfortune (e.g., Amato-von Hemert 1998; Ammerman, 1997; Eng and Hatch 1991; Harris 1995, 1996; Hogstel and Davis 1996; Humphrey 1980; Morrison 1991; Olson, Reis, Murphy, and Gehm 1988; Rawlings and Schrock 1996). Yet, are Mississippi religious communities in a position to expand current aid offerings or launch new service programs—perhaps with block grant monies—in an age of temporary public assistance? How, if at all, are such efforts expected to compare with public assistance programs offered by the state alone?

In one of the few previous studies of congregational orientations toward charitable choice, Chaves (1999) found that approximately one third of 1236 faith communities surveyed throughout the nation would consider participating in a charitable choice program. Liberal and moderate congregations, as well as African-American faith communities, were more likely to evaluate positively the prospects for charitable choice initiatives.

Our investigation extends Chaves' study by focusing specifically on the viability of rerouting welfare services through religious congregations in rural Mississippi (specifically the GTR). To this end, we conducted in-depth interviews with key informants (typically pastors) representing 30 religious communities in northeastern Mississippi.[1] Our analyses of these interviews are informed by ethnographic data (not analyzed here) culled from a subsample of four churches in the GTR.

The GTR connects three Mississippi counties (Oktibbeha, Lowndes, and Clay), and their respective county seats (Starkville, Columbus, and West Point). Columbus is the largest of these small cities, with a population of approximately 24,000 residents. Starkville has about 18,000 residents, while West Point has a population of just over 10,000 (Mississippi Population Data Sheet 1993).

Mississippi is populated by whites (63%) and blacks (36%) (Mississippi Population Data Sheet 1993). Within the GTR, Clay County is 53.3% black, whereas Lowndes (37.2% black) and Oktibbeha (34.3% black) conform more closely to the ethnic composition in the state. Clay is by far the most rural of the three counties (48% farmland), when compared with Lowndes and Oktibbeha counties (39% and 28% farmland, respectively).

Why Mississippi?

In several respects, Mississippi provides an ideal test case in which to examine the feasibility of faith-based welfare reform. Apart from the challenge of providing social services to a geographically dispersed rural population, a plethora of statistical indicators underscore the pervasiveness of poverty and public assistance use in Mississippi at large and, more specifically, throughout much of the GTR.

Nearly 20% of all Mississippians and 32% of all children in the state live in poverty (1996 Statistical Abstract; Kids Count Data Book 1998). About 17% of Mississippi children live in extreme poverty (i.e., household income under half the poverty level), an indicator that is almost double the national rate (9%) (Kids Count Data Book 1998).

Income disparities between Mississippi's GTR and the U.S. are quite striking. Analyses of 1990 census data reveal that households earning $5,000 or less annually are over 3.5 times more common in the GTR (8.26%) than in the nation at large (2.34%). (Within Mississippi as a whole, 7.89% of households earn $5,000 or less annually.) Mississippi as a whole ranks last among all states in per capita money income ($16,531) (1996 Statistical Abstract). It is for such reasons that some scholars have described Mississippi as the poorest state in the nation (Howell 1997).

In addition, Mississippi features one of the highest rates of public assistance use in the country. In 1992 and 1995, Mississippi led the nation in receipt of public assistance (AFDC and SSI) (11.8%) (1995 Statistical Abstract) and in receipt of food stamps (19.26%) (1997 Statistical Abstract), respectively. Strikingly, public assistance use rates for Mississippi (15 public assistance recipients per 100 non-recipients) and the GTR (14 recipients per 100 non-recipients) have been recorded at more than twice the national average (6.5 recipients per 100 non-recipients). Clay County (19 public assistance recipients per 100 non-recipients) far outpaced the other two GTR counties (12 recipients per 100 non-recipients in Oktibbeha and 13 recipients per 100 non-recipients in Lowndes) in terms of public assistance use rates.

The pervasiveness of poverty in Mississippi and the GTR is complemented by a thriving local religious economy. Like much of the South, Mississippi's religious institutions figure prominently into many aspects of local social life (see Boles 1972; Harrell 1981; Harvey 1997; Johnson and Jersild 1996; Stowell 1998; White, and White 1995 for treatments of religion in the South). Throughout the GTR, churches—mostly Protestant and, particularly, Baptist and Methodist congregations—dot the landscape. In some rural locales, churches are the key institution through which local communities define themselves and forge social bonds.

Pastors representing 30 different faith communities in and around the GTR area participated in the in-depth interview portion of this study. One pastor served two churches, and one church at which a religious leader was interviewed failed to return its pre-interview survey. Therefore, 29 interviews were conducted in all. Profile data on the congregations are provided in Appendix I. (See Appendix II for the pre-interview survey instrument.) Sampled congregations were selected on the basis of several criteria coupled with a sensitivity to local social dynamics:

- *ethnic diversity,* including 16 Anglo churches, 11 black churches, a local Muslim mosque, and an itinerant Catholic ministry to Hispanic migrants;
- *denominational diversity,* with purposive sampling designed to account for the predominance of Baptist [N=9] and Methodist [N=9] churches in this region of Mississippi; and
- *congregational characteristics,* including membership size (ranging widely from 26 to 1,800 total members) and locale (urban areas, small towns, and rural areas).

In-depth interviews (see Appendix III for questionnaire) were conducted with religious leaders by one or more members of our research team using a semi-structured format. Although purposive non-probability samples do not permit generalizations to be applied outside the sample frame, data derived from this research strategy have a high degree of internal validity. Consequently, these data enable us to examine the meanings, motivations, and social processes associated with faith-based aid-provision and charitable choice in ways not permitted by a large, statistically random survey sample, with special attention to congregational dynamics in poor, rural areas. Our analytical orientation toward these qualitative data is consistent with the principles of interpretive social inquiry for policy-based research (e.g., Roe 1994). We used an emergent themes technique to analyze our data in the hopes of capturing the richness and nuances of the information provided in the interviews.

Study Findings

What Types of Relief Do Local Religious Congregations Currently Provide?

Pre-interview survey data on relief-provision among our purposive sample of congregations in Mississippi's GTR reveal that religious communities provide diverse forms of aid to the needy among their membership and in the local community. In Table 6.1, we present the percentages of all sampled congregations that engage in particular types of relief efforts. Mindful that these figures are presented only as background data, the following forms of relief are most commonly provided by congregations in our study: rental payment assistance (59%); utility payment assistance (69%); as well as the provision of groceries (72%), clothing (52%), and counseling services of various sorts (55%).

Table 6.1 also reveals that there are some differences in services offered by white churches in our sample when compared with their black counterparts. Interestingly, black churches in our sample provide emergency relief (i.e., cash assistance, temporary shelter) as well as educational or skills-based programs targeted at youngsters (e.g., tutoring, after-school programs) with greater frequency.

Religious leaders in this study are virtually unanimous in defining faith-based aid broadly enough to include both a material component and a non-material dimension. According to the religious leaders interviewed in this investigation, the provision of aid by religious communities should be a holistic endeavor that—unlike public assistance programs—aims to address the material needs of the disadvantaged while simultaneously providing the means for moral development and spiritual sustenance. A female pastor at an African-American Methodist Church in our sample suggested that her church's work with local elderly was quite successful precisely because this program assists older individuals "financially and then spiritually also." This black Methodist church has a jail ministry program founded on the same principle. The jail ministry entails not only visitation with the imprisoned, but a personal grooming service for them as well.

Many congregations meld material and non-material forms of relief in quite creative ways. Most religious communities in our sample offer special

Table 6.1: Percentages of Churches Providing Particular Types of Aid[a]

	% of All Churches (N=29)[b]	% of White Churches (N=16)	% of Black Churches (N=11)
Rent Assistance	59% (17)	69% (11)	55% (6)
Utilities Assistance	69% (20)	75% (12)	64% (7)
Grocery Assistance	72% (21)	81% (13)	73% (8)
Cash	24% (7)	19% (3)	36% (4)
Temporary Shelter	24% (7)	19% (3)	36% (4)
Affordable Housing	7% (2)	6% (1)	0% (0)
Clothing	52% (15)	50% (8)	55% (6)
Medical Services	28% (8)	25% (4)	27% (3)
Child Care	28% (8)	31% (5)	27% (3)
Hot Meals	17% (5)	19% (3)	18% (2)
Elder Care	24% (7)	25% (4)	27% (3)
Transportation	35% (10)	31% (5)	36% (4)
Counseling	55% (16)	50% (8)	64% (7)
Tutoring	28% (8)	13% (2)	55% (6)
After-School Programs	10% (3)	0% (0)	27% (3)
Other Aid	10% (3)	6% (1)	0% (0)

a: The figure bounded by parentheses within each cell is the number of churches in the numerator used to calculate the corresponding percentage.
b: All churches include white (N=16), Black (N=11), and other (N=2) congregations.

programs during various holiday seasons (e.g., Thanksgiving, Christmas, Easter). While these programs vary in their specifics, they generally complement the provision of material aid (e.g., free dinners at the church) with ritual activities (e.g., special worship services) for those who wish to attend them.

Even forms of aid that would seem—on the face of it—to be one-dimensional often subtly combine various types of relief work. For example, inasmuch as revivals are designed to inspire religious conviction among the un-churched and the regular church-goer alike, these special ministries would seem to center around the satiation of spiritual needs. Yet, the spiritual fervor often produced by such activities is often pointed toward a material outlet. At many revivals, special collections may be taken up for charitable organizations or a church's food pantry. In addition, these special services often provide pastors with a forum for the recruitment of church members into volunteer aid programs.

How Do Local Religious Communities Currently Provide Aid to the Needy?

Despite this general pattern of melding material and non-material forms of aid, many of the congregations in our study intentionally utilize one or more of four different aid-provision strategies:

- intensive and sustained interpersonal engagement with the poor;
- intermittent, direct relief to the needy;
- collaboration with para-church relief organizations;
- short-term mission trips to disadvantaged populations located in distant settings.

These four aid-provision strategies, described below, are not mutually exclusive. However, congregations often develop strong preferences for specific means of relief-provision.

Relief-Provision Strategy 1: Intensive and Sustained Interpersonal Engagement with the Poor

The first aid-provision strategy distilled from our study entails intensive, long-term interpersonal engagement with those in need. Faith communities located squarely in poverty-stricken areas frequently adopt this aid-provision strategy. For that reason, pastors who advocate this strategy of relief-provision typically do not need to look far to find the poor. In many instances, these pastors serve congregations whose own members face intersecting forms of social disadvantage ranging from racism, monthly economic shortfalls, and inadequate housing to educational deficiencies, unemployment, and job insecurity. These ministers defend what they perceive as the transformative consequences—for aid-giver and relief recipient alike—of sustaining intimate, face-to-face contact with the disadvantaged. These ministers and members of their congregations claim to cultivate lasting friendships and a sense of solidarity with the poor through providing basic necessities and emotional support to those who face persistent poverty.

Pastors whose congregations utilize this relief strategy claim that it is amazingly effective at fighting poverty and solving problems such as drug abuse. At the same time, several of the pastors who champion this strategy as the primary means of offering relief are explicitly critical of those who eschew sustained personal engagement with the poor. These pastors imply that "hands-off" religious entities offer "boardroom" relief bereft of personal engagement.

One pastor who advocates intensive and sustained interpersonal engagement with the poor ministers extensively to Hispanic migrant workers in the local area. During our interview with him, this pastor mimicked the voice of a "hands-off" religious leader who opts for cash-based assistance in lieu of more intensive personal engagement: "'We do a Good Samaritan program for them. But we make sure they don't come and eat with us.'" Then, adopting his own voice once again, this critical pastor offered his appraisal of this financial-donation-only relief strategy: "So, you know, the right hand is saying, 'Here is five-hundred dollars,' and the left hand is saying, 'Make sure you don't spend it around me, because I'd rather not talk to you.'"

Beyond the discomfort that some privileged congregants may feel in crossing social class lines to minister intensively to the poor, many churches that do not employ this relief-provision strategy argue that they simply cannot do so because it is so time-consuming and labor-intensive. Forming and sustaining relationships with the poor—particularly those who may live in a very different part of town than the aid-giver—requires considerable time and effort. Although many pastors whose congregations do not utilize this aid-provision strategy chose their words quite carefully, such intensive relief efforts can be seen as somewhat "inefficient" despite their effectiveness. It is for such reasons that many congregations—particularly those of privilege—often opt for other relief strategies.

Relief-Provision Strategy 2: Intermittent Direct Relief

A second aid-provision strategy in which many local congregations engage entails intermittent direct relief to the poor. This aid-giving strategy is quite popular among a wide range of churches—black and Anglo, working class and middle class—and takes many different forms. In a few instances, direct relief entails some form of long-term support such as "adopt-a-family" programs. In such cases, a religious congregation or some faction of members within it decides to remain in periodic contact with a particular family that has faced long-term disadvantage.

Our study suggests that these programs sometimes emerge through informal social networks in which there is a common point of contact between an affluent sponsoring congregation and the needy family. In one case, parents in a white affluent congregation heard that the family of their child's schoolteacher had run across a string of unfortunate circumstances (e.g., medical problems, financial shortfalls). In this instance, the child served as the common point of contact between the provider (the child's parents in the affluent congregation) and the recipient of aid (the student's schoolteacher).

More common by far than the scenario described above are churches that use this intermittent aid-provision strategy to provide one-time or short-term relief to known persons suffering a discrete crisis such as a house fire, a physical accident, or the death of a relative who had no savings or burial insurance. By contrast, individuals unfamiliar to the community whose struggles are less clearly defined by a discrete crisis are quite often (1) carefully screened by a range of church-imposed aid-giving standards (e.g., call-backs on their phone calls soliciting aid, visitation at the home of the needy person to inspect their resources, an escort to the grocery store rather than the provision of cash), or (2) referred to private or public agencies that specialize in providing the type of aid that is sought (discussed in the following section). Consequently, it is difficult to overemphasize the overriding significance of congregational social networks for the disbursement of intermittent aid.

Although the vast majority of pastors said that their religious communities would not turn away non-members, tight congregational networks can sometimes promote a "help-our-own" orientation in which resources are requested by a needy person or family within that group. In some cases, leaders in religious communities may even adopt pro-active strategies of aid-giving whereby needy members do not have to solicit relief.

A religious leader at a local mosque provided an illuminating account of the way in which such social networks can operate to the advantage of community members:

> Most of the people who are needy ... actually, they don't come and ask ... We know some individual, for example, has certain problems. But he is too shy or whatever ... He is too shy to ask for help. So we will go ask his friends ... If he is in the hospital, we will ask his or her friend, 'Does he or she have insurance?' Then if they say, 'Yes,' we will say, 'OK, does the insurance cover all of it? What is left over? Is he or she capable of doing that?' We go through friends and we ask.

The intracongregational provision of intermittent aid is perceived to offer two key advantages. First, the thorny problem of "deservingness" among those in need is made less ambiguous through pre-existing social networks. Prior knowledge of the person in need is viewed as a form of accountability—in a word, proof that the relief will be appreciated and used judiciously by the recipient. Second, intracongregational relief enables members of the faith community to witness firsthand the ways in which their aid-giving can transform the lives of people they value and call friends. In this way, the aid-*givers* become the *recipients* of renewed bonds of trust and faith within their own community—bonds which are affirmed by effectively meeting the needs of its members.

However, the power of social networks in some congregations is not solely affirmative, but can be exclusive as well. The same membership circles that enable churchgoers to support one another via this aid-provision strategy also provide the power, if needed, to deny aid requests to non-members. It is important to recognize that the term "non-member" is often code for an array of intersecting social cleavages. Because many local religious communities are such homogeneous organizations, a key outcome of this help-our-own orientation often entails the preservation of boundaries that insulate persons of different ethnic, social class, and denominational backgrounds from one another.

As might be expected, race is an especially salient theme in our interviews. Most pastors interviewed for this study conceded that race currently affects the way in which churches provide aid to the needy and would likely do so into the future. Several pastors even argued that racism is more entrenched within local churches—white and black congregations alike—than outside of them. Even those religious leaders who maintained that racial antagonism does not directly influence the provision of aid within their own churches recognized that such factors hold sway in neighboring congregations. We address this issue more thoroughly later when discussing pastoral affect toward charitable choice.

Relief-Provision Strategy 3: Collaboration with Para-Church Relief Agencies

A third aid-provision strategy entails congregational collaboration with para-church relief organizations. Such collaboration can take many forms: philanthropic support of a relief agency by local congregations, often coupled with church-based referrals to the relief agency to which congregational monies are directed. Churches that engage in philanthropic support often provide a long list of local interfaith relief agencies which they support through resources (e.g., money, clothes) donated by their members or via volunteer assistance. These churches may use other relief-provision strategies in addition to congregation-sponsored philanthropy, including intermittent direct relief (as described earlier). However, pastors sometimes argued that they can often most effectively provide aid to the needy through semi-professional para-church relief organizations rather than at their own church door.

Why would faith communities opt to refer aid solicitors to para-church relief agencies? Supply-and-demand considerations regarding aid often figure prominently into such decisions. On the "demand" side of the aid-provision relationship, these centralized and standardized agencies are believed to safeguard individual churches from fraudulent, self-serving, door-to-door requests for aid—which several pastors argued are quite common. The standardization and centralization of relief is typically used in an urban or semi-urban context where population density makes knowing one's neighbors difficult. These nonprofit agencies typically employ screening procedures, often maintain a centralized database on agency contributors and aid solicitors, are open regular hours, and are overseen by individuals judged to be competent staff workers.

In singing the praises of a local para-church relief agency, Outreach Ministries (a pseudonym), one pastor offered the following account:

> We [local churches] feed Outreach Ministries. Outreach Ministries, in turn, helps the needy. They are our screening process. If I have a question about somebody [pause]. Let me explain this to you. I am a sharp guy. I know how to read a phone book. I know how to go to the Yellow Pages

What is a Para-Church Relief Agency?

Para-church relief agencies are faith-based organizations that provide aid to the needy outside of a specific congregational structure. As described in our discussion of para-church agencies, local congregations often seek to coordinate their relief efforts with these organizations in ministering to needy populations. There is often a two-way relationship between para-church agencies and local congregations. Depending on their available resources, local churches may offer financial, material, or volunteer support to para-church relief agencies. In return, individual congregations may refer needy individuals to para-church relief agencies.

Some para-church relief agencies are interfaith or interdenominational in character (e.g., the Salvation Army); such organizations often have their own office and may draw staff from any of a number of different congregations. Other para-church relief efforts may be orchestrated within a particular religious denomination (see, e.g., the 1996 United Methodist Book of Discipline, pp. 423-424). There are several different para-church relief agencies in the northeastern Mississippi area. In this phase of our investigation, we are interested primarily in pastors' perceptions of their relationships with such agencies. In future work, we plan to collect and analyze data directly from local para-church relief organizations.

> under "churches." If I want to make five to ten thousand dollars in a week, I start calling every church in [county]. If I can get into every church in [county], 38 of them, it's feasible to come up with five or ten thousand dollars worth of food or things that I could sell ... By taking them to Outreach Ministries, there is a master file maintained there. That's one of the places I can call to check on people to see if they are abusers of the system.

Concerns about fraud are not the only reason that many congregations use para-church relief agencies. On the "supply" side of the aid-provision relationship, various types of congregational dynamics make para-church relief agencies an attractive option. First, some churches have limited benevolence funds, and are simply not able to address "desperate, dire" aid solicitations of over $300 to $500. In such cases, these churches will often provide a referral to a para-church relief agency rather than exhaust their benevolence funds completely.

Second, leaders in some churches that utilize this aid-provision strategy comment on the time constraints faced by their members—many of whom are in dual-earner households where couples struggle to meet their own family obligations. A religious leader from a large white Methodist church composed of middle-class members offered the following account of their membership: "We do have a lot of generous, giving people here who are very concerned about others. It is a very caring and loving church." However, when asked about the prospect of church members participating in expanded aid programs, she reacted with some caution and hesitancy. Although this church has some "gifted" retirees who are active in aid programs, she explained that many of her congregants are in families where both spouses are employed full-time: "You know, time, of course, is an issue for everyone nowadays with all of the working folks we have." In light of the fact that they support a plethora of nonprofit and interfaith relief agencies with philanthropic donations, this church often refers individuals requesting aid to these agencies. According to such reasoning, the church "already supports" aid to the needy through such donations and need not duplicate its efforts too vigorously with direct aid offerings.

When employed as a key mechanism for relief-provision, philanthropic aid-giving can inadvertently establish and maintain social distance between congregational members and the poor. Based on this aid-giving strategy, responsibility to assist the poor can unwittingly be shifted from the local congregation to a para-church relief agency that may function very differently from the former. This outcome is precisely the opposite of that which is desired by Marvin Olasky and other proponents of charitable choice—i.e., *a particular local religious community* acting as a conduit for the provision of material resources, social networks, and moral values through *face-to-face contact* with the poor.

Finally, pastoral referrals to para-church relief agencies may sometimes be motivated by a desire to quell membership concerns about the use of congregants' donations to the church. Are members' donations for relief efforts and church programs being used effectively? To be sure, no pastor admitted to providing referrals to para-church agencies simply because he or she feared confronting uncomfortable questions about the use of member donations. Nevertheless, such a scenario is not altogether unfathomable.

Our interviews are replete with references to the complex machinations of power that characterize the relationships between local pastors and the congregations they serve. Several pastors, especially those at Methodist and Baptist churches, even stated quite straightforwardly that the church belongs more to the congregants themselves—and longtime members in particular—than to pastors who often serve itinerant appointments in which they are transferred every few years. At times, power dynamics center squarely on the use of member donations. It is quite possible, then, that local skirmishes about the usage of donated funds sometimes encourage pastors to rely on para-church relief agencies—thereby circumventing the thorny fiscal issues that might otherwise emerge between pastors and the congregations they are charged to serve.

Relief-Provision Strategy 4: Short-Term Distant-Missions

Several churches employ a fourth aid-giving strategy by offering their membership the opportunity to participate in distant-missions—either to some location in the U.S. (typically a one-day trip by car) or to an impoverished country abroad. One large white affluent church offers a variety of missions on the domestic scene and abroad—a week's relief work at an inner-city mission in Texas; ministry to needy persons living in Appalachia; several weeks of participation at a Christian aid-giving agency in Central America, among others. This church employs a distant-missions relief strategy in combination with an array of other aid programs: "one-shot" funds for discrete crises, a grassroots adopt-a-family initiative begun in a Sunday school class, referrals to a local interfaith relief agency that this church helped to organize, and local volunteer efforts with (among other organizations) Habitat for Humanity.

Often, distant-mission trips are coordinated through pastors or adults who work with the youth in privileged congregations. Indeed, several churches in this study sponsor distant-missions for their youth that involve a "pilgrimage" to highly disadvantaged populations (e.g., inner-city children, residents of dilapidated homes in nearby cities). The aim of these missions is transformation on several levels.

First, the relief work performed on these distant-missions is designed to effect a small-scale social transformation of the disadvantaged community though intensive (though temporary) relief work performed by the volunteers. Second, distant-missions can promote spiritual transformation for aid recipients, as well as for the congregational members whose faith and camaraderie are enriched by the extraordinary challenges that they collectively confront on such sojourns. Third, some youth-oriented distant-missions are underwritten in part by young congregants' fund-raising activities (e.g., selling flowers to other members, which symbolically represent the "planting" of mission "seeds"). In such cases, these missions teach youngsters lessons about the cultivation of values such as hard work, thrift, and self-sufficiency.

Finally, such face-to-face ministry to the very poor serves as a "getaway"—i.e., a break from the everyday grind—for church youth that is at once educational, morally challenging, and even fun. Such mission trips often include a day or so of recreational activities in which participants consume distinctive aspects of the distant culture which might otherwise not be available to them in small Mississippi towns.

Like the first aid-provision strategy outlined in this section (i.e., intensive engagement), distant-missions require intimate contact with the poor and can promote spiritual transformation for all parties involved. Reflecting on the impact of these types of programs at his large Anglo church, one pastor concluded: "[The youth] become sensitive. When they have the opportunity to work with poor people, they begin to see people and not just the situation or something they have heard. They identify with people."

Such relief work can therefore subvert common misperceptions about poverty through experiential knowledge that attaches faces, bodies, and names to an otherwise abstract group of people—namely, "the poor"—who would otherwise appear foreign to those from a middle-class upbringing. However, at the same time, such outreach efforts entail a pilgrimage that propels the aid-giver *outside* of his or her own community.

Do these distant-mission pilgrimages lead to a more permanent transformation that manifests itself in local social action once the sojourner returns home? One local leader of distant-missions suggested that, while his church strives to effect permanent changes via these programs, such trips may enable members of affluent faith communities to avoid confronting the uncomfortable reality that local social hierarchies sustain their privileged position back at home.

Pastoral Perceptions Regarding the Feasibility of Charitable Choice: How Do Religious Leaders Assess the Prospect for Program Effectiveness If Charitable Choice Is Implemented?

Having explored the means of relief-provision currently utilized by local congregations, we now turn our attention to examining pastoral affect toward the implementation of charitable choice initiatives in Mississippi's

GTR. As part of our congregational profile of sampled churches, Appendix I reports thumbnail summaries of pastoral familiarity with and affect toward charitable choice. This information is distilled from interviews with local religious leaders.

A vast majority of pastors in our sample—23 to be exact—claimed familiarity with "the idea that churches might become more involved in the restructuring of public welfare." Four pastors were unfamiliar with this proposed initiative. Although only four pastors plainly stated their lack of familiarity with this proposal, a few pastors who claimed familiarity with political discussions of church-state relief partnerships had very limited knowledge of such an initiative. In such cases, we speculated that we may have introduced them to the idea for the first time during our interview and surmised that these religious leaders hesitated to acknowledge their unfamiliarity with this issue. Interestingly, some of these pastors were favorably disposed to the plan of faith-based welfare reform after we had apparently introduced the idea to them.

Pastors at 12 congregations were, in general, favorably disposed toward such an initiative. Yet, as discussed more fully in the sections that follow, even those pastors who were most favorably disposed toward charitable choice initiatives expressed reservations about this program. Religious leaders from 11 congregations expressed such a profound ambivalence toward faith-based welfare reform that their responses defied categorization as "favorably disposed" or "opposed." Many of these religious leaders simultaneously raised concerns and hopes regarding such an initiative. Four local pastors were expressly opposed to a church-state aid-provision partnership. These pastors either argued that their congregations would be unwilling to participate in this venture or harbored very serious reservations about church-state collaborations.

In addition, it is quite noteworthy that many more black pastors in our sample are quite favorably disposed toward charitable choice initiatives. Data on charitable choice familiarity and affect presented in Appendix I is summarized as a two-by-two diagram in Table 6.2. Pastors representing black churches favor charitable choice more frequently by a margin of over five to one. Among 14 white pastors for whom we have such interview data, two (14%) favor charitable choice. The majority of white pastors (57%) are quite ambivalent about such an initiative. Among the 11 African-American pastors in this study, eight (73%) are favorably disposed toward charitable choice.

These findings, based on our non-probability sample of religious leaders, are presented not for the purpose of generalizing from them. Rather, they serve as background information through which we can interpret charitable choice affect and related themes that emerge from a more thorough analysis of interview transcripts.

Table 6.2: Percentage of Pastors Familiar with and Favorably Disposed toward Charitable Choice by Race[a]

	Pastors Familiar with Charitable Choice	Pastors Favorably Disposed toward Charitable Choice
White Pastors (N=14)	79% (11)	14% (2)
Black Pastors (N=11)	91% (10)	73% (8)

a: *Percentages calculated on available interview transcript data using questions 6, 13, and 16 (see Appendix III). The figure bounded by parentheses within each cell is the number of churches in the numerator used to calculate the corresponding percentage. Because our data are drawn from a non-probability sample, these figures are designed simply to set the context for our analyses of interview transcripts.*

What Factors Shape Pastoral Affect toward Charitable Choice Initiatives?

With the foregoing overview in mind, we now seek to explore the nuances in local religious leaders' orientations toward charitable choice and discuss several factors affecting pastoral evaluations of this initiative. Our data suggest that pastoral affect toward charitable choice can be traced to several interrelated factors, including:

- evaluations of previous relief efforts complemented by specific congregational-denominational dynamics;
- attitudes concerning race-ethnicity, the poor, and social inequality; and
- beliefs about the government and its responsibility toward the poor.

In the remainder of this chapter, we discuss the relationship between each of these factors and pastoral affect toward charitable choice.

Notably, we do not contend that these factors "cause" pastors to favor or disfavor charitable choice in a lockstep fashion. Rather, we argue that pastors' perceptions and experiences regarding these topics act as interpretive frames through which these religious leaders gauge the prospects for charitable choice. Because pastors often have a range of perceptions and experiences about this complex set of issues, many of them advance conflicted feelings concerning the implementation of charitable choice initiatives despite an overall positive or negative orientation toward faith-based welfare reform. Where possible, we seek to highlight how such conflicted feelings manifest themselves. In doing so, we often illustrate our findings with reference to specific congregations in our study.

Previous Relief Experience and Congregational-Denominational Dynamics

During each of our interviews, pastors were asked to evaluate current and previous congregational relief efforts. These same religious leaders were also asked to describe several salient characteristics (e.g., church structure, decision-making processes) in their congregations. Both of these factors provide crucial lenses through which religious leaders assess the viability of implementing charitable choice programs in their congregation or in local religious communities. To begin, pastors who speak positively about their congregation's previous aid-provision efforts frequently are optimistic about the prospects for implementing effective charitable choice programs through their churches. At first blush, this finding is straightforward and intuitive: Those programs that were perceived to work effectively in the past are anticipated by religious leaders to be similarly effective under charitable choice.

Nancy Evans, a black female pastor at an African-American United Methodist church, serves as an excellent illustration of this perspective.[2] When asked if members of her congregation would be willing to participate in aid programs that involve the state, she said that her members are more than willing—they are also able and wish to live up to their distinctive congregational legacy. The "myriad of professional people in my church," she said, provide her with "a wealth of people that I can tap to oversee such programs." "People here want their church to be more involved," she contended. "They just don't want the door shut during the week. They want to be more involved. That church—they used to call it the Civil Rights church. That church has always ... been about improving."

Like many religious leaders who are favorably disposed toward charitable choice initiatives, Pastor Evans' church has also participated successfully in local para-church relief efforts. Pastors appointed at churches that have had generally positive experiences with para-church or interfaith relief agencies often express more optimism about the prospects for providing relief collaboratively with the government under charitable choice. In some cases, para-church connections have convinced pastors and congregants that they can cooperate effectively with persons situated outside of their congregation whose views may not mirror their own.

To be sure, para-church relief efforts are sometimes marked by conflicts based on theological or other denominational differences. Yet, in the end, many of the religious congregations in our study that remain active in such agencies argue that they can genuinely benefit the needy. Given the dearth of full-time black ministers in her small town, however, Pastor Evans warned that charitable choice monies routed only through para-church agencies could unwittingly promote racial stratification. Because black pastors in the area tend to be bi-vocational ministers who are employed outside the church, a para-church-only strategy for implementing charitable choice would unfairly favor congregations—specifically white congregations—with full-time professional clergy.

Interestingly, stories of relief program success offered by such pastors are often complemented by discussions about select program failures. Pastor Evans said that her church has indeed suffered some setbacks where aid-provision is concerned. Quite notably, though, she traces those setbacks not to a lack of time, skills, or motivation on the part of her congregants. Relief-provision in Methodist churches is based largely on fixed apportionments, and this particular church simply did not have enough funds available at key times to perform all desired relief work. One of the programs that had to be disbanded was a church-run child-care center. The money needed to bring the child-care center into compliance with local day-care standards was simply not available. Pastor Evans would also like to begin a program for victims of domestic violence—preferably with a trained counselor. If additional funds were made available to her church through charitable choice, these are the types of programs she would seek to reinstate or launch anew.

The source of such overriding optimism in this interview and others like it is located largely in perceptions about congregational dynamics within these pastors' churches. As noted above, Pastor Evans argued that her congregants have the time, ability, and motivation to engage in extensive relief-provision: "I am telling you there is so much they could do. There is so much they could do. And then I think they would be able to attract more people that way ... I mean, I have people who are in my congregation who know this community." Pastor Evans' optimism, however, is accompanied by a strong admonition concerning the implementation of charitable choice through local congregations—particularly Methodist churches:

> I think [government officials] need to be careful not to really allow the ministers to do everything, but allow the people [in the congregation] to get more involved ... In the United Methodist Church, they have what they call an itinerancy position. The ministers move constantly. If you want any program to be in place, to work, and to have long-term effects, you are going to have to have the people [in the congregation] involved more. The people who are in the church [need to be involved because] they are going to be there for longer amounts of time.

Such references to member involvement, often advanced by Methodist and Baptist ministers, underscore the importance of congregants in implementation of charitable choice initiatives. Many of these pastors readily concede that successful aid programs are predominantly dependent on member participation and the long-term commitment of congregants.

In other denominations where local religious leaders enjoy longer pastoral tenures, member involvement is still considered important for successful congregational relief. However, given their lengthier appointments, such pastors exercise more congregational authority than many of their itinerant counterparts in differently structured denominations. Such pastors might be in more of a position to oversee the implementation of charitable choice monies run through their congregations.

Elder Cornelius Smith, who has served as pastor of a large all-black congregation (Temple Zion–Church of God in Christ) for 18 years, is quite favorably disposed toward charitable choice. Much of his favorable disposition toward faith-based welfare reform stems from positive previous experiences. His church, which he said serves about 500 persons per month out of its food pantry, also claims great success in moving public assistance recipients out of welfare dependency. Elder Smith often addresses this very issue in his charismatic sermons:

> All I can tell you is two-thirds of our people when they came to us were on welfare. It is my Sunday morning sermon at some points [that is] on that [topic]. [I tell my congregants:] "If you are on welfare, get off as soon as you can because welfare is limiting your future. Welfare is hampering your success." That's how I teach it. I tell them this. "It is not God's will for you to be on welfare. And it insults God for Him to be our Father, [for] us to trust in Him, and we have to have a handout every day of our lives." So, therefore, I teach it is essential to us growing, to being proper witnesses, that we don't find ourselves on welfare. And I would dare to say [that] out of the numbers we called to you earlier [i.e., out of the two-thirds who came to the church on welfare], I would dare to say that less than 10 percent are on welfare.

How are these same factors—i.e., previous aid experience and congregational-denominational characteristics—related to pastoral pessimism toward charitable choice? Pastors who deem previous experiences with congregational relief as largely unsuccessful often carry this pessimism into their evaluations of prospective charitable choice initiatives.

Pastor James Holt, a United Methodist minister of a modest-sized white rural church, said that his church "should be" more involved in relief, even as he concludes "but I don't think it will be." Based on his experience, Pastor Holt argued that lofty theological ideals about Christian service to others simply do not motivate many of his members to participate in aid-provision programs. He suspects such patterns would continue under charitable choice:

> I think, in one sense of the word, churches ought to be very involved in this area out of concern for other people. But at the same time, I've had some reservations about whether we will become much more involved than we already are. A lot of time at the grassroots level, people may say, "Yes, we need to be involved." But as far as really volunteering for work or increas-

ing their giving to do so—that's where the problems usually begin. Not to mention agreeing on what those needs are that need to be met and who those people are that need to be helped. So as voluntary as the church is in depending on a consensus rather than a mandate, it is going to be difficult, I think, to get the churches involved in any significantly increased level.

Interestingly, then, Pastor Holt's account again highlights the importance of three keys for member involvement—time, ability, and willingness—in successful relief programs and, ostensibly, effective charitable choice initiatives. According to Pastor Holt, his congregants would lack the last of these elements and, for that reason, would be unlikely to participate. Indeed, this congregation has not participated in para-church relief efforts for many of the same reasons. Moreover, given the way in which decisions are made in this particular church—by "consensus rather than [by] a mandate"—disputes often preclude unified action. Finally, congregants in this church have to be stirred into action by an issue that *they* define as a problem, not issues that are defined *for them* as in need of a solution. Pastor Holt surmised: "At the present time? No, they would not have the motivation. The motivation would have to come. It would have to be—they would have to be challenged by something they really see as a problem ... A problem they care about before even the challenge comes."

Taken as a whole, our interview data reveal that pastoral affect toward charitable choice is partly contingent on religious leaders' appraisals of prior relief work. Evaluations of previous relief programs—conducted alone or in tandem with other congregations—often frame pastoral expectations about charitable choice. Moreover, each of three key elements—time availability, possession of skills, and willingness to participate—seem necessary for successful relief efforts and, by many accounts, would be needed for the implementation of effective charitable choice programs.

Finally, pastoral expectations of charitable choice also seem to be shaped by denominational and congregational norms ranging from pastoral tenure and relief-funding mechanisms to church-based decision-making patterns. Where the latter issue is concerned, congregant involvement in relief efforts seems to be a necessary ingredient for successful aid programs, but a thorough-going commitment to decision making by consensus can sometimes invite congregational paralysis.

Attitudes concerning Race-Ethnicity, the Poor, and Social Inequality

A second set of factors that appear to influence pastoral affect toward charitable choice initiatives centers on perceptions about race-ethnicity, the poor, and social inequality. Recall that many more African-American pastors in our sample are quite favorably disposed toward charitable choice than their white counterparts—the latter of whom are typically ambivalent about this initiative. Like charitable choice affect, references to racial attitudes among our sample of pastors are situated on a complex continuum.

Some white pastors argue that racism is still quite prominent in Mississippi and explain why charitable choice would not work for that very reason. As it turns out, impediments toward charitable choice participation at Pastor Holt's United Methodist congregation are not solely reducible to those specified above (i.e., evaluations of previous relief experience and congregational or denominational dynamics). Pastor Holt is one of the few pastors in our study who stated forthrightly that members in his rural, all-white congregation would likely view government standards mandating a color-blind allocation of aid as coercive. When asked if attitudes about race and ethnicity would affect the routing of welfare services through local congregations, Pastor Holt replied unabashedly:

> Yes, definitely. Well, it would affect it even in the beginning—if [charitable choice] was accepted to be [worthy of member participation]—for them to get involved. That is one way it would be affected. I don't feel my church would accept [block grant money] because of their attitude. They would simply turn it down. I feel there might be some churches, though, that might accept it. But their attitudes about the way they handled it and who they helped individually would shape [pause]. In other words, they might consider some persons unworthy of help and kind of refuse help. Or [they might] formulate their guidelines so that these people would be excluded. And their attitudes toward race might be one of those guidelines.

According to Pastor Holt, this racially insular implementation of charitable choice would simply be an extension of the way that church-based aid is currently provided. Like many pastors in our study (black and white), he said that current efforts at church-based relief are "most definitely" affected by attitudes about race and ethnicity. Notably, though, Pastor Holt charged that *his own* congregation would probably participate in such practices under charitable choice: "I have not seen them work across racial lines to help locally."

Interestingly, some white pastors argue that racism is no longer a prominent feature of Mississippi social life or, at least, maintain that racial prejudice does not mark congregational aid distribution. Such arguments could indirectly preclude these pastors from supporting charitable choice outright for reasons which, *prima facie*, seem unrelated to race.

Pastor Robert Davidson at Main Street Southern Baptist Church is ambivalent about charitable choice being routed through local churches—apparently for reasons other than race. Citing several instances of church fraud, he said that "sometimes the unscrupulous have a unique way of getting into those things." Pastor Davidson firmly believes that racism does not currently affect aid-provision in Mississippi churches and would not do so under charitable choice. When asked if race would affect the disbursement of funds to churches or, ultimately, to the needy, he responded point blank:

> No, because any group involved in [providing] aid today, to anyone, has long since dealt with that one ... I'm a Southerner. [I] grew up in the South, [and] have lived in a lot of other places, but [pause]. Southerners have always seen themselves as having to help, say, the black community. You know, the old plantation owner, he did it. The farmers did it. It's always been there. And so, race has—in my own lifetime—has never been a problem in relationships. Even when you had the active Ku Klux Klan and the marchers and everything, there's always been a desire to help. And I don't think that's ever been on a racial basis.

Using such language, Pastor Davidson suggested that even during tumultuous times—Klan activity and public protest (perhaps Civil Rights activity)—white Southerners have "always seen themselves as having to help ... the black community." One of the most striking features of this narrative is the way in which it portrays whites as the benevolent agents of aid-giving and depicts "old [Southern] plantation owners"—popularly viewed as a source of black oppression—in a positive light.

The vast majority of black pastors in our study, as noted, are favorably disposed toward charitable choice. Black religious leaders in general and a white Catholic priest with a ministry to impoverished Hispanic migrants argue that racism is persistent in Mississippi, but remain optimistic that certain safeguards could ensure that charitable choice initiatives address the needs of the poor. Elder Smith from Temple Zion–COGIC, an African-American congregation mentioned earlier, believes that race remains salient for Mississippi blacks and argued that charitable choice funds should be distributed based on need:

> A while back a large white church in Mississippi came to me ... [A pastor from that church inquired:] "Can we funnel our assistance programs through you?" I saw this as a great opportunity to get more money to more people. I said, "Certainly. What are you talking about putting through?" This was a large church. This church probably does three million [dollars] a year or more, so [it is] a large white church. And so I said, "What are you talking about money-wise?" And the pastor said to me, "We will give you $4,000 a year."
>
> I was insulted. I stood up and walked out, and he said, "What is the problem?" I said, "I am insulted." ... At this time our gross income was roughly two-hundred thousand [dollars] a year or a little better. I said, "We spend

> anywhere from $14,000 to $20,000 in helping people already. You mean to tell me you are going to offer me $4,000 a year to run all of your people through us? Your problem is you simply want to rid your lobby of a certain kind of people and put them in my lobby. You are not serious about the problem. So, when you want to spend some real money, we will talk." So I think the problem we are going to have is that if the government is going to do this, there has to be some real strict guidelines on how the money is appropriated at a state level so that it won't get into the wrong hands and the wrong churches [but] will get to where the people really need it.

As indicated by this quote, Elder Smith—who is quite favorably disposed toward charitable choice—has had previous experiences whereby some privileged churches have sought to "buy out" of social responsibility for very small sums. Given the racial dynamics evidenced in the foregoing narrative, Elder Smith concluded that if charitable choice is to be implemented, the program will require "some real strict guidelines ... so that [the funds] will get to where the people really need it."

Similarly, Father Dejean—an itinerant Catholic priest who ministers to Hispanic migrant workers in the local area—argued that there are currently many racial and class-based biases targeted at the poor. Yet, like Elder Smith, he also expressed a generally positive affect toward charitable choice. He began by describing racism as "prejudice plus power," but proceeded to argue that religious conviction can provide solutions to such social problems:

> We hear people ... say, "Why can't [the poor] be better off? Why can't they manage their money better? Why can't they get out of poverty? Why do we have to provide subsidies? Why do we have to help them?" You know, the prejudice and the racism is so ingrained. I define it as "racism is prejudice plus power" ... It's only when they have begun to share in their common humanity that the power stops, and the higher and lower people begin to be equal ... [which is] the message of the gospel.

Could the "message of the gospel" be spread more effectively under charitable choice despite local racism and antipathy toward the poor? Father Dejean is enthusiastic about the potential of such a program to motivate people to embody scriptural teachings more fully. He asserted that individuals in rural locales "have a greater sense of community than [their counterparts] have in larger churches in urban areas." If charitable choice were to be implemented, he imagines organizing "some government-sponsored programs for gardening [such as food cooperatives]. You don't have to carry the food for miles and miles. It's right here. Subsidize co-ops and gardens for good and reduce for the little people all these costs." He also spoke of expanding the churches' current aid programs for single mothers with children, as well as skills-based classes in bilingual education, self-esteem, cooking, sewing, parenting, and money management. He believes that there would be an abundance of volunteers nearby if federal funds were forthcoming.

In sum, is it noteworthy that black pastors we interviewed are much more favorably disposed toward charitable choice initiatives whereby public monies could be routed through local religious congregations. Although these pastors argue that racism remains a salient part of the African-American experience in Mississippi, many of them strongly believe that charitable choice—if implemented so that funds are delivered judiciously to those who need them most—could help to fight poverty on the local level. With few exceptions, then, pastors we interviewed argue that racial attitudes currently affect congregational relief-provision in local religious communities and will continue to do so under charitable choice. Among black pastors, such admissions rarely translate into negative affect toward possible church-state aid-provision partnerships.

Beliefs about the Government and Its Responsibility toward the Poor

A final factor that acts as an interpretive frame for charitable choice affect among pastors we interviewed may be best described as beliefs about the government and religious leaders' assumptions about government responsibility toward the poor. Many of the pastors in this study who are negatively disposed or ambivalent toward charitable choice cite the perceived fraud and waste associated with government assistance programs as a cause for concern with faith-based welfare reform.

Pastor Davidson, the white minister at Main Street Southern Baptist, is (like most Anglo pastors in our sample) ambivalent about charitable choice. Part of his ambivalence stems from the perceived outcome of public assistance programs begun during the War on Poverty: "We've basically raised up a culture that says, 'We really do deserve the money and you don't deserve anything from us.'" He added: "Since the 1960s, it has been a problem because we've developed a culture to allow people who really don't want any accountability required [of them]." He links this anti-accountability orientation to the problems his church has had in the Faith & Families of Mississippi program. Like a handful of other large white churches in our study, he said that the families his church selected from a list of Faith & Families profiles do not show up at the church when assigned to do so: "I think a lot of times, if a person realizes maybe if they are going to get involved in having a church and a mentorship, they are probably going to have to change some things in their lives. And they are going to have to face some responsibilities they don't want to face."

Pastor Davidson conceded that long-standing public assistance programs had altruism and "want[ing] to help" as the initial "basis of the program." Yet, he argued that this system has, since that time, become profoundly corrupt: "The welfare system basically operates in America today not for the poor person, but for the administrators." He asserts that such corruption is currently not incidental, but intrinsic to federal government programs: "What is it they say? That something like twenty-something percent of all federal welfare money is gulped up in fraud. In dishonesty." Consequently, Main Street's pastor reviles big government and strongly supports political devolution: "Most of those people [in the federal government] got those jobs through political appointments. They were put there to do just what they're doing—that's to lie, cheat, and steal ... I don't have a lot of appreciation for [federal government workers]."

Not all pastors who are ambivalent toward charitable choice—and, for that matter, not all white religious leaders—are so strongly supportive of political devolution or overtly critical of government poverty programs. A local religious leader of a predominantly white Latter-Day Saints congregation assessed public assistance programs like AFDC as "largely an excellent idea that has been, I guess, sloppily implemented." For both ethical and economic reasons, this pastor personally remains fully in favor of providing a "safety net" for the poor. However, he highlights the impersonal character of welfare programs by enlisting the provision of medical care as a metaphor:

> The reason that I say [welfare] has been sloppily implemented is that it's become a program that's very difficult to control and to make sure that the aid is going always to help people who need it ... And so, because of that sort of slack oversight, there's grown up to be a fairly significant abuse of the system. The difficulty with reforming it, then, is that you really don't want to wipe out the people that it's intended to help. And, of course, everybody says, "We'll just cut off the fat." But everybody has a different definition of fat, so that's a difficult thing.
>
> A comparison, I guess, that comes to my mind is that you would never ask a physician to prescribe addictive medication for somebody over the phone. And yet our welfare system is set up so that payments flow, in many cases, anonymously and continuously without—I mean, they fill things out and they have caseworkers, but there's not the person-to-person contact with people who are really involved in the [welfare recipients'] lives that you really need to administer the thing well.

This religious leader's ambivalence about charitable choice, then, combines hope and caution. Consistent with the views expressed above, he believes that churches—as local community organizations—may be able to administer aid more effectively. Yet, he is quick to concede the difficulty associated with predicting the viability of such a potentially complicated collaborative relationship.

Black pastors are equally critical, and often times more so, regarding public assistance programs that predated welfare reform. However, such criticisms of pre-PRWORA government programs are often coupled with defenses of particular aspects of public assistance. Overall, such assessments of public assistance programs did not erode these pastors' favorable disposition toward charitable choice. How are we to explain these distinctive findings?

To begin, popular images of "welfare fraud" and the stereotypical "welfare recipient" are quite often criticized by black pastors. While several black pastors concede abuse among welfare recipients of various ethnic backgrounds, many of these same religious leaders argue that "welfare fraud" is all too often narrowly understood. Indeed, several of these pastors allege instances in which welfare fraud—when understood in a broader and more practical sense—has been perpetrated by privileged whites who apparently extract benefits indirectly from welfare recipients. Among the most common examples cited are white landlords who artificially inflate rental prices in public housing for local blacks, and small-scale merchants who effectively keep retail prices high in order to absorb the monies of welfare recipients in nearby neighborhoods.

From this vantage point, both blacks and whites as well as both rich and poor have been beneficiaries of public assistance programs—programs, in the view of these pastors, that generate widespread abuse not restricted to the formal recipients of such state-sponsored aid. One black pastor who said he has personally seen such incidents commented on the centrality of public assistance monies to local economies and the financial fallout from welfare reform: "White people will be crying [about welfare reform]. It will be the mom-and-pop grocery stores who have been taking the food stamps and taking the welfare checks the first of every month [that will be adversely affected by welfare reform]. They will be going broke."

In addition, several of these black pastors cited welfare *dependency* as a major concern in previous public assistance programs but simultaneously suggest that "dependency" is a fact of life for devout Christians. One of these pastors argued outright that long-term reliance on public assistance is the wrong kind of dependency, whereas dependency on God is justifiable and necessary. Such notions lend themselves to support for charitable choice if this initiative is viewed as a program that promotes a socially productive dependency on God or one's co-religionists—rather than an unproductive dependency on the state—while using public monies to achieve these ends.

Finally, in offering a counterpoint to those who argue that "big government" is the source of all social ills, some black pastors defended continued government involvement in anti-poverty work. Like all pastors in our study, Elder Smith has some misgivings about charitable choice. However, his generally favorable disposition toward it stems in part from his experience as a black Southerner who came of age during the Jim Crow era. Given his own life experiences, Elder Smith saw the positive involvement of the federal government in facilitating the demise of blatant Jim Crow segregation in the South:

> Whenever I hear people in Congress and the senators say things like, "We have to make government smaller and giver power back to state governments" [pause]. To a Southern black person [pause]. Whenever I hear them say those kinds of terms, I know that means that [political power and resource control] is going to be put in the hands of the good old boys. It is going to be handled the way it was handled all the time. And the people who need [help] most won't get it. And so for that reason, I opt to say, "Let's keep the government [big]." I too would like to see a small government. But I would like to see a more fair system to where the government could be smaller because we have rectified the problem [of] each state being able to discriminate when they want to.

In sum, charitable choice affect is influenced by pastoral views of the government and religious leaders' assessments of prior public assistance programs. Several of the pastors who are opposed to or ambivalent about the prospects for charitable choice find crucial flaws in previous public assistance programs, and some of these religious leaders express anxiety about collaborating with the government for this very reason.

Pastors who are quite favorably disposed toward charitable choice often concede that previous public assistance programs were marked by significant shortcomings. However, these pastors—many of them black religious leaders—also contend that a thorough-going reversal of public policy will not necessarily redress poverty-related problems. It is in this spirit that many African-American pastors express support for charitable choice, a program that would entail collaborative anti-poverty work on the part of the state and local religious communities. Religious leaders who support charitable choice do indeed believe that potential problems could surface with such an initiative. But they also contend that religious communities could initiate or expand anti-poverty efforts with the infusion of resources that might be forthcoming under such a program.

Lessons Learned

This research study has sought to examine the feasibility of incorporating religious communities located in rural Mississippi's GTR into welfare reform. As noted, the "charitable choice" portion of the 1996 welfare reform law identifies religious congregations as a prospective provider of social services in states that consider routing block grant monies through local nonprofit agencies. Our feasibility study of charitable choice initiatives drew on analyses of in-depth interview data collected from pastors representing 30 religious congregations in GTR. Among the research questions we have sought to address are the following:

- What types of aid do faith communities currently provide, and how do local religious leaders define the concept of "aid" or "relief?"
- What are the strategies that local religious congregations currently utilize to provide relief to the needy? How are these aid-provision strategies perceived to differ from public assistance programs?
- In the wake of welfare reform, what are religious leaders' views of the prospects for charitable choice initiatives succeeding in poverty-stricken rural areas? What factors influence local religious leaders' perceptions concerning the prospect for charitable choice initiatives?

To summarize our findings, we found that pastors typically define religiously based aid in holistic terms that, ideally, should address both material and non-material needs. Yet, despite pastoral consensus on the general goals of religious relief-provision, local congregations currently employ an array of aid giving strategies to meet this goal. We detailed four relief-provision strategies used by local religious communities: (1) intensive and sustained interpersonal engagement with the poor; (2) intermittent direct relief to the needy; (3) collaboration with para-church relief agencies (e.g., via congregational philanthropy or referrals); and (4) short-term missions trips, often involving church youth, to the poor in distant locales.

Next, we found that although the preponderance of pastors in our sample are familiar with faith-based welfare reform initiatives, these religious leaders evince wide-ranging evaluations concerning the prospects for implementing charitable choice within their home congregations and local faith communities. Consistent with previous survey research on this topic, black pastors in our purposive in-depth interview sample express more positive affect toward charitable choice when compared with their white counterparts. However, regardless of their general orientation toward charitable choice, virtually all pastors express a mix of hope and trepidation about this initiative. Pastoral affect toward charitable choice can be traced to several factors, including:

- *evaluations of previous relief efforts complemented by specific congregational-denominational dynamics*—positive evaluations of prior experiences with relief-provision and the existence of key congregant resources (time, skills, and motivation) are linked to generally favorable pastoral dispositions toward charitable choice;

- *perceptions about race-ethnicity, the poor, and social inequality*—although most religious leaders concede that racism and social inequality are still salient features of social life in Mississippi, those who have seen religious convictions foster positive change in these areas were generally more optimistic about the prospects for charitable choice; and
- *beliefs about the government and its responsibility toward the poor*—although all pastors (black and white) expressed assorted criticisms of previous public assistance programs, those who recognized the positive role that the federal government can play in fighting poverty seemed more apt to consider entering into a charitable choice partnership with the government.

Our analyses of these in-depth interview data were not guided by the principles of variable analysis or cause-and-effect logic. Rather, we sought to reveal how pastoral experiences and perceptions serve as interpretive frames through which religious leaders evaluate the prospects for charitable choice. Given the recent genesis of charitable choice initiatives, additional research on this fast-evolving policy issue is certainly needed. Nevertheless, several significant lessons can be distilled from the present study.

Recommendations

1. State-level policy makers should recognize that there is no single type of congregation that is ideally suited to participate in charitable choice.

Our study has demonstrated that, even in a small geographical area, many different types of aid-provision strategies flourish across religious congregations. It is quite likely that congregations which dramatically vary in denomination, size, and preferred aid-provision strategies can participate effectively in charitable choice if a critical mass of members from these faith communities have the available time, skills, and willingness to do so. Consequently, state-level policy makers should consider the value of including a diverse range of congregations in charitable choice initiatives within any given area. Taken together, a diverse group of qualified congregations can offer a broad array of social services to the needy and may enlist a more variegated portion of the local religious population in relief efforts.

2. The preservation of religious diversity on the local scene should be an important consideration in awarding charitable choice funds.

Policy makers should not assume that the dominant faith tradition in a particular geographical area will be the most effective point of delivery for faith-based social services. Our study of religious communities in northeastern Mississippi revealed that relief-provision can be undertaken effectively by regionally dominant faith traditions (i.e., Baptist, Methodist), as well as by denominations which feature fewer local congregations in the rural South (e.g., Church of God in Christ, Roman Catholic, Muslim). Consequently, care should be taken to survey the religious landscape in an area without assuming that the congregation with the most members or the denomination with the most churches will function most effectively as social service providers.

Indeed, efforts designed to protect religious diversity in awarding charitable choice funds might improve the quality of relief that many local congregations provide. A great deal of sociological research suggests that congregations and denominations which function as an organizational monopoly in a local "religious market" actually operate less effectively—much like business monopolies—because of reduced competition for adherents. To be sure, sociological uses of a "religious marketplace" metaphor are limited inasmuch as congregations are not for-profit entities. However, including a diverse range of faith communities in charitable choice might prevent dominant faith traditions from further consolidating their advantage over other religious communities and may ensure that the anti-poverty commitment of many different local religious communities remains robust.

Because religious pluralism tends to promote greater involvement in and commitment to local faith communities writ large, policy makers should seek to ensure congregational and denominational diversity under charitable choice. Moreover, the dispersion of resources across various congregations and denominations might also ensure that the ethnic and socioeconomic homogeneity that is characteristic of many faith communities would not undermine one primary intent of charitable choice—namely, broad-based relief to diverse groups of people.

3. Faith communities should educate themselves about their rights and responsibilities as potential social service providers under charitable choice. In doing so, religious congregations can examine the avenues available to them for charitable choice participation while weighing the apparent advantages and disadvantages of this program.

Many of the religious leaders in our study were aware of aid-provision partnerships between the government and local religious communities because of Mississippi's path-breaking initiation of its Faith & Families program. Understandably, however, many religious leaders on the local and national scene do not understand all of the legal complexities—including faith communities' rights and responsibilities—associated with the charitable choice initiative outlined in Section 104 of the 1996 welfare reform law.

Faith communities can best gauge their opportunities and willingness to participate by familiarizing themselves with the dynamics of charitable choice legislation. An informative brochure on this topic (titled "A Guide to Charitable Choice") is available from the Center for Public Justice, a Christian civic education and policy research organization [phone: (410) 571-6300; postal address: P.O. Box 48368, Washington D.C. 20002-0368; online address www.cpjustice.org]. Local faith communities can also contact TANF (Temporary Assistance for Needy Families) representatives at their state's Department of Human Services to ascertain the status of charitable choice implementation within their area.

Faith communities should be mindful that the religious character of their organization cannot legally be used as a criterion to exclude them from competition for purchase-of-service contracts among local nonprofits—provided that their state purchases social services from local nonprofits. Regardless of the state-level opportunities for faith-based welfare reform, congregations should be aware that charitable choice legislation is currently supported by leading presidential candidates in both parties. The vagaries of candidate nominations and presidential elections notwithstanding, faith communities located in states that have not implemented charitable choice legislation thus far may have expanded opportunities to explore such options in the future. It is possible that political momentum for these programs will continue to build during the current election season.

4. Post-implementation evaluation studies of charitable choice may help identify positive and negative social outcomes of such programs. Evaluation studies might provide valuable insight into the improvement of welfare reform initiatives such as charitable choice.

Given the fact that charitable choice is a new policy initiative, we recommend that states which utilize religious communities as social service providers evaluate the outcomes of charitable choice partnerships using the same criteria employed to assess anti-poverty alliances between the government and nonprofit organizations from whom it purchases services. Post-implementation evaluation studies of charitable choice programs could be helpful to ensure that both public and congregational resources are being used in a manner that is beneficial to all involved parties (the faith community, the government, TANF recipients). In addition, such studies might call attention to some of the most innovative and effective anti-poverty strategies utilized by religious communities which participate in the program. Therefore, as charitable choice becomes an increasingly popular consideration for many different states in this era of welfare reform, government officials should be prepared to monitor carefully not only the economic outcomes associated with this program but also its social impact on grassroots religious organizations and local communities.

Postscript

With the inauguration of President George W. Bush in January 2001, additional momentum was given to faith-based initiatives at the federal level through the establishment of the White House Office of Faith-Based and Community Initiatives and the creation of satellite centers in six Cabinet departments—Justice, Labor, Health and Human Services, Housing and Urban Development, Education, and Agriculture. On the legislative front, the Bush administration proposed and strongly supported the Charitable Choice Act of 2001 and the CARE Act of 2003. Both of these legislative initiatives were substantially changed because of congressional concerns about direct public funding for religious organizations. Indirect support through tax credits, a strategy not favored by the administration, enjoyed broader appeal in Congress. Nevertheless, the expansion of charitable choice remains at the top of the President's domestic agenda. Key leaders in the administration, including Department of Health and Human Services Secretary Tommy Thompson and Attorney General John Ashcroft, share the President's vision and have remained strong supporters of charitable choice.

The federalization of charitable choice remains a priority for those who support this policy because state implementation to date has been uneven. A tracking report of charitable choice implementation conducted in late 2002 by the Hudson Institute revealed that only 14 states (28 percent) had formally taken advantage of charitable choice. And only about one-third of the states that implemented charitable choice had made any effort to monitor the evolving collaborations between themselves and faith-based providers. Careful monitoring and evaluation is thought to be evidence of a long-term commitment to state government collaborations with faith-based organizations. The only Southern states to have implemented charitable choice programs in a consistent fashion are Texas and Virginia.

More current evidence suggests that charitable choice is moving forward in other states as well. For its part, Mississippi has contracted out select social services to faith-based providers, and accepts bids from faith-based agencies in all outsourced services. However, like many states in the South and throughout the United States, Mississippi has neither a state-level Office of Faith-Based and Community Initiatives nor a faith-sector liaison in the governor's office.

In short, charitable choice is moving forward in many states, including Mississippi. But its impact has been felt most profoundly in states that have undertaken an orchestrated effort to include faith-based providers in the competitive bidding process.

John P. Bartkowski
Helen A. Regis
May 2003

Additional Information on Charitable Choice and Faith-Based Service Provision

Recent Books

Bartkowski, John P., and Helen A. Regis, 2003. *Faith, Hope, and Charitable Choice: Religion, Race, and Poverty in the Post–Welfare Era.* New York: New York University Press.

Cnaan, Ram A. 2002. *The Invisible Caring Hand: American Congregations and the Provision of Welfare.* New York: New York University Press.

Wineburg, Robert J. 2001. *A Limited Partnership: The Politics of Religion, Welfare, and Social Service.* New York: Columbia University Press.

Internet Resources on Charitable Choice

Faith In Communities
www.hudsonfaithincommunities.org

Sponsored by the Hudson Institute, this site seeks to inform and empower faith communities in the practice of social service delivery.

Roundtable on Religion and Social Welfare Policy
www.religionandsocialpolicy.org

Coordinated by the Rockefeller Institute of Government, this site tracks charitable choice implementation, provides legislative updates, and serves as a clearinghouse for the latest research on charitable choice.

White House Office of Faith-Based and Community Initiatives
www.whitehouse.gov/government/fbci

Sponsored by the Bush administration, this website provides guidance to faith-based and community organizations about the grant application process, highlights government-sponsored conferences for faith-based providers, and features links to each of the Cabinet-level Centers for Faith-Based and Community Initiatives.

Welfare Information Network (WIN)
www.financeprojectinfo.org/win

WIN serves as a clearinghouse for policy information and analysis, as well as technical assistance related to welfare, workforce development, and community services provided by faith-based and secular nonprofits.

Appendix I: Profile of Sampled Religious Communities[a]

Interview Number[b]	Denominational Affiliation	Pastor/Leader Characteristics	Membership Characteristics[c]	Location[d]	Facilities[e]	Budget	Types of Aid Provided[f]	Number of People Helped/Month	Charitable Choice Familiarity and Affect
1	United Methodist	White male 58 years old Seminary M.Div	White (99.5%) 1800 total members 1200 active members HH Inc: $50K+	Urban	8 offices 40 class-rooms Kitchen: 400	$1.3 million	1,2,3,5,9, 10,11	50	Familiar Ambivalent
2	United Methodist	White male 46 years old No seminary B.A.	White (100%) 550 total members 280 active members HH Inc: $30-50K	Urban	3 offices Kitchen: 200	$220,000	not specified	not specified	Unfamiliar Ambivalent
3	United Methodist (2 churches served by pastor, designated as CH1 and CH2)	White male 49 years old No seminary Some college	CH1: White (100%) 140 total members 65 active members HH Inc.: $30-50K CH2: White (100%) 110 total members 30 active members HH Inc: $20-30K	CH1: Semi-rural CH2: Semi-rural	CH1: 1 office 8 class-rooms Kitchen: 150 CH2: 3 class-rooms Kitchen: 100	CH1: $60,000 CH2: $42,000	CH1: 1,3,7,12 CH2: 7,12	CH1: 4 CH2: 0	Familiar Favorable

Note: *See page 206 for an explanation of a-f.*

Interview Number[b]	Denominational Affiliation	Pastor/Leader Characteristics	Membership Characteristics[c]	Location[d]	Facilities[e]	Budget	Types of Aid Provided[f]	Number of People Helped/ Month	Charitable Choice Familiarity and Affect
4	United Methodist	White male 55 years old Seminary M.Div.	White (100%) 96 total members 60 active members HH Inc: $10-20K	Rural	1 office 3 class-rooms Kitchen: 100	$50,000	not specified	"periodic help"	Familiar Unfavorable
5	Southern Baptist (SBC)	White male 58 years old Seminary M.Div., D.Min.	White (99.9%) 2300 total members 1600 active members HH Inc: $30-50K	Urban	10 offices 50 class-rooms Kitchen: 200	$1.4 million	1,2,3,5,8,13	20	Familiar Ambivalent
6	Southern Baptist (SBC)	White male 47 years old Seminary D.Min.	White (100%) 950 total members 375 active members HH Inc: $30-50K	Urban	8 offices 45 class-rooms Kitchen: 200	$630,000	1,2,3,9,11,13	130 (incl. 100 for day-care)	Familiar Unfavorable
7	Southern Baptist (SBC)	White male 40 years old Seminary Biblical Studies	White (100%) 372 total members 200 active members HH Inc: $20-30K	Rural	2 offices 20 class-rooms Kitchen: 200	$141,000	2,3,7,11, 12,13	8	Familiar Unfavorable

Interview Number[b]	Denominational Affiliation	Pastor/Leader Characteristics	Membership Characteristics[c]	Location[d]	Facilities[e]	Budget	Types of Aid Provided[f]	Number of People Helped/ Month	Charitable Choice Familiarity and Affect
8	Southern Baptist (SBC)	White male 36 years old Seminary M.Div.	White (100%) 150 total members 90 active members HH Inc: $20-30K	Semi-rural	2 offices 11 class-rooms Kitchen: 200	not specified	1,2,3,4,8,13	1	Unfamiliar Favorable
9	Catholic (Parish)	White male 46 years old Seminary Th.M.	Wh (84%); Bl (10%); Hisp (4%); Asian (2%) 1158 total members 740 active members HH Inc: $30-50K	Urban	5 offices 12 class-rooms Kitchen: 250	$480,000	1,2,3,4,5,7, 10,11,13	15-20	—
10	Catholic (Parish)	White male 49 years old Seminary M.A.	Wh (85%); Hisp (6%); Bl (3%); Asian (3%) 1600 total members 1000 active members HH Inc: not specified; upper-middle class	Urban	3 offices 12 class-rooms Kitchen: 200	$250,000	1,2,3,8,12,14	25	Familiar Ambivalent

Interview Number[b]	Denominational Affiliation	Pastor/Leader Characteristics	Membership Characteristics[c]	Location[d]	Facilities[e]	Budget	Types of Aid Provided[f]	Number of People Helped/ Month	Charitable Choice Familiarity and Affect
11	Latter-Day Saints	White male 35 years old No seminary Ph.D. (secular)	Wh (94%); Bl (3%); Asian (3%) 300 total members 120 active members HH Inc: $20-50K	Urban	1 office 13 class-rooms Kitchen: 150	$3,000	1,2,3,7,8,9, 10,12 (as needed)	2 families	Familiar Ambivalent
12	Presbyterian (PC-USA)	White female 47 years old Seminary M.Div.	White (99%) 265 total members 150 active members HH Inc: $30-50K	Urban	2 offices 10 class-rooms Kitchen: 175	$188,000	1,2,3,6,7,9, 13,16	10	Familiar Ambivalent
13	Presbyterian (PCA)	White male 32 years old Seminary M.Div.	White (100%) 350 total members 200 active members HH Inc: $30-50K	Urban	3 offices 20 class-rooms Kitchen: 100	$270,000	1,2,3,9,13	6-12	Unfamiliar Ambivalent
14	Presbyterian (PC-USA)	White male 51 years old Seminary M.Div.& D.Min.	White (99%) 170 total members 112 active members HH Inc: $30-50K	Urban	2 offices 9 class-rooms Kitchen: 200	$200,000	2,3,7	2-5 outsiders to church	Familiar Unfavorable

Interview Number[b]	Denominational Affiliation	Pastor/Leader Characteristics	Membership Characteristics[c]	Location[d]	Facilities[e]	Budget	Types of Aid Provided[f]	Number of People Helped/ Month	Charitable Choice Familiarity and Affect
15	Presbyterian (PC-USA)	White female 58 years old Seminary M.Div. & Th.M.	Wh (95%); Bl (5%) 26 total members 50 active members HH Inc: ranges from under $10K to over $50K	Urban	1 office 3 class-rooms Kitchen: 50	$70,000	1,2,3,4,7, 13,14	3	Familiar Ambivalent
16	United Methodist	Black male 44 years old Seminary M.Div.	Black (99%) 409 total members 225 active members HH Inc: $30-$50K	Urban	2 offices 10 class-rooms Kitchen: 100	$165,000	2,3,8,9,10 11,13,14,15	10-12	Familiar Favorable
17	United Methodist	Black female 60 years old Seminary Degree-seeking	Black (100%) 106 total members 50 active members HH Inc: $20-30K	Urban	1 office 5 class-rooms Kitchen: 150	not specified	1,2,3,4,7,14	3	Familiar Ambivalent
18	United Methodist	Black male 46 years old Seminary M.Div.	Black (98%) 205 total members 150 active members HH Inc: $30-50K	Urban	2 offices 8 class-rooms Kitchen: 150	$110,000	1,2,3,7,9, 10,11,12, 13,14,15	"infinite #"	Familiar Favorable

Interview Number[b]	Denominational Affiliation	Pastor/Leader Characteristics	Membership Characteristics[c]	Location[d]	Facilities[e]	Budget	Types of Aid Provided[f]	Number of People Helped/ Month	Charitable Choice Familiarity and Affect
19	United Methodist	Black female 45 years old Seminary M.Div.	Black (100%) 206 total members 150 active members HH Inc: $20-30K	Semi-rural	2 offices Kitchen: 100	$58,000	3,4,7,9,11, 12,13,14	10	Familiar Favorable
20	Missionary Baptist (National Baptist Convention)	Black male 57 years old Seminary B.A.	Bl (90%); Wh (5%) 525 total members 350 active members HH Inc: not specified; middle/upper-middle class	Urban	2 offices 8 class-rooms Kitchen: 300	not specified	1,2,3,5,8	5-10	Familiar Favorable
21	Baptist (National Baptist Convention)	Black male 43 years old Seminary Th.M.	Bl (95%); Wh (5%) 500 total members 375 active members HH Inc: $30-50K	Urban	2 offices 5 class-rooms Kitchen: 60	$120,000	2,3,5,12,13, 14,15	10	Familiar Ambivalent

Interview Number[b]	Denominational Affiliation	Pastor/Leader Characteristics	Membership Characteristics[c]	Location[d]	Facilities[e]	Budget	Types of Aid Provided[f]	Number of People Helped/ Month	Charitable Choice Familiarity and Affect
22	Missionary Baptist (National Baptist Convention)	Black male 69 years old Seminary B.A.	Black (100%) 300 total members 200 active members HH Inc: under $10K	Urban	2 offices 7 class-rooms Kitchen: 200	not specified	4	not specified	Familiar Favorable
23	Baptist (National Baptist Convention)	Black male 38 years old Seminary Certificate	Black (100%) 200 total members 125 active members HH Inc: $20-30K	Rural	1 office 3 class-rooms Kitchen	$60,000	1,2,3,7	25	Unfamiliar Favorable
24	Baptist (National Baptist Convention)	Black male 48 years old Seminary Degree not specified	Black (100%) 50 total members 35 active members HH Inc: $10-20K	Rural	1 office 2 class-rooms Kitchen: 50	not specified	7,13,14	4	Familiar Ambivalent
25	Church of God in Christ (COGIC)	Black male 45 years old No seminary	Black (99%) 400 total members 350 active members HH Inc: $30-50K	Urban	5 offices 16 class-rooms Kitchen: 300	$300,000	1,5,7,8,13	500-600	Familiar Favorable

Interview Number[b]	Denominational Affiliation	Pastor/Leader Characteristics	Membership Characteristics[c]	Location[d]	Facilities[e]	Budget	Types of Aid Provided[f]	Number of People Helped/ Month	Charitable Choice Familiarity and Affect
26	Church of God in Christ (COGIC)	Black male 43 years old No seminary	Black (100%) 200 total members 100 active members HH Inc: $10-20K	Urban	3 offices 4 class-rooms Kitchen: 75	not specified	1,2,3,4,5, 12,13	200+	Familiar Favorable
27	Muslim (North America Islamic Association)	Middle Eastern male 40 years old No formal religious training	International (71%); Asian (15%); Bl (10%); Wh (2%) 200 total members 150 active members HH Inc: $10-30K	Urban	2 offices 4 class-rooms Kitchen: 200	$5,000-$10,000	16 ("For needy according to their need; social support")	"Depends on # of needy"	Familiar Favorable
28	Catholic (Hispanic Ministry)	White male 49 years old Seminary M.Div.	Hispanic (98%) 300 total members 150 active members HH Inc: $10-20K	Rural	1 office 3 class-rooms	not specified	2,6,7,8,12, 13,16	20	Familiar Favorable

a: With the exception of the last column, this table was prepared from pre-interview survey information taken from pastors or religious leaders in our non-probability sample of local religious congregations. Charitable Choice Familiarity and Affect were estimated from responses to interview questions 6, 13, and 16 (see Appendix III). We use these multiple questions to estimate familiarity with and affect toward charitable choice in order to improve the validity of these data. The final row in this table (interview #28) counts a multi-church Hispanic Ministry as one entity for the purposes of our sample.

b: The assigned interview number does not reflect the order in which churches were surveyed or interviewed.

c: Where needed, "Wh," "Bl," and "Hisp" are used to abbreviate "White," "Black," and "Hispanic," respectively. "HH Inc" represents the typical household income within the congregation as reported by the key informant; the figure provided represents annual income, where $xK stands for x thousand dollars.

d: The term "urban" takes on a particular meaning in the rural South. Urban designates a church located in a county seat.

e: The figure following kitchen (e.g., "Kitchen: 200") describes the approximate number of persons that the kitchen facilities can serve.

f: The numerical references listed under "Types of Aid Provided" conform to the following key:

1 – HELP PAYING RENT
2 – HELP PAYING UTILITIES
3 – GROCERIES
4 – CASH
5 – TEMPORARY SHELTER
6 – LOW-COST HOUSING
7 – CLOTHING
8 – MEDICAL SERVICES
9 – CHILD CARE
10 – HOT MEALS
11 – CARE FOR THE ELDERLY
12 – TRANSPORTATION
13 – COUNSELING
14 – TUTORING
15 – AFTER-SCHOOL PROGRAMS
16 – OTHER (Specify)

Appendix II: Pre-Interview Survey Administered to Religious Leaders[3]

Interview Code No.:
Initials of interviewer:
Date:
Time:

Before we begin the interview, I would like to obtain some information about your religious congregation and your opinion about various topics. Please place an "X" in the appropriate spaces and fill in the blanks to the best of your ability.

Pastor Information

1. What is your: a. Age? b. Race/ethnicity? c. Gender? M__ F__
2. Beginning with first grade, how many years of schooling have you completed?
3. Were you trained at a religious institution/seminary? If so, where? What degree (if any) did you receive?
4. How long have you been pastor of this church?
5. Where did you serve as pastor before coming to this church (location, denomination)?
6. Is your church affiliated with a para-church group or larger religious network? If so, which one(s)?

Church Membership Information

Membership and Attendance

1. What is the total membership of the church?
2. How many of those members would you consider active members?
3. At a typical weekly service, approximately how many people are in attendance?
4. On which days of the week do you have services? (Sunday through Saturday provided as response categories)

5. What types of services do you have on each day?
6. Estimate what percentage of your congregation is in each age category:
   ___ % Under 20 ___ % 20-34 ___ % 35-49
   ___ % 50-65 ___ % over 65
7. Your church membership is approximately ___% male and ___% female.
8. Do you have any services that primarily draw men or women? If so, what are they?
9. At a typical service, your congregation is (estimate percentage)
   ___% European-American/White
   ___% African-American/Black
   ___ % Asian-American/Asian
   ___% Hispanic (Mexican, Puerto Rican, Cuban origins)
   ___% American Indian
   ___% Other (specify)________________________

Occupation

10. The most common occupations in your congregation are
    ___ white collar/professional
    ___ skilled workers/technicians
    ___ service workers/retail/sales
    ___ laborers
    ___ homemaker
    ___ unemployed
    ___ other (specify)________________________

Income

11. How would you describe your congregation?
    ___ working class/low-income
    ___ lower middle class
    ___ middle class
    ___ upper middle class
    ___ upper class

12. A typical household of your congregation earns:
    ___ under $10,000
    ___ $10-20,000
    ___ $20-30,000
    ___ $30-50,000
    ___ over $50,000

Aid Provided by the Church

13. Which of the following types of aid or services does your church provide on a regular basis?

___ HELP PAYING RENT	___ HOT MEALS
___ HELP PAYING UTILITIES	___ CARE FOR THE ELDERLY
___ GROCERIES	___ TRANSPORTATION
___ CASH	___ COUNSELING
___ TEMPORARY SHELTER	___ TUTORING
___ LOW-COST HOUSING	___ AFTER SCHOOL PROGRAMS
___ CLOTHING	___ OTHER (Specify)_______________
___ MEDICAL SERVICES	___________________________
___ CHILD CARE	___________________________

14. In a given month, how many people does your church help? _________

Annual Church Budget

15. The yearly budget of your church is $_________________.

Church Debt

16. Does your church have a debt?
17. If so, how large a debt do you have?
18. How many years will it take to pay it off?

Facilities

19. What is the size of church buildings (overall square footage)?
20. What is the seating capacity of your church?
21. How many classrooms does your church have?
22. How many offices does your church have?
23. Does your church have kitchen facilities? If so, how many people can be served out of your kitchen?
24. Does your church have a playground? If so, how many kids can it accommodate?
25. Does your church have bathroom facilities? If so, how many toilets?
26. Does your church have insurance? If so, what type(s) of insurance? What is the amount of coverage?

Appendix III: Interview Questionnaire for Religious Leaders[4]

1. To begin, tell me a bit about the history of your church and what your church stands for.
2. How is your church organized? What positions does your church have, and how are decisions made in your church?
3. What type of social service programs (e.g., outreach, mutual aid, relief or missionary work) does your church currently offer? How active are these programs? At whom are they targeted and by whom are they staffed? Is your congregation involved in any community based or inter-church relief programs? Have you heard of Mississippi Faith and Families? If so, what has been your experience with that program?
4. Which of the church's outreach or aid programs have been successful and which have not? What factors have contributed to their success or failure?
5. What do you think of government-sponsored public assistance that is currently in place in our society? Do you think churches might be able to provide aid in ways that the government cannot? How do churches provide aid differently than that provided by the government? (PROBE: Do churches provide *different* types of aid? Do churches use *different means* for delivering assistance to the needy?)
6. Have you heard of the idea that churches might become more involved in the restructuring of public welfare? What do you think of that idea? What do you think would be the outcome of such a program? Do you think the members of your congregation would or could support such a program?
7. Suppose your church was given a block grant from the state to provide additional aid to the needy in the community. What types of aid could your church provide with such a grant? How would the church use those funds? Who do you think should make decisions concerning how that money is used?
8. What standards do you use when deciding to give aid? Would those standards change if public money were used to expand your aid programs?
9. If welfare services were to be routed through local churches, do you think attitudes about race or ethnicity would affect the way in which such aid is distributed? Do you think that race currently affects the distribution of aid provided by Mississippi churches?
10. In deciding to take people off of aid, what rules do you currently apply? Do you think these rules would change if you had additional funds at your disposal to provide aid?

11. Do you think your church, or churches in general, can help people get off welfare? Do you think a joint effort among churches would be effective in this regard?
12. Many people living in poverty are single mothers and their children, as well as the elderly. Do you currently provide aid or services to these types of individuals? If so, how effective have these programs been? Would additional funding enable you to initiate or expand the aid provided to these groups of people?
13. If your church were to cooperate with the government in providing welfare services, would you have any concerns about such an arrangement? Would members of your congregation support this arrangement?
14. How will members of your congregation be affected once welfare support is no longer available to current recipients?
15. Suppose an increasing number of non-members came to your congregation seeking aid. What do you think would be the reaction of your church to these non-members' efforts to seek aid?
16. What are your views concerning the separation of church and state? If the church did play a role in providing welfare services, how might your views about the separation of church and state affect the program?
17. Thinking back over the past several years, what has been the single biggest change in the way you minister to your congregation? What has brought about this change?
18. Do you think that religion is more or less important in this country today than it was twenty years ago?
19. What programs does your church offer youth? In what ways, if any, does your church minister to the youth in your congregation?
20. Finally, I am curious about your general impressions of religion in America today. What do you think are the most important issues that are influencing religion at the national level? How do you think religious communities should respond to the issues/challenges you have identified?

Endnotes

1. Several notes bear mentioning at this juncture. First, our final sample of churches contains one black congregation located just outside of GTR proper. However, the demographic profile of the community in which this church is situated (not identified to preserve pastoral and congregational anonymity) is quite similar to those of small towns in GTR. Second, although we interviewed a leader from a local mosque, stylistic conventions dictate that we sometimes use the word "church" to refer to the religious communities in our sample. Third, one church is not featured in Appendix I. This church did not return a pre-interview survey initially provided during the in-depth interview.

2. The names used to refer to religious organizations and individual pastors in this chapter have been changed to preserve the anonymity of our subjects.

3. Pre-interview survey was self-administered prior to the interview. Given space considerations and readability, the survey was reformatted for this appendix. The specific questions asked on the pre-interview survey have been retained here.

4. Interview questionnaire adapted as needed to fit congregational context.

Bibliography

A Guide to Charitable Choice: The Rules of Section 104 of the 1996 Federal Welfare Law Governing State Cooperation with Faith-Based Social-Service Providers. 1997. Washington, D.C.: The Center for Public Justice, and Annandale, Virginia: The Christian Legal Society's Center for Law and Religious Freedom.

Amato-von Hemert, Kathleen. 1998. "Anti-Poverty Policy and Practice: Ethnographic Case Study of Churches in Appalachia, Kentucky and South-Central, Los Angeles." Working Paper, Joint Center for Poverty Research.

Ammerman, Nancy Tatom. 1997. *Congregation and Community*. New Brunswick: Rutgers University Press.

Boles, John B. 1972. *The Great Revival,* 1787-1805. Lexington: University of Kentucky Press.

Boston, Rob. 1998. "The 'Charitable Choice Charade.'" *Church and State* 51: 7-12.

Burger, Stephen E. 1996. "New Hope for Gospel Missions? Devil's in the Details." *USA Today,* September 3.

Chaves, Mark. 1999. "Religious Congregations and Welfare Reform: Who Will Take Advantage of 'Charitable Choice?'" *American Sociological Review,* vol. 64, no. 6.

Davis, Derek H., and Barry Hankins (eds.). 1999. *Welfare Reform and Faith-Based Organizations,* Waco: Baylor University J.M. Dawson Institute of Church-State Studies.

Eng, Eugenia, and John W. Hatch. 1991. "Networking between Agencies and Black Churches: The Lay Health Advisor Model." *Prevention in Human Services* 10: 123-146.

Faith & Families of Mississippi. nd-a. "Faith & Families of Mississippi: 'What is it?'" Jackson, MS: Faith & Families.

Faith & Families of Mississippi. nd-b. "From a Life of Dependency to a Life of Self Sufficiency." Jackson, MS: Faith & Families.

Fritz, Sara. 1999. "'Charitable Choice' Unites Church, State." *St. Petersburg Times,* June 18.

Harrell, David Edwin, Jr (ed.). 1981. *Varieties of Southern Evangelicalism.* Macon, GA: Mercer University Press.

Harris, Margaret. 1995. "Quiet Care: Welfare Work and Religious Congregations." *Journal of Social Policy* 24: 53-71.

________. 1996. "'An Inner Group of Willing, People': Volunteering in a Religious Context." *Social Policy and Administration* 30: 54-68.

Harrison, Erik. 1995a. "Religious Groups in Mississippi Take Poor Folks under Their Wings." *Houston Chronicle,* September 17.

______. 1995b. "Welfare Reform: Mississippi Experiment Puts Faith in Religious Groups." *Los Angeles Times,* August 29.

Harvey, Paul. 1997. *Redeeming the South: Religious Cultures and Racial Identities among Southern Baptists,* 1865-1925. Chapel Hill: University of North Carolina Press.

Hogstel, Mildred O., and C. Gail Davis. 1996. "Eldercare and Support in the Church." *Journal of Religious Gerontology* 9: 43-56.

Howell, Frank M. 1997. Mississippi Welfare Reform and Labor Market Capacity. Mississippi State University: SSRC Special Report Series, Mississippi State University.

Humphrey, Richard A. 1980. "Religion in Appalachia: Implications for Social Work Practice." *Journal of Humanics* 8: 4-18.

Jewish News. 1999. "Other Voices in the Valley." *The Arizona Republic,* May 24.

Johnson, Alonzo, and Paul Jersild (eds.). 1996. *"Ain't Gonna Lay My 'Ligion Down:" African-American Religion in the South.* Columbia: University of South Carolina Press.

Kids Count Data Book. 1998. State Profiles of Child Well-Being. Baltimore: The Annie E. Casey Foundation.

Mississippi Population Data Sheet. 1993. Social Science Research Center, Mississippi State University.

Morrison, John D. 1991. "The Black Church as a Support System for Black Elderly." *Journal of Gerontological Social Work* 17: 105-120.

Olasky, Marvin. 1992. *The Tragedy of American Compassion.* Washington, D.C.: Regnery Publishing.

Olson, Lynn M., Janet Reis, Larry Murphy, and Jennifer H. Gehm. 1988. "The Religious Community as a Partner in Health Care." *Journal of Community Health* 13: 249-257.

Pinkerton, James P. 1999. "Can Faith-Based Groups Resist Uncle Sam?" *The Buffalo News,* June 6.

Raasch, Chuck. 1999. "Religious Alliance Raises Concerns about Gore Idea." *USA Today,* May 26.

Rawlings, Charles W., and Janet W. Schrock. 1996. "The Role of the Religious Community in Shaping Community Partnerships for Health Care." *Journal of Long-Term Home Health Care* 15: 57-59.

Roe, Emery. 1994. *Narrative Policy Analysis: Theory and Practice.* Durham, NC: Duke University Press.

Sherwood, D.A. 1998. "Charitable Choice: Opportunity and Challenge for Christians in Social Work." *Social Work and Christianity* 25: 1-23.

Stowell, Daniel W. 1998. *Rebuilding Zion: The Religious Reconstruction of the South, 1863-1877.* New York: Oxford University Press.

White, O. Kendall, and Daryl White (eds). 1995. *Religion in the Contemporary South: Diversity, Community, and Identity*. Athens: University of Georgia Press.

Wolfe, Alan. 1993. "Whatever Happened to Compassion?" *Critical Review* 7: 497-503.

Yardley, Jim. 1996. "Focus on Overhauling Welfare...Mississippi Enlists Church Community." *The Atlanta Journal and Constitution,* April 30.

CHAPTER SEVEN

Business Improvement Districts and Innovative Service Delivery

Jerry Mitchell
Professor
School of Public Affairs
Baruch College, The City University of New York

This report was originally published in November 1999, revised May 2003.

Introduction

Downtown revitalization is at the top of the policy agenda in many American communities. Whether a response to urban sprawl or the judgment that vibrant commercial centers are essential for a quality community life, political and business leaders from across the political spectrum have been pushing for a return to the sidewalks of downtown.[1] So far, the evidence is that change is possible, illustrated best by the impressive renewal of Times Square in New York City. Equally important, the indication is that downtown renewal can be uniquely advanced through a new public-private partnership—the business improvement district (BID).

This chapter is an empirical study of BIDs. There are five sections: 1) an introduction to the BID concept, 2) a description of the methodology to survey the nation's BID managers, 3) the presentation of the research findings, 4) the identification of several recommendations to improve BIDs, and 5) a discussion of their future role in American society.

The BID Innovation

Local public administration has long been a source of creativity, from the elimination of spoils to the creation of city-manager governments to the privatization of public services. In recent years, this spirit of innovation has led to a fundamental reconsideration of municipal government, namely that government should be less involved in providing services and more involved in making sure services are provided. The book *Reinventing Government* put it this way, "Today's entrepreneurial leaders know their communities are healthy when their families, neighborhoods, schools, voluntary organizations, and businesses are healthy—and that government's most profound role is to steer these institutions to health."[2]

BIDs are a conspicuous illustration of creative thinking at the local level. Emerging in the 1980s and expanding in the 1990s to large and small cities throughout the nation, BIDs have essentially reformulated the concept of service delivery to commercial centers. While there are differences in the specific names, missions, and structures of BIDs from state to state, the basic approach is one in which a geographically defined majority of property owners and/or merchants agrees to provide an extra level of public service in a specific area by imposing an added tax or fee on all of the properties and/or businesses in the area. Examples of the services that may be provided include supplementary security, additional street cleaning, and the unique marketing of events. The job of local government is to legally establish the district, collect the special tax assessments or fees, and then transfer the funds over to a BID organization to use as it sees fit. BIDs are thus "a powerful combination of ingredients—business self-interest and vision, together with public financing unencumbered by urban politics."[3]

As entrepreneurial enterprises, BIDs are expected to "channel private-sector energy toward the solution of public problems."[4] Sometimes BIDs change the public image of commercial areas by putting up colorful signs, increasing trash pick-ups, and making façade improvements; in other cases they may draw shoppers downtown by producing special events, such as concerts or sidewalk sales; and in some instances they may encourage the creation of new businesses by supplying low-interest loans or working with local planning bodies to change zoning rules. By applying these and a variety of other economic revitalization techniques, BIDs have been credited with transforming many deserted, distressed downtown areas into exciting, interesting places where businesses want to relocate and people want to work, shop, live, and have fun.

BIDs have indeed become an integral part of American community life. *The New York Times,* for example, has proclaimed BIDs to be "one of the engines of New York City's renaissance,"[5] and The *Milwaukee Journal Sentinel* has likewise placed BIDs at the center of Milwaukee's "urban business renaissance."[6] More generally, the conclusion is that they are "more effective than government,"[7] "net contributors to public life,"[8] and "an urban revolution."[9] As BIDs have become more prominent, one 1998 survey found a growing optimism toward downtown areas in the U.S. among businesses, suburbanites, tourists, and others.[10]

The success of BIDs is perhaps best indicated by the fact that there were only a few such organizations in the country 20 years ago and now there are hundreds of them operating in 42 states[11] and the District of Columbia (see Table 7.1 for examples of BIDs). Self-assessment districts exist today in most of the nation's largest cites, including Chicago, Denver, Houston, Los Angeles, New Orleans, New York, Philadelphia, San Diego, Seattle, Tampa, and Washington, D.C. The expectation is that more will appear because new districts are under consideration in Boston, Jacksonville, Newark, and several other cities.

No two BIDs are exactly alike because each is an experiment in public administration for a particular area. In fact, there is not even any name consistency. For example, in Iowa they are called self-supported municipal improvement districts; in New Jersey they are known as special improvement districts; in Missouri they are called special business districts; in Texas they are labeled public improvement districts; in Oregon they are referred to as economic improvement districts; and in Washington they are termed parking and business improvement associations. Although California, New York, and most other states use the BID designation, any particular organization may still have a unique name, such as the Alliance for Downtown New York, Inc., or Downtown Visions, Inc. in Wilmington, Delaware.

Table 7.1: BID Examples

The **Alliance for Downtown New York, Inc.,** operates a BID in lower Manhattan in New York City. Covering the Wall Street financial district, the Alliance provides an array of services, such as providing funds for retailers to upgrade their storefronts, operating a jitney for downtown workers, and showcasing the area as a place to work, live, shop and dine.

The **Center City District** provides an assortment of supplemental services in downtown Philadelphia. With a budget of $9 million dollars, the District undertakes sidewalk cleaning, graffiti removal, landscape maintenance, crime prevention, and advertising and promotion. In a particularly innovative approach, the District produces ads contrasting the center city favorably with the suburbs in the quality and diversity of business services.

Central Atlanta Progress is responsible for an improvement district that seeks to make downtown Atlanta safe and clean, to increase the number of local jobs, and to promote the development of more market-rate downtown housing. To improve safety, the downtown district has a 50-person Ambassador Force that not only provides street patrols, but also conducts a hospitality campaign for conventioneers, visitors, and residents.

Downtown D.C. in Washington D.C. provides supplemental services to an area of approximately 120 blocks containing 825 properties that are subject to a self-assessment tax. Its goals include designing and implementing a consistent program of signage, developing promotion materials to better inform the public about downtown D.C., and enforcing a zero tolerance policy toward graffiti in the area.

The **Cleveland Theater District Development Corporation** (CTDDC) is the operating agent for the newly created BID in the Playhouse Square area. The CTDDC is responsible for maintaining a clean and attractive area; developing promotion materials; and providing additional security patrols on local streets.

The **Historic Third Ward Association** is responsible for BID #2 in the area adjacent to downtown Milwaukee. The BID area is home to over 350 business and 400 residences and is a nationally listed historic district. The Association has focused on developing a strategy for converting various manufacturing and warehousing structures into commercial and residential uses.

The **Hollywood Entertainment District** spans an 18-block stretch of Hollywood Boulevard and is funded by 240 property owners. The District provides security, cleaning, and marketing services. It is generally intended to make the area a visitor destination and an inviting location for business investment.

The **Mesa Town Center Corporation** (MTCC) works on behalf of 300 commercial properties and 600 business owners in the Town Center of Mesa, Arizona. A 501(c)6 nonprofit economic development corporation, the MTCC generates and provides downtown information and research; works with the local police department on security issues; and is actively involved in the retention and recruitment of new businesses.

Although there are differences among BIDs (the term used herein), the following general attributes are important:

- **BIDs are authorized by law.** Normally a state passes a statute that permits local governments to create BIDs. These statutes specify such things as how funds are to be collected, the types of services that may be provided, the size and makeup of the governing board, and the method by which property or business owners formally persuade government to create a BID.
- **BIDs are usually established through a petition process.** The initial impetus for creating a BID may come from real estate developers, property owners, merchants, downtown associations, or local government itself. To approve a BID in most jurisdictions, the affected property owners or businesses must vote for it in a petition submitted to the local governing body. Depending on the jurisdiction, the tests of approval range from 51% to 70% of those eligible to vote. In some places, such as New York, a BID may come into existence if a majority in the proposed district *do not* object to its creation. In a few states, such as New Jersey, the local government may establish a district without any petition vote.
- **BIDs receive most of their funding from an added assessment on the property owners and/or businesses within the boundary of the business district.** These self-assessments are mandatory, although there are often exemptions for residences. While there are extensive variations in tax rates around the nation, assessments are usually in the range of 1% to 3% of assessed valuation. Assessment formulas also vary widely, including square footage, a proportion of the benefits to be received, a frontage basis, or some combination of these. In some communities, fixed or conditional fees are paid by businesses instead of assessments. BIDs may also receive additional funds from economic development grants, voluntary donations, local subsidies, or the sale of goods and services. Institutions that pay no property tax, such as federal government offices and public hospitals, may provide in-kind or cash contributions.
- **BIDs may implement services through either a nonprofit organization, government corporation, or public-nonprofit partnership.** It is likely that a nonprofit BID may have begun as a voluntary merchant association. If a government agency is responsible, it is common for a BID to be controlled by a quasi-independent government corporation, although in small towns a planning department may be in charge if there is not enough revenue to warrant a separate organization. The partnership model, or so-called "holding company" approach, is relatively recent and typically involves a nonprofit membership entity that engages in downtown advocacy; a development corporation that finances

public facilities and infrastructure; and a not-for-profit or quasi-public management enterprise that provides security, maintenance, and other services.[12]

- **BIDs are expected to focus on what will be most effective for the business district.** A governing board, composed mostly of property or business owners in the area, oversees the district to maintain accountability, to establish a direction for its activities, and to select a manager to run the BID. Local government normally plays a limited role in the actual operation of a BID except to renew the district at particular time intervals and to monitor expenditures. The ideal is for the BID manager and the governing board to have the freedom and flexibility to discover what is the best way to enhance the district area.

Managing Innovation

BIDs separate off the management of public services from the normal structures and processes of government in a manner similar to special districts, government corporations, and independent regulatory agencies.[13] The advantages of BIDs include the following:[14]

- A dedicated, secure source of revenue is supplied for the provision of services and property or business owners are prevented from free-riding on the contributions of others.
- There is an independent power to act—to make plans, to hire people, to let contracts, to own and operate facilities, and to make physical improvements.
- A focus exists that allows business interests to think through problems and to come up with original solutions.

Underlying all of these benefits is that BIDs effectuate a "management tool for downtown."[15] With sufficient funding, highly skilled individuals can be paid to manage BIDs. With money and the power to act, BID managers can scan the environment to find the most effective ways to accomplish goals. And with a narrow focus, BID managers can put all of their attention towards promoting business interests and to developing partnerships with other community interests in order to implement solutions.

There are several ways to view BID management. To some, the model for BID management is a shopping mall or Disney World, involving the efficient supervision of day-to-day downtown activities.[16] To others, BID management is less about supervision and more about providing businesses with an ombudsman to the community, someone who can work with city hall and various local stakeholders.[17] Yet another perspective is to see BID management as "urban husbandry," that is, a single entrepreneur working in a small-scale organization who is continually seeking alternative ways "to reinvigorate and build on existing community assets in order to stimulate a place-based rejuvenation."[18]

Research Questions

There has been little research to identify how BID managers are actually approaching their jobs, or for that matter, to understand how BIDs are structured and what kinds of services they provide. While this lack of analysis can be partly attributed to the newness of the device, it is also because the emphasis thus far has been on describing the activities of selected BIDs;[19] trying to understand how best to create them;[20] considering how they fit into municipal governance;[21] and examining problems of accountability and oversight.[22] These issues are obviously important, but so too is a factual understanding of how the nation's BIDs are structured and managed. This is true for BID managers, who depend on information to enhance their performance, as well as for citizens and elected officials looking to create new BIDs or further the development of existing ones.

Three areas of research are important:

- **Structure:** What types of organizations are running BIDs? How large are they in terms of budgets, number of employees, and blocks covered? What is the size of their governing board?
- **Functions:** What kinds of services do they provide? Are there differences among BIDS in service delivery?
- **Management:** Who manages BIDs? How do BID managers approach their jobs? What are the knowledge areas and management skills required for success? How is BID performance evaluated?

Methodology

To examine the aforementioned research questions, a national mail survey of BID managers was undertaken. The target population was the top managers of BIDs (executive directors, presidents, etc.). The survey was implemented in the summer, 1999.

Population Identification

The initial step in the survey research process was to identify the population of BIDs to receive a questionnaire. This was no easy manner. Most state or local governments do not inventory BIDs, many of these organizations are not listed in telephone directories, and it is often difficult to discern the differences among voluntary merchant associations, economic development agencies, and BIDs. The International Downtown Association has estimated there are over 1,000 BIDs in North America, which includes approximately 300 Canadian organizations. The problem is that this estimate was derived from a compilation of what knowledgeable people *perceived* to be the number of operating BIDs, not from any process of systematic data collection.

To find BIDs for this study, it was necessary to determine the types of organizations that should be counted. The search was primarily for any independently managed organization in the United States whose funding came from mandatory taxes or fees paid by businesses or property owners, collected by government or the BID itself, and then spent by the BID on service delivery. Voluntary merchant associations were excluded because they lack the governmental authorization and special funding that makes BIDs unique. BIDs operating out of existing planning or economic departments were also excluded because it was too difficult to separate out BID functions from normal municipal functions. However, BIDs were included where there was a partnership between a specialized municipal unit (such as a parking authority) and a BID operating as a nonprofit organization. For purposes of data collection, a partnership arrangement was considered a single organization.

The following activities were undertaken to locate BIDs:

- The Internet was explored through 12 different search engines: Yahoo, MSN, Excite, Go To, Altavista, Infoseek, Snap, Lycos, Magellan, Netscape, Web Crawler, and Profusion. The search terms were "business improvement district," "public improvement district," "special improvement district," and "special services area." A total of 32 BID websites were investigated.
- A search was made for references to BIDs in books, newspaper stories, court cases, and journal articles. The major catalogs examined were from the City University of New York, the New York Public Library, Columbia University, and the Library of Congress. A database search was also conducted through Lexus-Nexus, Public Affairs Information Service, and Gale Encyclopedia of Associations.
- Letters asking for addresses and names of the executive directors of BIDs were mailed to 49 state municipal leagues, 50 state legislative research offices, 45 state economic development offices, and 50 municipal economic development offices in cities with over 100,000 population.
- Address and contact information was requested through either phone calls, letters, e-mails, or visits to 75 BIDs, 40 local government planning and economic development offices, and 15 professional associations,

including those concerned with downtown revitalization and the national main street program.

- Information was collected at the office of the International Downtown Association.
- *Downtown Idea Exchange* newsletters were examined for the years 1996 through 1998.

A total of 404 BIDs were identified from this data collection effort (see Table 7.2 for the distribution by state). California, New York, New Jersey, North Carolina, and Wisconsin were the states with the largest number of BIDs.

In most states, there is a high level of certainty that the numbers are accurate either because there were few communities where BIDs could be

Table 7.2: The Distribution of BIDs in the United States

	Number		Number
Alabama	1	Nebraska	1
Alaska	1	Nevada	1
Arizona	3	New Hampshire	1
Arkansas	2	New Jersey	35
California	73	New Mexico	0
Colorado	7	New York	63
Connecticut	3	North Carolina	32
Delaware	1	North Dakota	0
Florida	12	Ohio	7
Georgia	10	Oklahoma	1
Hawaii	0	Oregon	8
Idaho	2	Pennsylvania	11
Illinois	11	Rhode Island	0
Indiana	2	South Carolina	2
Iowa	10	South Dakota	0
Kansas	2	Tennessee	2
Kentucky	1	Texas	10
Louisiana	3	Utah	1
Maine	1	Vermont	1
Maryland	2	Virginia	10
Massachusetts	1	Washington	4
Michigan	0	West Virginia	0
Minnesota	3	Wisconsin	54
Mississippi	1	Wyoming	0
Missouri	3	Washington, D.C.	3
Montana	2		
		Total	**404**

created or there was a government agency or professional organization that provided an enumeration. However, since new BIDs are created all the time the population of BIDs may have changed as this research was ongoing. For example, 24 new BIDs were under consideration in Los Angeles alone. It is also conceivable that a few BIDs were missed because they could not be found through any of the aforementioned search techniques.

Overall, this population of BIDs is the most comprehensive list that exists to date. It includes BIDs from every section of the county; 42 states; all such organizations located in Chicago, Los Angeles, and New York City; and the entire BID membership of the International Downtown Association.

Questionnaire Construction

To determine the questions to ask BID managers, two previous BID surveys were reviewed, one conducted by the Pittsburgh Downtown Partnership involving 23 BIDs[23] and another undertaken by Lawrence O. Houstoun, Jr., involving 24 BIDs.[24] For comparative purposes, there was also an analysis of previous surveys of government corporation executives and city administrators.

In addition to secondary sources, the subject matter for the questionnaire was considered during several in-person interviews. Unstructured interviews were conducted with 12 BID managers from different sections of the country, as well as with two management consultants and two leaders of professional associations.

The final survey instrument is included in the Appendix.

Survey Implementation

The questionnaire was mailed to the top managers of the 404 BIDs on June 23, 1999. A cover letter with a postage-paid reply envelope was included with each survey.[25] The cover letter explained the purpose of the survey and guaranteed the respondents confidentiality. On July 9, a follow-up reminder postcard was mailed to the nonrespondents. On July 25, another letter and survey was mailed to those who had not yet responded. On August 8, one final mailing was completed. The survey research process ended on August 24 with the receipt of 264 completed questionnaires. This is a response rate of 65%.

Study Findings

The analysis of the survey responses was undertaken with the aim of making the results straightforward and easy to assess. Consequently, some question categories were combined and several responses were recoded to provide averages and other summary statistics. In the tables, the frequencies are less than the sample size of 264 because some of the questions were not answered by all of the respondents.

Structures

BIDs are new. Almost 60% were created since 1990. Nearly 28% were established since 1995.

Large, medium, and small communities have BIDs. The median city size for the population of BIDs was 104,445; the median size for the response sample was 105,301. The city size range in the BID population was from approximately 1,000 to over 7,000,000; in the response sample, it was from a little more than 2,000 to over 7,000,000. One-fourth of the BIDs in the sample were from an urban area with greater than 700,000 people.

Among the BIDs, 61% were operated by nonprofit organizations, 13% were the responsibility of public sector bodies, and 26% were run by a public-nonprofit partnership. Generally, the smaller the community the more likely the BID was run by a public agency; the larger the community the more likely it was the responsibility of a nonprofit organization.

No matter the type of organization, most BIDs employ few persons on a full-time basis (excluding contract workers or those on loan from local government). The median number of employees was two, the average was eight, and the range of full-time employees went from none to 155. In those BIDs with no full-time workers, the BID manager served in a part-time capacity. Slightly more than 32% of the BIDs had two employees and 16% had three workers. Only 5% had more than 50 full-time personnel.

BID managers control relatively large budgets. Annual expenditures ranged from $8,000 to $15 million. The median budget was $200,000. One consequence of a larger budget was the ability to hire more workers. The correlation between BID budgets and the number of employees was .71. Budget size was only moderately correlated with city size (.33) and with the number of blocks in a BID (.47).

All of the BIDs in the sample were funded by self-assessments because of the selection methodology. For other sources of revenue, 50% of the BIDs received voluntary donations; 27% obtained federal or state subsidies; 24% acquired funds from local government; and 21% sold goods or services. Only 7% issued bonds. While this survey did not address to what extent different sources of funding contribute to the overall budgets of BIDs, previous research in New York has determined that self-assessments make up by far the largest percentage.[26] Similarly, a 1995 survey of 23 BIDs by the Pittsburgh Downtown Partnership found self-assessments made up at least 84% of any budget.[27]

The median and average number of blocks in a BID was 20. The number of blocks ranged from one to 300. There was a small correlation between the number of blocks in a BID and the size of the governing board (.30). The median size of boards was 15 and the average was 16. The smallest board had three members and the largest had 51.

Functions

To assess the functions of BIDs, the respondents were asked to indicate their level of involvement with nine services:

- **Capital Improvements:** installing pedestrian-scale lighting and street furniture; planting trees and shrubbery.
- **Consumer Marketing:** producing festivals and events; coordinating sales promotions; producing maps and newsletters.
- **Economic Development:** offering incentives (such as tax abatements or loans) to new and expanding businesses.
- **Maintenance:** collecting rubbish; removing litter and graffiti; washing sidewalks; shoveling snow; trimming trees.
- **Parking and Transportation:** managing a public parking system; maintaining transit shelters.
- **Policy Advocacy:** promoting public policies to the community; lobbying government on behalf of business interests.
- **Public Space Regulation:** managing sidewalk vending; discouraging panhandling; controlling vehicle loading.
- **Security:** providing supplementary security guards; buying and installing electronic security systems; working with the city police force.
- **Social Services:** aiding the homeless; providing job training; supplying youth services.

Table 7.3 presents the service delivery results. More than three-fourths of the BIDs were very involved with consumer marketing. More than half were very involved with capital improvements, maintenance, and policy advocacy. Less than half were very involved with economic development, parking/transportation, public space regulation, and security. Only 6% were very involved with social services.

Three aspects of the service delivery findings stand out:

- "Clean and safe" is a phrase often associated with BIDs, but according to the survey, maintenance and security activities were not as important as consumer marketing, at least for the entire sample.

Table 7.3: BID Services Distribution

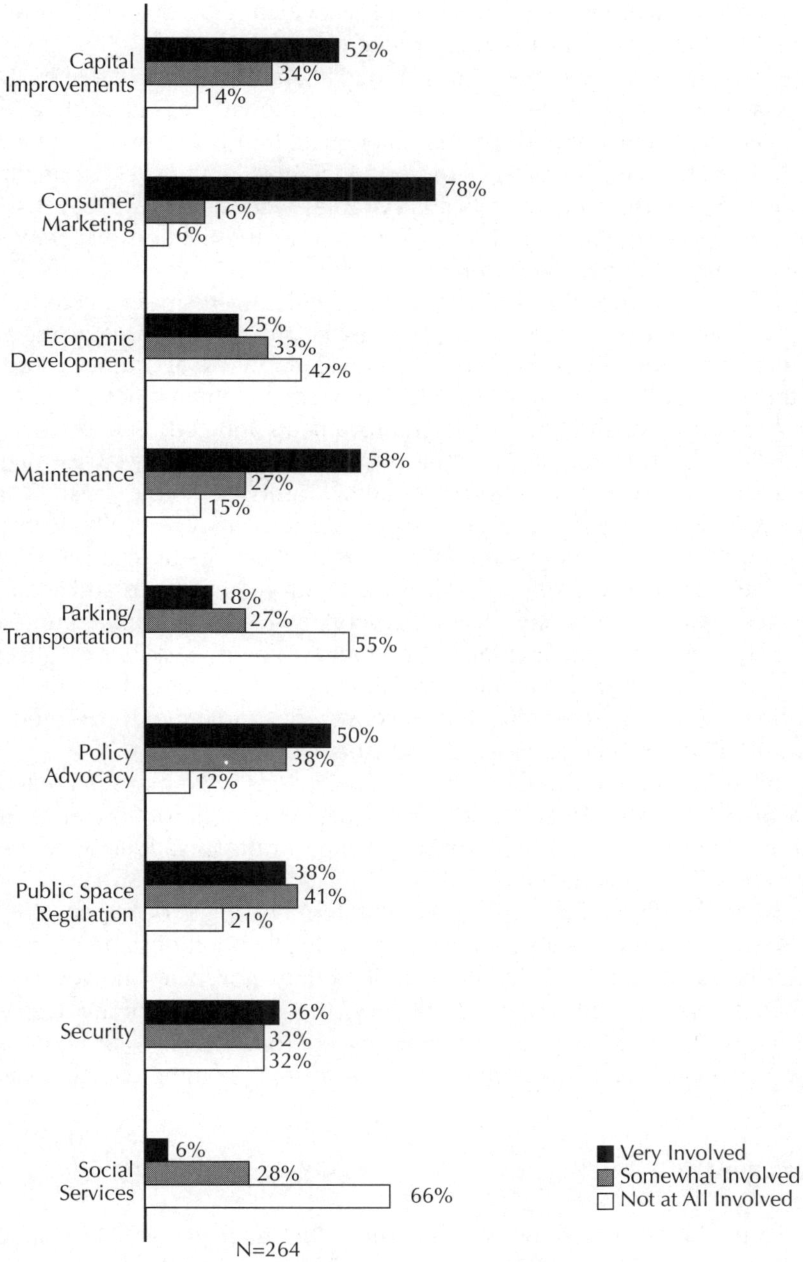

- The number of BIDs that engaged in policy advocacy was relatively high. BIDs are known for providing services such as landscaping and sidewalk cleaning, but it has been less evident that they act almost as interest groups in the political sphere.
- Few BIDs were very involved with parking/transportation services. This was unexpected since the decline of downtown areas is partly attributed to insufficient parking and inadequate transportation alternatives.

When the nine services were cross-tabulated with several organizational characteristics, the significant variables were city size, budget size, and the type of organization. Table 7.4 presents the relationship between service delivery and these factors.

Table 7.4 shows that BIDs from large cities were more likely to be involved with the entire range of services, especially consumer marketing and maintenance. Security and public space regulation were also much more of a concern for BIDs in large cities. BIDS from small communities were more apt to be very involved with capital improvements and consumer marketing.

While this research did not measure which type of funds (assessments, donations, etc.) were used to pay for particular services, Table 7.4 indicates BIDs with large budgets were more likely to be very involved with the entire range of services except for capital improvements. Large-budget BIDs were nearly three times as likely to be involved with maintenance and security services. Again, many small BIDs were very involved with capital improvements (which could be as minor as putting up flower baskets on light fixtures or as major as installing new streetlights). Of note, these findings confirm previous research that discovered fundamental differences between BIDs with large and small budgets.[28]

Table 7.4 also shows that public organizations were more likely to be very involved with capital improvements than were nonprofit organizations or mixed public-nonprofit enterprises. Nonprofit organizations were more involved with maintenance.

Overall, BID service delivery is not uniform. As might be expected with an innovative form of public administration, local conditions and organizational factors affected service delivery. This does not mean, however, that BIDs are narrowly specialized. If anything, the wide extent of involvement of BIDs with a range of public services (except for social services) confirms that they are a broad-based means for transforming commercial centers.

Management

Four areas were examined concerning BID management: 1) manager attributes, 2) management styles, 3) knowledge and skills requirements), and 4) performance evaluation methods.

Table 7.4: The Relationship Between Service Delivery and City Size, Budget Size, and Type of Organization*

	City Size			
Very Involved with Service	**2,000-24,458**	**24,459-105,301**	**105,302 736,014**	**736,015-7,000,000**
Capital Improvements	64%	50%	44%	49%
Consumer Marketing	80%	83%	88%	71%
Economic Development	27%	33%	18%	23%
Maintenance	32%	49%	69%	85%
Parking/Transportation	12%	12%	24%	26%
Policy Advocacy	39%	46%	64%	54%
Public Space Regulation	21%	27%	49%	56%
Security	11%	22%	58%	59%
Social Services	2%	2%	5%	16%
	Budget Size			
Very Involved with Service	**1,000-100,000**	**100,001-200,000**	**200,001-718,500**	**718,501-15,000,000**
Capital Improvements	61%	63%	40%	43%
Consumer Marketing	68%	88%	81%	77%
Economic Development	20%	29%	30%	23%
Maintenance	35%	46%	73%	82%
Parking/Transportation	14%	18%	13%	31%
Policy Advocacy	29%	49%	64%	63%
Public Space Regulation	23%	44%	35%	52%
Security	9%	18%	51%	72%
Social Services	0%	2%	8%	15%
	Type of Organization			
Very Involved with Service	**Nonprofit**	**Public**	**Mixed Public Nonprofit**	**Sample Totals**
Capital Improvements	66%	46%	58%	52%
Consumer Marketing	68%	79%	81%	78%
Economic Development	25%	28%	20%	25%
Maintenance	63%	59%	55%	58%
Parking/Transportation	26%	15%	23%	18%
Policy Advocacy	40%	51%	55%	50%
Public Space Regulation	40%	41%	32%	38%
Security	34%	38%	35%	36%
Social Services	6%	6%	6%	6%

**N = 259; the city size and budget size variables are sub-divided into quartiles.*

Manager Attributes

The average BID director was 45 years of age and had served four and one-half years. Males comprised 59% of the sample. Before their current job, 43% had worked in the private sector, 36% had been employed in the nonprofit sector, and 22% had come from the public sector. The BID managers were highly educated: 4% were high school graduates, 11% had attended some college, 45% held a bachelor's degree, and 40% had completed or were in the process of completing a postgraduate degree. Some common postgraduate degrees listed by the respondents included the Master of Business Administration, Master of Public Administration, and Master of Urban Planning.

Management Approaches

The managers were asked in the survey to rank three approaches to BID management:

- **Supervisor:** designing organizational structures; entering into contracts; making budgets; hiring employees; conducting performance evaluations.
- **Public Servant:** following the directions of elected officials and/or board members; responding to complaints and requests for information or services from businesses, citizens, and the media.
- **Entrepreneur:** finding new services to provide; designing programs; marketing services; developing new sources of revenue.

No style was overwhelmingly dominant in the survey results. The entrepreneur approach was ranked first by 46% of the respondents, the public servant approach was ranked first by 34%, and the supervisor approach was ranked first by 20%.

Most organizational characteristics (budget, board size, etc.) and personal characteristics (age, gender, tenure, etc.) were not related to the rankings. Only two factors were important—the type of BID organization and the educational achievement of the respondents.

- The entrepreneur approach was ranked first by 52% of nonprofit managers and 51% of public managers, but by only 41% of those from mixed enterprises. The public servant approach was ranked first by 40% of those from public-private partnerships, but by only 32% of those from public agencies and 31% of those from nonprofit organizations. Organizational factors played no role in who ranked the supervision approach first, although almost half of public managers ranked it second, compared to a third of managers from the other two types of organizations.
- Educational achievement was also a relevant factor. The supervisor approach was ranked first by those with a high school degree (44%), the public servant approach was ranked first by those with some college (44%), and the entrepreneur approach was ranked first by those

with a college degree (49%) or postgraduate education (50%). This later finding is perhaps because of the steady emphasis placed on reinventing government in graduate programs during the past two decades.

Each of the management approaches was somewhat related to service delivery. While it is not obvious whether management affects service delivery or vice versa, when using management as an independent variable, the supervisor approach was much more associated with maintenance and security than were the other two approaches; the public servant approach was more related to the capital improvements than were the other two; and the entrepreneur approach was slightly more connected to policy advocacy.

Knowledge and Skills

The survey also asked the managers to rate how important various knowledge areas and skill requirements were to the management of a BID. Table 7.5 indicates that the top executives gave the highest score to speaking effectively to audiences. Job analysis and employee performance evaluations were the least important.

Organizational factors (budgets, board size, etc.) were not very important when it came to the knowledge and skills requirements. There was, however, a relationship with the three management approaches. Those who ranked the entrepreneur approach first rated speaking and writing skills as most important (3.54). When the public servant approach was ranked first,

Table 7.5: Average Rankings of Knowledge and Skills Requirements*
(4=Most Important; 1=Least Important)

	Average	Standard Deviation
Speaking effectively to audiences	3.51	.85
Financial analysis and budgeting	3.48	.80
Planning for and designing projects	3.48	.83
Situation and political analysis	3.35	.88
Bargaining and negotiating methods	3.28	.94
Writing policy statements and reports	3.20	.84
Impact analysis and evaluation	3.15	.86
Research methods and data analysis	2.95	.84
Job analysis and performance evaluation	2.92	.89

*$N = 257$

the highest knowledge and skill requirement was for financial analysis and budgeting (3.62). For those who placed the most emphasis on the supervisor approach, the highest rating was for planning skills (3.49).

Performance Measurement

One of the most important activities of any manager is to evaluate organizational performance. While there is no agreed on measure of performance for all organizations, the assumption is that benchmarks can improve service delivery. A benchmark is a point of reference for comparison or measurement purposes. With a benchmark, managers can "measure the performance gap between where they are and where they want to be and track their progress in closing that gap."[29]

In the survey, 54% of the BIDs had set benchmarks, 42% had not set any, and 4% of the managers were unsure. This reconfirms a 1995 New York City Council study that found "most BIDs have failed to establish and utilize performance indicators that specifically measure BID performance."[30]

Generally, the larger the BID organization, the more likely that benchmarks were set. Benchmarks were set by 76% of BIDs with very large budgets (over $700,000); 61% of BIDs with more than the average number of blocks (20); and 67% of BIDs with more than the average number of employees (eight). BIDs that had been created in the last year were less likely to have set benchmarks (although several respondents from new BIDs did note on the survey instrument that they were in the process of establishing performance standards).

Two performance measures were used most by BIDs: occupancy rates (55%) and citizen attitude surveys (42%). Other measures were used much less: crime rates (35%), lease rates (31%), taxable retail sales (19%), number of jobs created (28%), pedestrian/visitor counts (31%), and business license revenues (12%). A few BID managers did write on the questionnaire that they had also used cleanliness measures.

The relationship between performance measures and service delivery is presented in Table 7.6. The interesting aspect of these findings is the mismatch between the major service provided by BIDs and the way they assessed performance. While over three-quarters of the BIDs were involved with consumer marketing, slightly less than half of the sample measured performance with customer surveys and only a third conducted pedestrian/visitor counts.

Approximately 15% of the sample had recently used three or more of the performance measures. For those BIDs that had set benchmarks, there was a greater likelihood that performance was assessed with occupancy rates and citizen attitude surveys.

BIDs with large budgets in large cities, compared to those with small budgets in small cities, were more likely to use two performance measures: citizen surveys (56% to 28%) and crime rates (57% to 11%). Occupancy

Table 7.6: The Relationship Between Performance Measures and BID Service Delivery*

Use of Performance Measures	Very Involved with Services				
	Capital Improvements	Consumer Marketing	Economic Development	Maintenance	Parking Transportation
Crime Rates	31%	34%	31%	49%	48%
Lease Rates	33%	34%	42%	31%	33%
Taxable Retail Sales	18%	22%	27%	17%	28%
Customer Attitude Surveys	42%	43%	55%	52%	50%
Number of Jobs Created	36%	31%	61%	24%	28%
Occupancy Rates	57%	60%	73%	54%	61%
Pedestrian/Visitor Counts	30%	34%	38%	34%	37%
Business License Revenue	12%	15%	16%	9%	13%
Sample Totals	**52%**	**78%**	**25%**	**58%**	**18%**

Use of Performance Measures	Very Involved with Services				
	Policy Advocacy	Public Space Regulation	Security	Social Services	Sample Totals
Crime Rates	41%	50%	68%	80%	35%
Lease Rates	36%	34%	38%	40%	31%
Taxable Retail Sales	23%	22%	15%	27%	19%
Customer Attitude Surveys	47%	52%	68%	67%	42%
Number of Jobs Created	28%	25%	20%	47%	28%
Occupancy Rates	57%	60%	56%	47%	55%
Pedestrian/Visitor Counts	40%	35%	38%	40%	31%
Business License Revenue	15%	17%	6%	7%	12%
Sample Totals	**50%**	**38%**	**36%**	**6%**	

*N = 259

rates were favored by those in small communities with below average budgets (65%).

Table 7.7 assesses the extent to which the three management approaches were related to the use of performance measures. The supervisor approach was associated overall with a greater use of performance measures. This could be expected since organizational analysis defines the supervisor approach.

Table 7.7: The Relationship Between Performance Measures and BID Management Approaches*

Use of Performance Measures	Management Approaches			Sample Totals
	Supervisor	Public Servant	Entrepreneur	
Crime Rates	64%	46%	56%	35%
Lease Rates	51%	34%	32%	31%
Taxable Retail Sales	39%	26%	33%	19%
Customer Attitude Surveys	51%	37%	43%	42%
Number of Jobs Created	28%	31%	26%	28%
Occupancy Rates	61%	53%	52%	55%
Pedestrian/Visitor Counts	31%	28%	34%	31%
Business License Revenue	12%	13%	11%	12%
Sample Totals	**46%**	**34%**	**20%**	

**N = 259*

Recommendations

This survey has provided a picture of BIDs in the United States. As with any picture, it is only a snapshot in time. Adjustments will occur as additional BIDs are established, existing ones evolve, and new managers assume responsibility for them. Drawing on the survey results, four recommendations may improve the operation of BIDs.

Evaluate Organizational Design

Serious thought should be given to the type of organization that can best accomplish the goals of the business district and the community. This may occur when state governments draft BID legislation, when local governments first create BIDs, or when existing BIDs are renewed. Such an assessment is necessary because of the relationship that has developed between organizational design and service delivery. This survey found public agencies were more likely to be very involved with capital improvements, while nonprofits were more likely to be very involved with maintenance and security services. In the future, research should focus on the types of organizations that deliver particular services the most efficiently and effectively.

Recognize the Service Delivery Potential

The finding that so many BIDs from both large and small cities were new, but already very or somewhat involved with services ranging from promotion to security, suggests their potential is great. Given that parking and transportation issues are critical for downtown areas, but not that important to BIDs today, perhaps these services should become more of a focus.[31] There are many other service areas that BIDs could also become involved in, such as developing Internet websites that market downtown areas, creating new entertainment options, and promoting mixed-use development. The general idea is to make downtown a good place to work and shop, as well as an inviting place to live and enjoy amusements such as sporting events and concerts. The assumption is that entertainment and residential development can reinforce and advance the commercial and employment potential of an area.[32]

Enhance BID Management

Attention to the professional growth of the BID executive is especially important given the nature of the position. The BID manager may very well be one of a few full-time employees. Moreover, he or she may be responsible for implementing a wide range of services, working with a large governing board, and controlling a sizable budget. While the International Downtown Association and state-level associations hold conferences where BID leaders can share ideas, there are no manuals or guides that thoroughly describe what BID management entails. Such publications are especially relevant for new managers and for students considering a career in downtown development. The model for BIDs could be the publications provided by the

Foundation Center for nonprofit board members or the various documents produced by the International City/County Management Association for city administrators. Materials for BIDs could be supplied through training programs provided by professional associations, universities, and/or by BID councils.

This survey has identified a portion of the subject matter for written materials and training sessions. In considering management approaches, the focus should be wide-ranging, including basic administrative tasks, the development of political relationships, and entrepreneurship. The knowledge and skills areas most important are communications, budgeting, and planning. Human resource management is less of an issue. While not specifically addressed by the survey, the development of a "best practices" inventory would also be helpful.

Measure Performance

This research found that about half of the BIDs have not established benchmarks, and many performance measures are underutilized. While performance measurement takes time and money, it is necessary if organizations are to understand what they are doing well, what they are doing poorly, and where they can change to make things work better. Without good performance evaluations, BIDs could reach a point where they do not recognize when they are providing services as inadequately as the local government agencies they are intended to supplement. On a larger scale, without good data it is very difficult to promote the overall utility of the BID innovation.[33]

There are many ways to evaluate performance, such as before-and-after studies using secondary data or cross-sectional surveys of citizens, businesses, and elected officials. When conducting evaluations, the measurement approach should be realistic. For instance, to what extent is it possible to determine how much a BID contributes to a reduction in downtown crime rates? The evaluation methodology should also match the type of services delivered. For example, community-wide citizen surveys and pedestrian intercept studies should be used to assess the effectiveness of consumer marketing efforts.[34]

The potential significance of performance standards and frequent performance measurement for discovering what is and is not successful should provide a rationale for the managers of self-assessment districts to instigate and continue a system of self-evaluation. As BIDs mature and discover new services to provide, performance measurement may very well determine whether they continue as important innovations in the revitalization of commercial centers.

The Future of BIDS

BIDs have definitely become an integral part of the service delivery system of municipalities across the country. They are engaged with a diverse set of programs and projects, and even though the evidence is limited, they seem to be doing very well. It is obvious when walking around these districts that most of them are more visually appealing. No longer plagued by trash and grime, garish facades, deteriorated sidewalks, rundown parks, and nefarious individuals, there is a sense that the commercial centers of small, medium, and large size communities have come back to life. But clearly there is much more to be done.

America remains a nation largely dominated by the shopping mall, the strip mall, the suburban life-style, and the automobile. Even on revived main streets in small towns, there is no comparison to the deluge of activity in the Wal-Mart located on the distant bypass highway. In the downtown areas of medium-size cities, storefronts are still boarded-up as retailers continue to relocate to shopping malls on the outskirts. And while the commercial sidewalks of large cities may be teeming during the workday, in the evenings and weekends they are all too often empty of people.

In the future, the larger challenge for BIDs will be to effect change in the very culture of American community life which has been the essential reason for their creation. BIDs are uniquely positioned to take a leadership role in sociological change because they can advocate a consistent, focused downtown development strategy that stands in sharp contrast to typical municipal planning and the need to balance competing political, economic, and social interests. Moreover, BID managers have already proven that creative thinking and sufficient funding can make a big difference in areas that had long ago been written off as a lost cause. And, since many BID managers have gained a measure of respect for their ability to provide an array of innovative services, as well as to advocate sensible policies, they may be heard by citizens, the media, and municipal officials.

How can BIDs work to change the culture of communities? Since many BIDs are already very involved with consumer marketing, one way may be to take an advertising campaign to the suburbs and beyond. This approach has recently been embraced by the Center City District in Philadelphia in ads that point out the positive differences of the city compared to the suburbs.

Yet another idea is to work with economic development corporations and planning agencies to target community development toward teenagers, young families, and senior citizens. A pedestrian-friendly central business district may hold a special appeal to each of these groups—to teenagers bored with the sameness of shopping malls, to young families seeking affordable housing near to good employment opportunities, and to senior citizens looking for a special sense of community within walking distance.

BIDs could also become leading policy advocates for limiting the expansion of highways through cities, for creating so-called "green-belts" that encourage the enlargement of park lands instead of commercial activity on city boundaries, and for rezoning old manufacturing districts into new mixed-use developments.

BIDs should listen to a broad cross-section of citizens. One of the criticisms of BIDs is that they are unaccountable, that they tend not to bring any outsiders into their decision-making processes. Whether BIDs are any more or less accountable than traditional public agencies or private firms is debatable, yet it is evident that most have not established specific mechanisms for gaining citizen input. As this research has discovered, only about half utilize citizen surveys and few conduct pedestrian counts. It would be to the advantage of BIDs to rely on surveys, focus groups, public hearings, and other means to understand consumer opinions. How else can strategies be developed for bringing people back to central business districts if their views are not fully considered?

No matter the approach that is taken, there are many exciting opportunities for BIDs to continue the revitalization of America's cities and towns. The outlook should remain positive in the years to come if:

- local officials sustain the idea that their purpose is not to tell BIDs how to provide service, but to make sure that a high quality service is provided;
- BID managers stay active by looking for ways to improve what they do, such as setting benchmarks; and
- the theme of the BID movement is to foster a positive attitude toward downtown life.

Postscript

Since the survey of business improvement districts, or BIDs, was originally published by the Endowment in 1999, the number of BIDs has grown and their responsibilities have expanded. One city after another has recognized that a necessary way to change city places is to put in place an innovative public-private implementation device that can be devoted to making revitalization a reality. While BIDs cannot do everything, elected officials and business leaders certainly believe that they can make city places safer, cleaner, and more marketable. This said, it is still not entirely clear to what extent particular BID activities are effective or ineffective.

The population of BIDs keeps growing. The number of BIDs is now estimated to be over 450. New York City has added two more BIDs, giving it 44, and has two more in the works. As of 2003, there are 32 in Los Angeles and another 21 under consideration. Michigan adopted BID legislation in 2001, and the Gateway BID in Detroit is up and running. Other cities with new BIDs include Boulder, Colorado; Hyannis Port, Massachusetts; and Yonkers, New York.

BIDs continue to be predominantly independently financed through self-assessments, yet there are increasingly more partnership arrangements whereby BIDs work with kindred organizations. For example, in 2001 the BID in Portland, Oregon, partnered with the local Chamber of Commerce to create the Portland Business Alliance. Partnership arrangements can now be found in such places as Anchorage, Baltimore, Little Rock, Memphis, Philadelphia, Phoenix, and Sacramento. The umbrella format permits like-minded organizations to share administrative costs, to reap collectively the advantages of different organizational exigencies, and to coordinate activities.

Led by managers who focus on entrepreneurial projects, BID activities continue to expand in innovative directions. BIDs highlight the vibrancy of city nightlife. The Center City District in Philadelphia produced an ad campaign highlighting its after-hours allure, noting that you can "find romance virtually anywhere in Center City."[35]

BIDs are also continuing to do everything they can to make city places clean. In one year, the Times Square BID spent 780 hours hand-scraping lampposts to remove 2,300 stickers and placards advertising everything from locksmiths to quick-fix dating services.[36] BIDs are also trying to change the character of cities. In a Disney-like manner, the Cranford, New Jersey, Special Improvement District has joined with the city government to re-create the downtown central business district around a Victorian theme, including antique lampposts, brick sidewalks, pedestrian benches, flower beds, and a clock tower.[37] BIDs are seeking to bring order to city places by preventing and eliminating the crimes and behaviors that contribute to negative impressions. In Philadelphia's Center City District, the BID's officers and the local police work as a partnership: They share the same lockers, jointly stand roll each morning, and jointly plan daily deployment strategies.[38]

BIDs are becoming increasingly more involved with economic development projects. The Lower East Side BID in Manhattan has a business incubator to stimulate retail trade in the area, including business training and space for start-up fashion entrepreneurs.[39] BIDs are also entering into the political arena to improve city places. Three BIDs in Texas' largest cities effectively lobbied for state legislation creating stiffer penalties for those repeatedly found guilty of public intoxication and disorderly conduct on city streets.[40] BIDs are playing a civic role in communities. The 14th Street-Union Square Local Development Corporation in Manhattan has partnered with a local high school to connect business mentors with students and to supply information about how to pursue a career in business.[41]

A major conclusion of this chapter was that BIDs were not doing enough to measure their performance nor was anyone else conducting studies of their effectiveness. This state of affairs remains. While BIDs are busy and businesses seem supportive of their activities, we still do not know with any certitude if they are doing a good job or not.

Many BIDs continue to demonstrate that they are doing a good job by enumerating what they do. For example, the Downtown Improvement District in Dallas reported that it had in a three-month period collected over 50,000 gallons of trash, and the Fashion District in Los Angeles noted in one year that it had responded to 943 illegal vending incidents.[42] Other BIDs conduct surveys that show the public has a generally positive view of BIDs. The missing piece of information remains whether inputs and outputs are correlated. We don't know if street cleaning leads to greater retail sales, new business openings, less crime, reduced vacancies, more pedestrian traffic, and positive consumer attitudes.

The complexity of BID organizational structure remains a problem in assessing the true effectiveness of BIDs. It is often difficult to isolate the effects of BIDs from the other organizations and social events. A BID may very well overlap a historic district, a state enterprise zone, or one or more tax increment financing districts. It may also be impacted by overall economic conditions, local government budgets, and changing demographics. The role of BIDs in city places may even be affected by the passage of time.

One recent academic study of BIDs by Lorlene Hoyt of the Massachusetts Institute of Technology compared crime statistics in BID and non-BID areas in Philadelphia. Controlling for various social and economics factors through regression analysis, she found crime went down more in BID areas than in non-BID areas and that statistically the visibility of BID security personnel was an effective crime deterrent.[43]

There clearly is a need for more systematic study of BID outcomes. Innovation should not preclude evaluation. There is a need to go beyond "if you believe it works, then it works." Research can isolate effects; it is done all the time in equally complicated policy areas. BIDs, the International Downtown Association, and research centers should step forward to support and conduct elaborate studies that can tell what BIDs are doing well and what they are doing poorly. BIDs will continue to expand; the question is whether they will expand in an intelligent way.

Jerry Mitchell
May 2003

Appendix:
BID Management Survey

Organizational Characteristics:

1. In what year was your organization established? ______________
2. Your organization has how many full-time employees? __________
3. Approximately, what is its annual budget? ____________________
4. How many members are on your governing board? ____________
5. Roughly, how many city blocks does your organization cover? _____
6. Which of the following best characterizes your organization? (please check one)
   ☐ Government Agency ☐ Nonprofit
   ☐ Combination of Government and Nonprofit
7. Which of the following are sources of funding for your organization? (please check all that apply)
   ☐ Special Tax Assessment on Property and/or Business
   ☐ Voluntary Donations or In-Kind Contributions
   ☐ Subsidies or Grants from Federal or State Govt.
   ☐ Bonds (public or private)
   ☐ City General Tax Revenues
   ☐ Sale of Goods or Services
   ☐ Other (please specify):______________________________

Service Delivery:

8. To what extent is your organization involved in providing each of the following services? (circle a number by each)

	Very Involved	Somewhat Involved	Not at all Involved
Capital Improvements: i.e. installing pedestrian-scale lighting and street furniture; planting trees and shrubbery	1	2	3
Consumer Marketing: i.e. producing festivals and events; coordinating sales promotions; producing maps and newsletters	1	2	3

	Very Involved	Somewhat Involved	Not at all Involved
Economic Development: i.e. offering incentives (such as tax abatements or loans) to new and expanding businesses	1	2	3
Maintenance: i.e. collecting rubbish; removing litter and graffiti; washing sidewalks; shoveling snow; trimming trees	1	2	3
Parking and Transportation: i.e. managing a public parking system; maintaining transit shelters	1	2	3
Policy Advocacy: i.e. promoting public policies to the community; lobbying government on behalf of business interests	1	2	3
Public Space Regulation: i.e. managing sidewalk vending; discouraging panhandling; controlling vehicle loading	1	2	3
Security: i.e. providing supplementary security guards; buying and installing electronic security systems; working with city police force	1	2	3
Social Services: i.e. aiding the homeless; providing job training; supplying youth services	1	2	3

Other (please specify):__________________________________

Management Practices:

9. To what extent do you consider the following knowledge areas or skills as important to your management of a business district? (circle a number by each)

	Very Important	Somewhat Important	Of Little Importance	Not Important
Bargaining and negotiating methods	1	2	3	4
Financial analysis and budgeting	1	2	3	4

	Very Important	Somewhat Important	Of Little Importance	Not Important
Impact analysis and evaluation	1	2	3	4
Job analysis and performance evaluation	1	2	3	4
Planning for and designing projects	1	2	3	4
Research methods and data analysis	1	2	3	4
Situation and political analysis	1	2	3	4
Speaking effectively to audiences	1	2	3	4
Writing policy statements and reports	1	2	3	4

10. There are obviously many ways to administer a business district. From your managerial perspective, please prioritize the relative importance of the following administrative approaches (you should rank the statements with "1" the most important; "2" the second most important, and "3" the least important).

    ____ **Supervisor:** i.e. designing organizational structures; entering into contracts; making budgets; hiring employees; conducting performance evaluations

    ____ **Public Servant:** i.e. following the directions of elected officials and/or board members; responding to complaints and requests for information or services from businesses, citizens, and the media

    ____ **Entrepreneur:** i.e. finding new services to provide; designing programs; marketing services; developing new sources of revenue

11. Has your organization established standards of performance ("benchmarks") from which to evaluate its outcomes?

    ☐ Yes ☐ No ☐ Unsure

12. During the past year, which of the following has been used as a measure of organizational performance? (check all that apply)

    ☐ Crime Rates ☐ Taxable Retail Sales
    ☐ Number of Jobs Created ☐ Pedestrian/ Visitor Counts
    ☐ Lease Rates ☐ Customer Attitude Surveys
    ☐ Occupancy Rate ☐ Business License Revenue
    Other (please specify):____________________

Personal Information:

13. What is your age? _________
14. What is your gender? ☐ Male ☐ Female
15. How long have you served in your current position? _______________
16. Prior to your present job, in which sector did you work?
    ☐ Public ☐ Private ☐ Nonprofit
17. What is your highest completed educational degree?_______________

Endnotes

1. The importance of downtown districts has been explored by John O. Norquist, *The Wealth of Cities: Revitalizing the Centers of American Life,* (Reading, MA: Addison-Wesley, 1998). Also, see Peter Katz, *The New Urbanism: Toward an Architecture of Community,* (New York: McGraw-Hill, 1994).

2. David Osborne and Ted Gaebler, *Reinventing Government: How the Entrepreneurial Spirit is Transforming the Public Sector,* (New York: Plume, 1993), p. 30.

3. Lawrence O. Houstoun, Jr., *BIDs: Business Improvement Districts,* (Washington, D.C.: Urban Land Institute, 1997), p. 38.

4. Heather MacDonald, "BIDS Really Work," *City Journal,* (Spring 1996), p. 42.

5. *The New York Times,* "The Mayor vs the BIDs," (May 1, 1998), Internet Edition.

6. *Milwaukee Journal Sentinel,* "Urban Revival Spreads Across the Country," (June 23, 1999), Internet Edition.

7. James Traub, "Can Associations of Businesses be True Community-Builders?" *The Responsive Community,* (Spring 1996), p. 29, 31.

8. Richard Briffault, "A Government for Our Time? Business Improvement Districts and Urban Governance," *Columbia Law Review,* (March 1999), p. 477.

9. Brian Mackle, "Growing, Without Pains," *Our Town,* (July 15, 1999), p 4.

10. Alexander Communications, "Downtown Vitality is on the Mend," *Downtown Idea Exchange,* (August 15, 1998), p. 1.

11. At least five other states have BID legislation, but have not yet created any BIDs. Three others are considering BID legislation.

12. For a description of the mixed model, see Bradley Segel, "A New Generation of Downtown Management Organizations," unpublished monograph from the Progressive Urban Management Associates, 1998.

13. BIDs are comparable to special districts, see Kari Hudson, "Special District Governments," *American City & County,* (September 1996), pp. 54-71; they are similar to government corporations, see Jerry Mitchell, *The American Experiment with Government Corporations,* (Armonk, NY: M.E. Sharpe, 1999); and they reflect many of the advantages of nonprofits, see Lester M. Salamon, *America's Nonprofit Sector,* (New York: The Foundation Center, 1999).

14. For an early analysis of the advantages of downtown revitalization districts, see Laurence A. Alexander, *Downtown Improvement Districts: Creating Money and Power for Downtown Action,* (New York: Downtown Research and Development Center, 1979), pp. 13-14.

15. Alexander, p. 7.

16. Briffault, p. 470.

17. This was a point made in reference to a small BID in Brooklyn, NY. See *The New York Times,* "Improvements on a Small Scale," (February 20, 1999), p. B1.

18. Roberta Brandes Gratz and Norman Mintz, *Cities Back from the Edge: New Life for Downtown,* (New York: John Wiley, 1998), p. 61.

19. See Houstoun, Jr., BIDs, (1997). Also, see Richard G, Williams, "Business Improvement Districts—Main Street Asset Management," *Journal of Property Management* (May/June, 1996).

20. Two examples of guides to BID creation are the Massachusetts Department of Housing and Community Development's *Business Improvement Districts: A Guide to Establishing a BID in Massachusetts,* (Boston: Division of Community Services, 1998) and the Oregon Downtown Development Association's *EID/BID Handbook,* (Salem, OR: The Association, 1999).

21. See Briffault, pp. 430-475. Also, see James Krohe, Jr., "Why Reform Government? Replace It," *Across the Board,* (December 1992), pp. 40-45.

22. For a thorough discussion of the accountability issue, see two reports from New York City Council's Committee on Finance, *Managing the Micropolis: Proposals to Strengthen BID Performance and Accountability,* (1997) and *Cities Within Cities: Business Improvement District and the Emergence of the Micropolis,* (1995). Also, see *The New York Times,* "Business Districts Grow at Price of Accountability," (November 29, 1994).

23. Pittsburgh Downtown Partnership, *Survey of Business Improvement Districts,* (Pittsburgh: The Partnership, 1995).

24. Lawrence O. Houstoun, Jr., "Betting on BIDs," *Urban Land,* (June, 1994), pp. 13-18.

25. Each step in the BID survey was based on the process recommended by Don A. Dillman, *Mail and Telephone Surveys: The Total Design Method,* (New York: John Wiley, 1978).

26. New York City Council's Committee on Finance (1997).

27. Pittsburgh Downtown Partnership, (1995), p. 1.

28. Houstoun, Jr., *BIDs,* (1997), p. 11.

29. David N. Ammons, "A Proper Mentality for Benchmarking," *Public Administration Review,* (March/April 1999), p. 107.

30. New York City Council's Committee on Finance, (1995), p. ix.

31. A similar point was made by Lawrence O. Houstoun, Jr., "Are BIDs Working?" *Urban Land,* (January 1997), p. 58.

32. For a series of questions about the utility of BIDs, see Janet Rothenberg Pack, "BIDS, DIDS, SIDS, SADS, Private Government in America," *The Brookings Review,* (Fall 1992), pp. 18-21.

33. Houstoun, Jr., BIDs, (1997), p. 105. Also, see James Howard Kunstler, *Home from Nowhere: Remaking our Everyday World for the 21st Century,* (New York: Touchstone, 1996).

34. An example of such research was conducted by KRC Research and Consulting, *Street Intercept Survey: Perceptions of Business Improvement Districts and Conditions in the Grand Central, Bryant Park, and 34th Street Areas,* (New York: KRC, 1994).

35. Center City District, *Newsletter,* (Summer 2000), p. 7.

36. Times Square BID, *Annual Report* (2001).

37. *New Jersey Online*, "Cranford's Revitalized Downtown a Model for Others to Follow," (July 2002), Internet Edition.

38. Paul Levy, "Making Downtowns Competitive," *Planning,* (April 2001), p. 17.

39. *The New York Times,* "Taking the Plunge, Gown and All, (March 28, 2002), p. B1.

40. Dallas Downtown Improvement District, *Quarterly Report,* (1999).

41. Brochure from the 14th Street-Union Square Development Corporation (2000).

42. Dallas Downtown Improvement District, *Quarterly Report,* (1999), and The Fashion District of Los Angeles, *Monthly Report Operations Summary,* (May 2001), p. 3.

43. Lorlene Hoyt, "Collecting Private Funds for Safer Public Spaces: An Empirical Examination of the Business Improvement District Concept," (Unpublished manuscript).

PART III

Transforming the Delivery of Environmental Programs

CHAPTER EIGHT

An Assessment of Brownfield Redevelopment Policies: The Michigan Experience

Richard C. Hula
Professor and Chair
Department of Political Science
and Urban Affairs
Michigan State University

This report was originally published in November 1999, revised May 2003.

Introduction[1]

Brownfield redevelopment has become an important theme in environmental policy as both federal and state governments rush to implement new programs to redevelop land parcels that are "abandoned, idled, or underused industrial and commercial facilities where expansion or redevelopment is complicated by a real or perceived environment contamination."[2] A number of characteristics of these efforts are intriguing. Perhaps most interesting is the diverse coalition supporting brownfield redevelopment. It is a coalition that defies traditional expectation, cutting across political party, ideology, and region.

The problem set which brownfield redevelopment is thought to address is equally diverse. Obviously it includes site remediation, but also incorporates other important goals. For urban policy makers, the dedication of contaminated sites to future industrial and commercial use transforms brownfield redevelopment into an economic development tool. To the extent that brownfield redevelopment reduces development pressure on rural and agricultural land, it serves as a greenspace preservation effort. Indeed, brownfields are seen by some as a means to achieve key elements of comprehensive land use policy without the need to actually impose direct regulation.

Brownfield programs reflect a shift in the fundamental assumptions driving the design and implementation of American environmental policy since the 1960s. It is a shift not only in substantive policy, but includes a refocusing of authority. Through brownfield redevelopment, a number of states are successfully challenging long established federal dominance in environmental policy. This chapter explores efforts by the state of Michigan

What Is a Brownfield?

The federal Environmental Protection Agency defines a brownfield as "abandoned, idled, or underused industrial and commercial facilities where expansion or redevelopment is complicated by a real or perceived environment contamination."

Contamination at a brownfield site is insufficient to place the site in the federal Superfund program.

The actual level of contamination at brownfield sites is often unknown since the property has often been abandoned because of a fear about what "might" be on the site.

Estimates of the number of brownfield sites in the United States vary from 50,000 to over one million.

Brownfield sites are typically the responsibility of state environmental agencies.

to craft one such brownfield initiative. Although the primary focus here is the experience of a single state, the lessons to be learned from this case have national implications. Michigan is a leader in brownfield programs, but it is hardly unique. Many states are designing and implementing aggressive brownfield programs that challenge traditional federal policy (Consumers Renaissance Redevelopment Corporation, 1998). The impact of such programs will almost certainly have a profound impact on overall environmental policy in the coming years.

More than two dozen pieces of federal legislation regulate toxic materials in the United States. Of these, three define the broad regulatory framework that has controlled toxic substances for the past 20 years. They are the Toxic Substance Control Act of 1976 (TSCA), the Resource Conservation and Recovery Act of 1976 (RCRA), and the Comprehensive Response, Compensation and Liability Act of 1980 (CERCLA). Each is targeted to a different period in the life cycle of hazardous material. TSCA attempts to set out rules for the review and analysis of new chemicals. The goal is to identify dangerous chemicals as they are developed so that appropriate control strategies can be devised before they cause human harm. RCRA charges the EPA to develop standards for current waste management. CERCLA is targeted to the cleaning of existing toxic-waste sites. Together these laws create a complex network of regulations that attempt to control toxic materials from inception to disposal.[3]

The largest and most controversial of these efforts is CERCLA. Generally known as Superfund, CERCLA (and its 1986 reauthorization, Superfund Amendments and Reauthorization Act, SARA) outlines the general parameters of toxic-waste-cleanup policy in the United States. Key to understanding

Key Administrative Characteristics of Superfund (CERCLA)

Goals	Land-based toxic contamination is defined as a public health issue.
Responsibility	Federal authorities are assigned to lead efforts to clean toxic-waste sites.
Response Model	The EPA is given authority to act quickly in cases where the public health is threatened. In such cases the initial cleanup can draw on interim public funding.
Liability	Places responsibility for paying cleanup costs squarely on those who caused the contamination
Bureaucratic Organization	Regulations are framed within a traditional command and control structure.

CERCLA is its focus on central (federal) decision making, the legislative commitment to restoring sites to a "natural" condition, and the assumption that those responsible for pollution are responsible for all costs associated with cleanup. CERCLA has been mired in controversy since its passage. Currently debates are occurring within the EPA, in Congress, and in various state houses across the country as to how toxic-waste policy might be revised.

At the federal level there are efforts within both EPA and Congress to restructure important elements of toxic-waste policy. Policy entrepreneurs within EPA have sought to mute public criticism of CERCLA through a number of administrative reforms and public relations initiatives. For example, independent of legislative mandates, the EPA has sought to soften some elements of the CERCLA liability standards. Beyond efforts to improve the agency's processing of Superfund sites, the EPA has also begun to implement an interesting shift (or least an expansion) in CERCLA goals by initiating a number of pilot efforts to encourage the redevelopment of less contaminated sites that do not qualify for CERCLA intervention.

Federal brownfield initiatives modify past toxic-waste policy in a number of important ways. Unlike Superfund sites, brownfields are seen in much more instrumental terms. That is, decisions to invest in a brownfield cleanup are driven not so much by the level of on-site contamination, but by the economic potential of the site. Thus, estimated economic viability of the redevelopment plan is a key factor in evaluating applications for EPA brownfield pilot programs.

Unlike much of the history of Superfund, the design of the EPA brownfield initiative is based on cooperation, consensus, and self-interest. The command-control logic that drives Superfund cleanups has largely been replaced in the brownfield initiative by voluntary agreements backed by grants and tax credits. Funding is based on incentives rather than a punitive liability scheme.[4] A striking aspect of the Brownfield initiative is the explicit acknowledgment of the leading role of state and local officials in cleanup efforts. Some regional EPA offices have been particularly aggressive in allowing state authorities to take a leading role on specific sites. This increased federal flexibility has been instrumental in promoting state-level innovation in brownfield policy.

Congressional dissatisfaction with CERCLA is dramatically revealed in its repeated failure to reauthorize the legislation. The taxing authority that financed the Superfund expired in 1995, and no one has yet been able to form a coalition capable of passing a revised CERCLA. Currently the future of reauthorization remains unclear. However, the concept of brownfield redevelopment clearly enjoys strong support in Congress. A good deal of additional legislation to support brownfield programs has been introduced. However, most has been stalled by the continuing debate on CERCLA reauthorization.

Study Objectives and Methods

This chapter is primarily based on 24 semi-structured field interviews of practitioners active in brownfield redevelopment.

Four general groups were sampled: local-level officials (some were sponsors of Brownfield Redevelopment Authorities, others were active in the authorities themselves), legislative actors who crafted the legal framework for the brownfield program, state-level officials in the Michigan Department of Environmental Quality charged with state-level program implementation, and private developers active in specific redevelopment projects.

Although the interview schedule was modified for particular groups of respondents, a number of issues were discussed with all. These include; (1) a general sense of how the state brownfield program operates; (2) an evaluation of how well the program works (including a review of specific projects), and; (3) thoughts about how the program might be improved.

In spite of announced EPA policy changes, many state and local policy makers remain skeptical. They see the federal program as continuing to be too rigid and overly adversarial. They remain critical of CERCLA's history of huge administrative and legal costs and very modest record of completed cleanups. Recent federal initiatives are seen as ineffective and half-hearted efforts targeted to the margins of toxic cleanup policy. As a result, many state authorities have initiated brownfield programs at the state-level. A review of such efforts identified 41 states that had significant voluntary cleanup/brownfield redevelopment programs (Consumers Renaissance Redevelopment Corporation, 1998). Eleven of these states have signed memoranda of agreements with the federal EPA in which federal authorities essentially agree to grant the state full authority over all non-Superfund sites that enter state-run programs. These state programs provide an important laboratory for future environmental policy in the United States.

The Michigan Experience

In contrast to the deadlock in Washington over broad toxic-waste policy, the state of Michigan has implemented one of the most comprehensive state-level programs to encourage brownfield redevelopment. The policy has been created through new laws passed by the state legislature as well as a number of executive actions taken by the governor. While these changes were justified, in part, as an effort to improve the cleanup capacity of the state, there is little doubt that the changes also reflect a new political agenda. No longer would cleanups be the unitary variable driving environmental policy. The connection of environmental and economic development goals was made quite explicit by former Michigan Governor John Engler:

> The cornerstone of any urban revitalization strategy must be an aggressive brownfield redevelopment program. We have made brownfields attractive by reforming the cleanup laws and offering tax credits and low interest loans to our communities. More than anything, our success comes from making brownfield redevelopment a top economic and environmental priority in the state of Michigan. (Consumers Renaissance Redevelopment Corporation, 1998).

Although the changes in Michigan environmental policy are broadly consistent with new federal initiatives, the magnitude of the state changes is much greater. Each of these policy innovations is a fairly direct effort to respond to long-standing criticisms of federal policy.

Liability Protection

The most fundamental contrast between Michigan and federal policy is that of liability. Basically, the state has incorporated the key features of past convenants not to sue into a relatively automatic framework. If a landowner is not responsible for site contamination, then he or she is not liable for a cleanup.[5] For parties responsible for the original contamination, liability remains in force. Indeed, current law has created a new affirmative responsibility of landowners to identify and remediate contaminated sites. The Michigan Department of Environmental Quality (MDEQ) is empowered to seek penalties and fines of up to $10,000 a day from any responsible party if they have not "diligently pursued" the cleanup of contaminated sites which they own.[6]

Private/Voluntary Action

To avoid liability, new owners of potentially contaminated property are required to perform a Baseline Environmental Assessment (BEA) on their property. The BEA is an assessment of existing contamination levels on the property. The result of this assessment must be filed with the MDEQ within 45 days of the purchase, occupancy, or foreclosure, whichever comes first.

New owners have full liability for contamination beyond that reported in the baseline assessment.[7] Owners have the option of filing a petition with

Key Elements of Michigan Brownfield Policy

Innovation	Description
Liability protection	Prior to the 1996 Natural Resources and Environmental Protection Act (NREPA) amendments, Michigan statutes followed the federal lead in imposing a strict liability framework for site contamination. This essentially held that ownership of a property carried with it the liability for cleaning that site. Changes in the law now allow purchasers to escape liability for contamination for which they are not directly responsible.
Increased reliance on private/voluntary action	New owners of potentially contaminated property can secure exemption from cleanup liability by filing a Baseline Environment Assessment (BEA) with the Michigan Department of Environmental Quality. This baseline data is to serve as a basis from which to evaluate state claims against the landowner. The completion of the BEA is largely a private action, with limited state oversight.
Flexible cleanup standards	Brownfield redevelopment rests on the assumption that contaminated properties ought to be cleaned to levels appropriate for future use. Industrial properties need not be cleaned to residential levels. This introduction of differential cleanup standards represents a significant departure from earlier environmental regulations, which demanded a total removal of all contaminants.
Public funding	The Brownfield Financing Act (1996) permits municipalities to create Brownfield Redevelopment Authorities. These authorities are allowed to dedicate state and local taxes generated by the redevelopment into financing remedial cleanup action on the site. Developers are also granted a tax credit on their single business tax. In addition, the state has dedicated a total of $335 million in bond funds for brownfield redevelopment.

MDEQ requesting written documentation that they qualify for the liability exemption. This petition may also request a determination that the owners' proposed use of the facility is consistent with statuary demands that land-use not exacerbate contamination at the site.[8]

Flexible Cleanup Standards

The state has also reconfigured cleanup standards. A key element of this change is tying the level of cleanup to the proposed use of the land. Thus, MDEQ has created separate standards for residential, commercial, or industrial properties. Not surprisingly, the commercial and industrial standards are less demanding than those for residential development.

In an effort to simplify the requirements for redevelopment, the new standards are general for the state, rather than being tied to a site-specific risk analysis. As part of the reconfiguration, overall risk standards were reduced. For example, the cleanup levels for known carcinogens have been set at a risk level of 1:100,000 rather than the earlier standard of 1:1,000,000. Groundwater cleanup standards have also been revised to what are generally less stringent levels. Finally, the state has recognized institutional controls on land use as an acceptable alternative to cleaning a site to the highest possible standard.

Public Funding

The state has also developed a number of alternative sources of financing for local brownfield projects. Although Michigan law has increased public resources for site redevelopment, funding is typically not from general funds; rather, specific revenue streams have been directed to redevelopment efforts. Two revenue sources are of particular importance: Brownfield redevelopment authorities, and the Clean Michigan bond issue.

Michigan law permits municipalities to create a brownfield redevelopment authority (BRA). These authorities create a specialized institutional structure to promote local planning and implementation of brownfield redevelopment. The Brownfield Redevelopment Financing Act grants authorities a number of fiduciary powers including paying or reimbursing private or public parties for cleanup activities; leasing, purchasing, or conveying property; accepting grants and donations of property, labor or "other things of value" from public or private sources; investing the authority's money; borrowing money; and engaging in lending and mortgage activities associated with property it acquires (Davis and Margolis, 1997). Authorities may also create revolving loan funds to finance projects.

Each authority must develop a plan for redeveloping eligible properties within its jurisdiction. Elements of this plan include the identification of specific target parcels in the district, a comprehensive financial plan, and strategies for dealing with possible citizen displacement resulting from redevelopment efforts. The brownfield plan must be approved by the chartering municipality before tax increment financing is available to the authority. School tax increments become available only after the Michigan Department of Environmental Quality has approved the plan.[9]

Brownfield redevelopment authorities have the legal capacity to raise revenue in several ways. They are permitted to capture increases in state and local (including school) taxes that result from the redevelopment of a brownfield. These tax increment funds can be used for evaluation and feasibility studies of specific sites, on-site demolition of buildings, necessary on-site construction, and for the combining of contaminated property with adjacent parcels. The existence of an authority allows a developer/taxpayer a tax credit on Michigan's single business tax (limited to 10 percent of capital investment or an absolute cap of $1 million).[10]

A recent state bond issue provides a second important funding source for brownfield work. In 1998 Michigan voters approved a $675 million environmental bond issue, Clean Michigan. The bond issued included $335 million that was targeted directly to brownfield remediation. There will be a number of ways in which local authorities will be able to access these funds. Some projects will be directly funded by the state. These sites will be selected from a set nominated by local authorities.[11] Other funds will be allocated through several remediation and assessment programs administered by the Michigan Department of Environmental Quality. In addition, grant funds from a number of other state agencies have often been used to support specific projects.

Implementing Michigan's Brownfield Program

The design of the Michigan brownfield initiative requires the cooperation of state government, local government, and private developers. Thus, the substantive impact of changes in Michigan toxic-waste policy depends on three broad implementation issues. First, do state policy makers have the capacity to reorient key state bureaucracies to support revised programmatic goals? Since the brownfield program does not require local action but only encourages it, program outcomes also depend on local interest and capacity to implement a redevelopment effort. The willingness of the private sector to invest in brownfield properties defines the final and key link to program success.

The Role of State Bureaucracy

Michigan's brownfield initiative challenges responsible state administrators in a number of important ways. First is the clear shift in the focus of toxic-waste policy. As noted above, the introduction of economic development as an important component of toxic-waste policy represents an expansion of formal agency goals. Related to this change in substantive focus is a shift in role. Prior to the brownfield initiative, state environmental staff was largely seen as an enforcement agency. More recently, state staff has been defined as facilitators promoting economic development. Rather than imposing solutions on target communities, state environmental actors are now expected to nurture cooperative links across the public and private sector.

A key issue is whether there has been a real change in the behavior of state-level bureaucrats charged with implementing toxic-waste policy. Certainly the notion of mission or agency culture is, at best, difficult to define and measure. Yet, speaking to individuals working in and with the Michigan Department of Environmental Quality (MDEQ), it is difficult not to feel that a mission shift has occurred. Asked about how the department achieved this culture change, a senior administrator in MDEQ remarked:

> A really good word would be "challenging." We are on this payroll to implement laws passed by the legislature. The new law required us to take a new approach. Our focus is still getting property cleaned up so that it is safe for the people that use it. But because the law is aimed at a land use...we've had to start retraining ourselves to consider a developer view.

Elected state political authorities, particularly those in the governors' office, put a good deal of pressure on agency staff to change environmental enforcement procedures. Pressures were also quite explicit in the department:

> If you feel that as an employee of the department that there are certain things that need to be done to protect the environment, including cleaning up a property or groundwater, to the point where it can be put to use because that's the way it should be, you are in the wrong department. You don't fit in anymore. And, in fact, if you maintain that outlook, some sort of action will be taken to either move you to a less sensitive job, or some encouragement to change your outlook of one form or another, because it doesn't work in this program. And I would say, that it is better now than it was. We are getting more done and providing as much protection. The difference is that if you have a view that contamination that we put there has to come out in order to make it right, that viewpoint doesn't work anymore.

Compliance was enhanced by two rather dramatic administrative strategies. In an effort to reduce the state workforce, employees were offered an attractive early retirement package. Not surprisingly, observers report many of those who were most opposed to the governors policy initiatives chose to leave state government. In addition, the governor reorganized executive departments so that environmental regulation would be centered in a new Michigan Department of Environmental Quality. Obviously the new department had many workers quite familiar with traditional environmental regulation. However, these workers were joined by a set of state workers more focused on community development:

> This happened at the same time that there were changes in other Michigan departments. As you know, the Michigan Department of Commerce used to handle both industrial and community development issues. When the Department of Commerce split, the majority of the people went to the Jobs Commission to focus on industrial development and not community development, not retail, not downtown activities, not tourism and such. And so there was a concern about community development at the same time there was a switch in the environmental law that allowed individuals to look at community development sites. Almost by default...the Department of Environmental Quality became the Community Development branch of the State of Michigan, because nobody else was doing that. It actually was a good fit because we were now looking at the cleanup based on what the land use was going to be.

The result has been, at least, a formal compliance with the new environmental policy. For many employees of the MDEQ there seems to be a genuine commitment to the new departmental goals:

> I think there's no question there's been a major culture change. When it first came about, there wasn't unity in the way we were heading. I think it's an evolutionary process. Once you see what you can do and see the rewards of what you've created, it becomes a hell of a lot more palatable to follow that same path. We've evolved to the point where we are because we've had a lot of success stories.

Both central and regional office personnel are anxious to frame their actions both in terms of economic development and environmental protection. There is no question that environmental protection remains a key value for MDEQ. It clearly is. But it is also clear that other values are also now important. A number of observers across the state acknowledged this. One local development specialist captured this view when he tried to summarize how MDEQ has changed:

> They realized that for whatever reasons, they really stood in the way of economic development for years and there were ways that they could partner with business and industry and still achieve their initial goals of protecting the environment and human health and safety without being a burden and a hindrance to business. And so a lot of people call the Department of Environmental Quality today the "Department of Economic Development," because they wholly, at least at the upper administrative levels, totally embraced the idea of doing whatever it takes to encourage business while still protecting the environment.

The Role of Local Political Authorities

Local political leaders have been important supporters of the Michigan brownfield initiative. A mayor of one of Michigan's older industrial cities described the important role that the state mayors played in supporting the effort.

> The urban-core mayors were the key allies of the governor in changing Public Act 305. We carried the water for him. So we saw ourselves as key players. It was important for him, it was important for us. He needed something for the environment, and it was a safe environmental issue for him, because he had all these urban Democrat mayors carrying the water. I considered the state on this issue to be an ally, and this is a tool that they have helped create. And it is an important tool and it has been helpful.

> We (the mayors) supported the Clean Michigan Initiative. I went out there and cut TV ads; all of the urban mayors did that in the regions. So we wanted to put our imprimatur on it.

Data collected from local government authorities picture an enthusiastic response to opportunities created by state brownfield statutes. In July of 1996, the MDEQ published an initial one-year evaluation of the new redevelopment policies based on an informal telephone survey of 40 municipalities (Michigan Department of Environmental Quality, 1996). Of the 33 responding cities, 29 claimed an increased interest in redeveloping contaminated properties in their cities. Twenty municipalities reported a total of $221,573,000 in private investment and the creation of 2,379 new jobs.

In a follow-up survey in June of 1999, 23 authorities (out of a total of 115) reported $93,100,000 in new industrial investment, $149,600,000 in new commercial investment, and $106,750,000 in new residential investment (Michigan Department of Environmental Quality 1999). Municipal spokesmen attribute this increased investment to the new liability protection and revised land-use-based cleanup standards. One local official noted that the program had changed how the city viewed brownfields: "We now have this ethos where we believe that our brownfields are assets."

Further evidence of local enthusiasm for brownfield redevelopment is provided by the speed at which eligible local government units have created Brownfield Redevelopment Authorities. As of January 30, 1998, 59 municipalities had created authorities. By June of 1999, 121 authorities were operating in the state. While the creation of a BRA is only a first step in creating an active local program, it does strongly suggest that municipal authorities are anxious to begin the process.

Even more than their state counterparts, local officials have accepted the important role of private investment in brownfield redevelopment. One official described the planning process for the city's brownfield program as follows:

> One of the first things that came out of those meetings was everybody agreed that the economic development part of the program is going to drive the environmental cleanup. Everybody realized that we couldn't just go and pick a site and start cleaning up for no reason if the site doesn't have any basis for development or any business interest.

Although there is broad agreement on the general assumptions of the program, there is significant variation in how the program was administered. A review of local programs shows that local jurisdictions have used the program's flexibility to construct a number of alternative implementation strategies. Significant structural variation exists across the state on at least two important dimensions: implementation agencies and program scope.

Municipalities have assigned brownfield redevelopment to a variety of agencies. Some jurisdictions have centered their efforts in established line departments, usually planning or economic development offices. Others have experimented with a remarkable degree of privatization. In one case, the local brownfield authority is staffed completely by private employees of the local Chamber of Commerce. Specific programs also vary in geographic scope. Some cities focus their efforts within city boundaries. Others see redevelopment as more of a regional issue, and therefore focus their efforts through regional-level organizations.

There are two important points to be made about these implementation strategies. First, the distinctions are not simply theoretical. There are examples of active programs in each cell. Even more important is the finding that local officials report success using each type of model. Thus, "best practice" varies from site to site. Such findings do not suggest that state and federal officials should give up oversight efforts in the name of local autonomy, but they do argue for an increased reliance on outcome assessment and greater tolerance of alternative implementation strategies.

Alternative Local Implementation Strategies

Focus	Implementation Agent Public	Implementation Agent Private
Local	Administered by standing city agency. Focus within city boundaries.	Administered by private sector (or public-private partnership). Focus within city boundaries.
Regional	Administered by standing city agency. Regional focus.	Administered by private sector (or public-private partnership). Regional focus.

The Role of Private Actors

A final assumption embedded within the Michigan brownfield effort is that, given the right set of incentives and protections, private sector actors will become active in brownfield redevelopment. Note this expectation is not based on any appeal to civic obligation or good citizenship, but simply on the claim that brownfields are sound business investments. Once again, there is some modest evidence that the effort has been successful. For example, the relatively high rate of Baseline Environmental Assessment (BEA) filings gives clear evidence that there is significant economic demand for some potentially contaminated properties. By July 1996 the MDEQ reported that 425 Baseline Environmental Assessments had been received. This was 10 times the total number of property transfers brought about by negotiated covenants not to sue for the previous five years. Moreover, BEA filings continue to increase. By April 1999 MDEQ had received a total of 2,635 applications (Kummler and Card, 1999).

Not surprisingly, the willingness of private developers to become involved in brownfield projects is very much tied to the perceived economic opportunities that specific projects present. A number of redevelopment officials observed that developers in general are very sensitive to new investment opportunities. Following the passage of legislation promoting brownfield work, some developers independently sought out city officials to identify brownfield opportunities. When asked how the city identified potential developers, one economic development specialist admitted:

> We haven't really had to do any formal marketing yet. It is interesting that as state-issued environmental cleanup guidelines have changed, and their various programs have come to be, the state goes to a lot of con-

> ferences around the state inviting developers, environmental consultants, and attorneys and so forth. The state runs conferences, private sector consultants run some, attorneys sponsor some, and we've gone to a fair amount of those, spoken to a fair amount of them, and we've gotten a lot of attention that way.

In areas where the local economy is particularly robust, brownfield specialists report that redevelopment is occurring with relatively little public intervention. Revised liability and cleanup standards have apparently promoted a sharp increase in entirely private redevelopment projects. One city redevelopment official expressed frank surprise at the willingness of private developers to take advantage of the new regulatory climate independent of city assistance:

> With the publicity associated with the creation of the authority, we thought that there was going to be more interest by companies wanting to utilize the authority in one way or another. That has not proven to be the case. The real estate development community comes across stuff. They just say…we'll deal with it. We don't need you. It's reassuring …I think, of the free enterprise system, where they say we will deal with it, …thanks for the offer. We'll deal with it. We'll take care of it, and the cost associated with the baseline work, and the remedial efforts that need to be done they just do it and pass the cost on. They absorb the cost. It's a transactional cost associated with the development or redevelopment of a piece of property. It's very gratifying in most instances. In spite of what we have done, they just plod ahead. "Thanks but no thanks. We'll take care of it."

More often, however, local authorities actively recruit developers. One developer commented:

> I've got a dozen proposals sitting back here; the city of this, the city of that—trying to contact developers to get them to come in and build something in and around vacant land, old, deserted, demolished or, empty buildings from downtown. We've got the city of…after us because we just bought a building down there, and they want us to look at some other opportunities. The economic development people are trying to get people into their area, and they latch onto developers all the time. We get proposal after proposal. "We want to build a shopping center, we want to build an outlet center, we want to build this, we want to build that, would you be interested," that type of thing.

Asked whether he would be willing to become involved in a brownfield project, a developer was clear about the decision rule for his company:

> Depends on the piece. If we think it's a good location—and that's the beauty of the brownfield areas, is that they are in good locations—if it's a good location and we can fill a need of the city, why not? It just depends on how much you're going to put into it. We'll look at any opportunities.

The strong interest in brownfields expressed by developers, combined with the relatively high rate of BEA filings, suggests that a significant number of sites are being redeveloped independent of public sector intervention. This would seem most likely for those sites where the actual level of contamination turned out to be modest. Unfortunately, there is no reliable data available to either conform or disconfirm this hypothesis.

It is clear that where the local economy is weak, there is relatively little interest on the part of developers to invest in brownfield property.[12] Current incentives are simply insufficient to attract such interest. At a minimum, these communities will require a deeper public subsidy to entice private sector investment.[13]

Recommendations

Policy evaluation seldom offers definitive results. The world is simply too complex to identify strong and unambiguous causal linkages. Nevertheless, the Michigan brownfield initiative does offer some important insights about the impact of specific toxic-waste policies on redevelopment efforts. Such insights do lead to a set of concrete recommendations as to how state and local officials can encourage the redevelopment of brownfield sites.

However, decisions to implement such recommendations will inevitably lead to tradeoffs with respect to other reasonable policy goals. It is essential that policy evaluation not only specifies positive policy outcomes, but also illuminates these tradeoffs.

Recommendation 1: Restrict liability associated with potentially contaminated land parcels.

The notion that those who pollute a site should be responsible for cleaning it has served as a key element of national toxic-waste policy for almost 20 years. It is an intuitively appealing approach that attempts to tie liability with responsibility. However, in practice the application of such strict liability has raised a number of questions. Some center on the practical difficulties of implementation. For example, most sites had multiple sources of pollution. In such cases, how does one allocate responsibility for cleanup costs? Indeed, it is often difficult to even know who contributed to the pollution of a site. It is also impossible to sanction responsible parties that no longer exist. The fairness of strict liability has also been questioned. Many argue that if actions were legal when they were performed, it is unreasonable to declare them illegal at some later point. Critics also argue that it is unreasonable to assess the full cost of a cleanup to what is almost always a subset of guilty parties. Finally, many question whether ownership alone should create a liability for the actions of others.

A less discussed critique of strict liability is the fact that it creates a set of severe negative externalities that impose significant but unintended social costs on the community in which the property is found. This claim is based on the view that strict liability creates a negative incentive structure that virtually force developers to not even consider siting projects on older industrial or commercial sites. Rather, projects are targeted to previously undeveloped properties.

The argument as to why this occurs is straightforward. It is simply not rational to site a project on property that may carry a significant liability when other available properties have no such risk. Indeed, even if a developer had an interest in a potential brownfield site, owners of that property may be unwilling to sell the property since liability for site cleanup remains with past owners even after the property is sold. As long as there is a possibility that a major cleanup will be required, economic rationality demands that the property simply be left unused. Note that this logic would apply not simply to sites with known significant contamination, but to all sites with possible contamination. Essentially this predicts the collapse of the commercial and industrial real estate market in older industrial cities.

The Michigan brownfield initiative provides convincing evidence that such externalities do exist. Certainly providing liability protection for new property owners has had the effect of revitalizing a long dormant urban real estate market. The large number of Baseline Environmental Assessments filed with the Michigan Department of Environmental Quality documents a sharp increase in market exchanges. Interestingly, the BEA statements reveal many of these properties had only modest environmental problems. This gives further support to the notion that strict liability depresses the entire market for older industrial and commercial properties, including many parcels without significant environmental problems.

It is important to stress that this finding does not lead unambiguously to a recommendation for relaxed liability in toxic-waste cleanups. As noted, important tradeoffs often cannot be avoided. The Michigan Brownfield initiative illustrates that these tradeoffs may be quite complex. A decision to impose cleanup costs on "guilty parties" also imposes a set of broad social and economic costs to a much wider population in terms of a collapsed real estate market and forgone economic opportunities. Whether that cost is justified remains a political decision to be made by responsible policy makers.

Recommendation 2: Offer selective incentives to encourage the redevelopment of specific brownfield sites.

Michigan's financial commitment to its brownfield initiative makes it stand out from efforts of other states. Financial incentives included substantial bond funds targeted to assessment and remediation, authorization for local governments to use increment tax financing to support remediation, and direct tax incentives for businesses willing to develop brownfield sites. There is a widespread perception at the local level that if such funding were not available, a significant number of brownfield sites that have been redeveloped would have remained derelict. A number of localities have particularly promoted the reduction in the state's single property tax in seeking to persuade businesses to explore the potential of brownfield locations.

Recommendation 3: Allow local officials sufficient flexibility to respond to market-driven redevelopment opportunities.

Federal and state environmental officials often maintain that the design and implementation of site redevelopment projects should occur within the framework of an overall development plan. The Michigan brownfield initiative provides a contrast to this public rhetoric. With its focus on private sector investment, the initiative gives little encouragement to comprehensive community planning. Projects are typically designed and implemented on a parcel-by-parcel basis. Project selection is driven more by developer preferences than local strategic objectives.

Indeed, this focus is institutionalized in a number of state brownfield assessment and cleanup programs that require local authorities to identify an interested developer before funds can be allocated to a proposed project. There is no empirical evidence that the parcels most attractive to that private sector are those of greatest concern to the community. Moreover, given that the proposed end use is driven by economic return, there is little reason to assume that such a use would be consistent with the overall preferences of the community.

The Michigan brownfield initiative has created, or in some cases reinforced, a set of cooperative linkages between state and local development and environmental officials. In some communities it has also reinforced ties between political decision-makers and private sector developers. These linkages expand the capacity of local government to promote the sort of public-private ventures that drive the brownfield initiative. However, they tend to de-emphasize the traditional planning function within local government. In addition, efforts to promote community engagement in brownfield redevelopment are quite modest, most often taking the form of "informational" community meetings.

Recommendation 4: Allow the use of institutional controls as a means to mitigate health risks from existing contamination.

The amount of actual cleanup work at most projects generated by the Michigan brownfield initiative has been actually quite modest. This is due to a set of three interrelated factors. First is the somewhat surprising finding that a relatively large proportion of the brownfield sites actually have had less contamination than expected. A second important factor is that new state standards require less rigorous cleaning. Finally, where contamination does exist, developers almost always rely on institutional controls rather than actual site cleanups to meet state environmental standards.

The logic of this process is clear. As private economic actors, developers seek to minimize costs whenever possible. Direct costs generated by institutional controls are almost always less than actual site cleanups. Thus, it is logical to use such controls even if there might be a significant long-term social cost in doing so. This is not to suggest that developers act headless of community interest and the common good. Rather, they are responding to strong structural pressures to minimize their own costs.

The reliance on institutional controls reveals some tension between a brownfield program that emphasizes public health and one that focuses on economic development. Institutional controls do reduce short-term costs, and they seem to promote economic development. Less clear are the long-term public health implications of such controls. This policy dilemma raises an important set of unresolved issues that are discussed further in the next section.

Recommendation 5: Provide local jurisdictions with the capacity to design and implement redevelopment plans that reflect local conditions and political culture.

Local governments have adopted a wide variety of implementation strategies in their redevelopment efforts. For example, in traditionally conservative areas of the state, an effort has been made to not only engage the private sector, but to have private actors assume strong leadership roles in the program. In other cities, public officials have taken key leaderships roles. Sometimes leadership is provided by the traditional planning or economic development department. At other times it is located in other city agencies. Where regional cooperation is common, brownfield programs are often regional in scope. Where regional cooperation is less common, programs are more likely to focus on a single jurisdiction. An important finding of this review is that no single approach stands out as most effective. The best programs are those designed with an eye to local conditions and preferences.

The ability and willingness of local jurisdictions to design their brownfield programs lends support to the general decentralization assumptions built into the state initiative. It suggests that future state policy should continue to be directed to desired outcomes, without an exact specification of how local governments are to reach these goals. These findings also support similar federal decentralization efforts. However, state and federal officials must continue to have an oversight role since not all local programs are successful. Indeed, the development of effective oversight and evaluation tools is a critical task if policy decentralization is to continue.

Continuing Policy Dilemmas

Long-Term Empirical Questions

The Michigan brownfield initiative raises a number of unresolved policy questions. First, there remain a number of empirical questions about the long-term effectiveness of specific policies. These issues can be clarified by a continued monitoring of efforts like the Michigan initiative. Three important evaluation issues are listed below:

Are current contamination standards sufficient to protect public health?

The key to spurring economic development projects has been cutting developers' costs in meeting state environmental standards. These cost reductions have been achieved through an overall lowering of standards and an increased use of institutional controls as an alternative to actual site cleanup. There is little question that these changes have reduced developer costs. Less clear, however, is the adequacy of the new standards to protect public health. While most public and private officials maintain that existing standards will protect human health, this view is not universally shared. A few officials noted with concern that standards had been lowered with relatively little scientific evidence to support such changes.

How stable are institutional property controls?

Institutional controls through land-use, zoning, and on-site construction (such as parking lots) provide an important means to reduce the cost of redevelopment. Currently neither the federal government nor the state government has much experience in maintaining such controls over long periods of time. As a result, it is impossible to know how stable such controls are. Although institutional controls do appear to meet short-run public health concerns, their long-term viability is more problematic. At a minimum, it is essential that state and local governments create more capacity to monitor the long-term stability of these institutional controls.

Does targeted publicly supported brownfield redevelopment promote spontaneous economic expansion?

There is little doubt that the Michigan brownfield initiative has been instrumental in generating a number of redevelopment projects across the state of Michigan. Long-vacant properties are being targeted for development projects. Informed observers agree that state policy has been successful in increasing developer interest in brownfield projects through a net reduction of private sector costs associated with such projects. Nor is there much dispute that these projects have had a generally positive impact in their community. At a minimum, site redevelopment means that a community is able to rid itself of a nonproductive eyesore. There are usually economic advantages as well. For example, some modest employment growth often follows redevelopment.

However, no case was found where an initial brownfield investment plausibly led to a significant secondary development as predicted by brownfield renewal enthusiasts. Of course, linkages between economic development efforts and general growth are notoriously difficult to demonstrate. In addition to the complexity of the causal linkages involved in economic development policies, the modest economic impact of the Michigan brownfield initiative may also be a function of the relatively short time the initiative has been in existence. For example, a number of municipalities report that they have just begun their efforts, and it is unlikely that long-term impacts would be observable.

It is important to remember that a number of the Michigan reforms also promoted private development as well as public projects. Thus, it might be the case that while publicly supported projects have only a modest impact on overall economic expansion, the reforms that drive the public projects also promote a significant investment in the private sector. For example, limiting liability may have the effect of reintegrating properties once thought to be contaminated, but in fact were not, into a viable real estate market. Strictly speaking, such an outcome would not be public brownfield redevelopment. Nevertheless, the local economic advantage of such a reintegration is obvious. Therefore, any future attempts to measure the economic impact of the Michigan program will need to explicitly consider the impact of such private market transactions.

Broad Policy Questions

In addition to these empirical questions, the brownfield program presents a set of issues that pose fundamental policy choices. While further evaluation can certainly help identify options, it cannot specify a "best option." Ultimately these issues can only be resolved in the political process. Three examples of such issues are given below. The first two explore specific elements of the brownfield initiative. The final example raises a more general issue of state and federal policy decentralization.

What is the appropriate role of community preferences?

There is little formal requirement for community or neighborhood involvement in brownfield project planning. Most communities have, nevertheless, attempted to create a forum for some neighborhood-level participation. Usually this participation provides for neighborhood review rather than initiation of projects. This finding raises the question of the appropriate role of citizens most directly impacted by brownfield projects. To what extent should local communities be involved in a local redevelopment effort, and how does one bring about the desired level? Note that there is an inherent tension between efforts to promote private sector investment based on the market potential of specific parcels and efforts to design and implement an overall community plan. In a number of cities it was found that developers were unwilling to invest in specific facilities that were most desired by community residents.

How should policy makers deal with demands for increased environmental justice?

Brownfield sites are most likely to be in low and moderate income, and minority neighborhoods. Critics of the Michigan brownfield initiative see the implementation of reduced contamination standards and institutional controls as creating patterns of environmental injustice. That is, minority and low-income citizens are put at greater health risks simply because of their proximity to sites to be redeveloped. Others—very often local elected officials—stress the critical need for economic development within these communities. For example, recently the mayors in Michigan's core cities led the fight against federal environmental justice standards that would have reduced the capacity of cities to promote redevelopment projects.

What is to be done with unsuccessful programs?

Although the long-term impact of the brownfield initiative remains problematic, there is evidence that it has spurred redevelopment projects across the state. Obviously this success has not been universal. Failures do occur. Indeed, failures can occur at both the site and community level. Site-level failures occur when local jurisdictions are unable to attract investment to specific parcels. Such problem parcels may suffer from relatively high levels of contamination or may be undesirable for development because of location, size, or other factors.

Failure can also be community-wide. In this case a community is unable to attract significant private investment in any local brownfield sites. Community failure can also be traced to a variety of factors. Some communities simply do not have the capacity or the political will to implement brownfield programs. In other communities the available economic incentives are not sufficient to attract developers to local projects.

Such local policy failures pose important issues for state policy makers. For example, should more incentives be made available for so called "problem sites"? If so, how can one identify these sites? The issue of community program failure is even more complex. How, for example, can one differentiate city needs? Should the state take a more direct lead in redevelopment efforts in such jurisdictions, or should the state focus on those jurisdictions capable of generating private investment?

Concluding Thoughts

This case study of the Michigan brownfield initiative reminds us of how complex the policy process actually is. Although formally a state program, the heart of the initiative is a set of over 100 local programs, many having multiple projects. Each project typically involves an array of local officials, developers, and community members. Moreover, projects and local programs have complex and overlapping ties with a variety of state officials.

Unfortunately, it is impossible to understand the impact of the brownfield initiative without relatively detailed analysis of these specific local projects. It is the impact of such projects that must ultimately drive the evaluation of the overall brownfield program. While the number and value of local initiatives can—and certainly will—be reported in a variety of aggregate statistics, the central evaluation issue is the return that specific redevelopment projects bring to the communities in which they occur. To monitor such local impacts requires an extraordinary effort, and often a rather messy and unsystematic research design. However, there is no alternative if we are serious in our efforts to learn from current policy initiatives.

This chapter illustrates the importance of such local-level analysis. It shows that within a single legislative framework, municipalities have constructed a variety of implementation strategies. Students of organizations sometimes decry such complexity, arguing that this variation introduces inefficiency into the policy system. A review of program outcomes suggests that such a fear may not be warranted. There is little evidence that there exists a single best municipal strategy. There was, in fact, substantial evidence that the initiative has had a positive impact in a number of Michigan cities across a variety of implementation strategies. However, this success carries two important qualifications.

First, it is clear that the program in its present form introduces some policy tradeoffs that may not be acceptable to some communities. Specifically, a reliance on private developers almost automatically reduces opportunities for inclusive community participation and planning. It is also clear that program outcomes are modest. While it is certainly possible to identify specific sites that have been redeveloped through the program, there is no evidence of a broader pattern of redevelopment.

Second, certainly there is little to suggest that current brownfield programs can meet the very ambitious goals articulated by the programs more optimistic supporters. The initiative is neither revitalizing older industrial cities nor halting urban sprawl. Whether the program can evolve toward meeting these more ambitious goals will depend in part on the willingness of policy officials to subject their efforts to a careful assessment and then apply gained knowledge to the design of future redevelopment programs. Given this effort, brownfield redevelopment can become an even more effective economic development tool for Michigan cities in the future.

Postscript

Interest in brownfield redevelopment has continued both at the federal level and in the state of Michigan since the original publication of this report in 1999. The Small Business Liability Relief and Brownfields Revitalization Act of 2002 provides protection from Superfund liability for perspective purchasers, owners of contiguous property, and landowners not responsible for contamination. It also expands federal funding for state and local programs to assess and clean up brownfield sites. The Michigan program was expanded in a series of Brownfield Amendments enacted in 2000. These amendments increase the level of tax subsidies available to development on brownfield sites. In addition, the legal definition of brownfields was significantly expanded to include "obsolete" property in 88 core cities across the state. Thus, in the state of Michigan it is now possible to have a brownfield with no actual site contamination.

There is a remarkably high level of support for redevelopment efforts in Michigan. Public endorsements of specific elements of the program often exceed 90 percent. However, there continues to be a need to engage community actors in planning redevelopment projects. For example, there is little public support for using different standards for different land uses. The public continues to feel that all sites should be cleaned to the same standards. In addition, there are some important differences in public attitudes by income that point to potential long-term political threats to the program.

There continues to be a good deal of anecdotal evidence that the Michigan program is having significant success. Unfortunately, there is little systematic data to confirm this assertion. Key policy issues identified in the initial research remain important unanswered questions.

Richard C. Hula
May 2003

Additional Background Information

Hula, R. C. (2003). *Citizen Assessment of the Michigan Brownfield Initiative: A Report to the Institute for Public Policy and Social Research,* Michigan State University.

Hula, R. C. (2003). *The Michigan Brownfield Initiative and Private Market Redevelopment: An Assessment: A Report to the Institute for Public Policy and Social Research,* Michigan State University.

Szymecko, L. A., and T. C. Voice (2002). *Brownfield Redevelopment: Guidebook for Michigan.* Chicago, Brownfield News.

Endnotes

1. This project would not have been possible without the generous support of the IBM Endowment for The Business of Government. Preliminary funding was provided by the Michigan Applied Public Policy Fund. A special thanks is due to the many practitioners who graciously gave their time and insights to make this chapter possible. Thanks also to Brian McGrain for his able research assistance, and to Mark A. Abramson of the IBM Endowment for The Business of Government for a careful reading of an earlier draft. Of course, any errors of fact or interpretation remain my own.

2. This is the definition of brownfields commonly cited by the federal Environmental Protection Agency (EPA). See Kaiser (1998).

3. For a more complete discussion of RCRA and TSCA see Rosenbaum (1995, p. 232-262).

4. Congress has observed this shifting set of goals with some ambivalence. On one hand, there is wide support for the overall concept and direction the EPA has taken. However, some concern has been expressed that EPA has moved beyond its statutory authority in using CERCLA trust funds to implement certain aspects of the brownfield effort. For example, Congress expressly prohibited the EPA from using any of its resources to underwrite local and state revolving loan funds to finance actual cleanup on brownfield sites. See United States General Accounting Office (1998), and Reisch (1998).

5. Michigan actors note that there are two major elements of liability that continue to retard redevelopment of brownfield sites. Both are associated with CERCLA liability. Obviously the state cannot grant immunity from federal action against property owners. As noted above, the EPA has reduced these concerns by entering a set of agreements not to sue based on a lack of responsibility for on-site contamination. A second concern is the potential of responsible parties to bring suit against new owners under CERCLA liability. Interestingly, while this concern is widely cited as a block to redevelopment, there seems to be no reported instance of such suits actually being filed. See Environmental Financial Advisory Board(1998).

6. Such penalties can also be assessed to new landowners if the new owners do not takes steps to identify and report current levels of site contamination. See Woodruff et. al.(1998).

7. The BEA filing essentially replaces a much more complex process in which a developer might escape liability. Prior to the amendments to Part 201 the only way to relieve a developer/purchaser from liability from existing contamination was a "covenant not to sue." This was almost always a very slow and complicated process. For example, between 1991 and 1995, only 37 such covenants were implemented. See Michigan Department of Environmental Quality(1996).

8. Note that while new owners are no longer responsible for site cleanup they are required to meet the "do-care" requirements that the public be protected from contamination. Indeed, such "do-care" requirements have been extended to all owners of contaminated sites. This actually represents an extension of past liability in that potentially responsible parties now have an affirmative responsibility to show "due care" whether or not the site has been identified as a potential public health threat by some public agency.

9. Unfortunately, these plans reveal less than might be expected. A number of jurisdictions have adopted a strategy of including a parcel into their brownfield plan only after they have identified a developer interested in the property.

10. Woodruff et. al.(1998) suggest that even if the municipality is unable or does not want to capture tax increments, the single business tax credit is cause enough for the municipality to form a Brownfield Redevelopment Authority. Field interviews show that

some BRAs have been formed primarily to have local business qualify for the single business tax.

11. MDEQ accepts local nominations, develops a ranking, and submits a priority list to the state legislature. The legislature either modifies or accepts DEC recommendations. Respondents at MDEQ report that they could not remember when the legislature had not followed departmental recommendations under an earlier bond issue. Some concern was expressed that this pattern might change as the brownfield initiative has significantly expanded the criteria for project selection. Thus creating a basis for political disputes.

12. There is an interesting exception in some very depressed communities. Some large corporations that have in the past engaged in significant disinvestment in the community, but retain a presence, are sometimes willing to make community investment beyond what one would expect from straightforward market calculations. Note that such corporate "citizenship" is both limited and relatively rare.

13. In some of Michigan's poorest communities there remains a strong emphasis on more traditional federal aid programs to promote economic redevelopment. Relatively large federal investment can be seen as a means to secure these relatively large subsidies.

Bibliography

Consumers Renaissance Redevelopment Corporation (1998). Michigan's Brownfield Redevelopment Program: First in the Nation, Consumers Renaissance Redevelopment Corporation.

Consumers Renaissance Redevelopment Corporation (1998). National Comparative Analysis of Brownfield Redevelopment Programs, Consumers Renaissance Redevelopment Corporation.

Davis, T. S. and K. D. Margolis (1997). *Brownfields: A Comprehensive Guide to Redeveloping Contaminated Property*. Chicago, American Bar Association.

Environmental Financial Advisory Board (1998). Expediting Clean-Up and Redevelopment of Brownfields: Addressing Major Barriers to Private Sector Involvement—Real or Perceived. Washington D.C., United States Environmental Protection Agency.

Kaiser, S.E. (1998). "Brownfields National Partnership: The Federal Role in Brownfield Redevelopment." *Public Works Management and Policy* 2(3): 196-201.

Kummler, R. H. and D. S. Card (1999). Brownfield Redevelopment: The Michigan Strategy, College of Urban, Labor & Metropolitan Affairs, Wayne State University.

Michigan Department of Environmental Quality (1996). The Part 201 Amendments: One Year Later.

Michigan Department of Environmental Quality (1999). Brownfield Redeveloping Financing Acts: Three Years Later.

Reisch, M. (1998). Superfund Reauthorization Issues in the 105th Congress, Congressional Research Service.

Rosenbaum, W. A. (1995). *Environmental Politics and Policy.* Washington D.C., Congressional Quarterly.

United States General Accounting Office (1998). Superfund: EPA's Use of Funds for Brownfield Revitalization.

Woodruff, F. M., C. M. Denton, et al. (1998). Michigan's Brownfield Redevelopment Initiative: A Primer on How to Make the Most of It. Grand Rapids, Varun, Riddering, Schmidt and Howlett.

CHAPTER NINE

Rethinking U.S. Environmental Protection Policy: Management Challenges for the Bush Administration

Dennis A. Rondinelli
Director, Center for Global Business Research
The Frank Hawkins Kenan Institute of Private Enterprise
Kenan-Flagler Business School
University of North Carolina at Chapel Hill

This report was originally published in November 2000, revised May 2003.

Introduction

A large and diverse group of organizations in the United States is calling for a review and revision of federal and state governments' environmental policy. A remarkable convergence of opinion in both the public and the private sectors is evolving about the need to supplement regulatory policies with environmental management systems that focus more strongly on pollution prevention and eco-efficiency.

Environmental policy now predominantly relies on a regulatory approach that requires the private sector to use the "best available" technology to control environmentally harmful air, water, and solid waste emissions from industrial and business facilities. Observers both inside and outside of government generally agree that environmental regulations have greatly reduced air, water, and soil pollution in the United States since the early 1970s. Many note, however, that the regulatory system is not always effective in controlling non-point sources of pollution. Moreover, single media environmental regulations (separate laws for each type of pollution) do not address complex environmental problems that involve more than one source. Nor are regulations always cost effective or based on scientific findings. Both business leaders and state and local government officials often point out that national regulations result in a "one-size-fits-all" approach that can be relatively inflexible and sometimes unresponsive to conditions and needs in different areas of the country, in different communities, and in different industries.

The Limitations of Command-and-Control Management

Although regulations are usually effective in reducing emissions from large and obvious point sources, they do not allow the U.S. Environmental Protection Agency (EPA) and state regulators the flexibility to reduce pollution among numerous small sources that account for a significant portion of all environmental degradation. National environmental regulations are numerous, complex, fragmented, and ever-changing, making it difficult for both the regulators and the regulated to keep pace with new requirements and to achieve and maintain compliance. The number of federal, state, and local environmental rules and regulations in the United States grew from about 2,000 in the 1970s to more than 100,000 at the end of the 1990s. Environmental regulations are now listed in over 789 parts of the Code of Federal Regulations. At the same time that environmental regulations were becoming more complex, they became more costly for governments to enforce and businesses to comply.

The total cost of compliance with environmental laws since 1970 now exceeds $1.5 trillion. Studies indicate that by 1990, the cost of pollution abatement had "emerged as a major claimant on the resources of the U.S. economy," reaching more than 10 percent of the total cost of government purchases of goods and services.[1] Individuals, businesses, and governments now spend more than $120 billion annually on pollution abatement and control alone. Clearly, the reduction of environmental pollution has significant social and economic benefits, but alternatives to command-and-control regulation may be more effective and less costly.

The Need for Pollution Prevention

Many of those who have assessed the performance of environmental management in the United States conclude that, in a post-industrial nation in which legal controls are already quite stringent, federal and state environmental protection agencies must use a wide array of policy, technical, and management instruments to achieve continuous improvements in environmental quality in the future.[2] Many of those calling for a review of environmental policy note that greater returns on public and private investment can be obtained from management practices that, while maintaining a sound regulatory system, place much more emphasis on promoting pollution prevention and eco-efficiency. Environmental conditions can best be improved by encouraging business and industry to eliminate the sources of environmental degradation rather than continuing to try to clean up pollution at the "end of the pipeline."

Pollution prevention is not, of course, a new idea. Many corporations are pursuing pollution prevention, clean manufacturing, and the responsible use of resources through voluntary environmental management systems that make use of eco-efficiency practices. (See "The P2/E2 Concept" on page 282.)

Corporations in some industries have been practicing pollution prevention for more than 25 years. But environmental protection policy based on P2/E2 has never been widely adopted in the United States because it requires flexibility and a multimedia approach that the current regulatory system does not easily accommodate.

A "Win-Win Strategy" for Environmental Management

The arguments for increasing the emphasis on promoting P2/E2 in environmental management policy are compelling for both government and the private sector. P2/E2 can be a "win-win" solution for both government and the private sector. Eliminating pollution from production systems and from goods and services and conserving natural resources and energy would

The P2/E2 Concept

Pollution prevention (P2) is a set of technologies and processes that help organizations to reduce or eliminate waste at the source rather than controlling emissions at the "end of the pipeline." The World Business Council for Sustainable Development (WBCSD), the Organization for Economic Cooperation and Development (OECD), and the United Nations Environment Program (UNEP) all recommend that manufacturing industries adopt "eco-efficiency" (E2) practices that seek not only to reduce waste in manufacturing, but also to reduce environmental impacts and conserve resources throughout a business's entire operations, from the acquisition of inputs and raw materials to the final disposal of products by consumers.

The WBCSD defines eco-efficiency as the "delivery of competitively priced goods and services that satisfy human needs and bring quality of life, while progressively reducing ecological impacts and resource intensity throughout the life cycle, to a level at least in line with the earth's estimated carrying capacity."*

Eco-efficiency encourages businesses to become more competitive, innovative, and environmentally responsible by pursuing both environmental protection and productive commercial activities. Organizations attain eco-efficiency by:

- reducing the material requirements of goods and services;
- reducing the energy intensity of goods and services;
- reducing toxic dispersion;
- enhancing material recyclability;
- maximizing sustainable use of renewable resources;
- extending product durability;
- increasing the service intensity of goods and services.

The terms "pollution prevention" and "eco-efficiency" are complementary and are sometimes used interchangeably, but E2 is generally broader in scope than just waste reduction or elimination of waste at the source. The combination of management and technical tools inherent in pollution prevention and eco-efficiency provide a strong thrust for multimedia environmental performance improvement in the private sector.

* *Source: C. Keffer, R. Shimp, and M. Lehni, "Eco-Efficiency Indicators and Reporting," (Geneva: WBCSD, 2000), quote at p. 1.*

reduce substantially the volume of pollutants that would have to be controlled at the end of the pipeline. In government, billions of dollars could be saved that now go to administration and enforcement of regulations at federal, state, and local levels, and to monitoring compliance, prosecuting violators, and defending legal challenges to new rules and to civil and criminal penalties. P2/E2 would reduce workers' exposure to toxic materials and health-threatening emissions, degradation of the environment in communities where companies' facilities are located, and pressures on local landfills and on water, air, and land resources.

To the extent that harmful emissions and wastes can be removed from products and manufacturing processes, companies would save money, increase their efficiency, improve the quality of the products they make, and enhance customer satisfaction. Cleaner production would result in cost savings through energy and water conservation, materials substitution, and recycling and reuse of "waste materials." By eliminating or significantly reducing pollution at the source, companies could more easily comply with environmental laws, saving them money in fines, penalties, and compliance costs. By lowering their risks, firms could save on legal and insurance costs. Lower legal liabilities would help to satisfy stakeholder concerns about corporations' environmental impacts and to improve their images as socially responsible organizations. Eco-efficiency practices would help companies improve the quality of their products and give them competitive advantages in global markets.

A P2/E2 Policy in Government

These arguments are, of course, well known in Congress, EPA, and state regulatory agencies. Indeed, in 1990, Congress mandated the EPA to focus its efforts on pollution prevention. (See "The Pollution Prevention Act of 1990" on page 284.) Yet, Congress never really followed up with significant reform of environmental laws to allow EPA the flexibility, or gave it the budgetary resources, to make pollution prevention the focus of its activities. EPA officials recognize the limitations of the conventional regulatory approaches to management, and emphasize in the agency's *Strategic Plan 2000* that end-of-pipe pollution control must be supplemented in the future with new and different alternatives.[3] "EPA increasingly finds diminishing returns in its traditional approaches to regulating large and obvious sources of pollution," its strategic plan points out. EPA claims that its "strategy of first choice is to prevent pollution before it occurs. Pollution prevention precludes environmental damage and necessity for costly cleanups."

EPA officials recognize the need to "promote the use of pollution prevention (P2) for meeting environmental goals by ... increasing adoption of environmentally protective business practices such as environmental accounting practices and P2 opportunity assessments ... [and] increasing integration of P2 into EPA's regulatory, enforcement, and compliance programs...."[4] EPA attempts to promote innovations in pollution prevention by testing market-based solutions, providing compliance assistance, developing partnerships with industry to address environmental problems, encouraging breakthroughs in science and technology, and promoting "pollution prevention and reduction by developing more environmentally compatible technologies and facilitating their introduction into the marketplace."[5]

The Pollution Prevention Act of 1990

The Congress finds that:

- (1)The United States of America annually produces millions of tons of pollution and spends tens of billions of dollars per year controlling this pollution.

- (2) There are significant opportunities for industry to reduce or prevent pollution at the source through cost-effective changes in production, operation, and raw materials use. Such changes offer industry substantial savings in reduced raw material, pollution control, and liability costs as well as help protect the environment and reduce risks to worker health and safety.

- (3) The opportunities for source reduction are often not realized because existing regulations, and the industrial resources they require for compliance, focus upon treatment and disposal, rather than source reduction; existing regulations do not emphasize multimedia management of pollution; and businesses need information and technical assistance to overcome institutional barriers to the adoption of source reduction practices.

- (4) Source reduction is fundamentally different and more desirable than waste management and pollution control. The Environmental Protection Agency needs to address the historical lack of attention to source reduction.

- (5) As a first step in preventing pollution through source reduction, the Environmental Protection Agency must establish a source reduction program which collects and disseminates information, provides financial assistance to States, and implements the other activities provided for in this chapter.

Policy

The Congress hereby declares it to be the national policy of the United States that pollution should be prevented or reduced at the source whenever feasible; pollution that cannot be prevented should be recycled in an environmentally safe manner, whenever feasible; pollution that cannot be prevented or recycled should be treated in an environmentally safe manner whenever feasible; and disposal or other release into the environment should be employed only as a last resort and should be conducted in an environmentally safe manner.

Source: United States Code, Title 42, "The Public Health and Welfare," Chapter 133: Pollution Prevention, 1990.

EPA initiated several programs during the 1990s to work with the private sector on voluntary pollution prevention. Through the Common Sense Initiative (CSI), EPA elicited the participation of stakeholders from industry, environmental justice organizations, labor organizations, environmental organizations, as well as federal, state, and local governments to address environmental issues facing companies in the automobile manufacturing, computer and electronics, iron and steel, metal finishing, petroleum refining, and printing industries. EPA's Climate Wise and Energy Star programs help industry to practice energy efficiency and conservation. Its "Design for Environment" program helps businesses take environmental considerations into their design of products, processes, and management systems. Project XL is a pilot program that encourages corporations to test innovative ways of achieving more cost-effective environmental performance. In addition, the EPA has programs promoting environmental accounting and sustainable development practices in specific industries.

However, the agency is not organized or staffed effectively to work with the private sector nor is it supported adequately with legislative authority to do so. EPA has not been able to commit sufficient financial resources to increase its focus on P2/E2. EPA programs for pollution prevention and industrial partnership have been limited in scope and impact. Only a small percentage of EPA's budget goes to promoting pollution prevention in the private sector. In fiscal years 1998, 1999, and 2000, EPA's total expenditures for pollution prevention programs were less than 4 percent of its budget each year, and only a small part of those expenditures targeted industry. In FY 2000, programs for preventing pollution accounted for less than $278 million (3.6 percent) of a $7.5 billion budget.[6]

An Opportunity for Change

New opportunities have emerged to review and revise environmental protection policy in the United States for the 21st century. Regulation is a necessary part of environmental policy, but it may be reaching the limits of its capacity to improve environmental conditions effectively. A stronger emphasis on programs that encourage businesses and industries to prevent pollution, reduce or eliminate waste, and adopt principles of eco-efficiency can supplement the regulatory system in creative ways to achieve continuous improvements. The National Research Council (NRC) points out that "the environmental problems of today are often difficult to diagnose and treat; they cross state and national boundaries, entail difficult tradeoffs, and sporadically present unpleasant surprises."[7] Relying simply on regulatory solutions will not address the complexities of environmental protection in the 21st century. "Past illusions about simple and easy solutions to environmental problems," the NRC report emphasizes, "have been replaced by the realization that environmental protection is often complicated and challenging."

Implementing a policy of environmental management more strongly focused on P2/E2 will require a better understanding by environmental protection agencies of trends in the private sector to adopt beyond-compliance environmental management systems and P2/E2, and of their motivations for doing so. At the same time, if P2/E2 is to play a stronger role in U.S. environmental management, beyond-compliance practices will have to be disseminated more widely in the private sector. Although many large corporations are innovating with new technologies and processes for achieving eco-efficiency, commitment to beyond-compliance management varies from industry to industry, and among companies within industries. Often these innovative processes and technologies do not filter down from large companies to medium- and small-sized enterprises. Some companies, both large and small, still see environmental management as a cost and regulations as burdens to be avoided or complied with minimally. Supplementing "end of pipeline" emissions-control regulations with a system of environmental management based on pollution prevention and eco-efficiency will require both public agencies and private businesses to experiment with and develop innovative processes and technologies for improving environmental quality and find new ways of disseminating them more widely.[8]

The findings of this chapter show what companies can do in pollution prevention and eco-efficiency, what motivates them to do it, and the types of interventions governments can make to spread these practices from large corporations to small and medium-sized enterprises.

Study Findings

If regulatory approaches to environmental protection are to be supplemented by a stronger focus on P2/E2, how should environmental policy be managed in the future? A large number of studies undertaken over the past decade generally conclude that the success of pollution prevention programs depends on developing a deeper understanding among political and legislative leaders and regulatory personnel at the federal and state levels of "best practices" in the private sector to achieve eco-efficiency, and the motivations of business leaders for adopting beyond-compliance environmental management systems.

To understand better what must be done to shift from a predominantly command-and-control approach to environmental management to one that focuses more strongly on P2/E2 requires first a brief summary of the limitations of the regulatory approach and then a review of the types of practices being adopted in the private sector.

The Limitations of Regulatory Approaches to Environmental Management

Public, private, and nonprofit organizations in the United States have been calling for changes in federal and state environmental policy for more than a decade. Many of the problems of the current system arise from the intrinsic nature of regulation.[9] Frequently observed weaknesses of the command-and-control approach to environmental management include the following:

- Environmental regulations are numerous, complex, and frequently amended, making it costly and difficult for regulated entities to stay abreast of requirements and compliance.
- Regulations are punitive rather than incentive-driven, creating tensions (and sometimes hostility) between government and regulated entities rather than positive incentives for change.
- The slowness of regulatory and bureaucratic processes makes it difficult for government to stay ahead of environmental threats and to make pollution prevention rather than emission control the focus of environmental policy.
- A command-and-control approach to environmental protection encourages regulated entities to comply with the minimum requirements set in regulatory standards rather than exploring managerial and technological innovations that go beyond compliance.
- Regulations result in a uniform set of standards that are not flexible enough to address variations in industry conditions and local needs for solving environmental problems.
- Media-specific environmental regulations are inadequate to deal with the increasingly significant "non-point" sources of environmental degradation.
- Changes in environmental regulations are often based on administrative or political criteria rather than sound scientific evidence, causing suspicion of or opposition to seemingly arbitrary changes in standards.
- Regulations for which benefits are not obvious, widespread, or clearly in excess of financial costs undermine compliance and encourage regulated entities to find ways of evading them or complying minimally.
- The command-and-control approach to environmental protection reinforces an adversarial relationship between government and the private sector that subjects regulatory changes to political backlash and legal challenges.

The U.S. General Accounting Office (GAO) concludes that although the current system of environmental regulation in the United States is the most advanced in the world, its volume and complexity "often results in conflict and gridlock."[10] Between 1970 and the mid-1990s the federal government promulgated more than 11,000 pages of environmental regulations resulting in more than $1.5 trillion in compliance costs for industry.[11] The GAO points out that this regulatory structure impairs the EPA's "ability to experiment with innovative and more cost-effective ways of reducing pollution (such as preventing pollution by eliminating or minimizing it at its source, instead of containing it at the end of the pipe) or using market-based incentives (such as pollution or trading emission rights)." In turn, federal regulatory restrictions make it more difficult for states and localities to solve creatively environmental problems in their jurisdictions.

Numerous problems arise from the fact that environmental regulations focus separately on individual media of pollution (air, land, and water) and categories of pollutants (toxic substances, hazardous wastes, pesticides), rather than on overall environmental quality.[12] New laws have been enacted and amendments have been made to environmental regulations over a 30-year period, usually independently of each other and sometimes in conflict with already existing standards. Rarely are requirements for one medium coordinated with requirements for others either in legislation or in administrative rule making. Often the regulation of one medium (e.g., air) increases pollution in other media (e.g., water or soil).

Restrictions on one category of pollutants sometimes lead to increases in other types of emissions or degradation. Because Congress passes environmental legislation piecemeal, consolidates diverse environmental regulations under EPA's control, and adds new environmental rules and regulations without reviewing the scope and impacts of previous laws, the federal government lacks a coherent environmental mission and a clear direction. More than 40 committees and subcommittees of Congress have some type of oversight responsibility for or jurisdiction over EPA. More than a dozen statutes govern EPA's mandate to control pollution and require the agency to organize into numerous offices with different environmental management philosophies, control strategies, and "legal cultures." Frequent changes in federal and state environmental regulations make it difficult for companies, especially smaller ones, to keep abreast of requirements and to comply.[13] Environmental protection agencies sometimes do not use accepted scientific findings as the basis for regulations, explain their decisions realistically in terms of risk, or take into account the compliance costs to government or the private sector.[14] The Enterprise for the Environment Committee, led by former EPA Administrator William Ruckelshaus, emphasizes that "the environmental protection system of the next century must become as efficient and low cost as possible without compromising environmental progress."[15]

Since the early 1990s, many corporations have taken new initiatives in managing their environmental impacts. They seek new ways to reduce their costs, increase their efficiency, lower their liabilities, and enhance their competitiveness while reducing pollution, conserving resources, and eliminating waste. These P2/E2 practices in the private sector can be the foundation for government programs that identify, test, disseminate, and encourage pollution prevention in an environmental protection policy for the 21st century.

Corporate Environmental Management: Moving Toward P2/E2

Increasing the focus on P2/E2 in environmental policy requires policymakers and regulators to understand better how progressive companies are seeking to apply beyond-compliance practices and what motivates them to do so. Most large corporations in the United States are implementing voluntary environmental management systems (EMS) that go well beyond legal requirements, and many are adopting international standards of environmental management, such as ISO 14000, that transcend or exceed national environmental regulations. The challenge for federal and state government regulators is to understand better what companies are doing, why they are doing it, how to reinforce those that are moving toward pollution prevention and eco-efficiency, and how to encourage other companies to do the same.

Figure 9.1 summarizes the P2/E2 management practices that many companies are embracing:

Environmental Management Systems (EMS)

Large corporations in North America and Europe are adopting environmental management systems that integrate eco-efficiency practices into their overall business operations. By early 1999 more than 330 organizations in 37 states had officially joined more than 8,000 other organizations worldwide in certifying their EMS under ISO 14001, an international standard that was developed by the International Organization of Standardization in Geneva and implemented in the United States by the American National Standards Institute (ANSI). Many companies are using ISO 14001 guidelines to design or improve their environmental management systems without seeking official certification.

ISO 14001 provides a framework for environmental management that focuses on five major components. First, the facility or firm seeking certification must develop and adopt an environmental policy to which senior management is committed. Second, it must establish a planning process that identifies all of the environmental aspects of a facility's operations, legal and other requirements, a set of clearly defined objectives and targets for environmental improvement, and a set of environmental management programs. Third, it must create a clear structure of responsibility for environmental management; programs for training, awareness and competence among all employees of the facility; and internal and external communication of the EMS; a system of environmental management documentation; a

Figure 9.1: Components of Corporate P2/E2 Management

Environmental Management System

1. Environmental Policy
2. Objectives and Targets
3. Responsibility Structure, Implementation Program and Documentation System
4. Monitoring Environmental Impacts and Reporting Plan
5. Management Review Process

Management and Financial Tools

- Environmental Monitoring and Auditing
- Environmental Accounting

Operations and Product Improvement Tools

- Environmental Life Cycle Analysis
- Environmental Design of Products and Process
- Extended Product Responsibility/Stewardship
- Supply Chain Environmental Management

Materials and Resource Management Tools

- Waste Reduction
- Materials Substitution, Recycling, Reuse
- Air Emissions Reduction/Elimination
- Energy and Water Conservation

documentation control system; and procedures for operational controls of environmental impacts and emergency preparedness and response. Fourth, the facility or organization must monitor and measure environmental impacts, report non-conformance and take corrective and preventive action; keep environmental management records; and carry out environmental audits. Fifth, it must establish a review process through which senior management reassesses the suitability, effectiveness, and adequacy of the EMS at appropriate intervals to assure continuous improvement.

Some companies have been implementing environmental management systems that go beyond regulatory requirements for more than two decades. The 3M Corporation long ago committed itself to solving its own environmental problems, preventing pollution at the source wherever possible, developing products that have minimal effect on the environment, conserving natural resources, meeting and sustaining government regulations, and, where possible, assisting government agencies in environmental activities.[16]

Other corporations such as Texaco, Kodak, SmithKlein Beecham, Goodyear, Bristol-Myers Squibb, and Alcoa developed their EMS based on their own corporate environmental, health, and safety standards that exceed U.S. standards and international guidelines. These corporate standards are often more stringent than the requirements adopted by governments. Texaco's EMS addresses product stewardship, air emissions, spill prevention and control, and waste management, as well as health and industrial hygiene and personnel and contractor safety. Texaco applies its environment, health, and safety policies not only in its facilities in the United States but in all of its global business operations.[17]

Some companies have their EMS certified for the entire corporation; others for strategic facilities, products, or processes. IBM certified an EMS for the entire corporation to the ISO 14001 standard, with all of its manufacturing and hardware development sites having completed the audit process by 1999.[18] Lucent Technologies implemented its EMS for 98 percent of its products, services, operations, and facilities in 1999 and certified 63 percent of its facilities.[19] Motorola plants in the United States and around the world use a common environmental, health, and safety management system framework that satisfies ISO 14001 requirements; the corporation seeks to have all of its manufacturing plants certified by 2001.[20] General Motors, Ford, Toyota North America, and other automobile manufacturers not only require all of their plants to certify their EMS but also to encourage or require their suppliers to certify as well. Indeed, General Motors' EMS includes all of the ISO 14001 requirements plus several others that require plants to provide higher levels of support for environmental performance, cost reduction, and system auditing.

Xerox has completely integrated its EMS with health, safety, and operational processes and is continuously improving its environmental performance through beyond-compliance practices. Figure 9.2 shows how Xerox's Environment, Health, and Safety (EH&S) system focuses on achieving sustainable growth by internally managing environmental impacts, reducing the corporation's external environmental "footprint," and partnering with customers and suppliers to improve environmental performance. Since the 1980s when the corporation focused on ensuring regulatory compliance, Xerox has moved steadily from voluntary assessment and remediation of contaminated sites to developing and implementing waste reduction programs for its factories, products, and offices, and initiating product take-back and recycling programs.[21] (See Figure 9.3.)

During the mid-1990s, Xerox began to pursue an eco-efficiency strategy that focuses on sustainable product design, development of an EMS, and the extension of environmental management programs and projects throughout its supply chain. From 2000 to 2005, Xerox aims to achieve sustainable growth objectives by integrating environmental, health, and safety practices into all of its businesses and services, achieving a zero injury target, minimizing use of natural resources, and adopting knowledge management solutions. Xerox has registered all of its major manufacturing and logistics facilities to ISO 40001 environmental management standards.

Figure 9.2: Environmental Management at Xerox

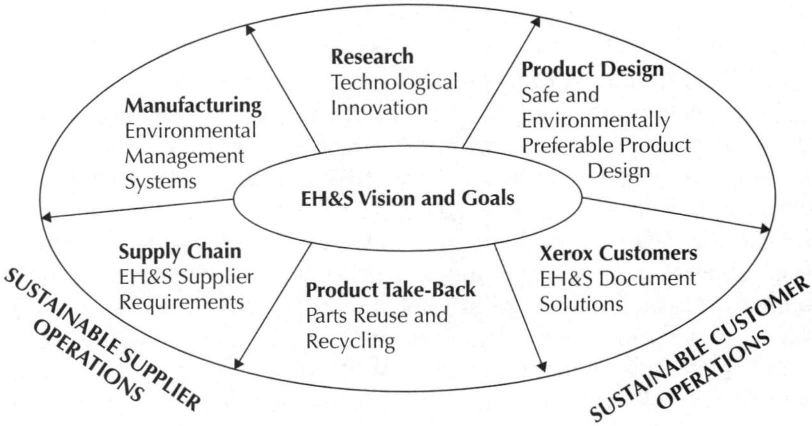

Source: Xerox, 1999 Environment, Health and Safety Progress Report

Figure 9.3: Environmental Progress at Xerox

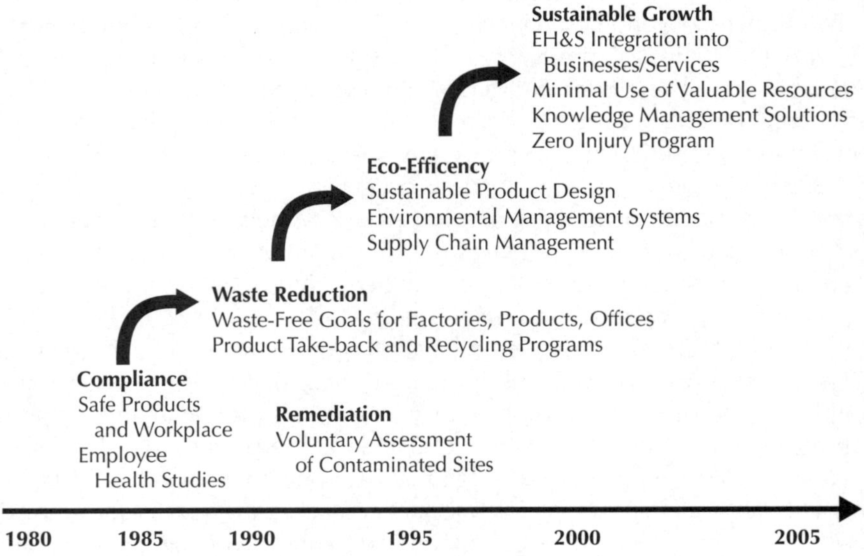

Source: Xerox, 1999 Environment, Health and Safety Progress Report

Environmental Monitoring and Auditing

An essential element of P2/E2 is monitoring, auditing, and measuring environmental performance. An increasing number of corporations are now voluntarily monitoring and auditing their environmental impacts regularly in order to prevent problems or correct them quickly. General Motors assesses air emissions, wastewater discharges, solid and hazardous materials handling and waste disposal, and emergency response capabilities for all facilities, plus other impacts that are regulated in specific jurisdictions.[22] Kodak uses a "Business Unit Evaluation Guide" to measure semi-annually how well unit managers integrate environmental responsibility into business plans and track progress in environmental performance.[23] SmithKlein Beecham and Kodak assess each of their facilities' environmental performance against legislation and corporate standards at least once every three years. Kodak evaluates all of its sites worldwide on a regular basis by 28 performance criteria and for compliance with local laws and regulations. In addition, Kodak has integrated environmental performance progress criteria into pay raise evaluations for senior corporate and business unit managers. Bristol-Myers Squibb developed a self-assessment process for measuring its performance against 16 principles of the International Code Council Business Charter for Sustainable Development and its own EH&S codes of practice that encompass ISO 14001 standards. Baxter International, for example, requires all of its operating units to perform environmental self-audits annually and outside auditors to evaluate 25 percent of its divisions each year using the company's rigorous environmental audit protocol. Baxter's headquarters holds operating unit managers responsible for closing audit action items quickly.

All of Alcoa's business units formulate annual action plans for environmental management and set specific targets. All of its facilities are audited at least once every three years. The audits—conducted by multi-functional teams of central-resource experts, business-unit managers, and external representatives—identify environmental problems or deficiencies and make recommendations for improvements. Audit teams diagnose each site's environmental conditions and report unsatisfactory performance. Facility managers must provide an analysis of the deficiencies, outline corrective action that will be taken, and submit quarterly progress reports. Sites with unsatisfactory ratings are audited again within a year.[24]

Environmental Accounting

Increasingly, American corporations are attempting to identify the costs of their environmental impacts and expenditures, and the savings from reducing the use of materials, energy, and water, as well as the costs of regulatory compliance and penalties. Environmental accounting is a management tool that firms use to identify, quantify, and allocate the direct and indirect costs of operations and to determine the real costs of producing a product. Environmental cost accounting identifies and quantifies not only the direct costs of environmental management (labor, capital, and raw materials), but also the hidden costs (monitoring and reporting), contingent liability costs such as fines and remedial action, and intangible costs such as public relations and goodwill.

Baxter International was a pioneer in the development of a corporate environmental financial statement that accounts for the costs of basic environmental programs, remediation, waste, and other environmental responses, and for income, savings, and cost avoidance related to environmental activities. Baxter keeps detailed accounts of its environmental costs and savings.[25] Its accounting system allows it to capture information about the administrative costs of basic environmental programs within the corporation and the costs of remediation, waste disposal, and other responses. It also calculates savings and costs each year for ozone-depleting substances, hazardous and non-hazardous waste disposal and material reductions, recycling, energy conservation, packaging, and water conservation.

General Motors, Amoco, 3M, DuPont, Allied Signal, Monsanto, and others have discovered ways of offsetting environmental costs with revenues by selling waste by-products, adopting clean technologies, and selling unused pollution allowances. Improving environmental performance in any area of business operations contributes to the overall effectiveness of a firm's environmental management system. General Motors, for example, uses environmental cost accounting information in internal decisions concerning the risks and impacts of its manufacturing processes and tracks cost information to assist in prioritizing its environmental management activities.

Environmental Life Cycle Analysis

An increasing number of firms are adopting principles of "extended product responsibility" that commit them to assessing the environmental, health, and safety impacts associated with their products and services throughout their life cycles. Life cycle analysis is a systematic means of measuring resource use and environmental releases to air, water, and soil from products, processes, and services. It helps companies to improve their understanding of how much resources their products consume in raw materials extraction, manufacturing, transportation, distribution, and final disposal, and the environmental impacts of production at each stage in the life cycle. Using life cycle analysis, corporations such as Dow Chemical, Intel, Hewlett-Packard, General Motors, International Paper, Xerox, and Nortel determine the environmental implications of producing, distributing, using, and disposing of a product and ways of improving the eco-efficiency of their operations, products, technologies, and practices. Life cycle analysis helps these firms reduce material intensity and create a smaller environmental "footprint" from their operations.

Many firms use life cycle analysis to study the environmental effects of products both within the factory during production and externally. Bristol-Myers Squibb is minimizing its environmental impacts by conducting product life cycle reviews of the company's major product lines.[26] During these life cycle reviews, cross-functional teams identify and reduce negative environmental, health, and safety impacts at all production and distribution stages. Baxter International uses checklists to forecast the environmental, health, and safety consequences for people who will handle all proposed new products and their packaging. 3M's life cycle management process helps executives to understand, manage, and systematically evaluate opportunities to improve the environmental impacts of its products. Using the life cycle process, product development teams designed recycling-compatible label materials for plastic electronic equipment, reduced the solvents used in manufacturing one of its electronically cut film products, and developed high-performance cloth for commercial use as a replacement for throw-away paper towels.

Environmental Design and Product Stewardship

Companies concerned about quality management are designing or redesigning their products to decrease or eliminate adverse effects on the environment. Many large firms are adopting "Design for Environment" (DfE) programs that allow them to redesign old products or to create new ones in ways that minimize their environmental impacts by using less raw materials or substituting inputs that are more environmentally benign. DfE guides designers to produce, package, and distribute products so that they conserve energy, water, and other resources. Companies use DfE to make components and finished products that can be recycled when customers no longer use them.

IBM created an "Environmentally Conscious Products" program in 1991 to help its engineers upgrade or extend product life by taking into consideration new ways of reusing or recycling them rather than disposing of them in landfills. The program guides IBM designers in finding ways to use recycled materials and to improve energy efficiency or reduce energy consumption in new or redesigned products. Other computer firms also adopted environmentally friendly design principles. Dell Computer Corporation developed a new personal computer chassis in 1996 that was not only 100 percent recyclable but also allowed the computer to be serviced and upgraded more easily.[27]

By designing the machine to be easily upgraded rather than replacing the entire computer, Dell can extend its life and reduce disposal problems.

Compaq also created a Design for Environment Resource Center, which is located on the company's intranet, giving all employees access to the best mechanical, electrical, and packaging design practices.[28] Compaq redesigned its manufacturing processes in order to increase reusable packaging and minimize waste, extend the life of computer products by making upgrading easier, and reduce their energy consumption. Other firms are innovating with new information technologies to guide DfE applications. Motorola adopted the software "Green Design Advisor," which allows product designers to compare materials and processes used to create a product and calculate the environmental impact of the product design for the materials selected. Motorola completely redesigned its Horizon Office products to be completely disassembled and divided into plastic housing, aluminum chassis, and electronic assembly for easy recycling. Lucent Technologies uses a formal DfE process to review and evaluate criteria for each of its products in order to minimize environmental impacts throughout their life. Lucent seeks to "dematerialize" products to use fewer components and raw materials, reduce energy in manufacturing and product use, "detoxify" products, and make them with more recyclable and reusable materials.

Supply Chain Environmental Management

Other companies are extending their environmental management practices and life cycle analyses throughout their supply chains and attempting to encourage suppliers, distributors, and customers to manage their environmental impacts more effectively. IBM requires all of its suppliers to comply with all applicable environmental laws and regulations in performing work for any of its units, and does environmental evaluations of those with environmental risks that are inherent in the work they do for IBM. IBM encourages its suppliers to pursue ISO 14001 certification and shares environmental management expertise and technology with them. Motorola asks its suppliers to provide environmentally preferred products—that is, those that are energy efficient, recyclable, and with significant amounts of recycled materials. Motorola plants also partner with suppliers to minimize product-packaging materials.[29]

Ford, General Motors, and Daimler-Chrysler are adopting pollution-prevention measures in production and distribution, and requiring their suppliers around the world to certify their environmental management systems by ISO 14001 standards. General Motors created a "GM Suppliers Environmental Advisory Team" to improve mutual understanding of environmental programs and efficiency and evaluate new ideas to promote eco-efficiency throughout its supply chain.[30] The Ford Motor Company works with suppliers to redesign parts and equipment to reduce adverse environmental impacts. Ford and its suppliers, for example, redesigned the alloy used in the production of heat exchangers to eliminate chromium coating and painting requirements and to replace a vapor degreasing process.[31]

Waste Reduction, and Materials Recycling and Reuse

Literally hundreds of examples can be found of how corporations are reducing inputs and recycling materials. The automobile industry has been especially attentive to reducing waste. General Motors' application of life cycle analysis helped it to find ways of recycling up to 200,000 pounds of fender scrap from its Saturn car line into wheel cap assemblies and to use 56,000 recycled tires per model year for making radiator side air baffles. GM uses more than 2,700 tons of recycled textile fabric each model year for floor insulation.

The carpet industry is also making significant progress in reducing waste. Shaw Industries, for example, reduced the amount of waste generated in manufacturing by adopting high-precision technology that cuts by 25 percent the amount of selvedge or residual edge trimming that had to be sent to local landfills. It reuses selvedge and carpet seams for making 100 percent recycled carpet pads that pass its industry trade association's "green label" requirements. Shaw engineers also recycled carpet fiber waste that would have had to be sent to landfills into reinforced concrete to make a product that is tougher, stronger, and more resistant to drying. Millikan Company is aggressively cutting waste from its carpet manufacturing plants. By 1999, 43 of its 55 locations in the United States achieved the company's "zero-waste-to-landfills" target. Millikan has reduced its waste output to landfills by 98 percent since 1988 and recycled 100 percent of its office paper since 1992. Interface, Inc. has a product take-back program for carpet that reclaims any brand, whether or not its owner is purchasing Interface products. The company recycles carpet tile and broadloom and reuses the material for carpet or other products so that waste will not end up in landfills.

Corporations in the retail and wholesale industries are also adopting waste reduction practices. J.C. Penney Company, for example, cut by more than 80 percent its paper, cardboard, wood, plastics, polystyrene and scrap metal at catalog customer service centers and catalog outlet stores. It refurbishes old cardboard cartons for reuse.[32] Home Depot uses recycled materials in its shopping bags, signage and office supplies, and it recycles all of its corrugated cardboard and wood pallets. It keeps drywall separators out of landfills by making them into other products.

Air Emissions Reduction/Elimination

Corporations are also finding new ways of reducing their harmful air emissions. Xerox cut its Toxic Release Inventory (TRI)-reportable air emissions by more than 92 percent and all TRI air emissions by nearly 86 percent by installing abatement technologies and improving production processes. DuPont's environmental management practices resulted in reductions of 65 percent in air toxic releases and 87 percent in air carcinogens since 1987.

The company is stretching from a 39 percent cut in greenhouse gas emissions in 1999 to a 45 percent reduction target. The Olin corporation, a specialty producer of chemicals, metals, and aerospace equipment, substantially reduced air emissions of carbon tetrachloride by applying technologies that reclaim the material for reuse in several of its production processes. Kodak's aggregate emissions declined by 40 percent, and its emissions from power plants by 20 percent from 1997 to 1999 alone.[33]

The 3M Corporation prevents pollution within its own plants and designs products that help customers reduce emissions. For example, it introduced hydrofluroether (HFE) fluids to replace chlorofluorocarbons (CFCs) and other ozone-depleting materials for commercial applications such as parts cleaning in the aerospace, computers, electronics, and medical products industries. 3M cut volatile organic air emissions by 80 percent since 1990 through a combination of pollution prevention practices and pollution control equipment. It reduced by one-third its greenhouse gases from fluorochemicals in manufacturing operations between 1995 and 1998 alone.

Energy and Water Conservation

Many corporations are decreasing their energy and water use in order to achieve significant cost savings and improve the efficiency of their operations. By using water-saving devices and selling some of its high water-consumption facilities, Nortel decreased its overall water consumption by 70 percent between 1993 and 1998.[34] Two Motorola plants in Arizona saved 138 million gallons of water in 1999 by reusing water sample streams, part of the reverse osmosis reject water, and modifying tools and software in their processing systems. United Parcel Service uses a variety of alternative fuels and engines, including compressed and liquid natural gas and propane- and electric-powered engines in its delivery trucks to lower their use of fossil fuels and vehicle fuel emissions. It has purchased thousands of electronic fuel injected engines to reduce gasoline consumption. PepsiCo initiated energy conservation programs that have saved more than 4.6 million kilowatts of electricity since their inception, preventing the emission of 1.5 pounds of carbon dioxide, 5.8 grams of sulfur dioxide, and 2.5 grams of nitrogen oxide for every kilowatt-hour saved.

Through effective environmental management practices, IBM has conserved more than 8 billion kilowatt-hours of electricity during the 1990s, and avoided more than 5.6 million tons of carbon dioxide emissions. Hughes Electronics is reducing water usage and using recycled wastewater in its manufacturing processes wherever practical. One of its businesses, Hughes Network Services, recycles nearly 27 percent of its water in manufacturing wave solder board wash machines, and another business, Hughes Electron Dynamics, recycles more than 18 percent of the water used as a cooling medium in cooling towers.[35] By using a turbine-powered co-generation plant at its Los Angeles refinery, the ARCO Corporation was able to double the productivity of its natural gas fuel. In addition, it achieved energy savings equal to 4,000 barrels of crude oil a day and reduced daily nitrogen oxide emissions by an equivalent of the emissions of 162,000 vehicles.

Why Corporations Adopt P2/E2 Practices

Corporations are adopting P2/E2 practices for a variety of reasons.[36] Four sets of forces are driving companies to pursue pollution prevention:

- **Increasing regulatory demands**—including more-stringent regulations, stronger enforcement of existing regulations, and increasing legal and civil liabilities for regulatory violations;
- **Stronger stakeholder pressures**—including stronger public demand for environmental protection, shareholder rejection of environmental risks, and customer demand for cleaner production processes and products;
- **Increasing costs and savings potential**—including increasing costs of emissions control, greater savings from pollution prevention, and the availability at lower costs of new technologies for waste reduction; and
- **Stronger competitive requirements**—including the need to adopt quality management principles in order to compete in global markets, new business opportunities for cleaner products and processes, the requirements of international trade agreements and standards to do business overseas, and the adoption of voluntary environmental management standards in major international markets.

Most firms try pollution prevention initially to get ahead of regulatory requirements or to obtain relief from regulatory burdens or because they find significant cost savings from waste reduction or elimination. IBM, for example, saved nearly $36 million in 1998 alone from energy conservation and cost avoidance efforts, and since 1990 has saved $518 million in energy costs from its reduced use of electricity. Xerox was able to achieve 88 percent solid waste recycling rates in 1998 and generated savings of more than $45 million that year alone from reducing, reusing, and recycling materials. DuPont cut waste in its polyester films throughout its value chain by reducing the components used in packaging, reusing as many components as possible, and recycling materials. In doing so, it kept 30 million pounds of materials out of landfills between 1997 and 2000 and saved $7.6 million in packaging costs.

Since 1980, 3M Corporation has carried out more than 4,600 pollution prevention projects that eliminated 1.6 million pounds of releases to air, water, and soil and produced savings of more than $810 million. Baxter International's pursuit of pollution prevention initiatives cut its costs by more than $100 million. By applying product life cycle analysis at all of its operating sites, Bristol-Myers Squibb identified potential savings in excess of $6.5 million. By re-engineering its carpet manufacturing process, Interface reduced waste from its production process, resulting in savings of more than $90 million since 1990.

Many companies are learning that pollution prevention not only helps them avoid the costs of regulation by eliminating harmful air and water emissions and by reducing wastes in their operations, but also that eco-efficiency has other business benefits. The adoption of a beyond-compliance EMS can help a company protect or enhance its ethical image, avoid serious legal liabilities, and satisfy the safety concerns of employees. For many firms, the challenge is to balance concerns with cash flow, profitability, and environmental protection in order to respond to the demands of stakeholders.

Companies such as 3M, Kodak, Xerox, Alcoa, and Procter & Gamble that adopted quality management programs during the 1980s to improve their competitive positions are also recognized by their shareholders and external stakeholders for exemplary environmental performance and social responsibility. Pharmacia's environmental policy, for example, declares that protecting the environment and the health and safety of its employees and the communities in which it operates "is central to our responsibility of a good corporate citizen. It is also good business, and ultimately benefits all of our stakeholders and shareholders."[37] The application of the corporation's environmental management standards worldwide is intended "to create a competitive advantage by maximizing operational effectiveness and minimizing environmental and safety impacts and their accompanying liabilities." Johnson & Johnson's reputation as a socially responsible company, developed over several decades, is reinforced by its environmental management policy.[38] "We are responsible to the communities in which we live and work and to the world community as well," its environmental performance report declares. "We must maintain in good order the property we are privileged to use, protecting the environment and natural resources."

Some firms have also found that applications of life cycle and supply chain analyses lead to the discovery of new business opportunities and new products, more efficient and effective production processes, and new sources of revenue. By adopting international standards of environmental management, such as ISO 14001, American corporations can more easily remain or become competitive in world markets. Through beyond-compliance environmental management practices, corporations are also finding ways of developing new products or improving existing products that make them more environmentally friendly, and marketing them on their "green" characteristics. According to the Marketing Intelligence Service, in 1998 and 1999 alone, the food industry introduced 641 new "green products," the beverage industry launched 266 new products with environmental features, the health and beauty aids industry came out with 560 green products, and the household products industry developed 193 environmentally improved products. Texaco has designed or reformulated products to reduce potential hazards, including biodegradable hydraulic fluids, non-chlorinated gear compounds, cleaner burning gasoline, ash-less lubricants, and long-life antifreezes.[39] Cooper Industries produces airtight recessed lighting fixtures for homes and offices to prevent energy leaks and reduce heating costs. Its industrial fluorescent lamps provide double the wattage output of incandescent lamps and last 13 times longer, thereby cutting energy use in factories.[40]

Recommendations and Conclusions

Calls for increasing the emphasis on pollution prevention and eco-efficiency in U.S. environmental policies are becoming more frequent and are emanating from a wider array of public and private organizations. Because regulations alone cannot achieve continuing improvements in environmental conditions during the 21st century, they must be supplemented with programs that promote P2/E2. Clearly, changes will be needed in the ways in which governments attempt to intervene to protect the environment and in the ways in which business executives perceive P2/E2 practices. Although federal and state governments alone cannot bring about a revolution in business practices, they can help to create conditions that encourage and promote beyond-compliance environmental management in the private sector. New federal environmental policies must combine cost-efficient, scientifically sound regulations with stronger programs to promote, reward, and disseminate new technologies and practices of eco-efficiency in the private sector to ensure continued improvement of environmental conditions in the United States during the 21st century.

Creating a Policy Framework for More Effective Environmental Management

Most public and business leaders accept the fact that a scientifically sound and cost-efficient regulatory system is the foundation for achieving environmental quality. But many observers argue that the regulatory system in the United States must be rethought and redesigned to leverage the resources of the private sector in achieving higher levels of environmental performance.[41] A new generation of environmental policy for the 21st century should include the components shown in Figure 9.4.

Figure 9.4: P2/E2 Environmental Management Policy

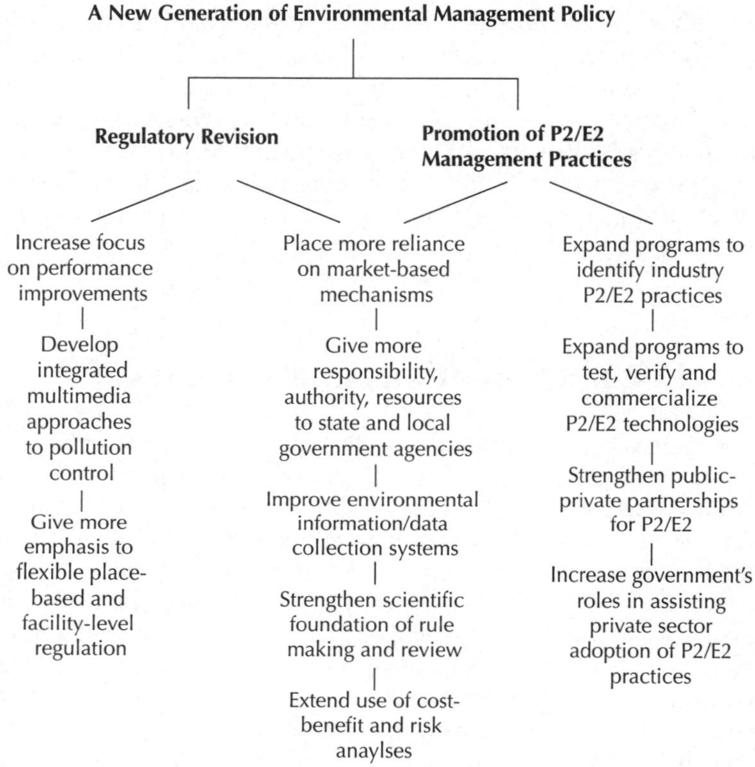

Among the most important management challenges for the executive branch and Congress will be to find ways to:

Increase the focus on pollution prevention and eco-efficiency for achieving environmental performance improvements in the private sector, while maintaining a sound regulatory system as the foundation for ensuring current levels of achievement.

For all of the reasons outlined earlier in this chapter, the promotion of pollution prevention and eco-efficiency practices should become a stronger focus of environmental policy in the United States during the 21st century. The Tellus Institute's assessment of environmental protection programs, however, points out that by the late 1990s pollution prevention had "by and large stalled in its evolution toward becoming the dominant regulatory ethic and framework," largely because the concept had not permeated the operations of regulatory agencies.[42]

The examples offered earlier show that many large corporations can and do apply pollution prevention and eco-efficiency practices. The spread of P2/E2 practices to other corporations and to small and medium-sized enterprises, however, requires policy revisions and new government programs that allow more businesses to develop flexible and innovative responses to reducing or eliminating harmful pollutants at the source. Government can play a crucial role in encouraging pollution prevention, recognizing innovative and effective practices, rewarding companies that adopt them, testing and verifying pollution prevention and eco-efficiency technologies and processes, supporting clearinghouses of information about best practices, and helping to commercialize those technologies that are proven effective.

Give greater attention to achieving performance improvements through multimedia, integrated, approaches to environmental management in both the public and private sectors.

A growing number of public and private organizations agree on the need to revise U.S. environmental policies in order to promote P2/E2 practices more widely. The U.S. General Accounting Office points out that "many state and industry officials have cited the need for statutory revisions, both in the near term to encourage experiments in alternative methods of achieving environmental compliance and in the longer term to achieve a more fundamental change in the conduct of environmental regulation."[43] A report of the Center for Strategic and International Studies concludes that the United States will find it more difficult to protect and restore the natural environment during the 21st century unless Congress and the Administration shift the current command-and-control approach "toward a more performance-based, information-rich, technology-spurring, flexible, accountable regulatory system." The report notes the need for "a broader array of policy tools that promote continuous environmental improvement, including environmental taxes, subsidy reform, emissions trading, and information disclosure; and toward stronger private-sector management systems that internalize the same stewardship ethics embodied in environmental statutes."[44]

In an internal report, a task force assessing EPA's source reduction efforts found "the importance of taking a multimedia approach was striking, yet a multimedia perspective is often not emphasized in the development and implementation of regulations at the agency."[45] The most frequently offered recommendation is that federal and state environmental laws be revised into a cross-cutting, three-dimensional (air, water, and land) policy framework that allows businesses and government to conceive of the environment as a whole rather than as separate environmental media.

Emphasize flexible place-based and facility-level regulation

Because the natural environment is composed of three inextricably interrelated media—air, water, and soil—what happens to one always affects the others. Segmented approaches to managing the environment are costly, inefficient, and ineffective, and invite continuing pollution displacement. One means of giving policies a multimedia focus is to adopt what the Ruckelshaus report calls "place-based" environmental protection that allows federal, state, and local governments to work together with the private sector and other stakeholders to find the most effective solutions within local communities and regions. (See "Place-Based Environmental Protection.") Another approach is to set facility performance targets and let business executives decide on the best methods for reaching the targets.

In order to promote P2/E2 more effectively, environmental protection agencies must place more emphasis on environmental performance than on regulatory compliance. EPA and the states must have the authority and ability to plan and budget their activities across media. Media-specific enforcement offices must be able to coordinate with each other and with regulated organizations to achieve facility-level improvements. They will have to retrain regulatory-oriented staff to understand and promote beyond-compliance technologies and processes in the private sector and find ways of setting compatible deadlines for rule making to allow for cross-media analysis and selection of appropriate technologies.

Increase the use of market-based mechanisms for encouraging the private sector to comply with environmental regulations and to move beyond compliance toward pollution prevention and eco-efficiency practices.

Economic incentives and rewards for innovation and creativity can entice more businesses to adopt new technologies that improve environmental performance than continued reliance on regulatory enforcement alone. A wide array of market-based tools is available that can supplement command-and-control instruments and create economic and financial incentives for companies to adopt P2/E2 practices. These instruments include polluters-pay fees and charges, tax incentives, subsidies, emissions trading mechanisms, fees for emissions monitoring and treatment, reporting requirements, and government procurement of products that have desirable environmental characteristics.[46]

Command-and-control policies do not adequately reward organizations adopting practices that lead to real, long-term solutions to environmental problems—such as the shift away from carbon-based economies—nor do they create business opportunities and make use of market forces to achieve improvements in environmental performance. States such as California, Massachusetts, Illinois, Colorado, New York, Michigan, Pennsylvania, and Maine have been experimenting with emissions trading and banking, pric-

Place-Based Environmental Protection

The Enterprise for the Environment committee headed by former EPA Administrator William D. Ruckelshaus recommends that environmental policy give greater attention to place-based environmental protection.

Place-based environmental policy involves identifying a geographic area, usually communities or distinct places defined by natural boundaries or ecological features; assessing the area for ecological, human health, economic, and socio-cultural aspects that relate to the environment; and involving diverse stakeholders in developing a vision, goals, priorities, and strategies.

Place-based environmental policy focuses on creating a collaborative process aimed at improving environmental, economic, and social conditions in a sustainable manner, building partnerships, and leveraging resources. It seeks to catalyze prescriptive, voluntary, and educational actions to achieve the goals. It requires monitoring environmental conditions, evaluating results, and redirecting efforts through adaptive management and developing processes that inform, assist, and involve the public.

Source: Enterprise for the Environment, The Environmental Protection System in Transition: Toward a More Desirable Future, *(Washington, D.C.: Center for Strategic and International Studies, 1997): pp. 44-45.*

ing programs, and other incentives that reallocate costs of pollution to the sources and give regulated entities more flexibility in achieving emissions reduction goals.

Give more responsibility, authority, and resources to state and local environmental agencies to encourage and reward organizations that adopt P2/E2 practices.

Giving states more authority and responsibility in environmental policymaking can help overcome the conflict and gridlock that sometimes characterize the current command-and-control system. The states now implement much of the federal government's enforcement of air, water, and waste regulations, but responsibilities are not always clearly and effectively defined. The relationship between the federal government and the states is often tense and characterized, as the GAO points out, by continuing disagreements over issues such as "state environmental agencies respective roles, appropriate priorities among state environmental programs, and the appropriate degree of federal oversight."[47]

The need for decentralizing and delegating more responsibility and discretion to state and local governments arises from the growing complexity of environmental pollution and the need for more-flexible responses to local conditions and needs. State and local governments are often better able than federal agencies to develop programs that appeal directly to corporate motivations for adopting P2/E2 practices. They may also be better able to restructure environmental policies to provide support for new combinations of regulatory and voluntary management systems that are more effective and less costly than current command-and-control approaches.

Regulations should focus on performance criteria that allow businesses and industries to develop the most appropriate means of achieving desired objectives. New Jersey's experiments with flexible, facility-level permitting has saved time and money for the state and for businesses. North Carolina's pollution prevention programs provide technical assistance to small and medium-sized businesses in adopting eco-efficiency practices that save them money and improve environmental performance. Wisconsin's award recognition program for innovative technologies and practices in source reduction provides models for other companies to follow in preventing pollution.

Several state environmental agencies have developed agreements with the U.S. Environmental Protection Agency that more clearly define their respective roles and responsibilities. Wisconsin's Department of Natural Resources (DNR), for example, established an environmental performance partnership with EPA for fiscal years 2000 and 2001 that facilitates joint planning and priority setting with EPA's regional office. The agreement includes provisions for the use of a new integrated work planning system, the development and use of a new environmental measurement system that is more relevant to Wisconsin's needs, the delegation of specific responsibilities to Wisconsin's DNR, and more consistent implementation of programs and regulations.

Although national regulations are needed to address "spillover effects" and regional impacts of pollution, many environmental problems can be solved more effectively at local and state levels through dialogue and interaction than by federal mandates. Local stakeholders generally understand local possibilities and constraints better than federal or state regulators. Business owners and managers often know the operational and economic realities of dealing with environmental problems at their facilities better than government officials. Federal regulations should be revised to allow EPA to set performance targets and allow businesses and state and local governments to determine the most effective ways of reaching them.

Improve federal and state environmental regulatory agencies' information and data collection systems.

The plausibility and acceptance of environmental rules and regulations depend in part on a sound information collection and analysis system that determines the types of harm caused to the environment and to public health by pollutants, the magnitude and scope of environmental threats, the risks inherent in continued or potential degradation, and technical requirements and economic costs involved in alternative solutions. Both public and private organizations insist that federal and state regulatory agencies need more comprehensive and sophisticated environmental information systems, more effective modeling capabilities, and more extensive environmental information dissemination programs.

Several states, including Ohio, Alabama, Illinois, Oregon, New York, Massachusetts, and New Jersey, are developing or expanding information collection systems that measure the integration of P2 practices in their compliance and technical assistance activities.[48] The information is aimed at determining how seriously environmental agencies are integrating P2 indicators in their regulatory, permitting, inspection, measurement, enforcement order, outcome tracking, and other activities.

The GAO points out that the federal government's existing environmental data management system "is outmoded in many ways. It continues to rely heavily on paper-based reporting, and its many separately designed databases are generally not technically compatible with one another."[49] The current environmental data management system, the GAO notes, makes it difficult to aggregate data from different databases to develop comprehensive information on environmental conditions, localities, industrial sectors, or even specific chemicals. The gaps in data make it difficult for regulatory agencies and the public to understand important human health and ecological effects.

Strengthen the scientific foundation for regulatory changes and rule making in federal and state environmental programs through support for science and technology research on environmental issues and through stronger external scientific peer review.

The willingness of the private sector and of the public to accept regulations or to adopt P2/E2 solutions depends on their faith in the scientific validity of decisions made by federal and state regulatory agencies. Federal and state environmental agencies must base rule making and standards on sound scientific evidence and on the results of scientific peer review. Confidence in P2/E2 practices also depends on government regulatory agencies' research and development, scientific review, and technology evaluation processes.

The National Research Council (NRC) points out that a stronger system of scientific review is needed in EPA to help determine which environmental problems threaten public health, quality of life, ecosystems, and the economy. EPA needs better scientific review procedures to avoid placing too much emphasis on problems that may be inconsequential and ignoring problems that may have significant impacts on public health and ecology. Better scientific information can help to reduce uncertainties in environmental decision making, identify emerging problems, deal with unanticipated threats, and develop cost-effective strategies to reduce risks.

The NRC calls on Congress to create a new position of deputy administrator for science and technology in EPA to strengthen overall responsibility for scientific and technical policy, coordinate scientific activity throughout the agency, and review potential rules and standards from a scientific perspective. EPA needs stronger capacity to identify and define important scientific issues facing the agency and in "developing and overseeing an integrated agency-wide strategy for acquiring, disseminating, and applying scientific information; and coordinating and overseeing scientific quality-assurance and peer review practices throughout the agency." EPA must create and strengthen processes to ensure that "appropriate scientific information is used in decision making through the agency, and ensuring that the scientific and technical information underlying each EPA regulatory decision is valid, appropriately characterized in terms of scientific uncertainty and cross-media issues, and appropriately applied."[50]

Extend the use of cost-benefit analysis, cost criteria, and risk assessment in environmental rule making.

Congress requires all regulatory agencies to take the costs of implementing new and more stringent rules into consideration. Current policies, however, do not require environmental agencies to use cost as a major criterion in promulgating and implementing regulations. Environmental regulations that are economically unrealistic can and do impose enormous costs on both businesses and state and local governments. In making decisions, businesses consider alternatives and balance value, quality, costs, and payback. In order to motivate the private sector to comply with regulations and adopt P2/E2 practices, environmental regulations must reflect similar criteria.

Environmental regulations based on unrealistic assumptions of risk in the face of scientific uncertainty do little more than encourage the practice of prudent avoidance. Risks are an integral part of human existence, and policies that seek to eliminate risks or minimize them at any cost quickly become unaffordable and lose their credibility. Environmental policies must make clear distinctions between real and perceived risks, and environmental protection agencies must make transparent the assumptions on which they base their estimates of environmental hazard. In order to improve risk assessment, New York's Department of Environmental Conservation (DEC), for example, is experimenting with a "Comparative Risk Project" that provides assessments that will help state government officials better understand which environmental problems create the highest potential risks to public health and safety, create strategies for reducing those risks, and select pollution prevention options.[51]

Expand programs to test, verify, and commercialize the results of new pollution prevention technology and eco-efficiency processes in the private sector.

Public confidence in P2/E2 practices will increase only if demonstrations show that new technologies and processes aimed at source reduction or elimination work effectively. In order to promote P2/E2, EPA and the states should explore more effective programs to test and verify the results of pollution prevention technologies and processes. The current federal environmental technology verification (ETV) program is slow, burdensome, and costly. The National Pollution Prevention Roundtable and other organizations recommend that the federal government create a simpler, lower-cost program for evaluating pollution prevention technologies. "A simpler protocol review process of existing data on critical performance and cost from multiple sites may be sufficient" for many pollution prevention technologies and more cost-efficient than the pilot programs EPA now uses. Massachusetts, for example, has a standard reporting and evaluation format for all technology development and verification activities that streamlines the process and helps disseminate results more quickly. Firms competing on quick manufacturing turnaround or short design and production cycles cannot afford to wait for time-consuming technology verification. EPA's program should also focus more strongly on identifying and disseminating information about the benefits of technology verification to developers and users.

If P2/E2 practices are to be disseminated more widely, companies must have easy access to affordable and effective technologies. Although many large corporations, research organizations, and engineering and consulting firms do develop technologies for pollution prevention, it is often difficult to commercialize them for general use. The U.S. Department of Commerce's Office of Technology Policy points out that there is often sufficient capital available for organizations to develop environmental technologies, but not for the stages between introduction and regulatory approval of use, when many technologies face a financial "valley of death" from which they never again emerge.[52]

Strengthen and extend public-private partnerships between federal, state, and local environmental agencies and the business community to explore, test, and apply P2/E2 practices.

More rapid dissemination of P2/E2 practices in the private sector requires government and private sector organizations to work together to identify, test, and apply effective technologies and processes for reducing or eliminating pollution at the source and the negative environmental impacts of products and services. Federal and state environmental agencies alone lack the expertise and information needed to promote P2/E2 practices, and the private sector is unlikely to take the initiative to disseminate successful practices on its own. Working together, state environmental agencies and private businesses can more effectively identify, test, verify, and disseminate P2/E2 technologies and processes.

Several states have been experimenting with public-private partnerships for pollution prevention since the early 1990s. Wisconsin's Department of Natural Resources, for example, develops joint agreements with industry-wide partners to work together voluntarily to reduce environmental emissions beyond levels required by regulations. Partnerships have been successfully developed with the pulp and paper, printing, and dry-cleaning industries. California's Environmental Technology Partnership is a joint program of the California EPA and the state's Trade and Commerce Agency that works with industry, academia, financial, and legal organizations and public interest groups to explore technological innovations and advances in knowledge for pollution prevention and to help commercialize promising approaches. The partnership seeks ways to encourage regulatory and user acceptance of new technology, and works with California companies to promote the export of environmental technology. The Pennsylvania Department of Environmental Protection (DEP) establishes partnerships with trade and professional associations to provide training and technical assistance to their members on pollution prevention and environmental management systems. It also works with environmental and management consulting firms and with banks, accounting, and insurance companies to introduce them to new business opportunities related to strategic environmental management.

At the federal level, EPA should expand and reorient its industry partnership programs. Initiatives such as Project XL, Waste Wise, Design for Environment, Energy Star, and Green Lights encourage industries to develop alternative pollution reduction strategies, but too often use regulatory compliance rather than the inherent benefits to business of better environmental performance as the benchmark of progress.[53] Federal and state environmental agencies must overcome a relatively high level of mistrust that exists between companies and regulators, and between corporations and external stakeholders, who are required to provide inputs. Many firms fear that involving stakeholders might lead to public criticism or legal actions by regulators. Paperwork involved in many of the federal programs is voluminous and tedious, requiring companies to commit substantial resources to participate. Negotiations between companies and environmental protection agencies can be long and drawn out. Fear that participation in voluntary programs sponsored by government agencies might lead to compliance actions has also limited private sector responses. Reorienting these programs toward the benefits to business of adopting P2/E2 practices can contribute to disseminating them more widely and more quickly.

Increase governments' roles in assisting private enterprises to adopt and integrate pollution prevention and eco-efficiency practices in their overall management systems, and provide regulatory relief and flexibility to companies that do so.

Complying with regulations, no matter how inefficient and costly, is now safer for many companies than risking prosecution for violations when they attempt to apply new technologies or processes that could lead to better environmental performance. EPA and Congress should commit significant budgetary resources to developing new programs that help private companies adopt voluntary environmental management systems and P2/E2 practices. The success of such programs depends on a clear recognition of the factors that shape decisions in the private sector.

Environmental protection agencies can play important roles in accelerating the adoption of environmental management systems by providing technical assistance and stimulating technology transfer, developing metrics that measure performance in terms of both environmental protection and economic impacts, and testing new technologies and processes that achieve environmental goals in cost-effective ways. P2/E2 promotion programs should be based initially on reinforcing and disseminating practices that corporations are already testing or using.

As noted earlier in this chapter, corporations can and are adopting voluntary environmental management systems and P2/E2 practices. Federal and state environmental agencies should develop programs that identify, recognize, and assist in adapting and disseminating eco-efficient technologies and processes. Support for trade association or university-based clearinghouses of information on pollution prevention and eco-efficiency practices would provide greater access for small- and medium-sized companies to practices that work. More programs are needed like those in Ohio, Maryland, Pennsylvania, and North Carolina that provide technical assistance to companies in adapting P2/E2 practices. (See "Pollution Prevention Program in North Carolina.")

In order for businesses to adopt P2/E2 practices they need assistance in developing accounting systems that allow for accurate identification and measurement of the value of natural resources and allocate responsibility for costs. Helping firms to adopt environmental accounting can have positive impacts on environmental performance because reducing or eliminating pollution will ultimately depend on changing the behavior of corporate executives and shareholders.

The success of P2/E2 programs depends in part on the capacity of environmental agencies to provide regulatory relief and flexibility to those companies that develop or adopt new technologies and processes. The National Academy of Public Administration recommends that EPA and state regulatory agencies encourage and reward companies that "draft multimedia,

Pollution Prevention Program in North Carolina

The Division of Pollution Prevention and Environmental Assistance (DPPEA) of the North Carolina Department of Environment and Natural Resources (DENR) has been providing industry with free non-regulatory assistance since 1984. It provides a staff of engineers and chemists with manufacturing, regulatory, and consulting backgrounds to help companies find cost-effective ways to eliminate, reduce, recycle, and reuse waste and conserve natural resources.

DPPEA experts analyze a company's operations and make suggestions on possible material substitutions, process improvements, water and chemical conservation, inventory management, preventative maintenance, housekeeping, and reuse and recycling opportunities.

After a site visit, DPPEA experts research technologies and management practices that the facility may be able to implement and then draft a summary report that contains the following elements: 1) summary of costs for waste generation and management; 2) summary of the plant survey including identification of sources of wastes; 3) a listing of pollution prevention practices or technologies the facility may want to consider; and 4) when possible, an economic assessment for each option. DPPEA is a non-regulatory program.

DENR's confidentiality policy prevents regulatory divisions from seeking information from DPPEA about the compliance status of any individual or company in order to take enforcement action. If areas of non-compliance are identified during a site visit, they are pointed out to facility personnel.

facility-wide plans to reduce their emissions to a point that might be significantly lower than national standards. EPA or a state environmental agency would formalize the plans by granting an integrated permit, which would stipulate the plant's total allowable emissions."[54] Under such a plan, the incentive for the firm is to find the least costly and most effective approach to improving environmental performance through appropriate combinations of emissions control and pollution prevention that meet its business needs and operational capabilities.

EPA and state regulatory agencies are now examining the possibility of integrating voluntary environmental management systems into their environmental policies. EPA and several states are pursuing pilot projects with both private and public organizations to test the EMS as an instrument for improving environmental performance.[55] EPA has developed a national tracking system based on successful experiments in New Jersey that can help determine the impacts of EMS implementation in private corporations and provide regulatory relief or compliance flexibility for companies that demonstrate better environmental performance.[56] These programs should be expanded and strengthened.

Expanding these programs at the federal level should be done carefully, however, because merely making what is now a voluntary management system part of the regulatory process can undermine the creative potential of businesses to protect the environment while reducing waste and gaining competitive advantage. A far more effective approach to promoting P2/E2 is for public agencies to provide incentives and rewards for companies that adopt beyond-compliance management systems. Those incentives should include facility-wide permitting, one-stop multimedia permitting, consistent industry-wide standards, permit streamlining, and concurrent compliance assistance, as is now done in New Jersey. Regulation should be used to change behavior, not to make it difficult for enterprises to comply or to punish executives that are trying new approaches to achieving beyond-compliance performance. More programs are needed like those in Oklahoma, Michigan, and Arizona that refund or reduce hazardous waste fees for pollution prevention activities. The State of Illinois gives preferred treatment in permitting and compliance problems to companies that develop toxic pollution prevention programs. Florida's Metro-Dade County lowers fees or allows more lenient time schedules in enforcement settlement agreements for organizations that implement pollution prevention projects.[57] Minnesota's Regulatory Innovation Act encourages assessment of pollution prevention strategies and authorizes flexibility to overcome unintended obstacles to P2 in existing statutes and rules.

Perhaps the most extensive P2/E2 experiments are being tried in Wisconsin, where the Department of Natural Resources has proposed a "Green Tier" program of performance contracts between the state and businesses that gives organizations a greater choice in how they meet statutorily set environmental standards.[58] The program evolved from ideas in regulatory reform studies and from experiments tried in Ireland, Germany, the Netherlands, and the European Union, and from programs tried in Oregon, California, New Jersey, Massachusetts, and Illinois. Recognizing that regulations, despite their volume and stringency, cover only about 20 percent of the environmental problems and opportunities in the United States, Wisconsin saw P2/E2 practices as a more effective way of addressing the 80 percent not covered by regulation. Although all businesses must meet regulatory requirements, those that sign agreements to move into the "Green Tier" of environmental protection select appropriate tools for reaching specific environmental performance targets, develop performance mileposts, monitor and report requirements, and accept sanctions for failing to meet targets. The amount of regulatory relief and its timing are determined for each organization based on its negotiated agreement. (See "Wisconsin's Green Tier Program for Environmental Management" for a summary of the program's main components.)

Wisconsin's Green Tier Program for Environmental Management

Vision: Business achieves greater environmental and economic performance through a cost-saving, voluntary regulatory system.
What's the problem? Government, business, and non-government parties may resist change, even knowing the regulatory system may have reached the limit of its effectiveness and all could benefit from more adaptive approaches.
What is the Green Tier System? It is a performance contract system to complement command-and-control regulations. The contract adapts to the needs of the firm, community, and environment.
How could it work? It's voluntary. Firms and the government negotiate contracts that are flexible, innovative, efficient, and enforceable. An environmental management system in the contract provides assurance of compliance, predictable performance, and due diligence. Self auditing, policing, and reporting may be approved under "mixed liability" accountability.
What's in it for business? Save time, reduce costs; encourage innovation; contain liability; adapt to market or supply chain demands; "trade" emissions within a "bubble"; incentives to prevent pollution first, and added credibility with citizens and customers.
What's in it for taxpayers? Reduces bureaucracy. Allows regulators to set standards and focus on more pressing problems and sub-performing regulated organizations. Some duties are "deputized."
What's in it for the community? More communication, involvement, and a cleaner environment.
What's in it for the environment? Produces greater environmental results by helping businesses and others do more than the minimum. Contracts may fit production lines, facilities, firms, areas, supply chains, sectors, products or pollutants and unregulated problems like land use, mobile air pollution sources, and runoff.

Source: Wisconsin Department of Natural Resources, 1999.

Conclusions

In brief, if the United States is to continue improving environmental conditions in the future, the current regulatory system must be augmented by a far stronger focus on pollution prevention and eco-efficiency practices in the private sector. In the future, significant gains in environmental quality are more likely to come from widespread adoption of P2/E2 practices than from more stringent control of "end-of-pipe" emissions.

New environmental management policies should focus on performance improvements rather than just regulatory compliance, use economic incentives to encourage clean manufacturing and the adoption of pollution prevention technologies and processes, and forge public-private partnerships for improving environmental quality. A new approach should reflect and reinforce the best practices that are being adopted by leading corporations in beyond-compliance environmental management. Governments have important roles to play in helping to reinforce innovation in the private sector, test and commercialize new pollution prevention technologies, and disseminate eco-efficiency practices from large companies to small and medium-sized firms and from the private sector to public organizations.

The recommendations described in this chapter provide a platform for a new generation of environmental policies in the United States that can protect the public health and natural resources through pollution prevention and eco-efficiency more effectively, less expensively, and more creatively than relying on a command-and-control regulatory system alone.

Postscript

Today, P2/E2 approaches to environmental protection and pollution prevention remain a minor part of federal and state environmental protection activities.

Since 2000, the Environmental Protection Agency has given additional attention to the National Waste Minimization Program, which encourages industrial organizations, government agencies, and communities to find ways to help companies reduce waste generation. This and other programs help companies to adopt less polluting manufacturing processes, promote green product design, sustain green markets, reduce the negative effects of the chemical supply chain, and develop new waste management technologies.

Recently, EPA's Environmental Accounting Project teamed with the Tellus Institute to develop new tools and documentation on environmental accounting. EPA is also creating a National Pollution Prevention and Toxics Advisory Committee to address issues of risk assessment and management, risk communications, and pollution prevention in chemicals management. It is expanding its pollution prevention information network and providing assistance for environmentally preferable purchasing.

Yet pollution prevention and eco-efficiency remain secondary concerns for both federal and state environmental agencies, which continue to rely primarily on regulatory controls. Programs to encourage private companies to prevent pollution and eliminate or reduce negative environmental impacts of their operations are still peripheral, compared to regulatory control, in federal and state environmental protection policies and budgets.

Dennis A. Rondinelli
May 2003

Endnotes

1. Dale W. Jorgenson and Peter J. Wilcoxen, "Environmental Regulation and U.S. Economic Growth," *RAND Journal of Economics,* Vol. 21 (Summer 1990): 314-340.

2. Enterprise for the Environment, *The Environmental Protection System in Transition: Toward a More Desirable Future,* (Washington, D.C.: Center for Strategic and International Studies, 1997); and Gary C. Bryner, "New Tools for Improving Government Regulation: An Assessment of Emissions Trading and Other Market-Based Regulatory Tools," Arlington, VA: The IBM Endowment for The Business of Government, 1999.

3. U.S. Environmental Protection Agency, *Draft 2000 Strategic Plan,* Washington, D.C.: USEPA, 2000.

4. Ibid., p. 26.

5. Ibid., p. 48.

6. U.S. Environmental Protection Agency, Summary of 2001 Budget, Washington, D.C.: USEPA, 2000.

7. National Research Council, *Strengthening Science at EPA: Research Management and Peer Review Practices,* (Washington, D.C.: National Academy Press, 2000): quote at p. 1.

8. Dennis A. Rondinelli and Michael A. Berry, "Corporate Environmental Management and Public Policy: Bridging the Gap," *The American Behavioral Scientist,* Vol. 44, No. 2 (2000): 168-187.

9. David Osborne and Ted Gaebler, *Reinventing Government: How the Entrepreneurial Spirit is Transforming the Public Sector,* (New York: Penguin Books, 1993): see pages 300-301.

10. United States General Accounting Office, "Regulatory Reinvention: EPA's Common Sense Initiative Needs an Improved Operating Framework and Progress Measures," GAO/RCED-97-164, (Washington, D.C.: USGAO, 1997): quote at p.12.

11. Kathi Futornick, "Total Quality Environmental Management: Managing Corporate Change," in Thomas E. Higgins (ed.) *Pollution Prevention Handbook,* (Boca Raton, FL: Lewis Publishers 1995): 57-76.

12. National Academy of Public Administration, *Setting Priorities, Getting Results: A New Direction for the Environmental Protection Agency,* Washington, D.C.: NAPA, 1995.

13. National Research Council, *Review of Research Progress of the Partnership for a New Generation of Vehicles—Sixth Report,* Washington, D.C.: National Academy Press, 2000.

14. Mark R. Powell, *Science at EPA: Information in the Regulatory Process,* (Washington, D.C.: Resources for the Future, 1999): quote at p. 112.

15. Enterprise for the Environment, *The Environmental Protection System in Transition,* (Washington, D.C.: Center for Strategic and International Studies, 1997); quote at p. 3.

16. 3M Corporation, "3M Environmental, Health and Safety Progress Report, 1998-1999," St. Paul, MN: 3M, 1999.

17. Texaco, Inc., "Environment, Health and Safety Review 1996," White Plains, NY: Texaco, 1997.

18. IBM, "Environment and Well-Being," Somers, NY: IBM, 1999.

19. Lucent Technologies, *1999 Annual Report—Environment, Health and Safety,* Murray Hill, NJ: Lucent Technologies, 2000.

20. Motorola Inc., "The Journey to a Sustainable World: Progress for 1999," Shaumburg, IL: Motorola, 2000.

21. Xerox Corporation, "1999 Environment, Health and Safety Progress Report," Webster, NY: Xerox Corporation, 1999.

22. General Motors Corporation, "1998 GM Environmental, Health and Safety Report," Detroit, MI: General Motors, 1999.

23. Eastman Kodak Corporation, "Health, Safety and Environment 1996 Report," Rochester, NY: Eastman Kodak Corporation, 1998.

24. Dennis A. Rondinelli and Gyula Vastag, "Private Investment and Environmental Protection: Alcoa-Kofem's Strategy in Hungary," *The European Management Journal,* 16, 4 (1998): 422-430.

25. Baxter International Corporation, "Environmental, Health and Safety Sustainability Report," Deerfield, IL: Baxter International, 1999.

26. Michael A. Berry and Dennis A. Rondinelli, "Environmental Management in the Pharmaceutical Industry: Integrating Corporate Responsibility and Business Strategy," *Environmental Quality Management,* 9, 3 (2000): 21-34.

27. Dell Computer Company, "Dell Observes Earth Day by Adding a Fully Recyclable Chassis to its Line of Business PCs," News Release, Austin, TX: Dell Corporation, 1996.

28. Compaq Corporation, "1999-2000 Environmental Health and Safety Leadership Report," Houston, TX: Compaq Corporation, 2000.

29. Motorola Inc., "The Journey to a Sustainable World: Progress for 1999," Shaumburg, IL: Motorola, 2000.

30. General Motors, "1997 GM Environmental, Health and Safety Report," Detroit, MI: General Motors, 1998.

31. Ford Motor Company, "1996 Environmental Report," Detroit, MI: Ford Motor Company, 1997.

32. Business for Social Responsibility Education Fund, "Retailers and the Environment," San Francisco: BSREF, 1999.

33. Eastman Kodak Company, "Environment, Health and Safety 1999 Annual Report," Rochester, NY: Eastman Kodak, 2000.

34. Nortel Networks, "1998 Progress Report on Environment, Health and Safety," Mississauga, Canada: Nortel, 1999.

35. Hughes Electronics Corporation, "Environment, Health and Safety Annual Report," El Segundo, CA: Hughes Electronics, 1999.

36. Dennis A. Rondinelli and Michael A. Berry, "Proactive Environmental Management: A New Industrial Revolution," The Academy of Management Executive, 12, 2(1998): 38-50.

37. Pharmacia & Upjohn, "Taking Care of Tomorrow: Environment and Safety," Bridgewater, NJ: Pharmacia & Upjohn, 1999.

38. Johnson & Johnson, "Environmental Report," New Brunswick, NJ: Johnson & Johnson, 1998.

39. Texaco Inc., "Environment, Health and Safety Review" 1996, White Plains, NY: Texaco, 1997.

40. Cooper Industries, "1996 Environmental Report," Houston, TX: Cooper Industries, 1998.

41. See Dennis A. Rondinelli and Michael A. Berry, "Corporate Environmental Management and Public Policy: Bridging the Gap," *American Behavioral Scientist,* 44, 2 (2000): 168-187.

42. Jeanne Herb, Allen White, and Susan Helms, "Pathways to State Pollution Prevention Regulatory Integration: The SPRINT Compendium," (Boston, MA: Tellus Institute, 1999): quote at p. 3.

43. United States General Accounting Office, "Environmental Protection: Challenges Facing EPA's Efforts to Reinvent Environmental Regulation," GAO/RCED-97-155, (Washington, D.C.: USGAO, 1997): quote at p. 10

44. Karl Hausker, "Reinventing Environmental Regulation: The Only Path to a Sustainable Future," (Washington, D.C.: Center for Strategic and International Studies, 1999); quote at p. 2.

45. Lynn R. Goldman, "Transmittal of Our Assessment of the Source Reduction Review Project," (Washington: USEPA, 1996): quote at p. 1.

46. For a more detailed discussion see Gary C. Bryner, "New Tools for Improving Government Regulation: An Assessment of Emissions Trading and Other Market-Based Regulatory Tools," Arlington, VA: The IBM Endowment for The Business of Government, 1999.

47. United States General Accounting Office, "Major Management Challenges and Program Risks: Environmental Protection Agency," GAO/OCG-99-17 (Washington, D.C.: GAO, 1999): quote at p. 28.

48. Tellus Institute, "Measuring Pollution Prevention (P2) Regulatory Integration," Boston, MA: Tellus Institute, 2000.

49. United States General Accounting Office, "Major Management Challenges and Program Risks: Environmental Protection Agency," GAO/OCG-99-17 (Washington, D.C.: GAO, 1999): quote at pp. 15-16.

50. National Research Council, "Strengthening Science at the U.S. Environmental Protection Agency," (Washington, D.C.: National Academy Press, 2000): quote at p. 6.

51. New York Department of Environmental Conservation, "New York State Comparative Risk Project," Albany, NY: NYDEC, 2000.

52. D.R. Berg, G. Ferrier, and J. Paugh, "The U.S. Environmental Industry," Washington, D.C.: USDOC, Office of Technology Policy, 1998.

53. Nancy S. Bryson and Richard J. Mannix, "Reinventing Project XL," *Environmental Quality Management,* Vol. 7, No. 3 (1998): 111-117.

54. National Academy of Public Administration, *Setting Priorities, Getting Results: A New Direction for the Environmental Protection Agency,* (Washington, D.C.: NAPA, 1995): quote at p. 31.

55. University of North Carolina at Chapel Hill and the Environmental Law Institute, "National Database on Environmental Management Systems," Washington, D.C.: Environmental Law Institute, 2000.

56. New Jersey Department of Environmental Protection, "Silver and Gold Track Program for Environmental Performance," Trenton, NJ: Office of Pollution Prevention and Permit Coordination, 2000.

57. National Pollution Prevention Roundtable, "White Paper on Government's Role in Pollution Prevention Technology Verification," Washington, D.C.: NPPR, 2000.

58. George E. Meyer, "A Green Tier for Greater Environmental Protection," Madison, WI: Wisconsin Department of Natural Resources, 1999.

CHAPTER TEN

New Tools for Improving Government Regulation: An Assessment of Emissions Trading and Other Market-Based Regulatory Tools

Gary C. Bryner
Professor, Public Policy Program
Brigham Young University
and
Research Associate
Natural Resources Law Center
School of Law
University of Colorado

This report was originally published in October 1999, revised May 2003.

Introduction[1]

Environmental policy in the United States is a study in paradox. Public opinion polls and other measures of public sentiment show strong support for environmental regulation.[2] Recent reports have found that significant progress has been made towards improving environmental quality; the nation's air and water is cleaner; national programs are helping implement new international agreements to reduce global environmental risks; threats to children's health posed by lead in the environment have diminished; farmers are reducing soil erosion and pesticide runoff into streams; and industries are reducing their release of toxic pollutants.[3]

Despite this progress, reforming environmental law and regulation has become a regular refrain of American politics and policy-making. As soon as the ink was dry on the first modern federal environmental laws, critics began questioning whether they were too expensive and intrusive. As the framework of environmental law developed into a complex maze of statutes, rules, and agencies, a growing number of voices from a variety of perspectives have called for changes in the way in which we regulate pollution and pursue environmental quality.

One of the most important and popular remedies for the ills that many believe plague environmental regulation is the use of market-based approaches to regulation. In the conventional, or command-and-control, approach to regulation, federal agencies issue national standards that apply to all sources in all areas, and agency officials mandate specific technologies and compliance actions. Market-based regulatory tools seek to create incentives for companies to find the most cost-effective ways of reducing emissions. This gives companies the flexibility to devise their own methods for achieving the reductions required of them.

There are several kinds of market-like mechanisms that might be employed in environmental regulation:

- monetary incentives, including taxes, fees, subsidies, and tax incentives;
- government-created markets for buying, selling, saving, and trading emissions;
- deposit/refund systems that discourage disposal and encourage collection or recycling of pollution-producing materials;
- disclosure of information to consumers;
- environmental auditing and releasing public data on kinds and levels of emissions;
- government procurement policies.[4]

The two most controversial instruments are pollution charges and emissions trading. Pollution charges, or taxes, are levied on emissions of pollutants or on input to activities producing pollutants. Polluters are charged a fee for each unit of pollution they emit. A pollution tax or fee, if it is high enough, can provide a strong incentive for companies to reduce their emissions in whatever way is most efficient for them, such as closing down some operations, using cleaner fuels, investing in control technologies, or changing work practices. It also provides a clear incentive for reducing emissions below permitted levels.

In emissions trading, polluters are allocated a limited number of allowances or units of emissions for release into the environment. Companies can either make the changes necessary to stay within the limits, or they can buy allowances from others. Tradable emission permits can be saved or banked for future use, or sold by polluting companies as long as limits on total emissions are not exceeded. Polluters have an incentive to reduce their emissions beyond the allowances given to them so that they can generate revenues through the sale of excess allowances.[5] Over time, decreasing the number of allowances distributed to pollution sources can reduce total emissions further.

Market-Based Tools for Environmental Regulation[6]

Deposit/Refund Systems	Payments required when purchasing products or containers that are refunded when products/containers are returned
Emissions Trading	Sources are allocated emission permits that can be bought, sold, or traded in order to meet levels of emissions permitted
Fees	Payments for services provided, such as monitoring of emissions or treatment of pollutants
Government Procurement	Purchases by governments of products that have desirable impacts on environmental quality
Reporting Requirements	Sources of emissions are required to disclose to the public information on the kinds and quantities of pollutants released
Subsidies	Direct payments to encourage or discourage emissions production, conservation, or other behavior
Tax Incentives	Reductions or increases in taxes to encourage or discourage behavior
Taxes (Pollution Charges)	Mandatory payments for the release of pollutants and wastes based on the quantity of discharges

The use of market-based regulatory tools raises three primary questions, which are addressed in this chapter.

1. How well do market-based approaches help achieve their goal of reducing the costs of compliance and making regulation more cost effective?

Given the billions of dollars spent on pollution control and cleanup ($140 billion a year according to some estimates) there are strong expectations that market-based tools can significantly reduce the cost of environmental regulation.

2. To what extent do these regulatory tools contribute to the achievement of environmental quality goals?

No matter how well market instruments reduce the costs of spending on pollution control, the primary question is whether environmental problems have been effectively remedied and natural resources protected.

3. How do market-based instruments facilitate the efficient and effective functioning of regulatory agencies, and contribute to the capacity of governments at all levels to achieve their policy goals?

The successes and failures of every major policy effort accumulate in ways that, over time, strengthen or weaken our ability to collectively solve common problems.

Emissions trading programs are the most popular market-based regulatory tools that the United States government is experimenting with, because of their promise to reduce compliance costs, increase the flexibility given regulated industries, improve the efficiency and effectiveness of regulatory agencies, and achieve environmental and public health goals. It is for these reasons that they are the primary focus of this chapter.

Emissions trading programs have been enthusiastically embraced by both regulated industries and policy makers, and have become part of virtually every policy proposal currently before Congress and state and federal environmental protection agencies. It is difficult to imagine a new regulatory program being proposed that does not include at least some form of emissions trading.

This chapter focuses on three categories of trading programs and proposals:

1. federal emissions trading programs under the federal Clean Air Act, including sulfur dioxide emissions in the acid rain program, and other national efforts, which were the earliest efforts to devise emissions trading programs;
2. state innovations, such as Southern California's South Coast Air Quality Management District's RECLAIM program for trading sulfur and nitrogen oxide emissions;
3. trading programs in other advanced industrialized democracies.

This mix of regulatory innovations at different levels of government, for different environmental problems, and for different countries provides a broad base for examining the advantages and disadvantages of market-based regulatory tools and their implications for improving the management of regulatory agencies.

Emissions trading programs are also being used to deal with other environmental problems, such as reducing water pollution and the generation and storage of hazardous wastes, but space does not permit a discussion of all trading programs here.[7] The experience of emissions trading in air pollution programs can provide important lessons for its use in addressing other pollution problems.

Emissions trading programs are quite new, so definitive studies of their costs and benefits will come in the future. But given the tremendous interest in them, this study seeks to assess the strengths and weaknesses of trading programs, based on the limited experience with them, and suggests questions that policy makers and others should ask before they embrace market-based tools, particularly emissions trading, as a way to improve the effectiveness of existing regulatory programs and design the next generation of environmental laws and policies.

Study Findings

Emissions Trading Programs in Place

Federal Government Emissions Trading Programs

The U.S. Environmental Protection Agency (EPA) has experimented with a number of emissions trading programs. Beginning in 1974, the agency instituted the first trading program, the Offset Program. The Offset Program required that new sources beginning operation in areas that have not met national air quality standards must buy enough emission reductions to offset their projected emissions, plus purchase an additional percentage of reductions in order to contribute to the attainment of the air quality standards. Most of the credits purchased for offsets have come from the closing of existing facilities. One study estimated that more than 10,000 tons of pollutants have been bought and sold through offsets for more than $2 billion, but it is difficult to gain information because these trades are private transactions.[8]

If new emissions come from an expansion of an existing source, the increase can be offset from internal sources through a process called "netting." Netting has become the most commonly used trading program, because it has fewer restrictions than offsets. Owners of existing facilities frequently construct new sources, and they can use the netting process to avoid the costs and delays associated with obtaining permits to operate new sources of pollution. One of the EPA's most recent innovations, the Environmental Excellence and Leadership Program, or "XL" program, includes pilot projects that allow facilities to alter their mix of emissions without having to obtain a new operating permit as long as total emissions do not exceed the facility's cap.[9]

The second EPA trading program, proposed in 1979 and put in place in 1986, was the bubble policy. This policy allowed companies to receive credit for emissions reductions in a specified area, as opposed to an individual location. Total emissions from each facility could be viewed as encapsulated within a large "bubble," rather than from individual smokestacks. Or two new adjoining power plants could use the bubble concept to combine their emissions. Regulatory officials established maximum total allowable emissions and left managers free to determine optimal emissions from individual sources, so that total compliance costs could be minimized. By the mid-1980s, the EPA had approved some 50 bubbles, and states had approved many more under their authority. Bubbles are still used to give facilities some flexibility in meeting emission limits.[10]

A third experiment with trading began with the phase out of lead in gasoline in 1979, when the EPA limited the average lead content permitted for large refiners. These refiners could average the content of leaded and unleaded gasoline in order to show compliance. In order to meet reduction goals required by 1982 and beyond, the EPA allowed refiners and importers of fuels who reduced the lead content of their fuel below the new EPA standards to sell earned credits to other refiners or importers. This was done by allowing them to average the lead content of leaded and unleaded fuel. Banking was discontinued in 1987, when all fuels were required to meet the standard, and the program was terminated in 1996 when all leaded gasoline for highway use was banned.

Other national programs authorized in the 1990 Clean Air Act Amendments have used trading mechanisms or variations. The Stratospheric Ozone Protection Program established a marketable permit system for producers and importers of chlorofluorocarbons (CFCs). Under this program, the EPA allows manufacturers of heavy-duty engines to meet emission standards by averaging emissions across their entire production and allows averaging between manufacturers. The Air Toxics Early Reduction Program allows sources of toxic pollutants that reduce emissions by 90 percent before national emission standards for hazardous air pollutants are proposed, to be able to delay their compliance with those standards when they are eventually issued.[11]

The EPA has also mandated emission limits for nitrogen oxide emissions (NOx) from electric utilities in the 12 Northeastern states and the District of Columbia in an effort to reduce ozone pollution. The Ozone

Emissions Trading in Federal Government Programs

Offsets	New sources beginning operation in areas that have not met national air quality standards buy enough emission reductions to offset the new source's projected emissions, plus an additional percentage of reductions so that the new source helps contribute to the attainment of the air quality standards.
Netting	If new emissions come from expansion of an existing source, the increase can be offset from internal sources, through netting, so that the facility's owners can avoid the costs and delays associated with obtaining permits to operate new sources of pollution.
Bubbles	Companies can receive credit for emissions reductions in some areas for higher emissions elsewhere; total emissions from each facility are viewed as encapsulated within a large "bubble," rather than from individual smokestacks.
Averaging	Producers of products being phased out, such as leaded gasoline and heavy-duty engines, have been allowed to show compliance by using an average of their products, rather than being required to show that every product complies with the standard.
Early Reduction	Sources of pollutants can gain credits or delay compliance with future standards if they reduce emissions before reductions are required.
Cap and Trade	Allowances are allocated to sources; a cap on total allowances is set and ratcheted down to meet environmental goals; sources can buy, sell, or trade allowances in order to meet their emission limits.

Transportation Commission's (OTC) NOx Budget Program is in effect from May to November of each year, beginning in 1999. NOx allowances are allocated to sources in each of the states and the District of Columbia. These units may set up trading systems to implement the program and achieve the emissions goals. The emissions trading program will spread to 22 states in 2003. Interstate emissions trading for the OTC states, and an additional 24 Eastern states, is also being developed.[12]

One of the most important innovations of the Clean Air Act of 1990 was the market-based incentive system to reduce acid-rain-producing emissions from coal-fired power plants through a nationwide cap and trade system. The first set of major rules to implement the sulfur dioxide (SO_2) allowance trading program was issued in 1993 and took effect in 1995. The heart of the acid rain emissions trading system is a cap on total emissions projected by the year 2010, which will result in a reduction of sulfur dioxide emissions of 10 million tons from 1980 levels. The plan is implemented in two phases. In phase one, 110 plants in 21 Midwestern and Eastern states were given allowances in the 1990 act. An allowance is a permit to emit one ton of sulfur dioxide. Allowances have been allocated for the years 1995 through 2030 (they cannot be used for compliance until the years for which they are designated). In phase two, the number of sources included in the program will be greatly expanded. The allowances for these sources are allocated by a formula based on the amount of fuel the plants used during a base-year period. The number of allowances will be capped at 8.95 million tons per year by 2010, when the program is fully implemented. Plants that are able to control emissions below the levels allocated to them can save them for future use, or trade or sell their excess emission permits to others who exceed their allowance. Transactions do not need to be approved by the EPA.

The first trade of acid rain allowances occurred in 1992. The EPA also auctions a small fraction of the total allowances allocated each year at an annual auction. The first auction of SO_2 allowances took place in 1993. Anyone can bid for allowances, and all allowances are sold each year. The proceeds of the auction are distributed to the sources from which the allowances were withheld. Auctions include spot allowances, which are only valid for the immediate year, and advance allowances, which are valid for future years. Participating sources must meet stringent monitoring requirements, usually through continuous emissions monitoring.

Emissions trading is also central to the developing U.S. policy for climate change. In October 1997, the Clinton administration proposed a five-year, $5 billion program of tax incentives and research and development aimed at reducing carbon dioxide emissions that included an emissions trading scheme for greenhouse gases that would cut emissions by 30 percent from projected levels in 2008. Sources that moved early to reduce emissions would get credits that they could use later when and if allowances are issued. The trading system would eventually expand internationally, and U.S. companies could buy and sell their allowances to emit greenhouse gases and encourage the most cost-effective ways of reducing emissions.[13] A 1998 Clinton administration plan called for achieving up to 75 percent of the reductions by purchasing allowances from Eastern Europe.[14]

A bipartisan group of senators introduced legislation that would amend the Clean Air Act to allow the president to make binding agreements with

U.S. businesses that reduce their greenhouse gas emissions to get credit for those reductions if and when a mandatory program is devised. The legislation's future is uncertain. Industry groups have sent conflicting signals to Congress. Some have opposed the early credit scheme because it may encourage the ratification of the Kyoto Protocol. Others favor it as a useful protection for companies that make early reductions voluntarily in case binding reductions are later mandated.[15]

State and Local Government Emissions Trading Programs

There is considerable variety across the states in terms of the specific elements of emissions trading programs. (See the Appendix).[16] As of 1999, 14 states had developed air pollution reduction programs that include some variation on the idea of emissions trading.[17] The programs were created between 1994 and 1998. The purpose of state-level programs is primarily to help bring the areas into attainment of national ambient air quality standards. The pollutants are particulate matter (PM), ozone, sulfur dioxide, nitrogen oxide, lead, and carbon monoxide. (Emissions of lead, the other pollutant regulated through national air quality standards, have fallen so dramatically, as a result of unleaded fuel, that lead is no longer a major concern of air pollution regulation.)

Most state programs are voluntary; regulated sources need not bank or sell or otherwise trade in emission allowances. If sources do choose to participate, they typically must demonstrate that reductions used to claim credits are quantifiable, real reductions in emissions, subject to enforceable requirements, surplus, and represent permanent reductions. Credits usually have a 10-year life. Some programs are limited to stationary sources, such as power plants and factories, while others include the creation of credits through vehicle scrappage programs, and some include reductions from area sources such as off-road equipment, consumer products, small commercial facilities, and other dispersed sources. Some states allow sources themselves to verify the creation of surplus allowances, while others require independent verification. Different states allow or prohibit inter-pollutant trading. Many states build into their trading program a requirement that the value of credits be reduced or discounted in order to decrease emissions over time and ensure that air quality improves.[18]

One of the most ambitious emissions trading schemes has been developed in southern California. The South Coast Air Quality Management District (SCAQMD), the agency responsible for addressing the greater Los Angeles area's air pollution problems, put in place an emissions trading program called the Regional Clean Air Incentives Market, or RECLAIM, in 1994. RECLAIM affects some 350 sources in the Los Angeles area that produce at least four tons of nitrogen or sulfur oxide emissions a year. These sources are required to reduce their emissions by a fixed percentage each year for the regulated pollutants. They are given an annual allocation of allowances and are free to find the most cost-effective means to reduce emissions. Sources that reduce emissions of nitrogen and sulfur oxide beyond the caps imposed on them may sell their excess credits, called Regional Trading Credits, to companies that have exceeded their limits.[19]

A brief mention should be made of a number of other market-based incentive programs that states have devised that do not involve trading systems, but are reflective of the range of possibilities for making environmental regulation more efficient. Maryland, for instance, was the first state to institute a "gas guzzler" law that imposes a surcharge on the sale of cars that consume high levels of fuel and gives a rebate to buyers of fuel-efficient automobiles.[20] Florida and California have developed congestion pricing programs that vary the price of traffic on toll roads, depending on the time of day and level of congestion. Since 1994, Maricopa County, Arizona, has had in place a trip reduction program that includes several market-based incentives such as parking charges, preferential parking for carpool vehicles, and subsidies and prize drawings to encourage the use of alternative modes of transportation.[21]

Other Countries' Experience with Emissions Trading Programs

As is true in the United States, European countries primarily rely on traditional, or command-and-control, approaches to environmental regulation. Most of the advanced industrialized democracies of Western Europe—countries that are members of the Organization for Economic Co-operation and Development (Canada, Japan, and the United States are also members of OECD)—have increasingly devised and implemented market-based innovations to regulation, but have selected approaches much different from the emissions trading programs that have been employed in the U.S.

In the 1970s and 1980s, a number of these countries instituted emissions taxes and charges. By 1987, approximately 80 different environmental taxes and charges were in place in 14 OECD countries. Between 1987 and 1993, the number of economic instruments used in environmental regulation increased by 50 percent. In the 1990s, OECD countries increasingly turned to "green" taxes to create financial incentives for environmental protection. The initial policy debate focused on whether countries should embrace traditional command-and-control regulation or market-based instruments. That question is now largely obsolete, as virtually every OECD country relies on a mix of both approaches, with market-based programs typically used as adjuncts to traditional regulatory schemes to create additional incentives for reducing emissions and/or to generate resources for other environmental protection efforts.[22]

Few European countries have followed the United States' lead in developing tradable emissions permit systems. German air pollution law allows

Examples of Market-Based Instruments in European Environmental Regulation

Water Effluent Charges	• France and other countries use these charges to finance pollution control facilities.
Ecotaxes	• Sweden uses taxes to encourage reduction of sulfur content of fuels. • Norway taxes carbon dioxide emissions from stationary sources and motor vehicles. • Denmark has increased taxes on non-hazardous wastes to encourage recycling. • Most countries impose high taxes on gasoline to encourage conservation.
Deposit/Refund Systems	• Several countries in Europe require deposits for aluminum cans, plastic containers, and glass beverage bottles.
Emissions Trading	• Rarely used; the Netherlands has a bubble policy in place.

sources to transfer emission reduction obligations, but that rarely occurs. The Netherlands has a bubble policy for power plants that allows facilities to treat all emissions from one facility as one source. Australia, Canada, and the United Kingdom have considered pollution trading policies, but no country has embraced the idea of emissions trading except the United States.

Europeans have chosen, instead, to focus on green taxes. Denmark, Finland, Norway, Sweden, and the Netherlands, for example, have all introduced carbon taxes. Many countries have imposed ecotaxes on leaded gasoline, pesticides, fertilizers, chemicals, batteries, lubricants, and packaging.

Europeans also have in place high energy taxes that lend themselves to restructuring for environmental purposes. They are also becoming increasingly interested in identifying tax and spending subsidies that result in environmental harm, such as free parking and company vehicles for employees, which encourages driving; reduced taxes for diesel fuels; subsidies for coal and water development; and agricultural payments.

Some countries, particularly the Scandinavian nations, are transforming their entire tax system to be more environmentally friendly. Sweden's 1991 tax reform law reduced income taxes and replaced the lost revenue with new taxes on carbon, sulfur, and nitrogen oxides. Denmark has shifted taxes from labor and income to pollution and scarce natural resources. The

Netherlands has a number of ecotaxes that generate about 2.5 percent of the nation's total tax revenue.[23]

Results of Emissions Trading Programs

Emissions trading is an important and useful innovation in environmental regulation in the United States. As the experience with this regulatory tool in federal and state environmental programs shows, pollution trading can reduce the compliance costs of regulated industries and give them more flexibility to meet emission goals, and can also help generate political support for new regulatory programs and serve as the basis for fashioning compromises acceptable to a wide range of interests. Carefully designed programs can simplify some of the regulatory tasks for government agencies and reduce compliance burdens that fall on regulated sources.

Trading programs may reduce the cost of achieving expensive environmental goals to acceptable levels, and may make it possible to take on environmental problems that otherwise are not addressed. They may encourage the diffusion of relatively inexpensive control technologies that reduce emissions enough to achieve environmental standards when combined with the purchase of emission credits. Most importantly, emissions trading can serve as a transition to a more effective set of market-based regulatory instruments.

However, trading should be used with caution. Emissions trading, if not carefully designed and integrated with minimum standards, can result in problems such as high concentrations of pollutants in some areas. Enthusiasm for its use may divert attention from decisions about what is required to achieve environmental goals. Trading may undermine the power of moral arguments that pollution should be reduced and conflicts with the expectation that all sources of pollution should take action to reduce emissions. It may fail to create incentives for continued technological innovation if pollution sources buy emission credits rather than invest in control equipment. Trading requires emissions monitoring capacity that may simply not exist. Some pollutants, particularly those where the total volume of pollution is the concern, are better suited for trading programs than pollutants posing localized health and environment threats. Introducing an emissions trading program, like any other policy change, creates some uncertainties and risks that regulatory officials and regulated industries may both resist.

Trading is not a panacea for all the difficulties posed by environmental regulation. It is not suitable for use in every regulatory program. The challenge is to determine when it should be used, and, when it is appropriate,

Strengths and Weaknesses of Emissions Trading

Strengths	Weaknesses
Usually reduces the cost of achieving regulatory goals	May result in hot spots—areas of concentrated emissions where sources buy permits from others instead of reducing emissions—if it is not carefully integrated with ambient air quality standards and if monitoring of these areas is inadequate
Usually gives regulated sources more flexibility and discretion in meeting the emission goals given them	May not require all sources to make at least some emissions reductions
Helps generate broad political support for new regulatory programs by promising to reduce the cost of meeting new environmental goals	Requires accurate monitoring data for emissions, but monitoring data or instruments may not exist; also requires aggressive enforcement of monitoring and reporting requirements
Reinforces the idea that regulation can help prices approximate true costs, including the environmental costs associated with producing goods and services	May fail to encourage the development and dissemination of new technologies and processes to reduce or eliminate emissions if companies simply choose to buy credits rather than invest in pollution control
Can simplify some administrative tasks of regulatory agencies by focusing on outputs rather than on mandates for control technologies and processes	May be opposed by agency and industry officials who fear the uncertainties and risks of failure associated with policy changes and the possibility that trading may not achieve the environmental goals in place
May encourage the development and broader use of control technologies that are cost-effective and might not otherwise be used because they don't produce compliance with emission standards	

how to design and implement trading in ways that ensure environmental protection and economic efficiency goals are achieved.

Reducing Regulatory Costs

Emissions trading programs generally reduce the cost of compliance for regulated industries. The acid rain control program is widely viewed as resulting in a significant reduction in the cost of pollution controls. The initial projections for meeting the goals of the acid rain program estimated compliance costs of $4.9 billion a year by 2010. The U.S. General Accounting Office's most recent estimate of those costs is now less than $2 billion a year in 2010.[24]

Industry groups estimated that the cost of reducing a ton of emissions under the traditional regulatory approach at about $1,500/ton; the EPA's estimate, about $650/ton. The actual prices of allowances available for purchase between 1993 and 1996 at the Chicago Board of Trade (where allowances are traded like other commodities) fell from $122 to $66. Transactions for more than 36 million allowances have been recorded, 25 million of which have been traded between different companies. Trades within companies are believed to be more numerous than those between firms (trades within firms are not yet required to be reported). The EPA has also auctioned over 500,000 allowances since 1993.[25]

According to a 1998 study by the president's National Science and Technology Council, the costs of administering the acid rain trading program are lower than traditional regulatory schemes because it "eliminates the need to devise source-specific emission limits and to review control technologies and detailed compliance schedules."[26] The EPA's decision to eliminate its case-by-case review and approval of each trade has also reduced the administrative and transaction costs. The program costs about $12 million a year to operate, which translates into an administrative cost of $1.50/ton of pollution reduced. Lower costs are attributed to "cost reduction efforts and improved performance of scrubbers and changes in fuel markets;" it is difficult to estimate "future technological improvements, the more efficient use of existing technologies, and future economic conditions," but technological innovation, prompted by competition, seems to have fueled cost savings.[27]

Southern California's emissions trading program also seems to have been successful in achieving its goal of decreasing the cost of reducing air pollution. A 1996 audit by the South Coast Air Quality Management District found that during its first two years, more than 100,000 tons of nitrogen and sulfur oxides had been traded for more than $10 million. The trading program was on track to meet its goal of reducing NOx emissions by 77 tons/day and SOx emissions by 15 tons/day by 2003. The price of NOx credits in 1994 was $24/ton and $132/ton for SOx, well under the $15,000/ton level that is the state of California's trigger point for reviewing the program's cost effectiveness.[28] During the following 15 months (1996 and the first quarter of 1997), more than $20 million worth of credits were traded.

However, emissions trading may not reduce compliance costs in every case. Not all emissions trading programs are simple. The EPA's bubble program is a complicated system that requires the agency to review each transaction. Transaction costs are relatively high—often $10,000 according to one estimate—which may be counterproductive for small trades.[29] It requires extensive emissions modeling, assessments of alternative control technologies, and compliance schedules, and is part of a complicated system of command-and-control emission limits and technological controls. What seems to work best is allowing trading within a facility, so that plant managers do not need to obtain new operating permits when production processes change, as long as the total emissions from the facility do not exceed its cap.

Achieving Environmental Goals

Emissions trading programs can be effective tools for improving environmental quality and preserving natural resources if sufficient information is available to policy designers to ensure that the emission targets they set will accomplish the environmental goals. If the targets are sound and the trading program is effectively monitored and enforced, the goals will likely be achieved. However, the national and state trading programs in place have not yet resolved the problems at which they were aimed. While it is too early to judge emissions trading definitively, there are some troubling indicators.

Under the acid rain program, sulfur dioxide emissions from the power plants in phase I of the program (1995-1999) were to decline each year for a total reduction of 3.5 million tons; during phase II (2000-2010), emissions are to fall another 5 million tons. Emissions in 1996 were 35 percent below the cap for that year. The program has reduced emissions and may prevent future damage, but emission reductions do not appear to be sufficient to restore lakes in the Adirondacks and elsewhere that are highly acidified. Lakes vary in their susceptibility to acid deposition, and some lakes are more damaged than others. The program's goal of reducing total emissions does not appear to be sufficient to provide protection for all lakes. Legislation before Congress in 1999 calls for a study to assess whether emissions reductions projected under the current acid rain program are sufficient to protect lakes in the Adirondacks and elsewhere.[30]

Despite the RECLAIM program, it is not clear that the Los Angeles area will ever achieve current air quality standards. At the start of the RECLAIM program, some critics argued that the initial allowances were too generous and that actual emissions could initially increase. Emissions did increase in 1995 over the 1993 baseline year, but District officials concluded that the increased trading in 1996 and 1997 was evidence that the surplus allowances built into the first years of the program were disappearing.[31]

More controversial was a proposal in 1995 to expand the RECLAIM program to include volatile organic compounds, pollutants that are precursors of ground-level ozone pollution. The proposal required all sources of

VOCs emitting at least four tons a year to keep their emissions under an assigned cap that would decline each year. In response to complaints by both industry and environmental groups, the District's board of directors rejected the proposal and in 1996 ordered the agency to institute technology-based standards for individual industries that use large amounts of chemicals that produce VOC fumes. Sources would be allowed to earn credits by reducing emissions from motor vehicles and area sources. Board members feared that the earlier proposal would limit economic growth in the area.

In August 1997, the California Air Resources Board, a state agency, suspended all rules that permitted the trading of VOC emissions because of complaints that the trading program had violated federal civil rights laws. The complaint argued that emissions trading in the Los Angeles area between stationary sources and motor vehicles resulted in disproportionately higher air pollution levels in minority communities near the facilities that purchased the credits.[32]

In theory, such problems should not be possible, since the Clean Air Act requires monitors to be located throughout airsheds and compels state officials to show attainment of the national standards at all monitors. But many people believe that national standards for pollutants like particulate matter and ozone are not sufficiently strong to protect humans from adverse health effects, so higher concentrations in minority communities, even if national standards are not exceeded, can be unfair.[33]

Emissions trading programs are a cost-effective means to accomplish the goals of environmental policies, but the goals themselves may not be sufficient to remedy the problems at which the policies are aimed. This is not the fault of emissions trading programs. They are policy tools that are neutral in terms of policy goals. If regulatory programs are not carefully designed to ensure that all areas meet minimum air quality standards, trading systems may not produce the environmental and health benefits expected of them.

Trading programs also clash with some important expectations held for environmental policy. In one sense, trading schemes are inconsistent with the "polluter pays" principle that is one of the key values underlying environmental regulation. Trading tends to distribute equally the cost of pollution controls across all sources, rather than imposing the greatest control costs on the sources that produce the greatest emissions. Some firms are able to externalize costs of production to other sources, rather than ensuring they account for all of those costs.[34] Trading programs may not reward sources that have reduced emissions voluntarily. If allowances are distributed based on past emission levels, high polluters will, in effect, be rewarded for their recalcitrance, while innovators who have already invested in emissions reductions will have fewer allowances to work with.

One of the underpinnings of environmental policy has been to encourage or force the development of cleaner, less polluting technologies. Despite the flaws in the conventional approach to regulation, it has often served to expand the use of cleaner technologies and to encourage the development of new technologies. This momentum can be lost if firms find emission credits available at a lower price than investing in newer, cleaner technologies. However, trading gives sources more flexibility in meeting standards, and they may be able to make more use of cheaper technologies. For example, trading encourages washing coal to reduce its sulfur content, a technology that alone will not lead to the achievement of emissions standards, but can be combined with other actions, such as purchasing credits, at a fraction of the cost of other control technologies.[35]

In contrast to emissions trading, pollution taxes provide a continuous incentive to devise new processes and technologies, since every time reductions are made, lower taxes result. Emissions trading programs, unless aggressively structured, may reduce the pressure for developments in technology. Trading programs, unlike pollution prevention efforts, may simply move pollution from one location to another rather than provide clear incentives to reduce emission levels. Credits earned by plant shutdowns may create incentives for regulated industries to close existing facilities and move to new, less regulated areas. Accurate past emissions from these sources may be difficult to obtain.

As the Los Angeles case shows, emissions trading programs may not adequately remedy the public health threats posed by pollution. They assume that there are safe levels of pollution for human health and ecosystems, but those estimates of safe thresholds of exposure are often difficult to make. They may result in increased exposures to some groups, particularly minority communities, who live near areas where sources find it cheaper to buy credits from others rather than reduce their emissions. Residents who are poor or lack the political clout to demand pollution reductions may be exposed to higher levels of toxic pollutants than their wealthier neighbors, and higher levels than before trading programs were instituted.[36]

Despite these shortcomings, emissions trading programs can contribute to broader shifts in policy towards true cost accounting. In a political economy fundamentally committed to market exchanges, regulatory strategies that help ensure that the real costs of production are included in the prices charged can make a critical contribution to achieving environmental protection goals and a sustainable economy. Economic goals of efficient use of resources are similarly fostered as prices are adjusted to reflect more accurately the real costs of production. No policy innovation will likely have a more significant impact on environmental quality and protection of natural resources than to move towards a system where the impacts on environmental factors are fully represented in prices paid.

Ending subsidies and reforming price structures are the key to a more effective regulatory system, and, ultimately, more effective environmental protection. Emissions trading programs are an incremental step toward that goal. The real importance of trading programs lies in their ability to help generate support for the idea of market-based incentives, generate some data on ecological costs and benefits, and pave the way for more fundamental policy reforms that will lead to ecologically sustainable economies.

The idea of ecological sustainability requires that renewable resources should be used only as fast as they can be renewed by natural resources. Nonrenewable resources should be used only as fast as renewable substitutes can be developed. Sustainability implies that public policies should encourage pollution prevention, reduced consumption of nonrenewable resources, increased reliance on alternative energy sources, and consumption of renewable resources that match renewal rates.[37]

These goals can be achieved through traditional regulation and economic incentives, ending subsidies that encourage the use of nonrenewable resources or consumption levels beyond sustainable yield levels, and other policies. Pollution prevention and waste reduction are the most important ways of protecting the health of the ecosphere, and the most effective ways of reducing emissions and wastes are to increase production costs to include all of the present and future costs of production including pollution, environmental degradation, and other effects.[38] Emissions trading programs can make an important contribution in facilitating the transition to the next generation of environmental policies.[39]

Enhancing Governmental Capacity

While there is little agreement over what environmental goals should be, once they are established, market-based regulatory tools can help generate support for these proposals. The debate over environmental goals is often extremely contentious. Conflicts could be softened if the costs of achieving those goals were reduced. The acid rain program is a classic example of how emissions trading made possible a new regulatory program with aggressive environmental goals.

If economic instruments can be devised to achieve environmental goals at lower cost than conventional command-and-control regulation, they will become one of the most important developments in public policy and will play a major role in the move toward more ecologically sustainable societies. They can help make possible the pursuit of environmental goals that appeared too expensive to achieve with conventional regulatory approaches.

Emissions trading programs can facilitate public debate by focusing discussion on overall environmental quality goals and total levels of emissions to be reduced, rather than embroiling interested parties in debates over what constitutes the best available control technologies and other bureaucratic rules and regulations. Economist Herman Daly has characterized the advantages of emissions trading programs this way. Emissions trading clarifies three fundamental economic problems. First, communities must decide how much pollution is to be tolerated, how much damage to be permitted. Second, they must decide how the ownership of rights to pollute will be distributed, who will be responsible for reducing emissions. The first two problems are addressed through political choices. The third problem, making reductions the most economically efficient way, then becomes a function of markets.[40]

Proposals for market instruments, while based on the virtue of the simplicity of the market, are often complex. Discussion about the details of trading plans may obscure broader questions about the amount of required emissions reductions and how much should be spent to improve environmental quality. Regulatory goals that are poorly designed or misdirected are not salvaged, because the cost of complying with them is reduced through trading programs. Trading schemes may become the focus of attention, as interests jockey over the specific provisions and mechanisms to be used. The environmental goals may be slighted or ignored, and discussions and analyses may turn to how the trading will work rather than whether it will actually reduce emissions and achieve environmental protection goals. A study of the Los Angeles RECLAIM program concluded that trading programs are inconsistent with democratic values since trading decisions are largely beyond public scrutiny.[41]

There are other political risks in using emissions trading and other market-based tools. The kind of regulatory instrument selected may have an impact on the political system and the policy-making process as well as on environmental quality.[42] The idea of buying permits to pollute may threaten the moral, symbolic power and appeal of pollution control. Environmental regulation is no longer seen as a moral imperative in protecting human health and those innocent third parties who enjoy few of the benefits of pollution-producing activity yet take on most of the burdens. Pollution simply becomes another cost of doing business. The efficiency promised by emissions trading might unwittingly produce equity problems. For instance, trading may result in increased pollution levels in areas where residents are poor or lack the political clout to demand pollution reductions instead of purchases of more pollution allowances. Some policy makers and environmental advocates are skeptical of emission trading policies, warning that they have been oriented more toward "regulatory relief than regulatory reform," and that these policies often lack "equivalency in accountability, enforceability, and environmental progress."[43] The changes involved in moving to a trading system raise risks for regulatory officials, who may be criticized for devising new approaches that may not work.

Reliance on pollution taxes and fees may also serve to weaken public commitment to a shared environmental ethic. As decisions are left to the marketplace, there is less need for educational and other collective efforts to foster public awareness of and concern for the environment. If trading systems are used to create property rights in pollution emissions, communities may have less opportunity to make decisions about what level of air pollution they are willing to accept. Market-like incentives may send the wrong signal that pollution is acceptable if the polluter is wealthy enough to pay for it.

The creation of a free market in pollution simply allows companies to buy permits when they choose not to install control measures or otherwise prevent pollution. Proponents of environmental regulation have long rested their arguments on the belief that individuals have the right to breathe clean, healthy air, and that public health and natural resource goals should be pursued independent of cost calculations. Clean air, clean water, national parks, and the environment in general are all part of a shared common endowment. Placing all of these values in a market may ultimately result in their unequal distribution and eventual devaluation.[44]

Conclusions and Recommendations

Emissions trading and other market incentives in regulation will likely become increasingly important in U.S. environmental policy making. Not only will they continue to play a central role in dealing with some problems like acid rain and ozone, but they are expected by many to be a central element of whatever efforts the United States and at least some other countries undertake to achieve the goals agreed to under the Framework Convention on Climate Change and the Kyoto Protocol. Emissions trading has two important advantages: It can lead to reduced compliance costs, and it can be the basis of broadening support for a new regulatory program.

The acid rain program of tradable permits is the most successful example of emissions trading reducing compliance costs. Several features have contributed to its success:

- The total level of emissions, rather than the location of sources, is critical. This characteristic facilitates trading.
- The time frame in which emissions occur is not critical, another factor that facilitates trading opportunities. The EPA does not need to be concerned with when exactly the allowances are used.
- Monitoring of emissions is critical. There is already in place a fairly extensive system of continuous emissions monitors for sulfur dioxide.
- The trading program was not transplanted onto a command-and-control system that complicated trading; it is a relatively simple system.

- The cap on total emissions and the allocation of allowances to each source is simpler than other regulatory programs. The EPA is required only to keep track of the allowances for each source and is not required to approve each transaction.
- The policy is seen by many as the result of a partnership between government and industry.
- The statutory authority for the acid rain emissions trading program is clear. Congress provided stringent default provisions in the event that the EPA failed to issue regulations on schedule. This gave regulated industries an incentive to support rather than fight EPA rule making. Congress also made adjustments in the allocation of allowances, rather than leaving that difficult task to the administrative process. This was done for political and distributional reasons.
- The allocation of extra allowances in the cap and trade system allowed policy makers to deal with distributional issues related to who would be responsible for making the reductions. This also helped to overcome resistance from political leaders representing areas responsible for cleanup costs.
- The trading system was so effective in reducing cost estimates that achieving the reductions in acid rain levels became politically feasible.[45]

Although the acid rain program has significantly reduced regulatory costs, it may still fail to resolve the problem of acid rain in many areas.

Despite their current popularity and potential for broadening political support for environmental regulation, emissions trading is a limited policy tool. The conclusions below suggest those tradable permits be used only in limited circumstances and not be used in many others. If they are to be used, emissions trading programs should be accompanied by several conditions. It is critical that the ground rules surrounding their creation, regulation, and eventual elimination are clearly understood. Finally, emissions trading programs should be seen as a temporary policy intervention that leads to the use of other policy tools that more effectively create incentives to reduce pollution and encourage more ecologically sustainable activity.

1. Emissions trading is a useful regulatory tool that can be used at all levels of government under the following circumstances:

- the same emissions have the same effect throughout the area in which they occur;
- minimum ambient concentrations are satisfied throughout the affected areas;
- emissions are quantifiable (emissions reductions can be determined and calculations replicated) and permanent;[46]
- emissions are relatively easy to measure and monitoring systems are in place so that emissions can be accurately measured;

- a limited number of major sources that can afford the transaction costs are involved (trading schemes do not work well when there are a large number of small sources, because the transaction costs will be too high);
- aggressively enforced penalties are in place for excess emissions, including fines and reductions in allowances for subsequent years;
- emission limits can be ratcheted down over time to ensure environmental quality goals are achieved;
- regulated industries see the trading system as stable and predictable;
- trading is combined with a requirement that each source make some minimum reduction in emissions, so that no source is seen as escaping at least some obligation to help solve the pollution problem; and
- there is clear understanding that allowances are only temporary permits to pollute; they are not permanent rights that can be changed as environmental conditions change.

2. Before employing an emissions trading program, policy makers should be able to answer affirmatively the following questions:

- Is there an accurate emissions inventory in place for determining the allocation of allowances? Will all sources be treated fairly?
- Is an appropriate baseline used? Does it fairly reflect economic ups and downs, breakdowns and other problems with maintenance and operation, investments in and performance of pollution control equipment, and a host of other factors?
- How are allowances allocated? Are sources that have already reduced their emissions treated fairly?
- Are there sufficient authority and resources for effective monitoring and enforcement? Can regulatory officials ensure that quantifiable emissions reductions can be determined and that reductions are surplus, quantifiable, permanent, and enforceable?
- Is trading among pollutants that pose different health and environmental risks prohibited?
- Are all sources required to make at least some reductions in emissions?
- Will trading programs encourage the development and diffusion of new control technologies?
- Will environmental quality be significantly improved? Will caps on emissions be sufficient to achieve environmental quality goals?

3. Emissions trading programs should lead to other, more powerful regulatory innovations that will more effectively encourage ecologically sustainable activities.

Emissions trading programs should be designed as a transition to a system of emissions fees or taxes and other efforts to reflect true costs in prices and to create more powerful incentives to reduce and prevent pollution. The ultimate test of an emissions trading program is its contribution to a more fundamental shift in practices aimed at reducing pollution, improving efficiency, and conserving resources.

Postscript

Interest in emissions trading as a regulatory strategy for achieving environmental goals continues to grow, especially in the area of climate change. Many corporations have made significant progress in reducing their emissions of carbon dioxide and other greenhouses gases, and numerous cities and states have adopted programs to reduce emissions of carbon dioxide from power plants, transportation, industry, and other sources.[47]

A central element of the strategy developed by businesses and governments to reduce greenhouse gas emissions is the development of emissions trading programs. Corporations, for example, are setting goals for reducing total greenhouse gas emissions and issue carbon allocations or targets to units of the company. Units achieve these goals through making changes in materials or processes, and by efficiency improvements that reduce emissions. The companies then allow these units to meet their goals by buying and selling these emission credits, and some allow them to purchase carbon credits from agricultural sequestration, tree planting, and other activities. Units that can reduce their emissions below their targets can sell their extra allocations to units that exceed their target because emissions reductions are more expensive for them than for other units. Companies encourage unit managers to aggressively pursue emissions reduction by tying compensation and promotion to achievement of these goals. Companies have found that steps they take to reduce carbon emissions also improve efficiency, reduce wastes and costs, and increase company profits.[48]

Governments are also enacting laws that require companies responsible for carbon dioxide releases to reduce their emissions and allow them to meet their goals by selling credits generated by exceeding their goals or purchasing credits from others to offset their excess. Several states have begun requiring reductions in power plants, motor vehicles, and other major sources of greenhouse gases. Cities have developed programs to ensure some activities are greenhouse gas neutral, where emissions in one area are offset by reductions elsewhere.

Some governments are also establishing goals for reducing carbon dioxide emissions from their own operations, with similar provisions that allow buying and selling of carbon allocations.[49] Under the Kyoto Protocol, expected to enter into force in 2003, participating countries can meet their greenhouse gas reduction goals through a number of trading programs, such as investing in emission reduction or clean energy projects in developing countries and then using the emission reductions from these projects as credits to be used in meeting their obligations.

Although the Bush administration announced its opposition to the Kyoto Protocol in 2001, emissions trading underlies its climate-change and clean-air policy initiatives. Part of its "Clear Skies" air pollution initiative is to establish a greenhouse gas registry to track the trading of emission credits and to reduce through voluntary measures the carbon intensity of the U.S. economy: Currently, 183 metric tons of carbon dioxide are released for every $1 million in GNP; the goal is to reduce that figure to 151 tons by 2012.[50] The Clear Skies proposal would also apply a cap and trade program, patterned after the acid rain program, to reduce sulfur dioxide, nitrogen oxides, and mercury from power plants.[51]

Gary C. Bryner
May 2003

Appendix: State Emissions Trading Programs

California allows sources that exceed emissions of volatile organic compounds (VOCs) for one product to offset them by "overcomplying" with the standards for other products. Regulations issued in 1997 provide guidelines for interchangeable air pollution emission reduction credits for local air pollution control districts. They establish a uniform credit currency, expressed in pounds of pollutant in the year generated, for trades between stationary, mobile, and area sources for all the criteria pollutants except lead. The state also has in place several market-based measures to encourage the early retirement of motor vehicles and the use of cleaner fuels.[52]

Colorado's generic emissions trading and banking program, adopted in 1996, allows sources to generate emission reduction credits by shutting down or curtailing production or by changing processes or materials. Mobile credits can be generated by scrapping high-emitting vehicles and replacing them with lower-emitting ones, switching to cleaner fuels, and trip reduction plans. One city, Telluride, requires residents who seek a permit to install new fireplaces or wood-burning stoves to turn into the city two existing fireplace/stove permits for every new permit granted.[53]

Connecticut began allowing trading and banking of nitrogen oxide emissions for both stationary and mobile sources in 1995. Credits generated outside of the summer ozone season cannot be used within the season. Mobile source credits are discounted by 10 percent.

Delaware's trading and banking program, adopted in 1996, includes NOx and VOCs; the state discounts credits by 10 percent in order to improve air quality. Reductions occurring after January 1, 1991, are eligible. Trading between mobile and stationary sources is permitted, as is trading with sources outside of the state and within the Northeast Ozone Transport Region.

Georgia, in a program approved in 1998, allows owners of vehicle fleets to earn credits for their vehicles that exceed federal clean-fueled fleet requirements; they can bank them for future use or sell them to other fleet owners. Fleets include 10 or more vehicles that are centrally fueled. Owners can earn credit by purchasing clean-fueled vehicles earlier than required, purchasing more than is required, or purchasing those with emissions cleaner than required by federal standards.

Illinois instituted a pilot program in 1993 of buying and scrapping pre-1980 automobiles. The state purchased vehicles for between $600 and $1,000 and measures the tailpipe emissions and fuel evaporation before destroying them.[54] The program now permits "allotment trading units" to be earned by scrapping vehicles. Stationary sources operating in areas that violate national air quality standards may buy these allotments and use them to meet emission limits.

A **Louisiana** trading program, promulgated in 1994, is in effect only in areas with current or past ozone pollution problems, and includes sources of NOx and VOCs. Stationary sources may obtain allowances by scrapping vehicles; motorists are paid the fair market value of their vehicles.

Maine approved in 1998 a trading program for stationary sources of NOx and VOCs. Credits can be generated by any permanent change in emissions and have an unlimited life—they can be banked and used anytime in the future. Credits obtained from another New England state require a 15 percent surcharge (if a source needing 100 tons of credits buys them from outside the state, it must purchase 115 tons of credit; if the source is outside of New England but still within the Northeast Ozone Transport Region, it must buy two times the required credits). NOx credits can be used to offset VOC emissions and vice versa.[55]

Massachusetts' Innovative Market Program for Air Credit Trading, for NOx, VOCs, and carbon monoxide (CO), was placed in operation in 1994 and is in effect statewide. Credits can be generated through implementing more stringent controls, source reduction, fuel switching, energy conservation, fleet conversions, lawn and garden equipment trade-in, vehicle scrappage, or ride sharing. Inter-pollutant trading is not allowed. Massachusetts was the first state to have its economic incentives program approved by the EPA; since October 1996, the state has not been required to gain EPA approval of each credit generated and used.[56]

Michigan's Emission Trading Program, established in 1996, applies to all criteria pollutants and is available to all stationary, mobile, and area sources. Credits are discounted by 10 percent in order to contribute to improved air quality and can be used for up to five years.

New Hampshire adopted an Emissions Reduction Credits Training Program in 1997 to reduce NOx, VOC, and CO emissions from stationary, mobile, and area sources. The goal of the program is not to reduce emissions but to give sources subject to control requirements flexibility and opportunities to reduce compliance costs. Credits generated by facility shutdowns cannot be traded; if the source does not use them, they become public credits that state officials can use to create or retain jobs in the state. Credits cannot be banked for future use.

New Jersey's Open Market Emissions Trading program, established in 1996, authorizes the creation, use, and trading of emissions reductions from stationary or mobile sources for NOx and VOCs. Credits must be verified by an independent party, such as a licensed professional engineer or certified public accountant. Inter-pollutant trades are not allowed. Credits are discounted by 10 percent. Sources may also purchase credits from sources in other states to the west or south.

New York's New Source Review Offset Program, promulgated in 1994, allows credits only to be used to offset the introduction of new sources. Credits are not discounted and have unlimited life. All types of emission reductions are allowed, including shutdowns.

Pennsylvania's Nitrogen Oxide Allowance Requirements Program, approved in 1997, operates during the summer ozone season. It is a mandatory cap-and-trade program: fossil-fuel-powered electric-generating plants are allocated a certain number of allowances each season; sources may trade allowances in demonstrating that their emissions are within the allowances allocated. Other kinds of sources may voluntarily opt-in the program.

Endnotes

1. I am pleased to acknowledge the many colleagues, scholars, government officials, and activists with whom I have discussed, over the past decade, market-based regulatory tools and other ideas for improving environmental regulation. I have received helpful comments and suggestions in exchanges with discussants and other participants at conferences of the American Political Science Association, Western Political Science Association, and the Association for Policy Analysis and Management; reviewers for and editors of books I have written on environmental policy with CQ Press, St. Martin's Press, and W.W. Norton and Company; policy analysts at the Office of Technology Assessment; members of the Clean Air Network; and Sheldon Kamieniecki, George A. Gonzalez, and Robert O. Vos, editors of Flashpoints in Environmental Policymaking, State University of New York Press, 1997. I wish to thank Mark A. Abramson for his interest in and support of the project, Susan Mitchell for the many improvements she made to the paper, Stuart Fribush and Barry Korb for many helpful comments and suggestions, and the IBM Endowment for The Business of Government for its interest in and commitment to improving the effectiveness of government.

2. Riley E. Dunlap, "Public Opinion in the 1980s: Clear Consensus, Ambiguous Commitment" *Environment* 33 (October 1992): 32.

3. See, for example, Council on Environmental Quality, *Environmental Quality: 25th Anniversary Report* (Washington, DC: Council on Environmental Quality, 1996).

4. National Commission on the Environment, *Choosing a Sustainable Future* (Washington, DC: Island Press, 1993.

5. See Robert W. Hahn, "Innovative Approaches for Revising the Clean Air Act," *Natural Resources Journal* 28 (winter 1988): 171-84.

6. For more on these other kinds of market-based regulatory tools, see U.S. Congress, Office of Technology Assessment, *Environmental Policy Tools: A User's Guide* (Washington, DC: Government Printing Office, 1995).

7. For a broader discussion of emissions trading and other market-based approaches to regulation, see Timothy E. Wirth and John Heinz, "Project 88, Harnessing Market Forces To Protect Our Environment" (unpublished report, December 1998); Wirth and Heinz, "Project 88–Round II, Incentives for Action: Designing Market-Based Environmental Strategies" (unpublished report, May 1991); Daniel J. Dudek and John Palmisano, "Emissions Trading: Why is this Thoroughbred Hobbled?" *Columbia Journal of Environmental Law*, vol. 13 (1988): 217-56; Robert Stavins, "Harnessing Market Forces to Protect the Environment," *Environment*, vol. 31, no. 1 (1989): 5-35.

8. Barry Korb, "U.S. Experience with Economic Incentives for Emissions Trading" in Organisation for Economic Co-operation and Development, *Applying Market-Based Instruments to Environmental Policies in China and OECD Countries* (Paris: OECD, 1998): 99-115, at p. 107.

9. Korb, "U.S. Experience with Economic Incentives for Emissions Trading," p. 105.

10. Korb, "U.S. Experience with Economic Incentives for Emissions Trading," pp. 108-09.

11. Korb, "U.S. Experience with Economic Incentives for Emissions Trading," p. 105.

12. U.S. General Accounting Office, "Overview and Issues on Emissions Allowance Trading Programs," GAO/T-RCED-97-183 (July 9, 1997): 10; "EPA Unlikely to Include Nuclear Generators in NOx Trading Plan," *Clean Air Report* (September 3, 1998): 4.

13. John Fialka and Jackie Calmes, "Clinton Proposes Global-Warming Plan." *The Wall Street Journal* (October 23, 1997): 2.

14. Christopher Flavin, "Last Tango in Buenos Aires" *World-Watch* 11 (November/ December 1998): 10-18, at 4-15.

15. Neil Franz, "Congress prepares for debate over global warming treaty." *Environment and Energy Update* (November 20, 1999).

16. More information on these state programs can be found at the U.S. EPA's "Market Incentives Resource Center," http://www.epa.gov/oms/transp/traqmkti.htm, accessed in June 1999.

17. See Georgia Institute of Technology, "Emissions Banking and Trading: A Survey of U.S. Programs" (unpublished manuscript, April 1994).

18. More information on these state programs can be found at the U.S. EPA's "Market Incentives Resource Center," http://www.epa.gov/oms/transp/traqmkti.htm, accessed in June 1999.

19. U.S. General Accounting Office, "Overview and Issues on Emissions Allowance Trading Programs," GAO/T-RCED-97-183 (July 9, 1997).

20. Peter Jensen, "'Gas guzzler law's value as tax source questioned," *The Baltimore Sun* (22 April 1992): 1A.

21. U.S. EPA, "Market Incentives Resource Center," http://www.epa.gov/oms/ transp/traqmkti.htm, accessed in June 1999.

22. Jean-Phillipe Barde, "Economic Instruments for Environmental Protection: Experience in OECD Countries," in Organisation for Economic Co-operation and Development, *Applying Market-Based Instruments to Environmental Policies in China and OECD Countries* (Paris: OECD, 1997): 31-58, at 34-36.

23. Barde, "Economic Instruments for Environmental Protection," pp. 37-41.

24. U.S. General Accounting Office, "Overview and Issues on Emissions Allowance Trading Programs," p. 6.

25. Korb, "U.S. Experience with Economic Incentives for Emissions Trading," p. 112.

26. National Science and Technology Council, "NAPA Biennial Report to Congress: An Integrated Assessment," (May 1998): 93.

27. National Science and Technology Council, "NAPA Biennial Report to Congress," p. 93.

28. South Coast Air Quality Management District, AQMD News (January 12, 1996) http://www.aqmd.gov/news1/Archives/recaudit.html (accessed June 1999).

29. Korb, "U.S. Experience with Economic Incentives for Emissions Trading," p. 107.

30. S. 172, 106th Congress.

31. U.S. General Accounting Office, "Overview and Issues on Emissions Allowance Trading Programs."

32. Roger Stevens, "Emissions-Trading Rules Suspended by California," *The Wall Street Journal* (August 29, 1997): A4.

33. Natural Resources Defense Council, *Breath Taking: Premature Mortality Due to Particulate Air Pollution in 238 American Cities* (New York: NRDC, May 1996).

34. Daniel A. Seligman, "Air Pollution Emissions Trading: Opportunity or Scam?" (Washington, DC: Sierra Club, unpublished paper, 1994): 8-10.

35. This example was provided by Barry Korb, meeting, August 14, 1999.

36. Richard Toshiyuki Drury, Michael E. Belliveau, J. Scott Kuhn, and Shipra Bansal, "Pollution Trading and Environmental Injustice: Los Angeles' Failed Experiment in Air Quality Policy," *Duke Environmental Law and Policy Forum*, vol. 9 (1999): 231-86, at 251-58.

37. For a recent assessment of sustainable development, see The President's Council on Sustainable Development, *Towards Sustainable America* (Washington, DC: President's Council on Sustainable Development, May 1999).

38. See Robert Repetto et al., *Green Fees: How a Tax Shift Can Work for the Environment and the Economy* (Washington, DC: World Resources Institute, 1992).

39. For a very thoughtful discussion of future directions in environmental policy, see Marian R. Chernow and Daniel C. Esty, eds., *Thinking Ecologically: The Next Generation of Environmental Policy* (New Haven: Yale University Press, 1997).

40. See "Sustainable Development, Part 5: Emissions Trading," *Rachel's Environment & Health Weekly #628* (December 10, 1998) (available through rachel@rachel.org).

41. Druy, Belliveau, Kuhn, and Bansal, "Pollution Trading and Environmental Justice," pp. 278-79.

42. Michael Gartner, "A Skeptic Speaks," *EPA Journal* Vol 18:2 (May/June 1992): 26.

43. *Environmental Reporter,* "California: Problems Seen Setting Baseline Levels in South Coast Emissions-Trading Program" (29 May 1992): 437.

44. Steven Kelman, *What Price Incentives?* (Boston: Auburn House, 1981).

45. Korb, "U.S. Experience with Economic Incentives for Emissions Trading," pp. 112-14.

46. U.S. EPA, "The New Generation of Environmental Protection," unpublished paper (April 15, 1994).

47. For accounts of innovative businesses, see Joseph J. Romm, *Cool Companies: How the Best Businesses Boost Practices and Productivity by Cutting Greenhouse Gas Emissions* (Washington, DC: Island Press, 1999); and Paul Hawken, Amory Lovins, and L. Hunter Lovins, *Natural Capitalism: Creating the Next Industrial Revolution* (Boston: Little, Brown and Company, 1999).

48. Case Study BP/Shell: Energy giants lead the way on emissions trading," *Environmental Finance* October 2000 supplement, xxvii-iii; Jeffrey Ball, "Companies Trade The Right to Emit Greenhouse Gases," *The Wall Street Journal* (January 16, 2003) A1.

49. Useful websites that provide information on carbon trading include the following:
www.unctad.org/ghg/index.html
www.gert.org/
www.greenhouse.gov.au/emissionstrading/
www.natsource.com/
www.ieta.org/About_IETA/Events/Members_Events/Greenhouse_Gas_new3.pdf
www.thecarbontrader.com
www.ieta.org/Library_Links/DocumentsforLibrary/Natsource_GHG_Pricing_Analysis.pdf
www.pewclimate.org

50. Andrew C. Revkin, "Bush Plan Expected to Slow, Not Halt, Gas Emission Rise," *The New York Times,* February 14, 2002, A1.

51. www.epa.gov/clearskies/clear_skies_factsheet.pdf, visited April 14, 2003.

52. South Coast Air Quality Management District, "Regional Clean Air Incentives Market, Summary Recommendations" (Spring 1992); South Coast Air Quality Management District, http://www.aqmd.gov/aqmp/97draft/eir/ch2.html (accessed June 1999).

53. Barry Korb, "U.S. Experience with Economic Incentives for Emissions Trading," p. 105.

54. Illinois Environmental Protection Agency, "Draft Proposal: Design for NOx Trading System" (unpublished manuscript, September 22, 1993); "Illinois Begins Pilot Project to Scrap Old, Polluting Cars in Chicago," *Clean Air Report* (8 October 1992, T-9).

55. Information updated through a telephone conversation with Judy Landers, Maine Department of Environmental Protection, 21 June 1999.

56. U.S. EPA, "First Emission Credit Trading Program Approved" (21 October 1996), Release #96-10-17.

About the Contributors

Mark A. Abramson is Executive Director of the IBM Endowment for The Business of Government, a position he has held since July 1998. Prior to the Endowment, he was chairman of Leadership Inc. From 1983 to 1994, Mr. Abramson served as the first president of the Council for Excellence in Government. Previously, Mr. Abramson served as a senior program evaluator in the Office of the Assistant Secretary for Planning and Evaluation, U.S. Department of Health and Human Services

He is a Fellow of the National Academy of Public Administration. In 1995, he served as president of the National Capital Area Chapter of the American Society for Public Administration. Mr. Abramson has taught at George Mason University and the Federal Executive Institute in Charlottesville, Virginia.

Mr. Abramson is the co-editor of *Transforming Organizations, E-Government 2001, Managing for Results 2002, Innovation, Human Capital 2002, Leaders, E-Government 2003,* and *The Procurement Revolution.* He also edited *Memos to the President: Management Advice from the Nation's Top Public Administrators* and *Toward a 21st Century Public Service: Reports from Four Forums*. He is the co-editor (with Joseph S. Wholey and Christopher Bellavita) of *Performance and Credibility: Developing Excellence in Public and Nonprofit Organizations*, and the author of *The Federal Funding of Social Knowledge Production and Application*.

He received his Bachelor of Arts degree from Florida State University. He received a Master of Arts degree in history from New York University and a Master of Arts degree in political science from the Maxwell School of Citizenship and Public Affairs, Syracuse University.

John P. Bartkowski is an Associate Professor of Sociology at Mississippi State University. Much of his current research examines the relationship between religious involvement, social inequality, and family life. Bartkowski is particularly interested in the social, cultural, and economic resources that religious congregations in rural areas provide to their membership and vulnerable populations within their local communities. His other research has examined the motivations and community-level impact of grassroots neighborhood activism in Austin, Texas. He is currently completing a research project exploring the impact of Promise Keeper affiliation on evangelical men and their family relationships.

His published work has appeared in *Social Forces, Social Science Quarterly, The Responsive Community, The Sociological Quarterly, Journal of Family Issues, Journal for the Scientific Study of Religion, Gender Issues, Sociology of Religion,* other scholarly journals, and various edited volumes. Bartkowski is the author of *Remaking the Godly Marriage: The Discourse and Negotiation of Gender Relations in Evangelical Families* and co-author of *Charitable Choices: Religion, Race, and Poverty in the Post-Welfare Era* (with Helen A. Regis).

Gary C. Bryner is Professor, Public Policy Program, Brigham Young University and a Research Associate at the Natural Resources Law Center, University of Colorado School of Law. He is a graduate of the University of Utah (economics), Cornell University (government), and Brigham Young University (law). He has been a guest fellow at the Brookings Institution, the National Academy of Public Administration, and the Natural Resources Defense Council. He has taught courses in policy analysis, environmental regulation, natural resources policy, international development policy, social policy, and the policy making process.

Bryner is the author of *Bureaucratic Discretion: Law and Policy in Federal Regulatory Agencies* (1987); *In Search of the Republic: Public Virtue and the Roots of American Government,* with Richard Vetterli (1987, 1995); *Blue Skies, Green Politics: The Clean Air Act of 1990 and its Implementation* (1992, 1995), *From Promises to Performance: Achieving Global Environmental Goals* (1997); *Environmental Politics: Domestic and Global Dimensions,* with Jacqueline Vaughn Switzer (1998); *Politics and Public Morality: The Great American Welfare Reform Debate* (1998); and *U.S. Land and Natural Resources Policy* (1998).

John J. Callahan is currently an Adjunct Professor, School of Public Affairs, University of Baltimore, and President, JJC Consulting Concepts. He was a Visiting Fellow at the Brookings Institution during 2001. He previously served as Assistant Secretary of Management and Budget, Chief Financial Officer, and Chief Information Officer of the U.S. Department of Health and Human Services from 1995 until 2001. During that time, he also served as Acting Commissioner of the Social Security Administration in 1997.

In 1997, Dr. Callahan served on the President's Management Council (PMC). He was appointed vice chairman of the Chief Financial Officers Council in 2000.

Prior to his work at HHS, Dr. Callahan held a variety of senior staff positions in the United States Senate from 1979 until 1995. During that time he was staff director for the Senate Subcommittee on Intergovernmental Relations, deputy staff director of the Senate Budget Committee, and chief of staff for Senator James Sasser.

Dr. Callahan has also seen service with the National Conference of State Legislatures, the U.S. Advisory Commission on Intergovernmental Relations (ACIR), and has been an assistant professor of education and planning at the University of Virginia.

Dr. Callahan received an M.R.P. and a Ph.D. in social science from the Maxwell School of Public Administration at Syracuse University. He is also a fellow of the National Academy of Public Administration.

Steven Cohen is the director of the Executive Master of Public Administration Program at Columbia University's School of International and Public Affairs. He is also director of Columbia University's Graduate Program in Earth Systems Science, Policy, and Management. Dr. Cohen teaches courses in public management, policy analysis, environmental policy, politics and management, and management innovation. From 1998 to 2000 he was Vice Dean of Columbia University's School of International and Public Affairs. From 1985 to 1998 he was Director of Columbia's Graduate Program in Public Policy and Administration, and from 1987 to 1998 he was Associate Dean for Faculty and Curriculum at the School of International and Public Affairs. He is a graduate of James Madison High School in Brooklyn (1970), Franklin College of Indiana (1974), and the State University of New York at Buffalo (M.A., 1977; Ph.D., 1979).

Cohen served as a policy analyst in the U.S. Environmental Protection Agency from 1977 to 1978 and from 1980 to 1981, and as consultant to the agency from 1981 to 1991, and from 1994 to 1996. Cohen is the author of *The Effective Public Manager* (1988), and the co-author of *Environmental Regulation Through Strategic Planning* (1991), *Total Quality Management in Government* (1993), *The New Effective Public Manager* (1995), *Tools for Innovators: Creative Strategies for Managing Public Sector Organizations* (1998), and numerous articles on public management innovation, public ethics, and environmental management.

William B. Eimicke is the director of the Picker Center for Executive Education of Columbia University's School of International and Public Affairs. Dr. Eimicke teaches courses in public management, policy analysis, management for international affairs, and management innovation. He also teaches at the Universidad Externado de Colombia in Bogota, Colombia.

He is a graduate of Syracuse University (1970) and holds an M.P.A. (1972) and Ph.D. (1973) from the Maxwell School of Syracuse University. He previously taught at Syracuse University, Indiana University, Russell Sage College, the State University of New York at Albany, and Baruch College of the City University of New York.

Dr. Eimicke served as director of Fiscal Studies for the New York State Senate from 1975 to 1978, assistant budget director of the City of New York from 1978 to 1979, and deputy commissioner of the New York City Department of Housing Preservation and Development from 1979 until 1982.

He served as New York Governor Cuomo's deputy secretary for Policy and Programs from 1983 through 1985. From 1985 until 1988, he served as housing "czar" of New York State, managing the state's six housing management, finance, and regulatory agencies. In 1993, he provided housing policy and management consulting services to Vice President Gore's National Performance Review.

Dr. Eimicke is the author of *Public Administration in a Democratic Context* (1974), and the co-author of *Tools for Innovators* (1998) and *The New Effective Public Manager* (1995), and has written numerous articles on public management innovation, ethics, competition and welfare-to-work programs.

Dr. Eimicke has also served as a management consultant to a wide array of public, private, and nonprofit agencies seeking to improve performance, reorganize, develop strategic planning, and improve productivity.

Richard C. Hula is Professor and Chair, Department of Political Science and Urban Affairs at Michigan State University. He is currently a co-director of MSU's Program in Urban Politics and Policy. He served as the director of Michigan State's Program in Public Policy and Administration from 1991 to 1996, and as an associate director in the Institute of Public Policy and Social Research from 1991 to 1998. Prior to joining the faculty at Michigan State, Hula held faculty appointments at the University of Maryland and the University of Texas-Dallas.

Dr. Hula received his B.A. from Michigan State University, and his Ph.D. from Northwestern University. While at Northwestern, Hula was a National Science Foundation Trainee (1969-72) and a Woodrow Wilson Dissertation Fellow (1972-73). He was named a distinguished scholar-teacher at the University of Maryland for 1986-1987.

Dr. Hula has been involved in a number of university programs to link university scholarship to the work of practice. These include a biannual policy institute for new Michigan legislators, a training program for citizens interested in political office, and numerous special workshops and symposia.

Dr. Hula is of author *The Politics of Crime and Conflict* with Ted Robert Gurr and Peter N. Grabosky (1977), *Market-Based Public Policy* (1988), *The Reconstruction of Family Policy* with Elaine A. Anderson (1991), and *The Color of School Reform* with Jeffrey Henig, Marion Orr and Desiree Pediscleaux (1999). Hula has published numerous articles on issues of housing policy, school reform, home credit, and environmental policy.

Dr. Hula teaches courses on urban politics and public policy.

Jocelyn M. Johnston is Assistant Professor of Public Administration at the University of Kansas, where she teaches public finance and intergovernmental relations. She received her Ph.D. in public administration in 1994 from the Maxwell School at Syracuse University. Her areas of research include government contracting, county finance, and property tax administration, as well as intergovernmental programs and policy. Professor Johnston's work has been published in numerous social science journals. She is co-editor, with H. George Frederickson, of *Public Management Reform and Innovation: Research, Theory and Application* (Alabama University Press, 1999).

Professor Johnston is a field research associate for the Rockefeller Institute's State Capacity Study, contributing to their national studies of welfare and Medicaid reform implementation in the states. She also administered county employment and training programs in New York State from 1978 to 1987.

Ann M. Kieffaber is Vice President, Public Sector, Global Strategy and Solutions, IBM Business Consulting Services. In this role, she is responsible for developing the unique solutions that help public sector clients transform their businesses. Prior to this position, Ms. Kieffaber was responsible for Technical Operations for Public Sector related to the strategic outsourcing line of business.

Throughout her career at IBM, she has held a series of positions in IBM Global Services working with clients in the federal government and in the health care, financial services, telecommunications, and manufacturing industries. She served as the first Business Information Executive for IBM Global Services. Prior to joining IBM, Ms. Kieffaber worked at Rolm Corporation and Honeywell. She has worked in the U.S. Fish and Wildlife Service, Department of the Interior.

Ms. Kieffaber has a B.A. degree in biology from the University of Minnesota and a master's in public and private management from Yale University.

Anne Laurent is the Deputy Editor of *Government Executive*, a national business magazine about the federal government. In addition, Ms. Laurent served as the lead writer of "The Manager's Edge," an executive guide to cutting-edge management challenges. She also served as Project Director of the Government Performance Project.

Ms. Laurent has written several articles for *Government Executive* that relate to the topic of entrepreneurial government. These articles include "Premium on Performance," "Let Contractors Take the Risks," "Revamping Reinvention," and "Management Magicians." In addition, Ms. Laurent has been a speaker at numerous seminars including Eastern Management Development Center: Seminar for New Managers, Executive Development Seminar, and Brookings Institution Seminars: Emerging Issues in Public Management.

Ms. Laurent is a graduate of the University of Michigan (B.A.) and Johns Hopkins University School of Advanced International Studies (M.A.).

Jerry Mitchell is a Professor in the School of Public Affairs at Baruch College, The City University of New York. He joined the CUNY faculty after receiving his Ph.D. in political science from the University of Kansas in 1987. He teaches courses in American government, research methods, policy analysis, and urban economic development policy. For several years, he also taught management courses for New York State's Public Service Training Program.

Professor Mitchell's research focuses on innovative forms of public administration, including business improvement districts, government corporations, and public boards. Seeking to explain the structure of these alternative arrangements and to describe how they can best be managed, his work has appeared in over 50 reports, papers, book chapters, essays, and journal articles. His most recent book is *The American Experiment with Government Corporations* (M.E. Sharpe, 1999). It evaluates the development and performance of semi-independent public agencies in the delivery of such services as economic development and transportation. His other books include *American Government in the Nation and New York* (McGraw-Hill, 1998) and *Public Authorities and Public Policy: The Business of Government* (Greenwood Press, 1992).

Elected to the governing council of the Policy Studies Organization in 1998, he is also a member of the American Political Science Association, American Society for Public Administration, and Urban Affairs Association.

Helen A. Regis is an Assistant Professor of Anthropology at Louisiana State University. Her key interests center on the relationship between the state and local communities, and the processes involved in the construction of civil society within the U.S. and abroad. She has conducted extensive ethnographic research on the interaction of medical practices, religious beliefs, family life, and public policy in Cameroon, Africa. Her recent book on this topic is titled *Fulbe Voices: Marriage, Islam, and Medicine in Northern Cameroon: Cultural Pluralism in Everyday Life* (Westview Press, 2002). On the domestic scene, Regis has explored the significance of social clubs and mutual aid societies among working-class African-Americans living in New Orleans. Her most recent work on this topic has appeared in *Cultural Anthropology,* and she is currently writing a monograph based on this research. Regis is also co-author of *Charitable Choices: Religion, Race, and Poverty in the Post-Welfare Era* (with John P. Bartkowski) based on the research reported in this volume.

Barbara S. Romzek is Professor of Public Administration at the University of Kansas, where she teaches public management and human resources management. She received her Ph.D. in political science in 1979 from the University of Texas at Austin. From 1988 to 1993, she served as chair of the Department of Public Administration. Her research focuses on the nature of public management and the career experiences of individuals who serve as public managers. She has concentrated her attention on the issues of accountability, government reform, privatization, and intergovernmental relations. Her work has encompassed a variety of work settings: from complex federal agencies like NASA, Congress, and the U.S. Air Force, to state social service agencies, as well as local governments and nonprofits.

Professor Romzek is a fellow of the National Academy of Public Administration, is listed in *Who's Who of American Women*, and received the Mosher Award from the American Society for Public Administration in 1988. Her most recent book is *New Governance for Rural America: Creating Intergovernmental Partnerships* (with Beryl Radin, Robert Agranoff, Ann Bowman, C. Gregory Buntz, Steven Ott and Robert Wilson, University Press of Kansas, 1996).

Dennis A. Rondinelli is the Glaxo Distinguished International Professor of Management, Kenan-Flagler Business School, and Director of the Center for Global Business Research at the Frank Hawkins Kenan Institute of Private Enterprise, University of North Carolina at Chapel Hill.

Dr. Rondinelli does research on corporate environmental management, international business management, economic development policy, and private enterprise development. He has carried out research in North America, Asia, Central Europe, Latin America, and Africa. He has authored or edited 16 books and published more than 200 book chapters and articles in scholarly and professional journals.

In addition, he has served as an advisor, consultant, or expert to the U.S. State Department's Agency for International Development, the World Bank, the Asian Development Bank, the Canadian International Development Agency, the International Labour Organization, the United Nations Development Program, and to private corporations. During the 1970s, Dr. Rondinelli was decorated by the government of the Republic of Vietnam for service as an advisor to the Ministry of Rural Development and for the ethnic minorities development program. In 1989, he received the Julio Lleras Order of Merit for outstanding service to the Central Mortgage Bank of the Republic of Colombia. He received the Warner Bloomberg Award for Excellence in Futures Studies in 1997 and the Weatherspoon Distinguished Research Award from the Kenan-Flagler Business School in the same year.

Prior to joining the University of North Carolina, Rondinelli was Principal Research Scientist and Senior Policy Analyst in the Office of International Programs at the Research Triangle Institute. He was also a professor at the Maxwell School of Citizenship and Public Affairs at Syracuse University and has held faculty positions at the Graduate School of Management at Vanderbilt University and at the University of Wisconsin, Milwaukee. He also served as a Senior Fellow at the Technology and Development Institute of the East-West Center in Honolulu.

Dr. Rondinelli received his undergraduate degree from Rutgers University and his Ph.D. from Cornell University.

About the IBM Endowment for The Business of Government

Through grants for research, the IBM Endowment for The Business of Government stimulates research and facilitates discussion of new approaches to improving the effectiveness of government at the federal, state, local, and international levels.

Research grants of $15,000 are awarded competitively to outstanding scholars in academic and nonprofit institutions across the United States. Each grantee is expected to produce a 30- to 40-page research report in one of the areas presented on pages 359–361. Grant reports will be published and disseminated by the Endowment. All the chapters presented in this book were originally prepared as grant reports to the Endowment.

Founded in 1998, the Endowment is one of the ways that IBM seeks to advance knowledge on how to improve public sector effectiveness. The IBM Endowment focuses on the future of the operations and management of the public sector.

Who is Eligible?

Individuals working in:

- Universities
- Nonprofit organizations
- Journalism

Description of Grant

Individuals receiving grants will be responsible for producing a 30- to 40-page research report in one of the areas presented on pages 359–361. The research paper should be completed within a six-month period from the start of the project. Grantees select the start and end dates of the research project.

Size of Grant

$15,000 for each research paper

Who Receives the Grant

Individuals will receive the grant, unless otherwise requested.

Application Process

Interested individuals should submit:

- A three-page description of the proposed research
- A résumé, including list of publications

Application Deadlines

There are two funding cycles annually, with deadlines of:

- The 15th of April
- The 15th of November

Applications must be postmarked or received online by the above dates.

Submitting Applications

Hard copy:

Mark A. Abramson
Executive Director
IBM Endowment for The Business of Government
1616 North Fort Myer Drive
Arlington, VA 22209

Online:

www.businessofgovernment.org/apply

Program Areas

E-Government

Specific areas of interest:

- Government to Business (G2B)
- Government to Citizen (G2C)
- Government to Employees (G2E)
- Government to Government (G2G)
- Capital investment strategies for e-government
- Enterprise architecture

Examples of previous grants in this area:

State Web Portals: Delivering and Financing E-Service by Diana Burley Gant, Jon P. Gant, and Craig L. Johnson (January 2002)

Leveraging Technology in the Service of Diplomacy: Innovation in the Department of State by Barry Fulton (March 2002)

Federal Intranet Work Sites: An Interim Assessment by Julianne G. Mahler and Priscilla M. Regan (June 2002)

Financial Management

Specific areas of interest:

- Cost accounting and management
- Financial and resource analysis
- Financial risk management and modeling
- Internal controls
- Financial auditing
- Contract management
- Reconciliation
- Erroneous payment recovery
- Asset management
- Systems modernization

Examples of previous grants in this area:

Credit Scoring and Loan Scoring: Tools for Improved Management of Federal Credit Programs by Thomas H. Stanton (July 1999)

Using Activity-Based Costing to Manage More Effectively by Michael H. Granof, David E. Platt, and Igor Vaysman (January 2000)

Audited Financial Statements: Getting and Sustaining "Clean" Opinions by Douglas A. Brook (July 2001)

Human Capital

Specific areas of interest:

- The components of human capital management required to accomplish an organization's mission (such as knowledge, skills, abilities, attitudes, and experience)
- Employee recruitment and retention
- Workforce planning and analysis
- Pay for performance

Examples of previous grants in this area:

Organizations Growing Leaders: Best Practices and Principles in the Public Service by Ray Blunt (December 2001)

A Weapon in the War for Talent: Using Special Authorities to Recruit Crucial Personnel by Hal G. Rainey (December 2001)

A Changing Workforce: Understanding Diversity Programs in the Federal Government by Katherine C. Naff and J. Edward Kellough (December 2001)

Managing for Results

Specific areas of interest:

- Policy, management, and resource allocation decisions that make use of performance and results information
- Balanced scorecards and measurement of customer service
- Collaboration between organizations to achieve common outcomes
- Performance-based budgeting

Examples of previous grants in this area:

Using Evaluation to Support Performance Management: A Guide for Federal Executives by Kathryn Newcomer and Mary Ann Scheirer (January 2001)

Managing for Outcomes: Milestone Contracting in Oklahoma by Peter Frumkin (January 2001)

Using Performance Data for Accountability: The New York City Police Department's CompStat Model of Police Management by Paul E. O'Connell (August 2001)

New Ways to Manage

Specific areas of interest:
- Contracting out
- Competition
- Outsourcing
- Privatization
- Public-private partnerships
- Innovations in management of public organizations

Examples of previous grants in this area:
Understanding Innovation: What Inspires It? What Makes It Successful? by Jonathan Walters (December 2001)

Making Performance-Based Contracting Perform: What the Federal Government Can Learn from State and Local Governments by Lawrence L. Martin (June 2002)

21st-Century Government and the Challenge of Homeland Defense by Elaine C. Kamarck (June 2002)

Transforming Organizations

Specific areas of interest:
- New organizational values in the public sector
- Changed public sector cultures
- Enhanced public sector performance
- Studies of outstanding public sector leaders

Examples of previous grants in this area:
Creating a Culture of Innovation: 10 Lessons from America's Best Run City by Janet Vinzant Denhardt and Robert B. Denhardt (January 2001)

Transforming Government: Dan Goldin and the Remaking of NASA by W. Henry Lambright (March 2001)

Managing Across Boundaries: A Case Study of Dr. Helene Gayle and the AIDS Epidemic by Norma M. Riccucci (January 2002)

For more information about the Endowment

Visit our website at: www.businessofgovernment.org
Send an e-mail to: endowment@businessofgovernment.org
Call: (703) 741-1077

Endowment Reports Available

GRANT REPORTS

E-Government

Supercharging the Employment Agency: An Investigation of the Use of Information and Communication Technology to Improve the Service of State Employment Agencies (December 2000)

Anthony M. Townsend

Assessing a State's Readiness for Global Electronic Commerce: Lessons from the Ohio Experience (January 2001)

J. Pari Sabety
Steven I. Gordon

Privacy Strategies for Electronic Government (January 2001)

Janine S. Hiller
France Bélanger

Commerce Comes to Government on the Desktop: E-Commerce Applications in the Public Sector (February 2001)

Genie N. L. Stowers

The Use of the Internet in Government Service Delivery (February 2001)

Steven Cohen
William Eimicke

State Web Portals: Delivering and Financing E-Service (January 2002)

Diana Burley Gant
Jon P. Gant
Craig L. Johnson

Internet Voting: Bringing Elections to the Desktop (February 2002)

Robert S. Done

Leveraging Technology in the Service of Diplomacy: Innovation in the Department of State (March 2002)

Barry Fulton

Federal Intranet Work Sites: An Interim Assessment (June 2002)

Julianne G. Mahler
Priscilla M. Regan

The State of Federal Websites: The Pursuit of Excellence (August 2002)

Genie N. L. Stowers

State Government E-Procurement in the Information Age: Issues, Practices, and Trends (September 2002)

M. Jae Moon

Preparing for Wireless and Mobile Technologies in Government (October 2002)

Ai-Mei Chang
P. K. Kannan

Public-Sector Information Security: A Call to Action for Public-Sector CIOs (October 2002, 2nd ed.)

Don Heiman

The Auction Model: How the Public Sector Can Leverage the Power of E-Commerce Through Dynamic Pricing (November 2002, 2nd ed.)

David C. Wyld

The Promise of E-Learning in Africa: The Potential for Public-Private Partnerships (January 2003)

Norman LaRocque
Michael Latham

To download or order a copy of a grant or special report, visit the Endowment website at: www.businessofgovernment.org

Digitally Integrating the Government Supply Chain: E-Procurement, E-Finance, and E-Logistics (February 2003)

Jacques S. Gansler
William Lucyshyn
Kimberly M. Ross

Using Technology to Increase Citizen Participation in Government: The Use of Models and Simulation (April 2003)

John O'Looney

Services Acquisition for America's Navy: Charting a New Course for SeaPort (June 2003)

David C. Wyld

Financial Management

Credit Scoring and Loan Scoring: Tools for Improved Management of Federal Credit Programs (July 1999)

Thomas H. Stanton

Using Activity-Based Costing to Manage More Effectively (January 2000)

Michael H. Granof
David E. Platt
Igor Vaysman

Audited Financial Statements: Getting and Sustaining "Clean" Opinions (July 2001)

Douglas A. Brook

An Introduction to Financial Risk Management in Government (August 2001)

Richard J. Buttimer, Jr.

Human Capital

Profiles in Excellence: Conversations with the Best of America's Career Executive Service (November 1999)

Mark W. Huddleston

Reflections on Mobility: Case Studies of Six Federal Executives (May 2000)

Michael D. Serlin

Managing Telecommuting in the Federal Government: An Interim Report (June 2000)

Gina Vega
Louis Brennan

Using Virtual Teams to Manage Complex Projects: A Case Study of the Radioactive Waste Management Project (August 2000)

Samuel M. DeMarie

A Learning-Based Approach to Leading Change (December 2000)

Barry Sugarman

Labor-Management Partnerships: A New Approach to Collaborative Management (July 2001)

Barry Rubin
Richard Rubin

Winning the Best and Brightest: Increasing the Attraction of Public Service (July 2001)

Carol Chetkovich

Organizations Growing Leaders: Best Practices and Principles in the Public Service (December 2001)

Ray Blunt

A Weapon in the War for Talent: Using Special Authorities to Recruit Crucial Personnel (December 2001)

Hal G. Rainey

A Changing Workforce: Understanding Diversity Programs in the Federal Government (December 2001)

Katherine C. Naff
J. Edward Kellough

To download or order a copy of a grant or special report, visit the Endowment website at: www.businessofgovernment.org

Life after Civil Service Reform: The Texas, Georgia, and Florida Experiences (October 2002)

Jonathan Walters

Leaders Growing Leaders: Preparing the Next Generation of Public Service Executives (November 2002, 3rd ed.)

Ray Blunt

The Defense Leadership and Management Program: Taking Career Development Seriously (December 2002)

Joseph A. Ferrara
Mark C. Rom

The Influence of Organizational Commitment on Officer Retention: A 12-Year Study of U.S. Army Officers (December 2002)

Stephanie C. Payne
Ann H. Huffman
Trueman R. Tremble, Jr.

Human Capital Reform: 21st Century Requirements for the United States Agency for International Development (March 2003)

Anthony C. E. Quainton
Amanda M. Fulmer

Modernizing Human Resource Management in the Federal Government: The IRS Model (April 2003)

James R. Thompson
Hal G. Rainey

Managing for Results

Corporate Strategic Planning in Government: Lessons from the United States Air Force (November 2000)

Colin Campbell

Using Evaluation to Support Performance Management: A Guide for Federal Executives (January 2001)

Kathryn Newcomer
Mary Ann Scheirer

Managing for Outcomes: Milestone Contracting in Oklahoma (January 2001)

Peter Frumkin

The Challenge of Developing Cross-Agency Measures: A Case Study of the Office of National Drug Control Policy (August 2001)

Patrick J. Murphy
John Carnevale

The Potential of the Government Performance and Results Act as a Tool to Manage Third-Party Government (August 2001)

David G. Frederickson

Using Performance Data for Accountability: The New York City Police Department's CompStat Model of Police Management (August 2001)

Paul E. O'Connell

Moving Toward More Capable Government: A Guide to Organizational Design (June 2002)

Thomas H. Stanton

Performance Management: A "Start Where You Are, Use What You Have" Guide (October 2002)

Chris Wye

How Federal Programs Use Outcome Information: Opportunities for Federal Managers (April 2003)

Harry P. Hatry
Elaine Morley
Shelli B. Rossman
Joseph S. Wholey

New Ways to Manage

Innovation

Managing Workfare: The Case of the Work Experience Program in the New York City Parks Department (June 1999)

Steven Cohen

New Tools for Improving Government Regulation: An Assessment of Emissions Trading and Other Market-Based Regulatory Tools (October 1999)

Gary C. Bryner

Religious Organizations, Anti-Poverty Relief, and Charitable Choice: A Feasibility Study of Faith-Based Welfare Reform in Mississippi (November 1999)

John P. Bartkowski
Helen A. Regis

Business Improvement Districts and Innovative Service Delivery (November 1999)

Jerry Mitchell

An Assessment of Brownfield Redevelopment Policies: The Michigan Experience (November 1999)

Richard C. Hula

San Diego County's Innovation Program: Using Competition and a Whole Lot More to Improve Public Services (January 2000)

William B. Eimicke

Innovation in the Administration of Public Airports (March 2000)

Scott E. Tarry

Entrepreneurial Government: Bureaucrats as Businesspeople (May 2000)

Anne Laurent

Rethinking U.S. Environmental Protection Policy: Management Challenges for a New Administration (November 2000)

Dennis A. Rondinelli

The Challenge of Innovating in Government (February 2001)

Sandford Borins

Understanding Innovation: What Inspires It? What Makes It Successful? (December 2001)

Jonathan Walters

Government Management of Information Mega-Technology: Lessons from the Internal Revenue Service's Tax Systems Modernization (March 2002)

Barry Bozeman

Procurement

Determining a Level Playing Field for Public-Private Competition (November 1999)

Lawrence L. Martin

Implementing State Contracts for Social Services: An Assessment of the Kansas Experience (May 2000)

Jocelyn M. Johnston
Barbara S. Romzek

A Vision of the Government as a World-Class Buyer: Major Procurement Issues for the Coming Decade (January 2002)

Jacques S. Gansler

Contracting for the 21st Century: A Partnership Model (January 2002)

Wendell C. Lawther

Franchise Funds in the Federal Government: Ending the Monopoly in Service Provision (February 2002)

John J. Callahan

Making Performance-Based Contracting Perform: What the Federal Government Can Learn from State and Local Governments (November 2002, 2nd ed.)

Lawrence L. Martin

Moving to Public-Private Partnerships: Learning from Experience around the World (February 2003)

Trefor P. Williams

IT Outsourcing: A Primer for Public Managers (February 2003)

Yu-Che Chen
James Perry

The Procurement Partnership Model: Moving to a Team-Based Approach (February 2003)

Kathryn G. Denhardt

Moving Toward Market-Based Government: The Changing Role of Government as the Provider (June 2003)

Jacques S. Gansler

Networks, Collaboration, and Partnerships

Leveraging Networks to Meet National Goals: FEMA and the Safe Construction Networks (March 2002)

William L. Waugh, Jr.

21st-Century Government and the Challenge of Homeland Defense (June 2002)

Elaine C. Kamarck

Assessing Partnerships: New Forms of Collaboration (March 2003)

Robert Klitgaard
Gregory F. Treverton

Leveraging Networks: A Guide for Public Managers Working across Organizations (March 2003)

Robert Agranoff

Extraordinary Results on National Goals: Networks and Partnerships in the Bureau of Primary Health Care's 100%/0 Campaign (March 2003)

John Scanlon

Managing "Big Science": The Challenge of Coordination (June 2003)

W. Henry Lambright

Transforming Organizations

The Importance of Leadership: The Role of School Principals (September 1999)

Paul Teske
Mark Schneider

Leadership for Change: Case Studies in American Local Government (September 1999)

Robert B. Denhardt
Janet Vinzant Denhardt

Managing Decentralized Departments: The Case of the U.S. Department of Health and Human Services (October 1999)

Beryl A. Radin

Transforming Government: The Renewal and Revitalization of the Federal Emergency Management Agency (April 2000)

R. Steven Daniels
Carolyn L. Clark-Daniels

Transforming Government: Creating the New Defense Procurement System (April 2000)

Kimberly A. Harokopus

Trans-Atlantic Experiences in Health Reform: The United Kingdom's National Health Service and the United States Veterans Health Administration (May 2000)

Marilyn A. DeLuca

Transforming Government: The Revitalization of the Veterans Health Administration (June 2000)

Gary J. Young

The Challenge of Managing Across Boundaries: The Case of the Office of the Secretary in the U.S. Department of Health and Human Services (November 2000)

Beryl A. Radin

Creating a Culture of Innovation: 10 Lessons from America's Best Run City (January 2001)

Janet Vinzant Denhardt
Robert B. Denhardt

Transforming Government: Dan Goldin and the Remaking of NASA (March 2001)

W. Henry Lambright

Managing Across Boundaries: A Case Study of Dr. Helene Gayle and the AIDS Epidemic (January 2002)

Norma M. Riccucci

Managing "Big Science": A Case Study of the Human Genome Project (March 2002)

W. Henry Lambright

The Power of Frontline Workers in Transforming Government: The Upstate New York Veterans Healthcare Network (April 2003)

Timothy J. Hoff

Making Public Sector Mergers Work: Lessons Learned (June 2003)

Peter Frumkin

SPECIAL REPORTS

Government in the 21st Century

David M. Walker

Results of the Government Leadership Survey: A 1999 Survey of Federal Executives (June 1999)

Mark A. Abramson
Steven A. Clyburn
Elizabeth Mercier

Creating a Government for the 21st Century (March 2000)

Stephen Goldsmith

The President's Management Council: An Important Management Innovation (December 2000)

Margaret L. Yao

Toward a 21st Century Public Service: Reports from Four Forums (January 2001)

Mark A. Abramson, Editor

Becoming an Effective Political Executive: 7 Lessons from Experienced Appointees (January 2001)

Judith E. Michaels

The Changing Role of Government: Implications for Managing in a New World (December 2001)

David Halberstam

To download or order a copy of a grant or special report, visit the Endowment website at: www.businessofgovernment.org

BOOKS*

E-Government 2001
(Rowman & Littlefield Publishers, Inc., 2001)

Mark A. Abramson and Grady E. Means, editors

E-Government 2003
(Rowman & Littlefield Publishers, Inc., 2002)

Mark A. Abramson and Therese L. Morin, editors

Human Capital 2002
(Rowman & Littlefield Publishers, Inc., 2002)

Mark A. Abramson and Nicole Willenz Gardner, editors

Innovation
(Rowman & Littlefield Publishers, Inc., 2002)

Mark A. Abramson and Ian Littman, editors

Leaders
(Rowman & Littlefield Publishers, Inc., 2002)

Mark A. Abramson and Kevin M. Bacon, editors

Managing for Results 2002
(Rowman & Littlefield Publishers, Inc., 2001)

Mark A. Abramson and John Kamensky, editors

Memos to the President: Management Advice from the Nation's Top Public Administrators
(Rowman & Littlefield Publishers, Inc., 2001)

Mark A. Abramson, editor

New Ways of Doing Business
(Rowman & Littlefield Publishers, Inc., 2003)

Mark A. Abramson and Ann M. Kieffaber, editors

The Procurement Revolution
(Rowman & Littlefield Publishers, Inc., 2003)

Mark A. Abramson and Roland S. Harris III, editors

Transforming Organizations
(Rowman & Littlefield Publishers, Inc., 2001)

Mark A. Abramson and Paul R. Lawrence, editors